PART TWO

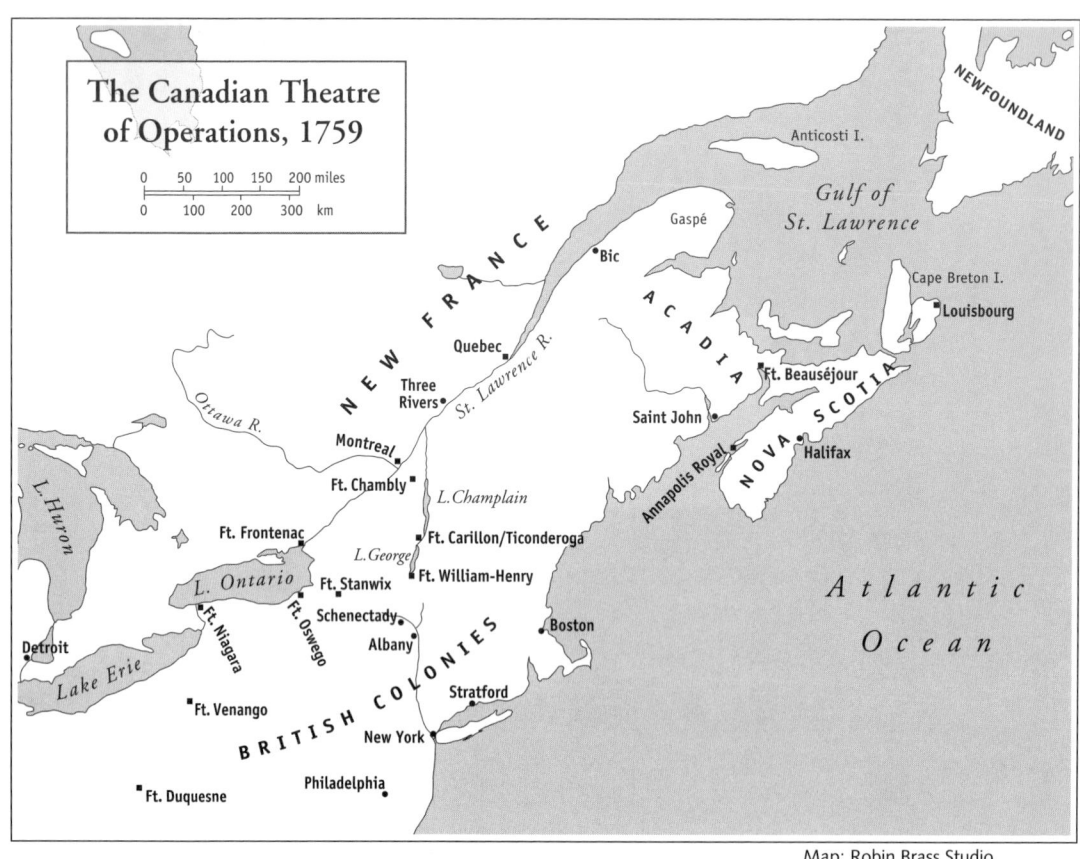

"WHACK WENT THE BROADSWORD!" THE REMINISCENCES OF SERGEANT JAMES THOMPSON

Having given a brief memoir of the sons of the family (nothing remarkable being attached to the history of the female branch), I now proceed to give this detail of various adventures as related by my Father, and in the order in which I suppose them to have occurred. I have endeavoured to preserve also his style and manner of recital.

James Thompson, Junior

Chapter 1 | Raised for Overseas Service, 1757

At the outbreak of the Seven Years' War in May 1756, the British army possessed 25 regiments of cavalry and 62 regiments of infantry, the great majority of which consisted of one battalion only (approximately 600 men on peacetime establishment). By the end of the war in 1763, the number of infantry regiments had more than doubled to 133 battalions in 126 marching regiments, plus seven battalions of Foot Guards and two corps of rangers. Ten of the new battalions were raised in the Highlands, some 12,000 men in total, two being deployed to North America while the other eight served in Europe and India. Between 1757 and 1763 more Highlanders wore the British red coat and tartan than ever followed the last Stuart prince.

On 4 January 1757 Lord Barrington, the Secretary of War, contacted SIMON FRASER, son of the executed Lord Lovat, and instructed him to "Raise a Highland Battalion of Foot, under your command, which is to Consist of Ten Companies of Four Serjeants, Four Corporals, Two Drummers, and One Hundred Effective Private Men in each Company, besides Commission Officers...." Fraser's commission made him lieutenant colonel commandant of the 2nd Highland Battalion of Foot, confirmed by Royal Warrant "the 5th Day of January 1757 in the 30th Year of our Reign." The 1st Highland Battalion of Foot was given to the Honourable Archibald Montgomery and both new units were numbered later in the year as the 62nd and 63rd Regiments of Foot and told off for North American service. Both were subsequently renumbered the 77th Foot (Montgomery's) and 78th Foot (Fraser's) the following year when several older established regiments of the British army had their second battalions turned into new stand-alone regiments.[1]

The Highland officers of these "North American service" battalions were to receive their initial commissions free and this created a flurry of willing candidates who actively lobbied their respective patrons. "It was a frenzy," recalled James Boswell, the famous diarist and colleague of Samuel Johnson. Half-pay officers of the Whig persuasion and former Jacobites all vied for the limited number of posts, citing their former service, experience and ability to raise men, and young Boswell was swept up in the excitement. Though only sixteen years of age at the time, and "timorous where firearms were concerned," Boswell confessed in later life that he was "set in a flame [and] wished to go among the Highlanders to America" in 1757. Wiser heads prevailed ["father prevented me"] and young Boswell remained at school.[2]

Other sprigs of Whig nobility who were not so well connected had to write to everyone they knew to advance their cause. Jacobite chieftains and lairds with forfeited estates also eagerly offered themselves or their sons with the requisite numbers of clansmen recruits for the posts they were seeking. While having good political connections or being a blood relative of one of the new colonel commandants was certainly a step up the ladder, the bottom line was the officer's actual ability to raise his quota of men commensurate with the rank and station he wished. For example, majors and captains were normally expected to be able to raise 100 men while a lieutenant was expected to provide a minimum of twenty-five recruits.

As these Highland troops spoke little or no English, Argyll writing to the Duke of Atholl in 1757 insisted that all officers whose names were forwarded for potential company commands must speak *Erse*, the prevailing term in the 18th century for the Gaelic or "Irish" language. More important than Gaelic-speaking officers, however, was the immediate requirement to train and discipline the raw recruits, and thus the selection of the non-commissioned officers, who would form the backbone of both battalions and ensure that the new battalions would

---

1. NAS, GD125/22: f.16 (3); NA SP44/189: ff.342–46; *London Magazine* (January 1757), 41–2. Both units were initially raised on a standard ten-company establishment. This was expanded to thirteen, and ultimately, fourteen companies.
2. James Boswell, *James Boswell: The Earlier Years, 1740–1769*, F. A. Pottle, ed. (New York, 1966), 31.

meet minimum standards as "British" regiments of foot, was even more critical to the success of the experiment.

Here Lord Barrington himself intervened to ensure the Highland regiments got off on the right footing. On 25 January 1757 he wrote to the senior officer commanding the Foot Guards, directing that twenty-five men who were ready to be sergeants were to be drafted from his regiment "who can speak the Highland language, Ten of whom are to be turned over to Lieu^t Col^o Montgomery's battalion and the remaining Fifteen to Lieu^t Col^o Fraser's Battalion." Furthermore, Barrington cautioned that all such non-commissioned officers (NCOs) were "to be draughted with their own Consent and approved of by the said Lieu^t Col^o appointed for that service." The same letter went out to eight other regiments (a good indication of how prevalent Highlanders serving in the regular British line regiments had become by the mid-18th century) directing each to provide a certain quota of "Highland-speaking NCOs" to the new Highland battalions for a total of 105 NCOs.[3]

For the majors and captains who would command Highland companies, more than just an ability to speak *Erse* or raise the required amount of men was required. Officers with previous military experience were essential and, to this end, Argyll recommended the active recruitment of officers who had served with the Protestant Dutch Scots Brigade in the Lowland countries or the transfer (and promotion, in some cases) of willing Scots officers from existing British line regiments, such as James Thompson's company commander, CHARLES BAILLIE, who had served as a lieutenant in the 21st Foot.[4] Most of the lieutenants serving in the 78th Foot also had previous military experience and it is only at the entry-level rank of ensign that one sees young gentlemen entering the service with no previous military knowledge, but allowed to do so on the expectation that they would learn on the job.

The Fraser officers were the cream of Jacobite gentry – Highland lairds, chiefs, brothers and sons of chiefs. There was the young MacNeil from the isle of Barra; RANALD OIG of Keppoch, 18th of his line, his father shot through both legs at the battle of Culloden; Sir Henry Seton of Culbeg, 4th Baronet Abercorn; and John Walkinshaw Craufurd, 21st of Craufurdland.

---

3. Lord Barrington to Foot Guards, 25 January 1757, WO 4, vol. 53 (Selections), LAC, Microfilm C-12585. Barrington was a keen advocate of using Scots in the British army. Just five years after the crushing of the clans at Culloden, he told Parliament in 1751: "I am for always having in our army as many Scottish soldiers as possible; not that I think them more brave than those of any other country we can recruit from, but because they are generally more hardy and less mutinous: and of all Scottish soldiers I should chose to have and keep in our army as many Highlanders as possible." Quoted in Linda Colley, *Britons: Forging the Nation, 1707–1837* (New Haven, 1992), 120.
4. Captain Charles Baillie, younger of Rosehall.

There was "Captain John of tree-rich Cluny," the brother-in-law of Lieutenant Colonel Simon Fraser and younger brother of Cluny Macpherson; Donald and Alexander Macdonell, younger brothers of the 18th Clanranald; and Charles Macdonell, brother of the 12th Glengarry. There was Lochgarry's oldest son, John Macdonell, whose father had cursed and thrown his dirk into the wake of his son's ship leaving Calais to return home and don the red coat of King George; and John Macleod, son of Macleod of Macleod, "Archie Roy" Campbell, youngest of Glenlyon, and Alexander Macdonald, youngest son of Coll Barrisdale, and so the roll went on.

The "gentleman volunteers" should also be mentioned. Essentially they were officer cadets, paid as soldiers and serving in the ranks to learn their trade, but messing with the officers. After a sanguinary battle, the most active and politically-connected of the surviving volunteers could optimistically expect to receive an ensign's commission without purchasing it. For example, James Thompson, the best friend of Charles Baillie, volunteered as a soldier when told all the officers' commissions were filled. He did so on the understanding that his friend would actively recommend him for the first vacant ensigncy and until that time Thompson would serve as a sergeant in the grenadier company. Unfortunately, Thompson's mentor and protector was one of the first killed at the Louisbourg landings in 1758, all hopes of preferment dying with Baillie.

In late March 1757, both Lieutenant Colonel Fraser and Lieutenant Colonel Archibald Montgomery received their instructions directly from William Pitt, Secretary for War, ordering both to "embarked at Corke, for North America" – Fraser's to "be landed at Halifax, in Nova Scotia" and Montgomery's battalion to "be landed at Charlestown in South Carolina."[5]

The 78th companies of recruits finally assembled at Inverness by 20 April 1757 and were soon marching for Glasgow via Fort Augustus. On arrival, the 78th were issued their weapons and underwent some basics of recruit training. This consisted of merely teaching the men foot drill and marching in order to get them quickly from one point to another. They were given no instructions on how to use their firelocks, as the British army's elaborate manual of arms could be taught on-board ship going over.[6] Simon Fraser would caution Lord Loudoun on arrival in North America, four months later, that while his young

---

5. William Pitt to Colonel Fraser, 31 March 1757, Whitehall; and, Pitt to Colonel Montgomery, 31 March 1757, Whitehall, in *The Correspondence of William Pitt ... with Colonial Governors and Military and Naval Commanders in America.*, Gertrude S. Kimball, ed., 2 vols. (London, 1906. Reprint New York, 1969), 26–8.
6. For the best account of basic recruit training through to advanced training for sieges or combined operations in the 18th-century British army, see Houlding, *Fit For Service,* 257–347.

battalion might resemble his Lordship's Highland regiment in its dress, there the similarities ended: "I have no doubt we shall resemble them in more respects when we are disciplined, for as yet, we have never been four days together."[7]

Thompson's regiment left Glasgow in early June, marching to Port Patrick, where they took troop ships to Ireland and then marched some 400 miles overland to Cork in the south, arriving in the latter part of June 1757. On 28 June 1757 the 78th Foot were aboard their transports,[8] but they waited an additional two days in Cork harbour for a fair wind. Finally, on 30 June 1757, they set sail for North America along with the 77th Foot (Montgomery's Highlanders), their large convoy of twenty transports escorted by three warships: *Falkland*, 50 guns; *Enterprise*, 40 guns; and the sloop *Stork*, 10 guns.[9]

Anecdote No. 1[10]
After I had got myself rigg'd out in the uniform of the Company[11] I had

---

7. Simon Fraser to Lord Loudoun, 25 August 1757, Halifax Harbour (Loudoun Papers, Huntington Library, San Marino, California, LO 4310). Loudoun's Highlanders, the 64th Foot, were raised in June 1745, and disbanded in June 1748. For detailed accounts on all items of Highland Weapons and Dress issued, see McCulloch, *SOTM*, II, Part Two.
8. In most cases, troop transports were chartered merchant ships suitably modified to convey troops. The transports used at this time were about 80–350 tons and carried between 25 and 260 men. Fraser's Highlanders were allocated a "transport allowance" (a formula whereby the number of troops aboard was related to the tonnage of the ship) of two tons per man. Two tons was a relatively generous allowance: at Rochefort in 1757 and Louisbourg in 1758, it was 1.5 tons per man (and even less for the voyage from Halifax to Louisbourg), thereby ensuring a cramped, smelly and very uncomfortable voyage.
9. *London Chronicle*, 9 July 1757, and *Public Advertiser*, 12 July 1757. Both newspapers mention that the three warships left Corke with "20 Sail of Transports, having the two Battalions of Highlanders on board...."
10. Many of the stories Thompson would recount to his listeners down over the decades, merged into one another. An example of Thompson mixing his stories is Anecdote 14, which occurs in two different geographic locations in two different years. These "unions" probably occurred when Thompson's memory started to fail him late in life when transcription actually occurred, or, his son James Thompson Jr., when transcribing the stories left out a paragraph or a page. Suffice it to say, the flow of the stories in their original order can be very confusing to someone unfamiliar with the regiment's history, campaigns and travels throughout North America. Therefore this book has been edited to reflect the proper chronological sequencing of Thompson's various tales and recollections that appear throughout the various anecdotes. With this in mind, the reader will find segments of various numbered anecdotes have been inserted earlier or later in the chronologically ordered chapters for the ease of the reader's comprehension. In most cases, introductory or bridging paragraphs have been added to some chapters to provide all-important missing context.
11. Thompson implies he received his uniform from the recruiting party in Tain. Recruits would not normally receive their uniform clothing until they joined their regiment and had passed a final inspection, although they could have received basic "necessaries" such as a shirt, stockings, shoes — all taken from their bounty. Newly raised regiments

volunteer'd with, that was rose by my friend Captain Baillie,[12] I marched alone from Tain,[13] my native place, to join my Company at Inverness,[14] and to call and see my Aunt, McRae,[15] the wife of a clergyman. She had two fine young women as daughters.

When I had knock'd at the door, and told who I was, and that I had come to take leave of my Aunt, one of the girls went upstairs with the message, at the same time I overheard her describing my dress. I waited some time, during which the young woman behaved kindly enough to me, but devil a nose of my Aunt would come down, because I had become a Soldier! and I never saw her after.

We staid some days at Inverness walking about the streets to shew ourselves, for we were very proud of our looks. It was a rule that the first time we met an officer, we took off our Bonnets to him, but did not take the least notice of him if we met him fifty times afterwards in the course of the day. The weekly pay-day came around, and our Paymaster, Sergeant ALEXANDER FERGUSON, wanted me to sign for my week's Pay, and offered me three and sixpence. I wouldn't take it.

What, says I, are you going to put me as a private Soldier? I'll have *none* of it, Sir – Why, says Ferguson, your pay appears on the Roll charged as a Private, and I hasn't heard that you were promoted. That may be, says I, but as I came

---

such as Fraser's Highlanders might have done things differently. It is also possible that since Thompson was a gentleman volunteer, he clothed and equipped himself. The faster a man could get into proscribed dress, and strut about, was as important then as it is now. As a grenadier soldier, Thompson would have worn a slightly different uniform than the other Highlanders in the regular marching companies. Besides the distinctive black bearskin grenadier mitre cap instead of the more typical Highland flat blue bonnet, Thompson's kilt may have had a coloured overstripe.

12. Captain Charles Baillie, younger of Rosehall.
13. Situated on the south shore of the Firth of Dornoch in northern Scotland, the Royal Burgh of Tain was the birthplace of James Thompson. When Thompson joined the newly embodied Fraser's Highlanders in 1757, Tain had a population of about 1,800. Today, it is a town of about 4,000 inhabitants.
14. Situated where the River Ness enters the Moray Firth in northern Scotland, Inverness has long been a natural transportation hub and is a distance of about 33 miles due south of Tain. In the 18th century, Inverness was a significant market town which enjoyed sea trade with the Low Countries. The town's main export was wool, and the textile industry contributed to Inverness's growth in the 18th century. In 1746 Inverness Castle and bridge were blown up by Jacobites, who were subsequently defeated at nearby Culloden Moor.
15. MacRae. The editors have been unable to track down a paternal (Thomson) or maternal (Stronach) aunt of Thompson who may have married a clergyman named McRae in Inverness. However, the minister of St. Duthus's Collegiate Church, Hugh Munro, who had previously been minister of nearby Tarbat, had a wife whose surname was Thomson, a relatively uncommon name in the area, but there are no records to show whether she was related to the Thomson family of Tain.

with the Captain, as a volunteer, I expect something better than that, and if you can't choose to give it, you may keep it, for I can manage to do without it. You see (continues my Father) I had great promises from my Captain, and had a little money with me, and felt myself too proud. This business made some inconvenience to the Paylists, and in a few days Ferguson offers me pay as a Sergeant. I don't know by what authority – however, I took it.

Anecdote No. 2

We crossed over from Port Patrick,[16] in Scotland, just after our breakfast, and arrived in time to Dine in Ireland. When we got to the town of Donaghadee,[17] which had only one principal street, but it was a long one, it was supposed that there would not be accommodation for us all, and after a good deal of consultation about this matter, we were made to form in Line, and it was left to each head of a Family to take as many as he thought he could find room for. Presently a person, having the appearance of a gentleman, comes up to our Grenadier Company, and told off five and twenty as his share, and was leading them away, when our Captain requested him to give up two of them, as he must allot two Non Commission'd Officers to take charge of them. Oh, says the gentleman, I'll take the two Non Commission'd Officers into the bargain. This choice happen'd to fall upon Sergeant JAMES SINCLAIR (x) and myself.

(x) General Sir James Hope's Grandfather.[18]

Then, away we went to some little distance from the Town. When we got to the House, we were shewn into a large apartment where there was a long table already laid to which we were all desir'd to come near, and the Master of the house, himself, sat at the head. After we had made a hearty Dinner for which we had

---

16. Portpatrick is a small port on the southwestern tip of Scotland, cradled at the foot of rocky cliffs. It has been used over the centuries by the ferry and mail packets to the port of Donaghdee, Ireland, 22 miles across the Irish Channel.
17. Donaghadee is a small coastal port on the northeastern side of Ireland, approximately 20 miles east of Belfast.
18. Footnote in the original Manuscript copy, identified with an **x**. A matching **x** indicated where it was to be inserted in the narrative. Sergeant Sinclair's grandson, through his daughter Elizabeth's marriage to Captain (later Major) Erskine Hope, 26th Foot, was General Sir James Archibald Hope (1786–1871). Sir James's gravestone at St. Peter's Church, Leckhampton, Cheltenham, Gloucester, reads: "General Sir James Archibald Hope, GCB. Late Colonel of the 9th Regiment of Foot East Norfolk. Born 14th April 1786. Died 30th December 1871." The grandson only returned to Canada with the rank of brigadier general in 1837, serving throughout the Lower Canada rebellion, a full seven years *after* James Thompson senior's death. This name-dropping in the anecdotes with regard to Sergeant Sinclair being the grandfather of General Hope is therefore directly attributable to James Jr., who personally knew General Hope during his time as deputy commissary general.

been well prepared with good appetites, and having drawn near towards dusk, our Landlord got a lanthorn, and led us to a Barn, where he had ordered straw to be laid to a good thickness, and he directed the men to a Bale of Blankets (which had not before been unpack'd) to be cut open, and told us to help ourselves. This circumstance led me to suppose that he was a wholesale merchant.

When all the men were dispos'd of for the night, he takes Sinclair and myself back with him to the House, and he would have us take a little *Punch* (a liqueur then very common in Ireland) and seeing that we were over come with sleep, he shewed us into a well-furnish'd room with comfortable beds. Well, to Bed we went, and as we had had a fatiguing day of it, we were not long falling to sleep. Presently we were woke up by the noise of scolding voices in the next room. I thought that it might be on account of our men in the Barn having done something or other to vex the Landlord. So I jump'd up and roll'd my Kilt about me, and stood a while list'ning to the talk, and I overheard a female voice saying, You have got upwards of twenty of the Scotch Soldiers to your share, and I have not been able to get one: this is treating me very ill, I think, after all the preparations I made for them. I'm told you have two Soldiers in this very house, and I insist upon having them go with me.

Our Landlady persisted she had no *Soldiers* in the house, and the Strange Lady persisted to the contrary: when our Landlady acknowledg'd there *was* two persons in the Bedroom, but that they were *not Soldiers*, they were both *Sergeants*. Mind what you say, said the Stranger, for they would not at all be obliged to you for saying they were *no Soldiers*. She, however continued to insist upon having the two Soldiers in that room woke up, that she might take them to her house, and 'afaith she obliged the Landlord to consent to knock us up. When I found she had gain'd upon him, I jump'd into bed again, and pretended to be fast asleep. Presently, our Landlord steps in and touches me upon the shoulder and, of course, I didn't feel it, but upon his repeating it, I starts up and call'd out, "what's the matter!"

He made an apology for disturbing us, and said that as there was a *lady* in question, we could not be displeased. Sinclair and myself had of course to get up and dress ourselves, which we did with a very bad grace – however, we soon turn'd out and join'd the folks in the outer room. There was abundance of apologies on all hands. We said we were sensible of her politeness, but we could not leave our men. She said her house was close by. In short it ended by the Strange Lady leading Sinclair and I, away with her.

We went but a short distance and came to a handsome house, and we were shew'd in to a room elegantly fitted up, and a table laid fit for a Governor to sit at. And, the lady desired us to draw near, and due to fatigue we could not have eat a morsel of victuals, and were oblig'd to displease our kind Hostess. We however took a little something to drink, and requested leave to retire as we were quite exhausted. She shewed us to our room, and 'afaith it was a noble one! and after wishing us a good night, she retired.

When we had snored away a part of the night, I was awaken'd by one of our Regimental Pipers[19] sounding the "Alarm"! I starts up, and the first idea that struck me was that our Party in the Barn had set fire to the Straw! However, after looking out, I found that it was a dwelling house, in flames, at the further extremity of the Town. Sinclair and I ran towards the spot, and we found the greatest confusion possible: no Buckets, no water, nobody to assist. Some of our officers set the Highlanders about it, and after gathering all the buckets and water they could, they went regularly to work, and the fire was confin'd to the house where it originated.

James Sinclair (and so did many others) saw a Woman at a corner cupboard fumbling about for something she could not find, at the same time that the ceiling of the room was blazing over her head, but nobody had courage enough to attempt her delivery. Sinclair starts in thro' a window and succeeded in dragging her away out of the danger, yet no sooner did he get her safe out than he discover'd her at the same work again! and, before he could have reach'd the spot, the ceiling fell in upon her and burn'd her to ashes!

After all was over, the people of the neighbourhood made up a subscription for the Highlanders that had work'd at the fire, and placed the money in the hands of our Sergeant FRASER,[20] requesting him to have the men refresh'd at the nearest tavern. Very few went, but for curiosity sake, Sinclair and myself step'd in, and after everyone who chose it, had taken a little something, Sergeant Fraser ask'd the Landlady for the reck'ning who said it amounted in all to three shillings! He gave her the three shillings and she return'd him threepence.

What! says Fraser, I thought you said the reck'ning was three shillings? So I did, replies the Landlady, and I have kept the three "thirteens"[21] you gave me,

---

19. Regimental Pipers. The written historical record is unclear on the number of pipers carried by Fraser's Highlanders over the period 1757–63, as pipers were not usually carried on the regiment's official establishment. Based on a strict interpretation of the historical record, as well as Thompson's above statement, some historians have claimed that the regiment had at most three pipers: Privates McIntyre, Macdonald and MacCrimmon. The latter fell sick in Ireland and never crossed over. In Stratford, Connecticut, the piper in the grenadier company was one Alexander McIntyre. Thompson states here that he was "awaken'd by *one* of our Regimental Pipers sounding the Alarm" (editors' emphasis). This statement clarifies that the regiment carried more than one piper at this time.
20. Sergeant John Fraser.
21. The English standard of 12 pence to the shilling arrived with the Normans, and a silver shilling coin was first struck in the 16th century. However, from 1460, Irish coinage was made with different metal contents to that of England and the values of the two currencies diverged. In 1701, the relationship between the Irish pound and sterling was fixed

and I return'd you the proper change. This was the first time that Sinclair and I came to the knowledge that one of our shillings would pass for thirteen pence. This business ran away with the night, and when we had taken breakfast the next morning and were going to quit, the Landlady, Mrs. MacLean, offered me some money to pay my way onwards, for which I thank'd her and said that King George gave me as much money as I wanted, and, if I was to judge of the hospitality of Ireland from what I had already experienced, I need never have a Copper in my pocket so long as I continued in that Country.

Anecdote No. 3
Out of the whole of our Regiment of Highlanders there remained only seven men on the Doctor's List, and I was left behind to take charge of them, and bring them forward as fast as they were able to bear the fatigue of the march. There were fourteen Companies of us altogether (×) and as there was two sent off each day at the dawn, it took seven days to get them forward without incommoding the houses along the line of march with too many billets at a time.[22] Somehow or another I contrived to get rid of all my invalids, but one, who managed to reach Dublin in a kind of carriage something like a Cart, and I walked the whole way. When we got there, I found that the 1st Battalion of the Royal Scots was quartered in the Town, in which Regiment was one of my brothers (William) as Lieutenant and Adjutant.[23] In going through the streets

---

with 13 Irish pounds being equivalent to 12 pounds sterling. With Irish copper coins being circulated with British silver coins, 13 Irish pence was equivalent to 1 British shilling.

22. Regiments were forced to move on 18th-century roads by "divisions" due to inadequate lodgings or facilities along the routes. See Houlding, *Fit for Service...*, 40–42.
23. This story does not ring true. There was no officer named William Thomson or Thompson serving in the 1st Battalion of the 1st Regiment of Foot (commonly referred to as "The Royal") at this time. The adjutant was one Thomas Frazer. There was, however, a Sergeant William Thomson in the 1st Foot (WO 25/209) according to John Houlding, and in the subsequent commissioning information he provided, confirmed that this was indeed James Thompson's older brother. Sergeant William Thomson (born 1715), who never adopted a "p" in his name like his younger brother James, was made adjutant of the Sutherland Regiment of Fencible Men (as the WO 25/209 Succession Book styles it) 11 September 1759 and remained in that post until it was disbanded. He was subsequently commissioned an ensign in the same regiment when a vacancy arose in 1760 and thus was a fully commissioned officer when it was reduced 3 March 1763 at the end of the War. As Fencibles were not entitled to half-pay, Ensign William Thomson returned to the service after an absence of five years as an ensign in the 41st Foot (Invalids) on 22 February 1768 and was promoted lieutenant 21 August 1780 in the 41st on a free augmentation vacancy. Records show Thomson remained in the 41st as late as 1793. As the commissioning rolls and succession books do not lie, we can thus with some certitude state that James Thompson's brother was serving as a sergeant at the exact same time Thompson was passing through Dublin on his way to America. Details of his older brother's military service got garbled through more than half a century of

I met with one of the men, and told him I would take it as a great favour, his directing me to their Barracks, and I ask'd him if he knew the Adjutant? "Oh," say's the man, "I know him d....'d [damned] well, for I have often felt the weight of his Rattan."[24] I was going to tell him that the Adjutant was my brother, but when I heard such an account of him, I said nothing about it. We jogg'd on together a little way, when the man shew'd me the door, and left me to find out the Barracks myself.

(×) being upwards of fourteen hundred strong[25]

When I got in, the people were very much surprised at my appearance, and after some enquiries I found out that the good Woman of the House was just then in child bed, and that my brother was gone out on the road I had just left behind me, in search of one – in this way we did not see each other for five days and until the night that I left Dublin, when we sat up together the whole of that night talking over our family affairs.

In strolling about the day before, who should I meet but my own dear Captain, Baillie! He ask'd me what I was doing so far in rear of my Division? (the Grenadiers). I told him I was kept back by one sick man out of the seven that was left in my charge at Donaghadee.

"Well, James," says Captain Baillie, "this won't do, you must start tomorrow at five in the morning." This was exactly what I wished for as I was quite low spirited on being divided from the Grenadiers. I went to my convalescent man and told him that I must quit him as I had orders to move forward at five next morning. The poor fellow was sorry to hear it for he had got as fond of me, nothing could be like it, and he said, "well, if you must go I'll go with you." So we started together, but he was still so weak that I was absolutely obliged to leave him on the side of the highroad, and make the best of my way alone.

---

storytelling, embellishment and the failing of memory.
24. Walking sticks, usually made from rattan (bamboo), were an essential part of a gentleman's wardrobe in the 18th century. A shorter version, known as a swagger stick, was carried by officers as well as regimental sergeant majors. They were often used as an instrument of punishment.
25. Footnote in the original Manuscript copy, identified with an ×. A matching × indicated where it was to be inserted in the narrative. Likely added by James Jr., the first editor, this number (1,400) is quite accurate. The original establishment of the 78th Foot was 1,145 all ranks (WO 24/326). At its first official inspection in Glasgow on 4 May 1757, the inspecting officers reported that the regiment was carrying 250 supernumeraries (i.e., those officers and men in excess of the establishment, but carried on the rolls until absorbed). This brings the regiment's total strength up to 1,395. Add a few pipers and we have the number stipulated by Thompson. (Of the 250 supernumeraries, 130 had been authorized by the War Office for use as reinforcements in America. Of the remaining 120 "unauthorized" supernumeraries, 80 would be transferred to another regiment, leaving a total of 170 taken to America.

I came up with several of our men still straggling along the road, and, Law! it made my heart *warm* to meet them again. My anxiety to join my own Company was such, that I did not break my fast until late in the day. I was fortunate enough, however, to get a comfortable dinner, by means of my billet, and I contriv'd to get into Cork[26] just at sundown, leaving sixty-four Irish miles behind me.[27]

The first person I enquir'd for was Sergeant James Sinclair who I found out at last, and he enquired of me where I had started from last? Why from Dublin, to be sure, said I. *"From Dublin!"* says Sinclair, "why that's impossible, for our Company was *five days* coming that distance"! You may talk as you like, but, I told him again, the same Sun that has just set had risen upon me and my brother this morning, at his Lodgings in Dublin. "Then," says Sinclair, "where's your Billet?" I have got none, I replied. "Then I can give you one," and this was a spare one he had about him.

Sinclair told me that there was a great Ball to be given to the Highlanders that night, and that I must go. What, says I, do you think I can be in the trim for Dancing after such a fatiguing march as I have had of it? "Never mind," says Sinclair, "you can sit down and look on." Well, I at last agreed to go but first and foremost I wanted to know where my Billet was. Sinclair shewed me the way to it, and it prov'd to be just on the opposite side of the street where the said Ball was to be. I thought this would do very well. I was shew'd by the Servant to a comfortable little room, and the Landlady was good enough to prepare some Tea for me, and she got me some water to bath my feet, and, by-the-law-Harry![28] I was as fresh, after this, as it nothing had happened.

I then told the good woman that I was invited to a Ball just opposite and perhaps would be out rather late. She said that was no matter. Well, to the Ball

---

26. Cork is a port city located on the southeastern tip of Ireland and was the principal staging area and embarkation point for British units shipping out to the Americas.
27. A good example of Thompson's tendency to embellish a good story. The walking distance between Dublin and Cork is about 150 miles, a distance which would take today's highly trained (and equipped) endurance walkers about two days. Thompson stated that he left Dublin at 5 a.m. and arrived in Cork "just at sundown." In June 1757 sunset in Dublin would have occurred about 9:30 p.m., so Thompson would have been on the road for about 16½ hours. This means that his walking speed would have averaged just over 9 mph! It is highly unlikely that Thompson, wearing his regulation army shoes, and carrying all of his equipment, could have maintained this pace for over 16½ hours. *The Penny Cyclopaedia of the Society for the Diffusion of Useful Knowledge* (London, 1837), seems to indicate that there was a difference between "Irish miles" and "English miles," specifically stating in one section that 94 Irish miles were equivalent to 119 English miles; thus Thompson's "64 Irish miles" would equate to about 81 English miles.
28. The expression "By the Law" or "By the Law Harry" was a common form of swearing in the 18th century. Old Harry, or Lord Harry, was a familiar name for the devil, and the use of "law" dodged the use of "Lord."

I went, and enjoy'd myself till two in the morning, when I went back across the street, and was agreeably surprised to find that the Servant had been made to sit up for me, by which means I did not disturb the family. I drank rather too much of Punch, a liquor I was not used to in my own Country but which I found very nice, which sour'd upon my Stomach, and, by-the-law, I had to lose the whole of it in the chimney-corner! However, after getting to bed, I slept like a Top, and was just as fresh as ever in the morning.

I forgot to tell you that my brother shew'd me a beautiful Silver Snuff Box that was given to him by my uncle who was a Lieutenant in "Sutherland's Rangers,"[29] and who had been the means of getting my brother into the Army (and who had made him a present of this same Snuff Box). When I got to Quebec, and after the first American War, my brother sent me this box by a merchant vessel bound to the place, but a rascal of a Yankee privateer captured the Vessel, Box and all! And I never saw it since I last saw it in my brother's own hands in Dublin. Oh! it was a thousand pities, for it was an elegant Box.

This same EARL OF SUTHERLAND who was Colonel of the Regiment[30] my uncle was in, got his first Commission in the Army in a funny way. His Father, the old Earl, was, with his Countess, passing some days with their friends in London, and she was far gone in the family-way, which was observed by "Geordy the Second," His Majesty, who slyly told the Earl that if the Countess carried a *Boy*, he would give him a Commission immediately. A Commission was accordingly prepared up, leaving the name blank. If it prov'd to be a Boy, his Christian name was to be inserted, and if a Girl, the thing was to be of no use. It turn'd out, however, to be a *Boy*, and the young Lord continued a long time to be a Subaltern in the Regiment, the old Earl not wishing to pay so bad a compliment to His Majesty's present as to further him on by Purchase. The King saw the inconvenience of it, at last, and gave the Earl authority to raise a Regiment of Fencibles, of

---

29. There is no historical evidence for a unit known as "Sutherland's Rangers." Thompson must be referring to one of the two Sutherland Independent Companies raised for service during the 1745 Uprising. A review of the officer rolls for those two companies shows no Thomsons or Stronachs serving in those units.

30. William Gordon, 18th Earl of Sutherland, was commissioned in the 1st Foot ("The Royal") from the early age of ten, serving as an ensign (29 November 1745) and lieutenant (22 January 1755). (He was *not*, as this oral history implies, Colonel of the 1st Foot.) He then secured a captaincy in the 56th Foot (Manners) before becoming a commandant of the Sutherland Regiment of Fencible Men raised in August 1759 (known thereafter as the 1st Sutherland Fencibles). It is fair to assume that Sergeant William Thomson and the young Earl served in the same "Royal" company for the one year the young gentleman was learning the duties of a lieutenant. What better man to have as an adjutant to supervise the training of the young inexperienced lieutenants in his own regiment, the Sutherland Fencibles, than ex-Sergeant William Thomson?

which he became the Colonel, and he took my Uncle with him as his Adjutant.[31] Soon after this we embark'd for Halifax.[32]

Anecdote No. 4
Our Regiment rendezvou'd at Cork, there to embark for Service, somewhere or other in North America. We sail'd with seal'd orders,[33] which were only to be open'd when we reach'd a certain latitude. The hir'd vessel I was embark'd in was call'd the "Martello," a beautiful new ship, and it was her first voyage.[34] The Captain did not know her trim, and the first few days after our sailing she would run away from the Commodore in no time, in spite of our short'ning sail, and for this high offense, which he couldn't help, the Captain had frequently a shot fired at him, to make him keep under the wing of the Commodore, the shot however, did no further injury than subject the Captain to a fine of six and eight pence for every shot.

One day we had a fine stiff breeze and our ship actually outsailed the whole

---

31. James Thompson Jr. unintentionally inserts himself into his father's oral narrative here when referring to his father's older brother, William, as "my Uncle." The adjutant was a battalion staff officer responsible for the commanding officer's paperwork in garrison, compiling the countless monthly returns, as well as issuing the daily regimental orders. His position, a paid appointment, was not a rank, so we find ensigns, lieutenants and even captains filling the post during the 18th century. Working closely with the major and the regimental sergeant major, the adjutant looked primarily after personnel, both officers and men, and thus concerned himself with enlistments, discharges, punishments, drill and the drawing up of duty rosters. He was also responsible, to a degree, for the discipline of the junior officers and their military training, especially ensigns and lieutenants.
32. Fraser's and Montgomery's Highlanders embarked on their transports 28 June but had to wait two days for fair winds and finally set sail for North America together on 30 June 1757.
33. This is incorrect, another embellishment by Thompson. Both Fraser's Highlanders and Montgomery's Highlanders had received their orders directly from William Pitt, Secretary for War, in late March 1757 instructing both to "embarked at Corke, for North America" – Fraser's to "be landed at Halifax, in Nova Scotia" and Montgomery's to "be landed at Charlestown in South Carolina."
34. Thompson's memory is a bit hazy. The actual name of his transport was most likely the *Martilla* (vice *Martello*) commanded by Captain Aust, which arrived at Deal (the anchorage called the Downs lay off this town in Kent in the southeast of England) from Virginia on 31 March 1758 "under convoy of his Majesty's ship Norwich" ("Port News" – *Lloyd's Evening Post*, 31 March 1758). It is safe to assume the *Martilla* was his actual ship for the voyage out to North America for several reasons as it had arrived in the company of other known transports used to convoy Fraser's Highlanders to Halifax the previous year (1757): viz. the *Ann* which not only conveyed Colonel Simon Fraser to Halifax, but subsequently was used to convey the regiment from Halifax to New York in October 1757, along with the transports *Brotherly Love, Kent, St. Cecilia, Duchess of Hambleton* and *Matilda* ("Embarkation Return, Halifax, 17 October 1757," NAS, GD125/22: f.17 [130]). The timing of the *Martilla's* return with its sister ships is in perfect alignment for these ships to have returned home to England by March 1758. See also footnote 8.

of the Fleet altho' only under bare poles. When the Commodore saw this he was satisfied it wasn't the Captain's fault, and he made him pay no more six-and-eight pence per shot. The ship was so tight that she didn't require pumping the whole of the voyage, which was a lucky circumstance indeed.

At last, we discover'd the Commodore's Signal for the whole of the Fleet to heave-to, and when we had done this as cleverly as we could, the Signal was made for all Commanding Officers of Corps to go on board the Commodore's ship. This was to make known our Destination, and to receive their Orders accordingly. We soon after found out that our place of destination was Halifax. As good luck would have it, the Fleet was safe, and soon after we cast our Anchor, our Captain was anxious to try the tightness of his ship and gave his orders to have her pump'd. The men had difficulty in getting the pumps to draw, and when, at last, water came, it was as black as my Bonnet,[35] and it produced such a stench, that it would soon have poison'd all the men on board. It turn'd out that instead of pumping *out,* 'afaith they were obliged to pump *in,* to prevent the Troops getting sick.

Chapter 2 | Winter Quarters, Connecticut Colony, 1757–58

James Thompson left us no oral accounts of his first impressions of North America. After eight weeks at sea, the first landfall of the 78th Foot was off Cape Sambro, Nova Scotia, and the first transports carrying seven of the ten Fraser companies dropped anchor in Halifax harbour on 23 August 1757. After a brief stay of only nine weeks in Nova Scotia, the Fraser Highlanders, totalling 1,135 all ranks, as well as 110 women and 29 children, were loaded onto eight transport ships and sailed south, bound for New York. According to their commanding officer, Simon Fraser, what should have been a short cruise turned into:

> … the most tedious and disagreeable voyage that has been known, in the course of which we had six very hard gales that your fresh water sailors would call storms. In one of these we were all separated, one ship drove upon Nantucket Shoal, another lost her Masts, a third her sails, and we who got off as well as any you may believe were not entirely at our ease during 26 hours that we drove with our helm lash'd under a balance mizen, however we thank God we have all got in one after another without any material loss, but from the Atlantic Ocean in the Month of November, *Libera nos Domine.*[36]

---

35. Here Thompson confirms that the grenadiers of his regiment wore black bearskin caps. For detailed accounts on all items of Highland weapons and dress issued, see McCulloch, *SOTM,* II, Part 2.
36. The numbers loaded on each ship were as follows: *Ann,* 94; *Kent,* 130; *Neptune,* 109; *Brotherly Love,* 233; *Myrilla,* 150 [*Martilla*?]; *St. Cecilia,* 134; *Duchess of Hambleton,*

People in New York had started to wonder what had become of the 78th Foot, Colonel John Forbes one of them. Writing to Lord Loudoun from Albany on 10 November 1757 – a "damn'd rainy foggy day" – the adjutant general for North America worried that "We have no accounts of Frazers Battalion." But on 23 November 1757, their battered transports, with broken spars and torn sails, dropped anchor in New York harbour while their colonel went ashore to wait upon Lieutenant Governor Oliver Delancey. There, Fraser was handed written orders from Forbes dated 18 October 1757, instructing him to "procure 16 Sloops" forthwith and "to victual them" for the short sail across Long Island Sound to the mainland. Once there he would march his Highlanders inland where they would be billeted on the people of Connecticut colony for the winter.[37]

"We don't, after all, remain here this Winter," Simon Fraser wrote disappointedly from New York on Christmas Day to a friend at home, "but go to Cantonments in Connecticut from 40 to 90 miles from hence among a set of Cromwelians [sic] imported [here] about the year 1640." His own company and James Thompson's grenadier company were quartered at Stratford while the remaining eight companies were billeted on the nearby towns of Norwalk, Fairfield, Milford and Stanford.[38]

The town selectmen were initially uneasy at the anticipated expense of quartering the Highlanders and wished that the soldiers might be more equitably distributed throughout the colony but soon realized "the compactness was necessary for the good of the troops." They agreed to provide rooms and houses, bedding, firewood, candles, cider, guard-houses and staffed hospitals, their full cooperation in quartering the King's troops a direct contrast to the shoddy reception encountered by the 77th Foot in Charles Town, South Carolina.[39]

All companies appear to have been snugly billeted well in time for Yule and Hogmanay, Grenadier Sergeant James Thompson crowing that in Stratford he "had the very good luck to get into a very good house own'd by one THOMAS

211; *Matilda,* 103. "Embarkation Returns, Halifax, 17 October 1757," NAS, GD125/22: f.17; Simon Fraser to Baillie James Fraser, 25 December 1757, New York, quoted in *Clan Fraser Society of Canada Newsletter.* "*Libera nos Domine*" translates to "Deliver us, O Lord."

37. Forbes to Loudoun, Albany, 10 November 1757, in *Writings of General John Forbes, Relating to His Service in North America,* Alfred Proctor James, ed. (Menasha, 1938),14 (also Loudoun Papers, Huntington Library, San Marino, California, LO 4803); and, Forbes to Fraser, New York, 18 October 1757, *Ibid.,* 14–15 (also LO 4665).

38. Simon Fraser to Baillie James Fraser, New York, 25 December 1757, *Ibid.* See also, "Report of the Quarters of His Majesty's 63rd or Second Highland Battalion as Canton'd in The Government of Connecticut in New England," NAS, GD45/2/41. As shown in this report, Fraser's Highland battalion mustered 42 officers and 1,100 other ranks.

39. Stanley Pargellis, *Lord Loudoun in North America* (New Haven, 1933), 225.

IVERS, a ropemaker, where I sat at as well a furnish'd table as my Colonel and as good wine and plenty of it.... I lived here like a fighting cock, without it costing me a Copper."

The 78th Foot spent a quiet but cold winter among the genial but God-fearing citizens of Connecticut. On 29 January 1758 the baptism of "Bettee, the daughter of Daniel Gunn, drum Major in Col. Frasier's regiment" in Stratford's Church of England passed almost unnoticed, everyone's attention being focused on the killing of a corporal in a guardhouse brawl just before Hogmanay, the Scottish New Year. Grenadier Sergeant ALEXANDER FRASER, the alleged perpetrator, was charged by the local magistrate in Stratford with the murder of one Grenadier Corporal James Macky, an incident Grenadier Sergeant James Thompson remembered only too well, for his dirk was the murder weapon and Fraser his best friend as will be seen in this chapter.

Colonel Simon Fraser tried desperately to have the civilian authorities turn Sergeant Fraser over to him for military justice through a court martial and appealed to Colonel John Forbes, the Adjutant General, to intercede with Lord Loudoun on the unfortunate sergeant's behalf: "for god's sake My Dear Sir, put my Lord in mind to do something about this poor unhappy man, whose life 'twere pity shou'd be in the hands of uncultivated creatures, for the King has not a better Soldier."[40] When the trial went ahead in a civilian court, the *Mac Shimi*[41] made sure he became directly involved with the proceedings. This intervention did not sit well with the Attorney General of Connecticut, Rob Walker, who insinuated that Colonel Fraser was trying to "screen" the prisoner. However, calmness prevailed and the court proceeded. The jury of twelve Connecticut men acquitted Fraser of the crime of willful murder by reason of self-defence. The not-guilty verdict was the cause for universal rejoicing in Fraser's Highlanders, or as related by James Thompson, "there was a terrible hullabaloo among the Highlanders...." A delighted Colonel Fraser proclaimed to Forbes on 25 February 1758 that "I must do them the Justice to say that Court & Jury behav'd with such moderation, decency & propriety as Surprized me. The Colony of Connecticut & the 2nd Highland Battalion are hand & glove."[42]

Returns from Stratford dated 14 December 1757 show that Sergeant Thompson's grenadier company, consisting of "1 Captain, 2 Lieutenants, 4 sergeants, 2

---

40. Simon Fraser to John Forbes, Stratford, 10 February 1758, NAS, GD45/2/29 f.4.
41. *Mac Shimi*, meaning "son of Simon," was the traditional patronymic of the Fraser chieftain.
42. Simon Fraser to John Forbes, Stratford, 25 February 1758, NAS, GD45/2/29 f.5. By this time, Fraser's Highlanders had been entered into the Order of Battle as the 63rd Regiment of Foot, but habits die hard as Colonel Fraser is still referring to his unit as the "2nd Highland Battalion."

drummers, 97 men, 7 women victuallers, Lieutenant Cuthbert's servant, Alexander McErtar [McIntyre] musician" shared the town with Colonel Fraser's own company numbering "1 Captain, 1 Lieutenant, 1 Ensign, 4 Sergeants, 3 drummers, 104 men, 6 women victuallers."[43]

Anecdote No. 13

The tents were order'd to be struck, and we were march'd into the town of Stratford[44] where we immediately got billets upon the inhabitants. I had the good luck to get into a very good house, own'd by one Thomas Ivers,[45] a ropemaker, where I sat at as well a furnish'd table as my Colonel, and as good Wine and plenty of it. Our breakfast was made from Indian meal and call'd "Soupaun" and 'afaith it was capital! I liv'd here like a fighting cock, without its costing me a Copper. My Landlord and Landlady were fine people, and they became so fond of me nothing could be like it. They had an only daughter, then about twelve years of age,[46] and Mr. Ivers proposed to me that if I should quit the Army, she should, at a proper age, become my wife, and that he would take me into partnership in the Rope-making business. I thank'd him for his good intentions, but said that as I had volunteer'd my Services to fight for my King and Country, it would look as if I had become faint hearted to quit the Army before I had been

---

43. NAS, GD125/22/17(20A) "A Return of Officers Quartered in Stratford & Milford" shows that the companies of John Macpherson and John Campbell *Barr Breac* were quartered at Milford. The list reads: "Hon. Col. Simon Frasier [sic], Captain John McPherson [sic], Captain John Campbell, Captain Charles Bailey [sic], Lt. John Cuthbert, Lt. Charles McDonald [sic], Lt. John Frasier, Lt. Alexander McLoud [sic], Lt. Simon Frasier, Lt. William McDonald, Lt. Hector McDonald, Ensign Simon Frasier, Ensign John Chisholm, Adjutant Hugh Frasier," quoted in Rev. Samuel Orcutt, *A History of the Old Town of Stratford* (Fairfield, 1896), 372.
44. Stratford. A coastal town in Fairfield County, Connecticut, on Long Island Sound at the mouth of the Housatonic River. In Stratford, the non-commissioned officers and men of Colonel Fraser's Company and Thompson's company of grenadiers were camped on the common at Watchhouse Hill, at the rear of Christ Episcopal Church. Colonel Fraser and his officers commandeered Parson Izrahiah Wetmore's new house on Main Street – so new that the minister hadn't even moved in. Stratford, then less than 3,600 inhabitants, had a hard time to supply the soldiers with firewood, water and food, and residents grumbled at the inconvenience. Stratford eventually received compensation the following October amounting to £449 16s 3p.
45. Thomas Ivers took in two soldiers. See "Report of the Quarters of His Majesty's 63rd or Second Highland Battalion as Canton'd in The Government of Connecticut in New England," NAS, GD45/2/41.
46. Thompson tells us that the daughter was twelve years old, thus born about 1745. Family records published in 2005, show one daughter, Elizabeth, born 19 July 1756, far too young to have been the daughter mentioned by Thompson. Another daughter, Anna, was baptized in 1761. Either Thompson's memory was faulty, or Ivers had another daughter, born twelve years earlier, who died.

in Battle; besides I could not think of any such thing without having first obtained the consent of Colonel Fraser.[47]

Then, said Mr. Ivers, if that's all that's wanting, and that I can obtain it for money, I shall offer such a sum as I am sure will be accepted. He accordingly went to the Colonel and stated his business. The Colonel said it was contrary to the rules of the Service to part with a man during the War, and, to let go a hearty young man such as Thompson was, would cost him his Commission. Poor Ivers came back to me with his finger in his mouth!

Anecdote No. 12
While we were quarter'd in Stratford, New England, I was sadly off for want of a Dirk,[48] and coax'd our regimental armourer to make me a blade of one, out of a Sword-blade which I got by accident. He said he would try his hand at it, and accordingly set to work – he found great difficulty in shaping it, on account of the hardness of the steel, but at length he contriv'd to finish it tolerably well. I myself, carv'd the handle, and got a Silversmith to mount it, from a pattern which I got for him.

Sergeant Fraser[49] of our Regiment having lent his dirk to one of the Officers of his Company, and having occasion to go somewhere or other on duty, he borrowed mine, and on his way he call'd at the Guardhouse which was mounted from our Highlanders and commanded by Corporal McKee,[50] who was also known as Mack-Chesney, and was then acting as Sergeant. Fraser had no particular business at the Guardhouse, but he went merely to warm his heels at the fire. As he was standing with his back to the fireplace, and was looking about him, he observes McKee lying down on the guard-bed, and his Regimental coat off. Fraser takes notice of it, and tells McKee that it was very unbecoming, and a bad example to the men. McKee who thought no small matter of himself, was

---

47. Lieutenant Colonel Simon Fraser, former Master of Lovat.
48. One of the deadliest weapons in a Highlander's arsenal was his dirk, a fighting dagger that had evolved purely and simply for fighting and killing with deadly efficiency. Combining elements of stabbing knives such as the ballock knives, *poignards* and *quillon* daggers used by medieval knights on the field of battle, the first known reference to a Highland dirk specifically by name occurs in 1617. There were no standard-issue dirks during the Seven Years' War, regulation dirks for pipers, bandsmen, and sergeants being issued in the following century. The 18th-century Highland dirk was a personal weapon and thus reflected the owner's tastes as well as means. It was worn on the right hip to counterbalance the broadsword on the left; a Highlander would draw it with his left hand after he had drawn his broadsword with the right. Dirk blades on average were from 10 to 18 inches long (the latter length usually a good indication that the weapon had been made from a cut-down sword).
49. Sergeant Alexander Fraser.
50. Corporal James Macky.

miff'd that the men should have overheard the rebuke, immediately took fire at this, and starting up, he ran to his Broadsword and made a lunge at Fraser with it, which gave him a devil of a gash on the head!

Fraser attempted to get away to have his head dress'd, but McKee seiz'd hold of him by the hair by one hand, and had got his other arm rais'd to give him another cut of his Broadsword, when, as good-luck would have it, Fraser got the guard door between him and McKee, and in that way they were struggling together, one to keep the door closed, and the other to drag it open by means of the grasp which he held of his adversary's hair which was worn long. By some chance, Fraser's hand that was free, came to touch the handle of my Dirk (which he had not thought of using during the scuffle) and the moment he felt it, he drew it with a back-handed grasp, and thrust it into McKee's belly, who fell that instant, and died on the spot! I happen'd accidentally to call at the Guardhouse just after McKee fell, and I was almost petrified at the sight of him lying dead on the floor, and his bowels coming out at the wound, and Fraser bleeding to death on the guard-bed, and the whole floor cover'd with blood.[51]

I ran after a Doctor, and was lucky in finding one immediately. Fraser was put into a private house, and remained there about one month under the Doctor's hands, and then he was put into the town-jail at Greenfield,[52] about eight miles off. When he was brought to trial[53] it was found that the Courthouse was too small for the crowd, as all the Regiment that could get leave to go was there, beside vast numbers of civilians. The Judges removed to the Church. As Fraser spoke scarcely a word of English, and the men who had mounted guard with McKee were the principal evidence, it was necessary to have an interpreter who could speak Gaelic, and the Colonel himself undertook the office.

In the course of the trial, the Attorney General observ'd to the Judges that all the evidence was so much to the same effect, that he could not refrain from taxing Colonel Fraser with wishing to screen the prisoner. The Colonel became

---

51. Actual testimony at the time stated that Fraser had mortally wounded James Macky with a thrust to "the neck and throat ... inclining downwards into the Trunk." George II vs Sergeant Alexander Fraser, December 1757 to February 1758, Fairfield County Superior Court Files, RG3, Box 5, 1750–1759, A-L.
52. Thompson's "Greenfield" is most likely today's Greenfield Hill, a neighbourhood of Fairfield. Greenfield Hill lies about eight miles west of Stratford.
53. The dirk fight occurred on Tuesday night, 27 December 1757. Sergeant Fraser was formally charged by the Colony of Connecticut with the murder of Corporal Macky on 23 February 1758, court documents stating that Fraser "was instigated by the devil and of his own preconceived malice." Fraser was tried and acquitted by the Fairfield Superior Court on the following day, 24 February 1758. George II vs Sergeant Alexander Fraser, December 1757 to February 1758, Fairfield County Superior Court Files, RG3, Box 5, 1750–1759, A-L.

"The deadly dirk." The Highland dagger was usually crafted from a broken sword, as was this one designed by James Thompson in 1757 and sketched by his son years later. Used by Thompson's friend and regimental colleague Alexander Fraser to defend himself against a drunken corporal of the guard at Stratford, Connecticut, in 1757, it became exhibit A at the subsequent murder trial of Fraser. He was quickly acquitted and the dirk returned to its rightful owner. It now resides in the 18th-century arms collection at the Canadian War Museum in Ottawa. Pen and ink sketch by James Thompson Jr. scanned from the manuscript letter-book. (Photo by Earl John Chapman)

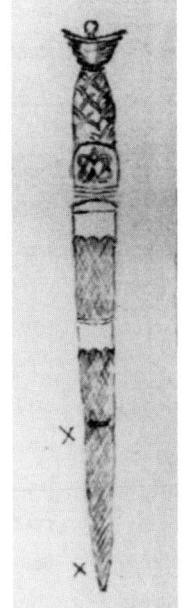

very indignant at the insinuation that he should attempt to conceal any part of the truth of the evidence, and appeal'd to the Judges to stop the trial, and give him an opportunity of bringing the Attorney General to accounts, and 'afaith he would have done so, as soon as look at him!

My landlord, good honest Thomas Ivers, and myself, went on horseback, on the day of trial, and Ivers took a second horse, which he led by the bridles, in order to bring Fraser home to his own house, if he should be discharg'd, and he had order'd a supper for twelve friends, to be in readiness at a tavern they call'd "the halfway house," and in order that they should not be disappointed, he promis'd that it should be paid for, whether eaten or not, however, we were all disappointed, for Fraser was remanded back to jail until the last day of the term, but there was one great consolation for the loss of the Supper, and that was, that the jury had acquitted him of the crime of willful murder, notwithstanding that the Attorney General tried all he could to persuade them to the contrary.

Well, when the day came, Ivers again gave me a horse to accompany him as before, and he took a spare one for Fraser, but he took no thought of the supper at *this* time. As soon as Fraser was again made free in the forest, there was a terrible hullabaloo among the Highlanders who should catch hold of him first, in order to give him a treat, and they wanted to carry him away on their shoulders. It was with great difficulty that Ivers and myself could get at him, and if it hadn't been for me poor Ivers would have got himself well thrash'd for his officious good nature, however, we got him at last upon horseback, and away we went, with the crowd hallooing after us.

We did not stop 'til we got home, where Mrs Ivers, a good body as ever liv'd, received my fellow-lodger with open arms, and she quoted the Scripture where it says "there is more rejoicing for the one lost sheep that is found again, than for the ninety and nine that never was in danger."[54] It was night when we got

---

54. It is possible that Thompson accurately recalled Mrs. Ivers' statement, and that she paraphrased the parable. The parable is from Matthew 18:12–14 (King James Version):

home, but we were so well entertain'd and so happy together, that it was morning before we thought of going to rest. So, you see, that that Dirk has done some mischief, but that's not all the work that it has done.[55]

Anecdote No. 13

When we were order'd away from Stratford, my parting with the family was very distressing indeed, both to me and themselves. Ivers made me promise that when the War was brought to a close I should go back to him, but altho' I made the promise I never perform'd it. This same Ivers was, afterwards, a Captain of Artillery in the army under General MONTGOMERY[56] that came in 1775 to the attack of Quebec, and altho' he was then our enemy I endeavour'd all in my power to find him out, and had some hopes that he was among the prisoners we took on that occasion when, if I had chanc'd to find him, I should have done every thing possible to make his situation comfortable, in consideration of the very great kindness he had shewn for me. To be sure our situation was somewhat chang'd, for when I knew him at Stratford, he was a British Subject, and now he was in a Rebel Army, but that was of no kind of matter to me.

Some years after the Conquest of Quebec, there came a General Officer who had Commanded a Regiment at Stratford and he accosted me in the Street with "haven't I seen you somewhere or other? Your face is very familiar to me?" Why, yes Sir, I replied, I think you must have seen me in Fraser's Highlanders while quarter'd at Stratford in New England, which is the place where I recollect to have seen you last. "Just so," said the General, "that was the very place." "Did ever you eat *Soupaun*[57] while you were there"? Oh yes I did, General, and I lik'd it very much indeed. Says the General, "I breakfasted upon nothing else while I was there, and I find it to agree so well with me, that I shall continue to use it as long as I live."

12: How think ye? if a man have an hundred sheep, and one of them be gone astray, doth he not leave the ninety and nine, and goeth into the mountains, and seeketh that which is gone astray?

13: And if so be that he find it, verily I say unto you, he rejoiceth more of that sheep, than of the ninety and nine which went not astray.

55. A note was found in the left-hand margin of this anecdote in the original Manuscript copy. Clearly added by James Thompson Jr., it explains that his father had made a second dirk, slightly longer than the first. Both dirks were given to his sons: the shorter dirk (the murder weapon) to William Alexander Thompson (see Part Three for Biographical Note); the longer dirk to James Jr. Both dirks were acquired by the Canadian War Museum, Ottawa.

56. Brigadier General Richard Montgomery.

57. *Soupaun* sounds like a Mohawk breakfast dish and not something from an established New England community.

Chapter 3 | The Siege and Capture of Louisbourg, 1758

On 11 March 1758 eight of the nine additional companies sent from Scotland to reinforce the three Highland battalions serving in North America arrived at New York together. The ninth company, carrying men destined for the 42nd Foot, had been blown by a storm southwards to the Caribbean. The three 78th companies that stepped ashore were commanded by Captains Sir Henry Seton of Culbeg, 4th Baronet of Abercorn; Thomas Ross of Calrossie; and ALEXANDER CAMERON of Dungallon respectively.

The ships also brought eagerly awaited dispatches. The first big news was that Lord Loudoun was relieved of command and replaced by Major General James Abercromby. The second was detailed orders outlining Pitt's new campaign strategy for offensive action in North America. It called for a three-pronged attack against New France on three separate routes or axes, and each of the three Highland regiments in North America found itself assigned to a separate army.

In the west, Brigadier General John Forbes would lead an expedition of some 1,500 regulars against the French fort on the Forks of the Ohio – Fort Duquesne (now Pittsburgh) – and would include the 77th Foot (Montgomery's Highlanders) who would soon be recalled from South Carolina for the task. In the centre, Major General Abercromby, the new commander-in-chief in North America, seconded by Brigadier George Augustus, Lord Howe, would command the largest of the three armies and launch north from Albany, New York. His ultimate objective was Montreal, but first he was ordered to move up the Lake George–Lake Champlain axis to capture the French forts at Carillon (Ticonderoga) and St. Frederic (Crown Point) respectively. For this, he assembled of force of some 17,000 troops comprising 6,000 regulars and 11,000 provincials from Massachusetts, New York, Connecticut, Rhode Island and New Jersey.

Thompson's regiment was initially assigned to this second army but was re-assigned at the eleventh hour by Abercromby to Major General JEFFERY AMHERST's 12,000-man army, whose mission was to capture the fortress of Louisbourg which guarded the approaches to the St. Lawrence River. This shift in assignments would dramatically change the lives of officers and men in the two affected regiments. The reason Abercromby gave for this change was that the Frasers in Connecticut were more suited to the amphibious expedition against Louisbourg as they were closer to the "place of embarkation, [Boston]; a shorter march for the men; and a saving in the expense,"[58] whereas it was more logical for the 42nd Foot in New York to move north and join his overland expedition in upstate New York. Amherst's army, if successful, was to move on and take

---

58. Abercromby to Pitt, New York, 28 April 1758, NA, CO5/50: f.7.

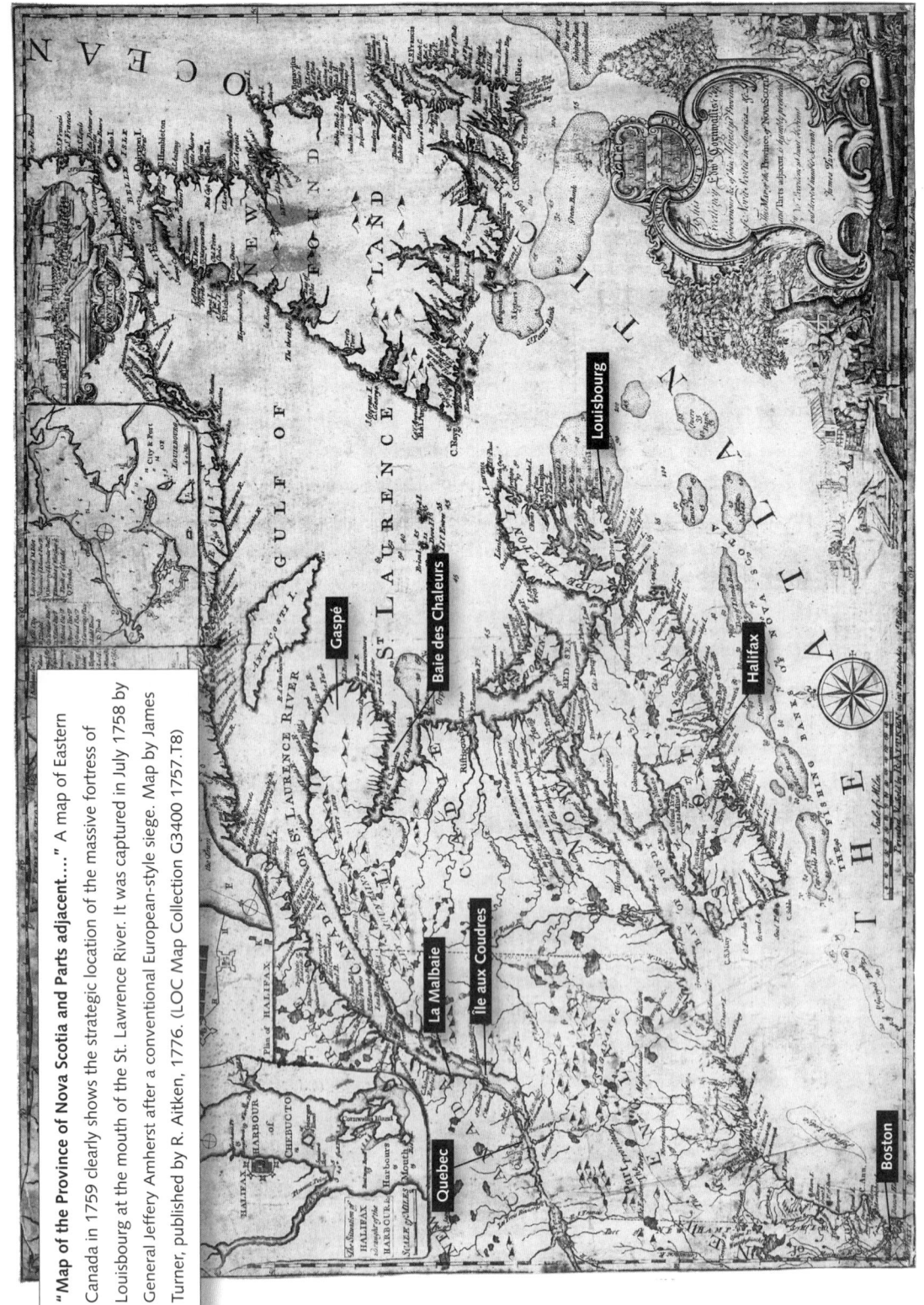

"**Map of the Province of Nova Scotia and Parts adjacent....**" A map of Eastern Canada in 1759 clearly shows the strategic location of the massive fortress of Louisbourg at the mouth of the St. Lawrence River. It was captured in July 1758 by General Jeffery Amherst after a conventional European-style siege. Map by James Turner, published by R. Aitken, 1776. (LOC Map Collection G3400 1757.T8)

The conqueror of Canada. A pensive Sir Jeffery Amherst leans on a map of Canada dressed in full armour (artistic licence and fashion of the day). In the background, his riverine army descends the rapids of the St. Lawrence River in boats to capture Montreal in the summer of 1760 and end the war on the North American continent. He eventually rose to the peerage and the rank of field marshal. Mezzotint after a painting by Sir Joshua Reynolds. (LOC LC-USZ62-45182)

Quebec if the season and circumstances permitted. A fleet of 41 warships and 116 transports under the command of Vice Admiral Edward "Dreadnought" Boscawen was to provide direct support.

The 78th Additional Companies crossed over from Long Island in late March, accompanied by the newly arrived chaplain, ROBERT *"Caipal Mhor"* MACPHERSON, reaching Connecticut just as the regiment was packing up in early April to march to Providence, Rhode Island, to take ship for Boston. The best account of the regiment's state of health, and its progress in training, comes from the pen of its commandant, Lieutenant Colonel Simon Fraser, writing to Lord Loudoun while waiting in Boston Harbour. His troops were "in general healthy, young & well-built, but not tall. Highlanders seldom are."

"As soldiers," he continued, his young Highlanders were "not what I would have them…" but they could "go thorough the platoon exercise pretty well … & they all march well & fire well at marks, which were the only things the cold would, for the greatest part of the winter, allow us to attempt."[59] A 19th-century town historian would attest to the Highlanders' prowess at shooting, claiming "Colonel Frasier's [*sic*] men amused themselves at times in shooting at the weathercock at the top of the Episcopal Church spire which they pierced several times."[60]

The *Mac Shimi* was also having a problem outfitting his men, citing that "four voyages within the year has put our cloathing much out of repair, but we are doing our best to refit it." Except for some missing Highland pistols,

---

59. Colonel Simon Fraser to Lord Loudoun, "from on board the Halifax, off Nantasket Lighthouse," 23 April 1758, Loudoun Papers, Huntingdon Library, San Marino, California, LO 5447.
60. Orcutt, *History of the Old Town of Stratford*, 372.

his weapons were "the carbines the horse had before they were reduced to Dragoons" and were "excellent arms in every respect, but that they are rather slight for hard use."[61]

The Frasers boarded their transports on St. Georges Day, 23 April 1758, in Boston, and sailed for Halifax in convoy under the protection of the sloop *Province*. Five days later their convoy entered Halifax harbour to be greeted by a forest of masts and a crowded anchorage. The 15th Foot had also just arrived, fresh from England, and once the 78th Foot's transports had dropped anchor, all newly arrived troops were informed they were to remain on board their transports.

Brigadier General JAMES WOLFE arrived with Admiral Boscawen and twelve warships on 9 May and three days later reported to Lord Sackville that "Fraser's and Brigadier Lawrence's Battalions were … in very good condition." He added with some admiration that "the Highlanders are very useful serviceable soldiers and commanded by the most manly corps of officers I ever saw."[62]

Commanding officers with troops cooped up on the transports in harbour had already been instructed a week earlier to ensure "those on board [were] kept extremely clean in their ships, carried frequently on shore and all possible means used to preserve them in health and vigour."[63] Finally, four days later, on 28 May 1758, the assembled army left Halifax harbour under the command of Admiral Boscawen only to meet their errant commander, Major General Jeffery Amherst, arriving in the warship *Dublin* at the entrance to Halifax Roads. Amherst quickly transferred his effects aboard Boscawen's flagship, the *Namur*, and the armada continued on its way to Louisbourg, making Gabarus Bay the morning of 1 June 1758.

Amherst's army was an impressive one – fourteen battalions of regular infantry, 500 rangers and a detachment and siege train of Royal Artillery – numbering nearly 12,000 men in all. The complement of seamen and marines in the fleet doubled the strength of the British force to over 24,000 men while, thanks to the navy's blockading efforts, the Louisbourg garrison could only muster four regular battalions, twenty-four *compagnies franche de la marine* (colonial troops) consisting of 1,200 men and a few hundred Acadian militiamen and Indians for

---

61. Colonel Simon Fraser to Lord Loudoun, "from on board the Halifax, off Nantasket Lighthouse," 23 April 1758, Loudoun Papers, Huntingdon Library, San Marino, California, LO 5447.
62. James Wolfe to Lord George Sackville, 12 May 1758, Halifax, in Beckles Willson, *The Life and Letters of James Wolfe* (New York, 1909), 363.
63. James Cunninghame to Lord Sackville, At Sea, 30 May 1758, noted that the light infantry had "exchanged their heavy Arms, for the light fusils of the additional companies of Frasers left at Halifax," quoted in J. S. McLennan, *Louisbourg: From its Foundation to its Fall, 1713–1758* (London, 1919. Reprint Halifax, 1979), 239 (hereafter McLennan, *Louisbourg*).

a total of some 3,500 men. There was also a French squadron of six frigates and five ships of the line cooped up in Louisbourg harbour, which theoretically added another 3,000 men to the manpower at Governor AUGUSTIN DE BOSCHENRY DRUCOUR's disposal, but the total French garrison could barely muster more than a quarter of the strength to oppose the combined British forces now dropping anchor off their coast.

The coast had been fortified, several miles east and west of Louisbourg, and there were only a few landing places along the rocky shore, mostly between Miré Bay on the east and the head of Gabarus Bay on the west. The shores of the latter sloped upwards from the beaches and rocky promontories to a considerable height except where swamps and moorland extended down to the shore. About 4,000 yards west of the town was L'Anse à la Coromandière (Cormorant's Cove), which French and English military planners alike had deemed the most suitable landing place for an amphibious force. Here the French had made their most elaborate preparations for defence.

It was a beautiful, sandy beach curving some 660 yards between two rocky headlands, the only marring feature a rocky outcrop that bisected it in the middle. The back of the long beach ended with an eroded earthen cliff some 15 to 20 feet in height. It was upon this firmer ground that the French dug their trenches and placed felled trees with sharpened branches pointing outwards to make an *abattis*, an 18th-century version of barbed wire designed to slow down attackers by entangling them. So closely had the trees been laid and intertwined that they appeared as a natural growth to British observers aboard their ships. The next two beaches down at Pointe Platte (Flat Point) and Pointe Blanche (White Point) were also strongly entrenched and guarded but none of the beaches were close enough to support one another, each separated by long stretches of rocky inaccessible cliffs.

The 78th, along with the other regiments, remained cooped up aboard their transports anchored in Gabarus Bay for another week while the uncooperative sea and the huge surf continued to run. After several false starts and attempts to load and unload the landing boats in the heavy swells, the weather finally abated several days later on Thursday, 8 June 1758, and Wolfe's assault force went in. He later wrote: "I couldn't recommend the bay of Gabarus for a descent, especially as we managed it!" In the same letter, he praised Thompson's unit, stating that "the Highlanders have behaved with distinction, [but] their company of Grenadiers has suffered, 3 of the officers killed and the fourth dangerously wounded."[64]

---

64. Wolfe to Major Walter Wolfe, "Camp before Louisbourg," 27 July 1758, Willson, *Letters of Wolfe ...*, 384–5; Wolfe to Lord George Sackville, Louisbourg, 30 July 1758, *Ibid.*, 388. Two 78th officers, Captain Charles Baillie and Lieutenant John Cuthbert, were killed in Sergeant Thompson's boat the day of the landing. Lieutenant Simon *Tenakyle*

Wolfe's Cove, Louisbourg, then. The "Red-haired Corporal" wades through surf at the head of a grenadier detachment to join the light infantry on the high ground dominating the main beach. A 20th-century watercolour by C.W. Jefferys. (LAC A/N 1972-26-1381)

Thompson, as will be seen in one of the ensuing anecdotes, reported that the 78th Foot broke ranks after they had landed on the beach and chased the enemy back to Louisbourg. However, two hours later, "they all came back again to a man," with Thompson adding that "almost every man brought in his prisoner and some had two...." By British army standards this was poor discipline indeed,

---

Fraser later died of wounds received during the landing and, according to Parson Robert Macpherson, was hit while standing beside Colonel Simon Fraser. Lieutenant James Murray of Macgregor was killed two days later in the trenches, unbeknownst to Wolfe. The two officers replacing Baillie and Cuthbert, the new Grenadier Captain Donald "Donull Gorm" Macdonell and Lieutenant Alexander Campbell, were also both wounded on the same day as Lieutenant Murray's death, while Lieutenant John Macdonald was wounded in the last few days of the siege.

Wolfe's Cove, Louisbourg, today. The small unguarded cove adjacent to the larger Cormorant Beach (rear) selected as the main landing place for Brigadier General James Wolfe's assault force. Light infantry seized the high ground (middle far right) and quickly brought flanking fire onto the French defenders' positions, causing them to retreat back to Louisbourg. Thompson and his fellow grenadiers subsequently landed unopposed on the main beach. (Photo by Susan Johnson McCulloch)

and in this same anecdote Thompson implies that some in the army viewed the 78th Foot as untrained irregulars. Jeffery Amherst, their commanding general, was not annoyed by his Highlanders' irregular behaviour. He later confessed in his journal that he too was impatient and more than a little put out that the Royal Navy had taken "so much time to land the Troops that it was impossible to pursue the Enemy so quick as could have been wished." The troops that had harried the fleeing enemy back to the town, in his opinion, had done well, pursuing their foe "through the roughest and worst ground I ever saw." Amherst also freely admitted that "the Pursuit ending with a Cannonading from the Town" was extremely useful "as it pointed out how near I could camp to invest it!"[65]

The psychological impact of having warlike Highlanders to use as shock troops was not lost on commanders like Wolfe and Amherst's brother, William. Wolfe had requested that the 78th be transferred from another brigade to beef up his assault force earlier in the week as the 78th Foot's light infantry and grenadiers already formed a goodly proportion of it. For this honour of being one of the first regiments to land, the 78th was eternally grateful to Wolfe and this does much to

---

65. 8 June 1758, *Journal of Jeffery Amherst: Recording the Military Career of General Amherst in America from 1758 to 1760* (hereafter Amherst, *Journal*), J.C. Webster, ed. (Toronto, 1931), 50–1.

Formalities of surrender. A French officer doffs his tricorne hat to Colonel William Amherst, the younger brother of General Jeffery Amherst, to report that Governor Drucour has accepted the terms of surrender for the fortress of Louisbourg and that hostilities are now at an end. A modern watercolour by Howard M. Pyle. (LAC C-008991)

explain his high esteem amongst the Highland officers and rank and file.

Once the British army had successfully landed on 8 June, the fate of Louisbourg was a foregone conclusion. One French naval officer assessing the situation four weeks later was blunt: "The place is in an evil state; it cannot sustain a siege!"[66] A week of bad weather at the outset, however, boded ill for things to come. The difficulty of landing the artillery and the attendant siege stores on the Cape Breton coast without the shelter of a harbour was enormous. Added to these technical difficulties was the personality of Amherst, who now after his ill-advised, rash enterprise of 8 June, was content to do everything by the book, much to the distaste of the eager-beaver Wolfe.

While guns were landed and the cautious and methodical Amherst dickered with his engineers on where to start the trenches and site batteries, Wolfe was detached with a small brigade of elite soldiers numbering some 1,200 men on 12 June 1758 to operate on the eastern side of the harbour opposite the town. Thompson's anecdotes cover several aspects of the siege. In particular he remembers the key role played by the French navy in supporting the defence of the fortress town.

On the afternoon of 21 July, Wolfe's shore batteries set fire to the French frigate *Célèbre*. With only a skeleton crew aboard, the fire quickly raged out of control and spread to the ships *Entreprenant* and the *Capricieux*. All three were lost, leaving only two French men-of-war still serviceable. They were dispatched four

---

66. M. de Beaussier, 15 July 1758, Louisbourg, quoted in Sir Julian Stafford Corbett, *England in the Seven Years' War: A Study in Combined Strategy*, I (London, 1907), 326.

nights later when "Dreadnought" Boscawen sent in two "cutting-out" parties of armed seamen under cover of darkness on the night of 25 July. They managed to burn the *Prudent* and capture the *Bienfaisant* before the French could react.

The Louisbourg garrison at the height of the siege was subjected to a constant bombardment by British batteries numbering some thirty-seven heavy guns and eleven mortars. They rained shells upon the town and ramparts, causing massive fires and serious breaches in the poorly maintained walls, the defenders virtually unable to react. On 26 July the French could see the British massing their scaling ladders and busily preparing for a major assault. The gallant and fairly stubborn French defence had run its course and William Amherst recorded with some satisfaction on the morning of 26 July 1758:

> … an Officer came out of the town, with a messenger from the Governor desiring a parley. The Admiral was on shore. The General made answer, signed likewise by the Admiral, which I carried to the Officer, giving the Governor notice that he must expect the consequence of a general attack by land and sea, if he did not surrender the Garrison Prisoners of War, and gave him an hour to consider it.[67]

The French tried at least two more times to negotiate more favourable terms but, seeing the British meant business, decided to surrender in accordance with Amherst's wishes. The next morning, at 8 o'clock sharp, the three "eldest" companies of grenadiers took possession of the Port Dauphin gate. At noon, General Amherst sent Edward Whitmore, his senior brigadier, into the town "to see the garrison lay down their Arms, to send the Arms out of the Town and to take what Guards were wanted for the Works, the Magazines and Stores from the Trenches. The garrison lay down their Arms at 12 o'clock, 5000 firelocks, 11 Colours. The Union was hoisted at the Citadel."[68]

Louisbourg was not much to speak of in its battered state, but Amherst proceeded to give orders for it to be repaired as regiments would garrison it for the winter. Amherst sent his brother back to England in the *Shannon* with dispatches of the British victory. For the next four weeks the Frasers and other regiments were employed in tearing down and filling in all their siege works, batteries and trenches. The fortress was now a British possession and it would not be proper to leave such works in place for any prospective enemy contemplating their own siege.

News of General Abercromby's decisive defeat by Montcalm at Ticonderoga on Lake Champlain caused General Amherst and Admiral Boscawen to re-evaluate plans to carry on to Quebec. Fraser's Highlanders soon learned they

---

67. 26 July 1758, Amherst, *Journal*, 32.
68. 27 July 1758, *Ibid.*, 71–2.

and four other regiments [2nd/1st Foot (The Royal); 17th Foot (Forbes's); 47th Foot (Lascelles); and the 48th Foot (Webb's)] were destined for New York as reinforcements to Abercromby's defeated army, and thus would not spend the winter at Louisbourg. The Frasers were chosen no doubt as they constituted Amherst's largest available regiment and had suffered light casualties during the landings and siege operations: four officers killed and three wounded; twelve privates killed and thirty-five wounded.[69]

Fraser's Highlanders packed up their tents and camp stores by 27 August 1758 and boarded their transports but, according to Amherst's journal, the wind was quite contrary and blew hard and they remained at anchor for another three days. They finally made it out of harbour on 30 August and fought against heavy headwinds for the next two days. When the wind abated, the convoy of forty sail found itself off Cape Sable on 8 September and well on its way to Boston, where they had started out four months earlier.

Anecdote No. 4[70]
When we landed at Halifax, we found our Commander-in-Chief General Wolfe[71] there, drilling away the men, and making fight sham-battles at a place round the Town called Deptford,[72] where the ground is level. We were not long at Halifax when we received Orders to set sail for the River Saint Lawrence,[73] and in a few days we came to anchor opposite the harbour of Louisbourg which we knew it was our business to try and take.

When all the Troops were got into the flat bottom'd Boats[74] which General

---

69. 16 August 1758, *Ibid*, 79; *Pennsylvania Gazette*, 7 September 1758 (1550), "Return of the Killed and Wounded in the Several Regim[nts] on the Island of Cape Breton from June 8 to the 26th of July, inclusive, 1758."
70. This anecdote on the Louisbourg landings was published in the Quebec newspaper the *Star and Commercial Advertiser* on 10 May 1828 under the headline "Anecdote of Wolfe's Army." While attributed only to "one of the Grenadier Company of Fraser's Highlanders, who was a volunteer in that service," it is clearly the words of James Thompson, extracted from Anecdote No. 4.
71. Brigadier General James Wolfe. Thompson's memory is faulty. Wolfe was not the commander in chief, but merely one of the four brigade commanders under the command of Major General Jeffery Amherst, the expedition commander. The C-in-C of North America was Major General James Abercromby, entrusted with the 1758 operation against the French forts at Ticonderoga and Crown Point on Lake Champlain, south of Montreal. See Part Three for Biographical Notes on both officers.
72. Thompson means Dartmouth, a small hamlet of woodcutters directly across the harbour from Halifax with some cleared fields. Open spaces behind a windmill provided room for the troops to practise their manoeuvres and bushcraft. It was to Dartmouth the regiment was sent to encamp with their tents after their first arrival in North America, 1757.
73. Thompson obviously means Cape Breton Island and not the St. Lawrence River.
74. Thompson is mistaken. There were no flat-bottomed boats built at Halifax in 1758 although whaleboats were constructed. Some flat-bottomed boats, however, were

Wolfe had ordered to be built at Halifax, and which we brought along with us, we presently after saw the Signal from the General's Barge (which was between us and the land) to push off towards shore. Now, as our Grenadier Company was very strong, we were so closely pack'd together, that there was only room to stand up, excepting in the back part of the boat where the Officers and Non-Commission'd Officers contrived to sit on the stern sheets and this left no room for Rowing, but we were taken in tow by a boat from a Seventy-four,[75] commanded by a Lieutenant whose name I could never get at.

As we were going very slow, we were among the last to land. All this time the French were peppering us from the Heights with Canister-shot, and musket-balls fired out of twenty-four-Pounders! and they came whistling about our ears, nothing could be like it. One 24-pound shot pass'd under my hams and kill'd Sergeant McKenzie who was sitting as close to my left as he could squeeze, and it carried away the basket of his Broadsword, which, along with the shot, passed through the body of Lieutenant Cuthbert,[76] who was on McKenzie's left, and tore his Body into shivers, and, after cutting off both the legs of the poor fellow that held the Tiller of the Boat, it struck fast in the sternpost. Altho' the shot did not *touch* me, yet all the hams of my thighs and the calves of my legs became as black as my Bonnet, and for some weeks I suffer'd a great deal of pain.

My Captain, poor fellow!… for whose sake I came away from Scotland, and who was my best and most intimate friend, poor Captain Baillie! He was sitting on the opposite side of the Boat, and was struck so mortally, that after gently leaning over his head upon the shoulder of the man next to him, he ex-

---

built in England in early 1758 and used at St. Malo, Cherbourg, etc. and others were built in North America in late 1758 / early 1759 for the 1759 Quebec campaign. They appear clearly in Richard Short's drawing "A General View of Quebec from Point Lévy" engraved by P. Canot in 1761 (LAC, C-118259).

75. At this time, Royal Navy warships were classified by the number of guns they carried which gave their "rate" from 1st rate (90–100 guns) down to 6th rate (20–28 guns). Ships of the line were ships powerful enough to fight in the main battle line and ranged between 1st and 4th rates. A ship with 74 guns would be classified as a 3rd rate, typically built with two gun decks. Years of experience proved that the 3rd-rate ships embodied the best compromise between sailing ability (speed, handling), firepower and cost. There were two 74-gun ships with Boscawen's fleet at Louisbourg: *Dublin* and *Terrible*.

76. Lieutenant John Cuthbert (1729–58), younger of Castlehill, son to George Cuthbert of Castlehill and Mary Mackintosh. John joined the Dutch Scots Brigade initially, resigning his commission in the Dutch service 25 April 1756. He was gazetted one of the two grenadier lieutenants in Captain Charles Baillie's company on 18 January 1757, when Archibald Macdonald declined the commission. Cuthbert was killed in James Thompson's boat at the Louisbourg landings, 8 June 1758. CBs; SBs; BALs; Papers Illustrating the History of the Scots Brigade in the Service of the United Netherlands 1572–1782, II, 390, 414, 421; Stewart, Col. D., *Sketches of the Character, Manners and Present State of the Highlanders of Scotland* …, 2 vols (Edinburgh, 1822), II, 20–1 (hereafter Stewart, *Sketches*).

pired without the least struggle: so much so, that the man thought he had lean'd down his head in that manner, in order to escape the Shot that were coming so thick upon us. Whilst we were in this predicament I had my eye on the boat that was towing us, anxious that she should get us forward as fast as possible, when I observed the Lieutenant (of the Navy) fumbling some time at the painter of our boat, without my knowing what he was at, but at last I saw him take a clasp knife out of his pocket, and cuts the Rope! and away he went, leaving us as a mark for the French Batteries to fire at![77]

As good luck would have it, our situation was soon noticed by a Frigate in the Fleet,[78] from which two boats were sent to our relief, and into which we were embark'd, and we had no sooner left our flat bottom'd vessel, than she sunk down to the gunnel, which was caused by the men withdrawing their plaids from out of the shot-holes, and the weight of the shot that stuck fast in her. In this state she was towed alongside the Frigate, and, I understood, was hoisted aboard, and taken Home to England, as a great curiosity, for she was completely riddled with shot-holes, and a bucket-full of musket-balls, and other small shot, was taken out of her. Had there been any other Troops than Highlanders in our situation, they must have gone to the bottom for the want of such a ready means of plugging up the shot-holes as we carried about us in our plaids.

The Right-hand man of our Company (and he was no little fellow) received a shot in his thigh which immediately swell'd up to the thickness of his body, & made him suffer exceeding-great pain: the idea was that the shot was poison'd. The poor devil scream'd the whole time that the boat was towing towards the Frigate, and when they were going to put him in slings to hoist him on board, his agony was so great, that he expired on the gunnel of the boat!

Well, as I was relating to you about the Landing, we were put into fresh boats, and, under the covering fire of our Ships of War, we at last got landed

---

77. The Reverend Robert Macpherson, the *Caipal Mhor* ("Big Chaplain") of the 78th Foot (see Part Three for Biographical Note), corroborates Thompson's story but states the tow ropes were shorn by the intense weight of shot: "the Granadiers were under the shole or Cover of a frigate [*Kennington*] that fir'd on the Trenches, Rowing briskly ashore. They at length came so near as to Receive not only the fire of the Canon but of Eight hundred men that lined the Trench. The Soldiers lay flat in the boats, the Sailors that Row'd were kill'd, Maim'd or gave up and [illegible] at last the rops [sic] that was towing the boats were cut by the Shote, the small towing boats immediately sail'd back & the long boats with the Men exposed without having it in their power to proceed or Retire, till at last the Soldiers with two oars instead of ten in all the longboats (there were two oars from first) made a Shift with great difficulty to get behind the frigate." Robert Macpherson to William Macpherson, Grand Camp before Louisbourg, 29 July 1758, LOC, James Grant Papers (hereafter, JGP).
78. Probably the 6th-rate frigate *Kennington*, 20 guns, commanded by Captain Maximilian Jacobs and tasked to provide close gunfire support to the landing.

on the West-side of the Town, altho' we were nearly swamp'd in the surf *and we had to wait a considerable time, until some axe-men were got to cut a passage for us through the abattis that lined the beach for about three miles long, to oppose our landing. With a great deal of difficulty we got to the top of the rock, and on our way to join the main Army, we came to the Battery that did us so much mischief, but it was desert'd, there was only one man found, and he had his head carried away, yet he held firm hold of a lighted lint-stock which one of our Highlanders tried in vain to force out of his grasp.*[79]

Our Fleet, as it appear'd to me from the shore, look'd as if the Bowsprit of one was made fast to the Stern of the next to it, and they seem'd to stretch across the whole Harbour.[80]

There was one Boat-load of Troops that was carried away out of her destination by the Surf, that rolled very heavily, and, after getting within it, pulled towards the East-side of the Town, and, the Troops in a second Boat, seeing the first going in that direction, thought that must be the right place to Land, and accordingly made after her, and these were the only two Boats that landed in that quarter. It happen'd that they had come opposite to a high rocky precipice, and no Road or footpath leading up.[81] However, with the help of one another, they all got safe to the top, which they found to be cover'd with brush-wood.

The next thing to be consider'd was how they were to join the remainder of

---

79. The section highlighted in italics above does *not* appear in the original Manuscript copy. However, these words were included in a version of this anecdote published in the Quebec *Star and Commercial Advertiser* on 10 May 1828 under the title "Anecdote of Wolfe's Army." While attributed only to "one of the Grenadier Company of Fraser's Highlanders, who was a volunteer in that service," it is clearly the words of James Thompson. This article was reprinted by LHSQ, Centenary Volume: 1824–1924, *Transactions,* New Series, No. 30 (1924), with the following note added by Lord Dalhousie: "This is the style, phrase, and very words of old Thompson of Quebec now in his 90th year; he was a sergeant in Fraser's Highlanders under Wolfe, and has recounted to me many such stories, with astonishing recollection and accuracy of detail – 'D'." The editors re-incorporate them here as we feel these anecdotes were copied and recopied so many times over the years for the use of Thompson's friends, acquaintances and newspaper editors (the side margins of the original Manuscript copy are full of notes explaining that a copy was given to so-and-so on a specific date), that this was part of the original storytelling missed in the 1830 transcription by James Thompson Jr.
80. Thompson was nowhere near the inner harbour of Louisbourg until after the siege was over. Here he is actually referring to Gabarus Bay near Louisbourg.
81. Governor Drucour in his dispatches on the landing stated that the British boats containing the light infantry found their landing spot either accidentally or "through a knowledge of the ground went into the cove of Nid de Pie twelve or fourteen yards across in sand surrounded by steep rocks situated between the Coromandiere after Sandy Cove and Flat Point, a place where there had been last year a detachment of twenty-five or thirty men and this year none." Drucour quoted in McLennan, *Louisbourg,* 260.

the Army. One of the Officers thought he would just look about him a little, and see the nature of the ground that lay between them and the Army, and, after going a short way, he finds himself at the edge of the brush-wood, and behold, to his great astonishment, the French Army form'd in their Trenches, in two lines, directly in a line with where he stood! He immediately returns to the Party, and relates what he had just seen, and after consulting what was best to be done, they agreed to form the men into Squads, each to sally out in turn from the brush-wood, and fire at the French, and then return to the rear to re-load, in order to conceal their real numbers.[82]

This they did only four times, when the French, supposing, as it was thought, that they were attack'd by a numerous body of our Troops, betook themselves to their Serap[h]ers,[83] and away they ran towards the Garrison which was about three miles distance from the trenches they had just quit. Some of the Highland Soldiers seeing the French running away, could not resist the temptation of giving them a chase (for they were a raw, undisciplined set, just raised, and un-used to restraint) and they stole away after them by two's and by three's, and presently, by whole Companies, and there soon remain'd only the Officers and Non-Commission'd Officers of our Regiment.

Upon the Quarter Master General (then Colonel Carleton)[84] coming to the

---

82. Young Robert ("Roby") Macpherson, a cousin of Parson Robert Macpherson, and serving as a volunteer cadet (as Thompson claimed to be), was one of the first Fraser Highlanders ashore and distinguished himself fighting with this light infantry advanced guard. "Parson Robert" proudly reported home that "The Volunteers of the Army with a part of Wolfe's detachment had to beat off the French from a rising ground we wanted to get possession of, they all run on briskly, stood 2 fires before they discharged their pieces, the boy was among the first of them when they fir'd and run on and wou'd not fire till he was sure of his mark, there he loaded several times, & was with Sandy Grant *Ducharn's* son / a very pretty lad one of the 3 officers that commanded the fifty Rangers that first landed. [Editors' note: Macpherson is mistakenly calling the light infantry "rangers," an interchangeable term similar to "irregular" used by many at Louisbourg in 1758, though in subsequent years of the war, they came to specifically mean those respective sub-units.] Roby and six more men with him were the first on top of the Hill and when they were like to be cut off by a force of French coming to Surround them; their friends not coming up so briskly as they might have done, the boy with the few others kept firing, 'till in charging or loading his piece, it turn'd so dirty his rammer broak & he made up to Grant who he was not then acquaint'd with & had the use of his, time about, till the Rascals, he said, were beat back off of it, and they kept the Hill till Wolfe and a few more came to their support and the enemy gave way. Grant shew'd the boy, whose connection with himself he was stranger to, he presented him to the general who seem'd vastly pleas'd with his behaviour." Robert Macpherson to William Macpherson, Grand Camp before Louisbourg, 29 July 1758, JGP.
83. Thompson's poetic meaning here is that their French foes' retreat was so quick that they were seraphic, evaporating like seraphim, beings of celestial light.
84. Thompson's memory is faulty. The deputy quarter master general (DQMG) at Louisbourg was James Robertson, not Guy Carleton, the latter being selected the

ground with the Orders to "Form Line" he was told they had already receiv'd Orders to that effect, which being explain'd to the Highlanders, they said among themselves, in Gaelic, "What! are we to stand and form Line, and quietly look at the Enemy running away? No! No! We can't understand that," and that from having actually ran off after the French, the Quarter Master General was heard to say, and I myself heard him say so, "I thought that they only wanted an opportunity and this is not more than I had expected of them." You see, (continues my Father) most of them had Serv'd in the Rebellion of '45,[85] and they were thought to be *not Game!*

In about an hour, or an hour and a half, or so, they all came back again, to a man, after having followed close at the heels of the French, up to the very Walls of the Town, and almost every man of them brought in his Prisoner, and some had two. Among the number, Duncan McFee[86] [*sic*] of our Company, a wicked rascal as ever lived, and as bold as a Lion, he overtakes a French Officer in the chase, who, according to Etiquette drops the point of his Sword in token of his Submission, and spoke something in French which Duncan did not understand. This wouldn't satisfy Duncan, but he seizes the Officer by the "skriff" of the Neck, and snatched away the Sword from out of his hand, and, in this way brought him into Camp, and deliver'd him over to our Adjutant[87] (this French Officer was a very fine gentle-manly-looking person) – but devil a bit would he give up the Sword for all the Adjutant could say. And, Duncan claps the French Officer's Sword in the frog of his Belt, alongside his own Broadsword, as a Trophy of War. The French Officer made great remonstrances at the treatment that he had received, and stated that it was not the rule of their Service that an officer, although a Prisoner of War, should be depriv'd of his Sword, it being sufficient that he was deprived of his Liberty, and he requested earnestly that the Adjutant would see him righted.

Upon this, the Adjutant who knew what kind of a Fellow he had to deal with, instead of attempting to force Duncan to give up the Sword, he goes

---

following year as James Wolfe's DQMG for the Quebec 1759 expedition. Robertson was another remarkable Scot serving in North America. Although from a good family, he began his military career in the ranks and ended as a lieutenant general commanding in New York at the end of the American Revolutionary War. At the time of the incident mentioned by Thompson, Robertson was a major in the 60th Foot (he was promoted to lieutenant colonel on 8 July 1758). Robertson returned to England in 1783 and died there in 1788. See Part Three for Biographical Note on Guy Carleton, who was later twice governor of Quebec during James Thompson's time as overseer of works.

85. This is "romantick" embellishment on the part of Thompson. Most junior officers and private soldiers (average age eighteen) were far too young to have fought in the '45 but were, for the most part, drawn from clans that had supported the Jacobite cause.
86. Sergeant Duncan McPhee. See Part Three for Biographical Note.
87. Lieutenant Hugh Fraser. See Part Three for Biographical Note.

up to Head Quarters (this is the first time that ever I heard the term used) to Colonel Fraser,[88] who understood how to manoeuvre him, and the Colonel's advice was to go back to Duncan, and undervalue the Sword, as being a paltry looking thing compared with his own Broadsword, and not worth his keeping (and indeed it was but a poor looking thing, with only a common brass Hilt) but to offer him a few Crowns for it, which he, the Colonel would take care to have repaid.

The Adjutant accordingly seeks out Duncan, who he finds strutting about, as proud as a Peacock, much to the annoyance of the French Officer, and he endeavoured, on behalf of the Colonel, to coax him out of the Sword. But No! devil a bit, Duncan would not part with his Prize. At length, whilst endeavouring to persuade him that it was not worth a single Crown, he ask'd him how many Crowns he would take for it? Duncan said he did not care a straw for the *money* it was the *honour* of the thing he most valued, but that if the Colonel would give twenty Crowns[89] for it, he might have the Sword. The Adjutant said that was too much, but that he would give him ten. To this Duncan voluntarily agreed, and the Sword was again put into the French Officer's possession.

The very next day as Duncan finds his way to the Colonel's Tent, and, what does he see passing by him, but the French Officer having his Sword at his side! He instantly rushes at him, and tears it away a second time, and, by my faith, it would have been no small matter to have got it back but for the influence of our Colonel, who explain'd to him the Custom-of-War, and that it was unbecoming a brave soldier to hurt the feelings of a Prisoner that might fall into his hands, and that instead of injuring him, he ought to treat him as he himself would wish to be treated if the Chances of War should place him in the same situation. After having gained upon him in this way, Duncan got cool again, gave up the Sword, and went his way, but rather down in the mouth.

Anecdote No. 9

During the landing at Louisbourg, there was a rascal of a Savage on top of a high rock that kept firing at the Boats as they came within his reach, and he kill'd volunteer Fraser of our Regiment who, in order to his getting one shilling instead of sixpence a day, was acting, like myself as Sergeant – he was a very genteel young man, and was to have been Commission'd the first vacancy. There sat next to Fraser in the boat, a silly fellow of a Highlander, but who was a good marksman for all that, and notwithstanding that there was a positive Order not to fire a shot during the landing, he couldn't resist the temptation of having a

---

88. Lieutenant Colonel Simon Fraser.
89. Before decimalization, the crown was a silver coin worth 5 shillings. At 20 shillings to the pound, 20 crowns were worth 5 pounds sterling.

slap at the Savage. So, the silly fellow levels his fuzee[90] at him, and in spite of the unsteadiness of the boat, for it was blowing hard at the time, 'afaith he brought him tumbling down like a sack into the water. As the matter so turn'd out, there was not a word said about it, but had it been otherwise he would have had his back scratch'd, if not something worse.[91]

This shot was the best I have ever seen, except that of Captain MOSES HAZEN,[92] who kill'd the French Officer that was leading on a Column on the Plains of Abram [sic], on the 28th April 1760. After we had all landed, and pitch'd our tents, General Wolfe, who had heard of the extraordinary size of this Savage, order'd his body had to be taken up and carried to the Camp, for all the troops to see it. He was an enormous fat fellow! I stood by him the whole time. He had been shot in the groin, and some of the Soldiers were passing their jokes upon it. He had many scars on his body, was tall and fat.[93]

After the men had all pass'd by, and seen him, he was again buried, but soon

---

90. A corruption of the French word *fusil*, a light flintlock musket carried by officers at this date. It was likely a carbine, and the "silly fellow" mentioned by Thompson was probably a member of the light infantry company. The 78th Foot arrived in North America in 1757 equipped with 37-inch carbines with iron ramrods, which according to Lieutenant Colonel Simon Fraser were "the Carabines the horse had before they were reduced to Dragoons, and are excellent Arms in every respect, but that they are rather slight for hard use...." The Highlanders' carbines were similar to those issued to the artillery and we find in various orders of the day those same carbines being re-issued to the various regimental light infantry companies. For example, before the 1758 Louisbourg campaign, the Highlanders of the three untrained additional companies of the 78th left behind in Halifax were ordered to exchange their carbines for Brown Bess muskets, one-for-one, with the light infantry of Major George Scott's Provisional Battalion.
91. The term "back scratching" refers to the practice of flogging, where a soldier would be tied and lashed with a short whip, usually by the strong arm of one of the regimental drummers. In 1807 the maximum number of lashes was reduced to 1,000 and by 1832 to 200. However, it was not abolished fully until 1881, and even then it took the death of yet another soldier after receiving a "mere" 25 lashes. Thompson was correct – express orders had been given soldiers forbidding them firing from the boats during the assault.
92. Captain Moses Hazen, Rogers' Rangers.
93. Thompson's story is corroborated by a story that appeared in the London newspaper the *Public Advertiser* on 25 September 1758: "Extract of a Letter from on board one of the Men of War arrived at Spithead from Louisbourg, dated Sept. 18. – On the 8th of June our Men, attempting to land in Gabarus Bay, were repulsed by the Enemy (who fired very briskly from the Batteries which they had erected on Shore) except Col. Frazer's Regiment who leap'd overboard, and swam to a Point of Rocks, on which (the Enemy having no Batteries there) they made good their Landing, and directly attacking the Enemy (French and Indians) with their Broad-Swords, caused them to fly, and thereby made way for our other Forces to land. Amongst the slain of the Enemy was an Indian six Feet nine Inches high. The Enemy, who called the Highlanders, English Savages, surrendered on the 26th of July to our Forces."

after taken up a second time at the desire of Admiral Saunders[94] and General Amherst, who had not yet seen him. It was supposed that his being shewn to the troops was to give them a dislike to the Savages, who were very numerous about the country.

A Report had gone about also, that this Savage had been dug up for the purpose of giving our Highlanders an opportunity of indulging in their favorite mode of inflicting casualties upon dead bodies, as they were consider'd to be mere Cannibals, and although the French women were constantly teazing our troops for something to appease their hunger, they could not be prevail'd upon to come near when any of the Highlanders were to be seen, until, at last, one of them who was more brave than the rest, ventured to come into our Camp, and we got our Master Tailor, KANAVAN (who was the only man in the Regiment that was not a Scotchman, and he could speak French well, having served his time to his brother in Paris) to interpret for the woman. She told us all about the fears they had, and getting plenty to eat, and being otherwise well treated, she left the Camp, and 'afaith it wasn't long before we had a great deal too many of the Canadian women amongst us begging for victuals, as they were in a starving state. And so it turn'd out that the Highlanders, instead of being eaters of human flesh, lived the same as other civilized people, and they soon afterwards proved to be the greatest favorites with the women.

Anecdote No. 10

After we got a footing at Louisbourg, there were three French Seventy-four's[95] and a Frigate that lay in the Bay, and that annoy'd us confoundedly particularly the Frigate,[96] and General Wolfe gave Orders that she should be watch'd at night, and if she made any move to get out, there should be a rocket set off by the Main Guard. There were two Sentries planted on the beach every night for this duty, and one night it came to the turn of two of our Highlanders, and one

---

94. Again, Thompson's memory is faulty. Vice Admiral Charles Saunders (1715–75) was the commander of the naval forces at Quebec the following year. At Louisbourg, Vice Admiral Edward Boscawen (1711–61) commanded the fleet and acted as Major General Jeffery Amherst's naval counterpart.
95. There were actually eleven French warships bottled up in Louisbourg harbour, of which only two were 74's: *Prudent* and *Entreprenant* (both burnt). The remaining nine ships were: *Capricieux*, 64 (burnt); *Célèbre*, 64 (burnt); *Bienfaisant*, 64 (captured); *Appollon*, 50 (sunk); *Aréthuse*, 36 (escaped); *Fidèle*, 36 (sunk); *Echo*, 32 (escaped, then captured); *Chevre*, 16 (sunk); and *Biche*, 16 (sunk).
96. The *Aréthuse*, 36, commanded by *capitaine de frégate* Jean Vauquelin. See Part Three for Biographical Note. This frigate caused many delays to the British building siege lines and gun batteries. Vauquelin moved his ship nearer to the town on 6 July, then slipped out of Louisbourg on the night of 15 July, the only French ship to escape the harbour and get clean away.

of these Sentries was Duncan McFee. He was the biggest thief in the world, and came to enlist with Colonel Fraser only to save his neck. He was in the practice of carrying off Cattle from the Lowlanders and selling them in England, and he told me that he was at this kind of business for seven years, without ever sleeping under the roof of a house. Oh! he was a terrible sad fellow! and would have faced the very devil!

Well, as I was telling you about the Sentries, when they were planted it was somewhat low water, but the tide soon began to rise, and as it did so, the other Sentry moved away, but devil a peg did Duncan budge from the spot where the relief had posted him. The other man seeing him stand fast calls to him to come out of the water. What for? says Duncan. Why, says the other, to keep yourself dry as I do. Then again says Duncan, did you ever get the Articles of War[97] explain'd to you, which says that it is Death for a Sentry to quit his Post? That may do very well says the other, but I'd rather be excus'd getting myself wet for nothing. Presently comes the Relief, and the Corporal finds but one man. He asks what's become of t'other Sentry? Why, says the man, he is somewhere *there* (pointing towards Duncan) and the Corporal could distinguish only his head and shoulders! So, he calls out to him to come forward. Upon his receiving the proper orders, Duncan came out of the water. This joke went all about the Camp, and at last it comes to the ears of General Wolfe, and he must needs see the fellow that could do such a thing. He accordingly had him pointed out, and he thought very highly of him.

Notwithstanding that the Frigate was so closely watch'd, 'afaith she managed, one dark night, to slip through our Fleet, and you would have thought it quite impossible, for they stretch'd across the whole of the outside harbour, and from where we were encamp'd you would have suppos'd that the bowsprit of one was made fast upon the poop of the next one to it. Immediately on its being found out, there were two of our Ships of war that slip'd their cables, and, supposing that the French Frigate must be gone to France, they went a considerable way down the River[98] after her to see and bring her back again, but 'afaith she was too cunning for them, and they couldn't get a sight of her.

Our two ships came back with but a fooling story to tell the King. We afterwards heard that the French Frigate had gone *up* instead of *down*, and had

---

97. *Articles of War* was the term used in the 18th century to describe the statutes governing military discipline and justice and were used by both the British army and the Royal Navy.
98. Thompson's geography and memory are faulty. The *Aréthuse* sailed to France and thus went nowhere near the St. Lawrence River. A few sentences later, Thompson repeats the story of the Governor's Lady which occurs with the *Echo* episode and not with Vauquelin's *Aréthuse*. See Part Three for Biographical Note on Madame Marie-Anne Aubert de Courserac, wife of Governor de Drucour.

arrived safe at Quebec, while it was yet in the hands of the French, and that she had taken the French Governor's Lady and all the Riches of Louisbourg along with her. It was this very Frigate that carried the news to Quebec that Louisbourg was taken by the English, and she it was that took away one Colonel Ross, Townsman of mine, who had served in the Rebellion of forty-five. He commanded a French Regiment at Quebec, and he began to think that he was not safe there, as the English Army were advancing upon that place by two different points.[99]

As General Wolfe was walking about our Camp he was 'spied by our men, and we nic-nam'd him the "red-headed Corporal," on account of his having red hair, and his wearing a Gold Equillette [sic][100] the same as the worsted ones of the Corporals of that time, and as the Army was always glad to see him, the men all turn'd out. He 'spies Duncan among the number, and this brings to his mind the escape of the French Frigate. He desires a Sergeant of ours to ask Duncan, in Gaelic, what he thought of that business? Duncan puts on a bold front, and says in reply to General Wolfe, "thank God that she did not escape through the *Woods*"! meaning, you see, that if she *did* get away, it was no fault of the *Army*. The Generals' fancy was highly tickled with this witty reply, and he whispered that Duncan was a fine fellow! This notice was not *lost* upon Duncan.

Some days afterwards, as General Wolfe was going reconnoitering alone towards the French Garrison, as was his custom, with only his fuzee slung over his shoulder, he observ'd a Highland Grenadier following him – (this was Duncan) – and he made a signal to him with his hand to keep back, but Duncan took no notice of it. Presently, the General again looks behind him and he sees the Grenadier still following him. General Wolfe, upon this, became somewhat vexed and stop'd short, repeating the signal for him to keep back – but no, the devil a keep-back would Duncan keep. When the General saw this, he went by the shortest way to the Guard-tent, where the Highlanders were encamp'd, and he calls for the Sergeant, and desires him to bring Duncan to him, and to demand of him the reason for his having disobey'd his orders in not keeping

---

99. No officer referred to as "Colonel Ross" can be found serving at Quebec in any of the French regular regiments or the *compagnies franches de la marine* (colonial troops). Everything Thompson knows about the mysterious and elusive "Colonel Ross" comes from his discussions with soldiers of the 42nd Foot when he visited their encampment at Montreal in 1760. Thompson may be alluding to James Johnstone, the Chevalier de Johnstone (see Part Three for Biographical Note), the best known Jacobite in the French army who served prominently as aide de camp to de Lévis and Montcalm respectively and was actually known to have had contact with British prisoners. It is possible that Johnstone did not use his real name when talking to prisoners.

100. Aiguillette. An ornamental braided cord, usually of gold or silver wire, with metal tips. They were worn as a badge of office by all officers, hanging from the right shoulder. Corporals also wore a similar set of cords but made from worsted white wool.

back as he made signal for him to do? Duncan says to the Sergeant, in Gaelic, "What! should I allow our General to go about alone, and perhaps some rascal of a Frenchman skulking behind a bush, or a stone, take it into his head to fire at him, and nobody at hand to take his part, and perhap we lose our General! No! No! that won't do." "You may tell the General (continues Duncan to the Sergeant) that whether he is pleas'd or not pleas'd I am determin'd to follow him whenever I can."

The Sergeant interpreted all this to the General, and he was so good-hearted a man that he couldn't be angry. So, he told the Sergeant to say that whenever he went about reconnoitering, for the future, Duncan should be allow'd to follow him as Orderly. This was exactly what Duncan lik'd. In a day or so Duncan, for this, was appointed in General Orders, "a Sergeant in the Army," never to be broke! a new kind of Appointment, and, as it so happen'd that he was in our Company, he gave me a good deal of trouble from his not knowing a single letter in the Alphabet.

Anecdote No. 5

The following little incident, altho' not connected with the above [i.e. with Anecdote No. 4], was related just afterwards, and was brought to my Fathers' recollection on his observing some little pranks of the Dog in the house, at the instant:

There was a little French Dog came away from the town of Louisbourg, and took-up with our Highlanders. He staid with us during the whole siege and the Men got to be very fond of him, and 'afaith he was well fed. The little animal stuck by us when we went to New England, and again came with us up as far as Quebec. He made his quarters at the main guardhouse. Our men had no other name for him than "François," to which he came when he was called. He was a sprightly little fellow, and very amusing from the tricks that the men taught him. He died in the Guardhouse at Quebec.

Anecdote No. 7

There was a good deal of jealousy in the Army that came against Canada, in regard to General Wolfe, on account of his having been made a General so young. His Father had commanded the 20th Regiment in which General Wolfe had been Serving, and at his Fathers' death he got the Command of this same Regiment.[101]

---

101. Thompson has confused James Wolfe, who commanded the 20th Foot as its lieutenant colonel, with his father, Edward Wolfe, who was a colonel in the 1st Regiment of Marines, later rising to the rank of lieutenant general. Lieutenant General Wolfe, the father, was also colonel of the 8th Foot (1745–59) which fought at Culloden, 1746.

After the Regiment I had volunteer'd with was raised, which, with the exception of the Master Tailor, an Irishman nam'd Kanavan, and was composed of fourteen hundred strapping, brawny, Highlanders, He, the General, offered our Colonel Fraser to exchange with him for the 20th Regiment, and it was surprising enough that he did so, for as we were raised only for a particular Service, the chances were that we soon would be reduced as a Fencible Regiment, altho' we were number'd the 78th (x) but perhaps General Wolfe thought that if *He* had the Command of us, he might prevent *that*, and it was perhaps upon this presumption that he made the offer.[102]

> (x) We had first been recruited as the 63rd and our pistols and Broadswords bear'd that number but owing to second Battalions which were made separate Regiments we were reduced to the 78th.[103]

Our's was, certainly, the most finest, beautiful Body of men that ever was raised for His Majesty The King of England, and General Wolfe had a good opportunity of knowing this, and he shew'd his attachment to us in a variety of ways. As regards myself individually, I received as much attention from him as if he had been a Father to me. He knew that I was a Volunteer. While before Louisbourg, the Siege of which lasted a period of seven weeks and three days, the Camp where our Regiment lay, was three miles distant from the General's, yet he almost every day came to see Us, when our men would turn out to him with the greatest alacrity, and the word that was passed on these occasions, in Gaelic, was, "here comes the red-headed Corporal" from the circumstance that he had red hair, and because he wore an Aiguillette similar to the worsted badge of distinction worn by the Corporals of that day, when every Mothers' son of them would have quit his "porritch" to be in time for the "turn-out."

> James Wolfe, the son, originally joined his father's marines as an ensign but quickly exchanged to a line regiment. In 1758 Wolfe was appointed colonel of the 67th Foot, a new regiment formed from the 2nd Battalion of the 20th Foot – the highest substantive rank he was to achieve.

102. There is no historical evidence (nor logic) to support Thompson's claim that Wolfe had offered to exchange with Simon Fraser.
103. Footnote in the original Manuscript copy, identified with an **x**. A matching **x** indicated where it was to be inserted in the narrative. This footnote (allegedly inserted for clarification by Thompson himself) is misleading. The two Highland regiments raised for service in North America were originally styled the 1st and 2nd Highland Battalions of Foot respectively, confirmed by Royal Warrant, "the 5th Day of January 1757 in the 30th Year of our Reign" (see Chapter One). The lower the number of a regiment, the better its chances of survival were at the end of the war when the most junior (higher numbered units) would be disbanded. At the conclusion of the Seven Years' War when all regiments above the number 70 were being reduced, Colonels Fraser and Montgomery petitioned to have their old regimental numbers reinstated so their battalions could be kept on the order of battle but to no avail.

The fresh water at Louisbourg had a particularly bad effect upon the whole Army, and I consequently did not escape it, but was attack'd by a disorder that in a few days brought me down to a mere skeleton. When I got over it sufficiently to crawl about, I used to walk a little way along the highroad and back again, in order to pick up a little flesh, and gain back some strength.

One day, as I was sauntering along after this manner, I saw a person coming towards me, in plain clothes, and who should this prove to be but General Wolfe! When he had come up to me he accosted me by the term "brother Soldier" – he did indeed – and this was his customary mode, as I afterwards learned, of addressing the men.

"Brother Soldier," said he, "you appear to be rather weakly, what is the matter"? Oh, General, I replied, I am indeed very weak, yet I was able to answer a number of other questions he put to me; at length discovering my situation, he continued, "I see that you are too weak to remain standing." "There," said he, pointing to a large fragment of rock that was standing in the highroad, "step across and sit you down upon that stone, and rest yourself awhile," and I sat down accordingly. And the General also sat himself down on the stone close alongside of me. He gave me a deal of good advice, and cautioned me to be very particular in what I ate, and more so in what I drank. After our sitting together in this manner for some time, and his having asked as many questions as he thought I was able to bear, he left me with the parting words which I shall never forget, saying, "Be of good cheer, brother Soldier"!

Anecdote No. 1

When we landed at Louisbourg there was a difficulty among the Sergeants of our Company in getting them to take Orders, for they could hardly write, and did not speak the best English, and I was selected by our new Captain, Donald MacDonald[104] (my friend Captain Baillie having being killed at the landing), to do Duty as Sergeant, as I spoke English and wrote a tolerably fair hand, but 'afaith I was nigh getting into a serious hobble for my Scholarship.

One of the Sergeants of the Company was one Duncan McFee [sic], who had behaved in a gallant manner in many ways, and so caught the attention of General Wolfe, and he became very fond of him, and appointed him a Sergeant for life, never to be broke! But as Duncan could hardly speak a word of English, and was illiterate, he could not take Orders without the help of some of the other Sergeants. It happened one day, during Duncan's week to be Orderly, that our Captain was down for Picket-guard, and he did not know of it, and he

---

104. Although Thompson refers to him as Captain MacDonald, he is in fact Captain Donald "Donull Gorm" Macdonell of Benbecula, the second son of Clanranald. See Part Three for Biographical Note.

had gone to dine with Colonel Fraser at Wolfe's Camp about three miles off. I knew of the circumstance, and wanted Duncan to get after the Captain with the book of Orders. He had shewed it to a good many of the Officers round about the place, but No – the devil a go would Duncan go after the Captain, but thought it was quite time enough to shew him the Orders when he came in his way.

Things remained in this state all the day, and towards dusk I began to feel uneasy, as I saw there was mischief a-brewing, and I myself went after the Captain, and found him, as I expected, in the Colonel's marquee[105] with some other officers drinking Wine together. I made signal that I wanted to speak to Captain MacDonald, and he came a-one-side. I then told him that he was put down for Picket that night, and that I had come to let him know it. His blood was up in a jiffy, and he says to me "this is a pretty time indeed to let me know the orders, why, Sir, did you not tell me this before"? I answer'd that I was not on Duty, but Sergeant McFee, and that I came to prevent mischief. The Captain orders me, in a harsh tone back to my quarters.

As I went along, I couldn't help thinking that I was badly paid for my trouble and good nature; but all this came from my being made a Sergeant, and my having lost my good friend Captain Baillie who wouldn't have allowed me to be treated so. I had scarcely got back, when there comes a Corporal to me to say that he had orders to confine me in the Quarter-guard. I told the Corporal that if I committed any crime I surely ought to be punish'd, but that all events I knew enough of the Service not to be confined by an Inferior, and I turns him about his business – presently I reflected that I was perhaps making Bad, *worse*, and I went to consult with Lieutenant McCallister[106] of our Company, telling him the whole story. He told me, Jim, you were right in refusing to be confined by an inferior and acted according to the Articles of War, but I would advise you to go to the quarter-guard, and confine yourself until morning, and I will see into the matter.[107]

---

105. Marquee. A large field tent. As it required wagon transportation, it was generally used only by high-ranking officers.
106. Lieutenant Archibald MacAllister (1741–1801). Born in 1741, 2nd son of Charles MacAllister of Loup, Kintyre. Gazetted an ensign on 13 January 1757; fought at Louisbourg, 1758; the Plains of Abraham, 1759; wounded at Sillery, 28 April 1760; a lieutenant in Captain John Macdonell's company on disbandment, he exchanged to half-pay December 1763. Returned to active duty in 1767 as a lieutenant in the 35th Foot, and three years later was appointed the regimental quarter master. He served in this capacity for five years before getting a company command. He officially became the battalion commander thirty-two years later in 1799 but had been made a lieutenant colonel "in the Army" five years previously. He died in 1801. BALs; CBs; *SBs*; Stewart, *Sketches*, II, 20–1.
107. See footnote 97. Captains were required to read the Articles of War to the men on

I went, and ask'd to speak to the Officer of the Guard and told him that I came to confine myself as his prisoner. The officer desired me to shew him any Crime for to enter it in his Report. I told him that I had committed no crime that I knew of, but was advis'd on account of some matters that had happen'd to deliver myself up. The officer said then I can't take charge of you, but as there is a Tent just here where there is a Sergeant a prisoner, you may go and pass the night along with him if you like, and if you don't like, you may let it alone. I went accordingly, and not a syllable passed between the Sergeant and myself.

While I was reflecting upon my situation, there was word passed about the Camp that the Grenadiers of Fraser's Highlanders, and some others that I now forget, were to go out that night upon Sharp-Service,[108] it immediately struck me that if I was known to confine myself, it would be said that I kept back from Cowardice. 'Afaith, thinks I, this will *never* do, so I bolted away from the quarter-guard without any body's leave, and went and fell in with my Company, but said not a word of what had passed, and never after heard any more of it.

The four Companies were already formed and paraded but without Haversacks, and besides Arms and Accoutrements, I observed that each man was served with a Pickaxe and shovel, the meaning of which I did *not* understand; however, away we went, in the dead of the night, and after passing over a crazy Bridge,[109] we were march'd high up on the French Glacis.[110] Two or three Engi-

---

a regular basis. As most of Fraser's Highlanders could not speak English, the Articles would have been translated into Gaelic. The Articles were available as a pocket-sized book, and Thompson may have obtained a copy and read them on his own. In any case, Thompson's interpretation is correct: a soldier or an officer could only be confined by a superior.

108. Their orders were to dig a final sap along the last northern ridgeline some 200 yards north of the Dauphin Gate. William Amherst, aide de camp to the commander, recorded in his journal that the grenadier detachments had taken post "along a little ridge of hills, & if they can work secure from the fire of the shipping on the other side of this post to the glacis, it will be lucky. A good communication will be made from the advance post upon the right to this, which will form a parallel." Entry 17 July 1758, Amherst, *Journal*, 28.

109. The *Barrachois*. Word of Basque origin (*barratxo* or *barrachoa*), meaning "little bar" or "sand bar." Later, it was adapted by the French and extended to mean a shallow body of fresh or salt water, sheltered from the sea by a sand spit or strip of land. Thomas Pichon, a British spy who operated inside Louisbourg prior to the siege, wrote in his 1760 book: "They give the name barachois in this country to small ponds near the sea, from which they are separated by only a causeway." The causeway is Thompson's "crazy bridge," probably rubbled and partially destroyed to prevent a quick crossing of the tidal-pond obstacle.

110. *Glacis*. The earthen slope fronting the stone walls or ramparts of a fortress to protect them from direct artillery fire and usually separated from the fortress by a dry ditch. *Glacis* were always kept free of buildings or trees in to afford defenders clear fields of fire

neers that came with us, put down several pickets in the ground, and we were order'd to make holes for ourselves, in a line with those pickets in order to cover us from the shot of the French Garrison, but the ground was so hard and shelvy, that we could *not* accomplish it that night, and we were withdrawn before break of day, to a low ground, where the French couldn't touch us.

Here we passed the whole of the daylight, and nothing could come to our relief and the next night we went back and fell to work again, and managed to intrench ourselves comfortably enough. For my part, I had work'd so hard, that my hands had the whole of the skin rubb'd off, and they kept bleeding and were very sore for three years after.

Our Captain[111] had a ball pass'd through his left wrist and nobody could tell how it came, and 'afaith he immediately shifted his position to the other end of the ground. A cannon shot also entered our trenches, and, funny enough, it struck the ground just under the slope of one of our men, who was in a sitting posture, and forced him up in the air, without doing him any harm, more than the fright it occasioned. This convinced us that we were not yet safe, and we set to work again to intrench ourselves deeper.

After all was got right again, there comes a *devil* of a large shell and lodged itself close in front of us, when, out runs one Corporal McPherson,[112] of our Company, and with his bare hand he twists out the blazing fuze, and held it over his head, to shew the French that he didn't care a button for them. This manoeuver must have saved a good many lives, and broken bones, for we were very much crowded together. Some one of the men ask'd McPherson how he could have thought of such a dangerous thing. "Oh!" says he, "I'm an old soldier and have often seen it done before."[113] Besides this, we hadn't tasted a morsel of victuals

---

from their gun batteries and parapets. It is highly doubtful Thompson and his grenadiers dug in on the French *glacis* as his son has dutifully transcribed. William Amherst is probably more correct in stating they dug in along a ridgeline overlooking the *glacis* and in dead ground to direct French fire.

111. In this anecdote Thompson hints that his captain, the infamous Donald "Donull Gorm" Macdonell may have been intentionally wounded or "fragged" by his own men due to his unpopularity. For a fuller essay on the hatred some men felt for this particular officer see "The Apparent Blue-Green Sheen of a Crow Flying Against the Sun": Two Oral Histories of Captain 'Donull Gorm' Macdonell, 78th Foot (Fraser's Highlanders)" in McCulloch, *SOTM*, II, 153–6.

112. Corporal Donald Macpherson. The same soldier appears in later anecdotes.

113. Corporal Macpherson's act of valour can be likened to one of the earliest gazetted awards of the Victoria Cross during the Crimean War when Lieutenant Charles Davis Lucas, RN, threw a shell with a burning fuse overboard from HMS *Hecla* during the 1854 bombardment of Bormarsund. Before the Crimean War there was no official standardized system for recognition of gallantry within the British armed forces. Officers were typically rewarded with an award of one of the junior grades of the Order of the Bath and/or brevet promotions, while a Mention in Despatches existed as an alternative

Mobile firepower. The cohorn mortar was an extremely light and mobile piece of artillery used at sieges to lob shells high over walls or one's own troops to drop upon the enemy. The one depicted here rested on a stout wooden platform of timbers which would have been carried from position to position by four men inserting poles fore and aft to carry it. (Editors Collection)

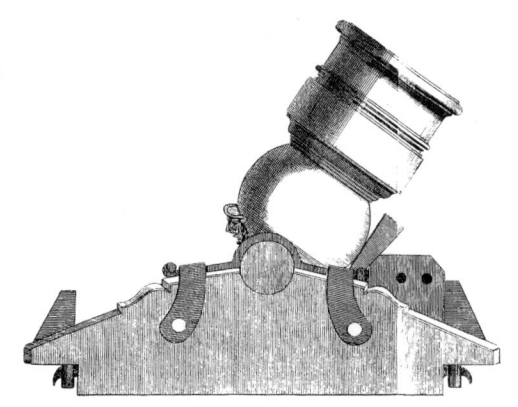

during the first forty-eight hours that we were away from the Camp.

They contrived, however, to get two other Companies to relieve us in the night, and as we were going to the rear, I came across a private man that had built a kind of an oven, and was baking a few loaves of soft bread. I immediately ask'd him to sell me a loaf, as the same time shew'd him a shilling; he took the shilling and I snatch'd away the loaf: it wasn't worth thruppence, but 'afaith I was glad to get it, and hot and raw as it was, I devour'd every morsel of it before I got back to the trenches. We got hard biscuit for our rations, so that I found this lump of raw dough a very great delicacy, but I could never find out the secret, where the man got the Flour!

When we had made a good lodgement, General Wolfe order'd a few Cohorns[114] to be planted in front of our trenches, and being within twenty yards of the crest of the glacis, as they were fir'd off we heard the French repeatedly crying out *"Garde La Bombe"!* and then we could distinguish that they were in

---

award for acts of lesser gallantry. That Corporal Macpherson was an "old soldier" is borne out by the fact that many experienced corporals like Macpherson were transferred over to the newly-raised 78th Foot from older regiments on the orders of Lord Barrington in January 1757. He directed that twenty-five men who were ready to be sergeants were to be draughted from the Foot Guards "who can speak the Highland language, Ten of whom are to be turned over to Lieu^t Col^o Montgomery's battalion and the remaining Fifteen to Lieu^t Col^o Fraser's Battalion." The same orders went out to eight other British regiments (a good indication of how prevalent Highlanders serving in the regular British line regiments had become by the mid-18th century) directing each to provide a certain quota of "Highland-speaking NCOs" to the new Highland battalions for a total of 105 NCOs. Lord Barrington to Foot Guards, 25 January 1757, WO 4, vol. 53 (Selections), LAC, Microfilm C-12585. (The abbreviation HMS, for His (or Her) Majesty's Ship, only became commonplace in the early 1800s, thus its use in this footnote is correct.)

114. Popular light artillery weapons, cohorn mortars were used extensively by both the French and English during the Seven Years' War. Each mortar weighed about 60–80 pounds and was carried into action and operated by a crew of two to four men, making it an ideal weapon for use in rugged terrain.

the greatest confusion, as we heard the clashing of their bayonets in rushing past each other. A French Frigate having escaped with the Governor's Lady[115] and valuables to Quebec, on the first night, the Governor did not put us to the trouble of repeating the dose, for he capitulated the very day after.[116]

Anecdote No. 6

After we took Louisbourg, there was an Order that none of the Army under the rank of Field Officer[117] should be permitted to go into the Garrison. There was our David Kanavan,[118] a Private in our Regiment, and he proposed to another of the men to go with him into the Garrison. The man replied that it was against Orders for any one under a Field Officer to go, and therefore that the thing was impossible. Kanavan then said, "if I put on such a Dress as to *appear* like a Field Officer, will you follow me as an Orderly"? The man agreed to this, and accordingly Kanavan rigs himself out as a Field Officer in a superfine Scarlet Coat which he had managed to cabbage from the Officers in his capacity of Master Tailor, and away he goes with his Orderly at his heels.

On coming to the West entrance gate there were two Sentries posted there,

---

115. While Thompson did not include the name of the frigate, there is no doubt that he is referring to the *Echo*, 32 guns. There is no definitive proof that Mme de Drucour tried to escape on the *Echo*. The "Governor's Lady" was of course Marie-Anne Aubert de Courserac. If Mme de Drucour was captured while attempting to escape, a highly significant incident, it was certainly not reported in extant despatches, journals, etc. The incident seems to rest on a report from a Captain Junkens in the 6 July 1758 edition of the *Boston Newsletter* which suggested that *Echo* was "… thought to be vastly rich having on board the Governor's Lady with some others of the French Gentry with their plate, jewels and most valuable effects being bound for France," an account quite similar to Thompson's. However, it would seem that the claim is nothing more than a camp rumour or legend – but camp gossip is exactly what James Thompson is passing on to us in this particular anecdote. Another possibility is that the "Governor's Lady" was not the wife, Mme de Drucour, but rather Drucour's mistress – which may help explain why the incident was gleefully retold by soldiers around their campfires.
116. Thompson's claim that the Governor "capitulated the very day after" Mme de Drucour allegedly escaped is false. The *Echo* escaped on 13 June but was returned to Admiral Boscawen in Louisbourg harbour six days later (as reported by the log of *Namur*) while Louisbourg capitulated the following month, 26 July 1758.
117. Field grade officers make up a battalion's command element and include the army ranks of major, lieutenant colonel and colonel. Since the early 1740s field officers in the Highland regiments wore lapels on their jackets while lapels were adopted by company grade officers (captains, lieutenants, and ensigns) only in 1760. These lapels would have been easily noticed at a distance, as described by Thompson in this anecdote. The coat worn by Kanavan had to be either Colonel Fraser's or Major James Clephane's. The other major, John Campbell, never crossed the ocean.
118. David Kanavan, the Irish master tailor of the 78th Foot. There was no soldier named Kanavan on the disbandment rolls but there was a Corporal Donald McKenivan, who also appears on a petition of discharged men of the 78th Foot requesting land grants in Quebec, 19 & 31 May 1765.

and they both presented Arms to him, which Kanavan return'd in proper style. Just at the right hand of the Gate there was a road leading to the top of the Ramp. Kanavan goes up this way, and on getting to the top, he meets with several French Officers speaking together, and he makes directly towards them, with bows and scrapes, exactly in the manner of the French. The Officers all salute him in return, and presently he got into close conversation with them, his Orderly standing off at a certain distance.

They were astonish'd to find that an English Officer should speak their Language, and they became so much taken with Kanavan nothing could be like it. Now, this same Kanavan had serv'd an Apprenticeship of 7 years to a brother of his, who was a Master Tailor in Paris where he became complete master of the language, and on his setting up for himself, he got into difficulties, and was obliged to quit the Country, which brought him over to Ireland, and he enlisted into our Regiment as we pass'd through on our way to Cork where we embark'd for Service in America.

Kanavan was an Irishman and the only one in our Regiment. He was a funny dog! and continually in hobbles.[119] While he was talking with the French Officers, Colonel Fraser happen'd to be going round the Ramparts in Company with several Field Officers of other Regiments and I was appointed to act as Orderly upon the Colonel which gave me an opportunity of seeing and hearing all that took place. One of the Officers observ'd to the Colonel that there was one of his Majors in Company with the French Officers. Oh! says the Colonel, that can't be, for both of our Majors are elderly men, and they don't wear the Kilt, and I don't know therefore what to think of the matter. Presently they all passed by the French Officers who saluted the Colonel and his Party, in which Kanavan join'd, and the Colonel return'd it without making any observation at the time, but pass'd down the Ramps and out at the Gate.

When they had got a little way on, the Colonel says to the Officers, "that Field Officer whom you saw speaking to the French Officers, is no less than our Master Tailor"! They thought it a very extraordinary circumstance indeed. The Colonel invites the Officers to dine with him, and by way of affording them some amusement he desires me to look out for Kanavan and bring him up to his marquee. I did as I was ordered, and told the Colonel that Kanavan was waiting his Commands on the outside.

Poor Kanavan thought he had got himself into another hobble for his frolic, and he felt very ugly indeed, and to mend the matter the Colonel kept him standing before all the Officers for some time before he spoke to him. All this

---

119. In the 18th century, one hobbled one's horse in order to prevent it from straying, and in this case hobble was used to mean "tripping up" or simply an "embarrassing situation."

time poor Kanavan look'd exceedingly foolish. At last the Colonel simply ask'd him if he was press'd with much work just then, as he wish'd to have some alterations done to a Regimental Coat, and then dismiss'd him.

Anecdote No. 15
About the time that we were carrying on operations against the Town of Louisbourg, the siege of which place lasted seven weeks and three days, our Army under General Amherst met with a defeat at Crown Point,[120] and among the prisoners taken, there was a number of the 42nd or Old Highlanders, as they were call'd, and they were sent by the French to Quebec.[121] There they received every kind of good treatment from Mr. DE LANAUDIÈRE[122] who was the Commissary of Prisoners, and who became so attach'd to them that he would pass whole days with them. He would not even allow them to drink the water of the Saint Lawrence, from its liability to affect the bowels, but he used to send for Rock-water for them, from a beautiful spring still on the high ground at the end of the Saint John Suburbs. The men all spoke highly of him, and said that a Father could not have paid them more attention than he did.

One of the French Regiments at Quebec happen'd to be commanded by a Townsman of mine, one Colonel Ross.[123] This Officer found means to procure Mr. De Lanaudière's permission to get admittance to the prisoners, and after a while, he asks them some simple questions in Gaelic about how they were, and good day, and so forth, which surprised them not a little, seeing that he was a French Officer, but when he enter'd into further conversation with them, they were quite astonish'd, and they, at last, became so fond of him nothing could be like it.

---

120. General Amherst was the commanding general at Louisbourg, 1758. Thompson means General James Abercromby and the battle he is referring to is Ticonderoga, not Crown Point. Crown Point was taken the following year by an army commanded by Amherst without a shot fired. For a full account of this battle and part played by the senior Highland Regiment, see McCulloch, *SOTM*, I, 84–111.
121. According to J. Murray Gibbon in his book *Scots in Canada* (Toronto, 1971), 78, "Some taken prisoner ... and expecting to be cruelly treated looked on in mournful silence. Presently a gigantic French officer walked up to them and whilst exchanging in a severe tone some remarks in French with some of his men suddenly addressed them in Gaelic. Surprise in the Highlanders soon turned to positive horror. Firmly believing that no Frenchman could ever speak Gaelic, they concluded his Satanic Majesty in person was before them." If this unsubstantiated anecdote is true, then the Jacobite officer in question was probably either John Douglas *aka* the Chevalier Jean Douglass de Bassignac, or his brother, Francis Douglas, *aka* Captain François-Prosper Douglass, both Jacobite officers serving in the French regulars.
122. Charles-François Tarieu de la Naudière.
123. See footnote 99.

One ask'd if he was not a Scotchman? to which he said that it was of no consequence what Countryman he was, but it was quite sufficient for him that he was his friend. He enquired what they got to drink with their victuals? and they told him that Mr. De Lanaudière was so kind as to procure them fine Rock water at a good deal of trouble. Then, says Colonel Ross, good water is a good thing in its way, but I shall see that every man of you shall have his pint of wine per day, and I shall send a hogshead of Wine for the purpose, and when that is honestly out, at the regular allowance, I shall send another.

He kept his word with them as to the first hogshead, but a circumstance happen'd that prevented him doing so with a second, it was this: A French Doctor by the name of LAJUSTE[124] (the same that attend'd my family for thirty years afterwards, and was very clever) having arrived over land, at Quebec, brought intelligence that Louisbourg was so closely besieg'd by General Wolfe's Army, that it would most probably Capitulate. This was very unpleasant news for the Colonel, for, you see, he had serv'd during the Rebellion of forty-five, in the army of the Pretender, after which he hid himself in the woods at Inverness, and was forc'd to fly for good-and-all to France, where he soon got a Commission, and got up, step by step, to be a Colonel.

Seeing that the English were gaining ground at the two extremities of the Colony, he thought that Quebec was not the place for him to remain in and he became very uneasy. It happen'd, and very fortunately for Colonel Ross, that a French Frigate which lay in the bay (I forget her name) at the west side of the harbor of Louisbourg, at the same time that our fleet stretch'd across the whole mouth of the harbour, so that you would have thought it impossible for anything to escape, actually slipp'd thro' them at night, after having taken on board the Governor's Lady, and all the riches of the place, and shap'd her course for Quebec, which made complete fools of the two Ships of war that were sent by the English Commodore to watch her, for they thought of course that if she manag'd to get through the fleet, she must naturally proceed *down* the River to France, and they thought that they would nab her. This frigate arriv'd safe however at Quebec, and she confirm'd the report brought by Doctor Lajuste, but she did not remain long, and it was on board of her that Colonel Ross (and many others) made his escape out of the Colony. Before he went away from Quebec, he call'd to see his friends of the 42nd and took leave of them with a heavy heart, and he gave every one of them a French Crown piece.

I got this story from several of the men themselves, who took great pleasure in relating it on my going to see their Camp the next year after we had taken Quebec, and proceeded to the reduction of Montreal, which Capitulated with-

---

124. Louis François Lajus (Lajuste).

out giving us much trouble. Our camp lay at the foot of the mountain, and that of the 42nd Highlanders about three miles higher up towards Lachine. We hadn't the means of making merry together, for 'afaith I recollected well that the General gave Orders to stop our gill of rum that very day!

Chapter 4 | Winter Quarters, New York Colony, 1758–59

Amherst's force arrived in Boston harbour and dropped anchor on 12 September 1758, and he sent orders for all regiments to be prepared to disembark the following day. "All the Regiments landed and camped on the Common joining the Town," wrote Amherst on 13 September, and eager to be on the march he "intended to have marched the next morning but the Commanding Officers all representing it as absolutely necessary for their providing necessaries for their men and taking care of their sick, baggage &c, I resolved to halt one day."[125]

It was a fatal error for a general in a hurry. On 14 September 1758, while Amherst attended "a Thanksgiving for the success of His Majesty's Arms by the taking of Louisbourg.... Thousands of people came to see [the regiments] and would give them Liquor and make the men Drunk in Spite of all that could be done." On his return, an irate Amherst ordered the crowds out immediately and established roving patrols around the perimeter, but the damage had been done.[126]

The next morning, when the army marched, many men were missing, either drunk, or worse, they had taken the opportunity to desert and melt away in the crowds. Amherst was more than annoyed with himself and made a mental note never to disembark an army under his command in a major city again. "I was obliged to leave the Q[uarter] Guards of all the Regts to take care of the [drunken men] & bring them up when sober." The next evening, "fifty men that were straggling behind owing to the Rum" rejoined the column encamped at Sudbury, Massachusetts.[127]

The grenadiers and the light infantry of Fraser's Highlanders were sent forward as an advanced guard with all the camp colour men of the regiments to prove the route and find the next night's camp site. This was Amherst's routine as he force-marched his five regiments across the colony, at first passing through well cultivated countryside with a good network of roads and well established towns. On the 20th they marched through Worcester, the town in "a very pretty situation, finely watered & the improvements very great," Amherst noted approvingly. "The Homes all built of wood, but this will probably change and

---

125. Jeffery Amherst, 14 September 1758, Amherst, *Journal*, 86.
126. 15 September 1758, *Ibid*.
127. 16–17 September 1758, *Ibid*.

in an 100 years, I imagine, this Country will want wood."[128]

Four days later they arrived at Springfield, having marched through "a woody Country, no part cleared, but the woods high with no underwood," Amherst recorded. Now the wide roads had become mere cart tracks and Indian trails. The officers and men were glad to stop at this frontier outpost with "Five parishes about 100 Families in each" housed in log cabins on both sides of the Connecticut River, "very fine, about 500 yards across."[129]

Amherst wrote on 25 September 1758 that he "got all the ferry boats that could be found & passed over the five battalions, and encamped on the other side to be ready to march the next day." However, there was no rest for Major James Clephane, the experienced second-in-command of the 78th Foot. He was ordered the same day to march westwards to Westfield with 200 Pioneers armed with axes and tools and Captain Alexander Cameron of Dungallon's light infantry company as a covering force. His orders were to prepare the eight-mile trail for the following day's march.[130]

The next week saw the five regiments marching westward through thick primeval green woods on very bad roads and trails, their wagons constantly bogging down or their axles breaking. One of Amherst's entries for 29 September reads: "Seven broken wagons left which we unloaded and brought the Baggage away; a Horse of Lascelle's [47th Foot] killed by a trea [sic] falling."[131] By 1 October 1758 the regiments were a mere seven miles from the Mohican town of Stockbridge in the Berkshire Hills. Two days later Fraser's Highlanders arrived at Greenbush near Albany, where they encountered the "green wood," and here James Thompson relates a tale in which General Amherst quickly learned that a Highland regiment's honour, especially one commanded by the former Master of Lovat, was of paramount importance.

While at Greenbush the regiment was ordered, according to "Parson Robert" Macpherson:

> ... to go to the Oneida Station or Great Carrying Place, a 150 miles further through an unpopulated and a good part of it Desert Country. we were to assist in building a fort and beating the French who the General was inform'd were coming to attack that place ... our destination was ... Fort Stanwix [with] as many of our men as that place can hold all winter, the next inhabited house to this 60 miles from it. The Rest of the Reg.ᵗ to be in little Forts up & down this River.[132]

---

128. 20 September 1758, Worcester, Mass., *Ibid.*, 87.
129. 24 September 1758, Springfield, Mass., *Ibid.*, 88.
130. 25 September 1758, *Ibid.*, 89.
131. 29 September 1758, *Ibid.*, 90.
132. Robert Macpherson to William Macpherson, "Schenectady on the Mohoe River 16 Miles bove Albany and a 160 above New York," 18 November 1759, JGP.

Four Fraser companies were eventually stationed at Fort Stanwix and would face mortal danger every day at the western end of the Mohawk Valley. Life for the rest of the regiment was more relaxed in the established and prosperous Dutch farming town of Schenectady. The six companies there were billeted with the townsfolk or on the neighboring farms, taking turns to mount the town guard. Two more companies were stationed mid-way at Fort Herkimer and another company was detached on garrison duties in Schoharie, south of Schenectady. Officers and men alike enjoyed weekly dances or frolics in the inhabitants' homes, skated on the frozen river and attended sleighing parties. One unforgettable highlight of the winter, according to James Thompson, was a contest to establish the champion swordsman of the regiment.

Anecdote No. 26
As we were marching, in Column, thro' a wilderness kind of place in New England, call'd "Green Wood,"[133] we arriv'd at an open space where there was a small House and somewhat of a Farm. The Drumbeaters of several of the Regiments, who are more at liberty than the rest of the Army, got together, and went to ask the Woman of the house for some milk. She accordingly gave each of them a drink, for which they gave her a few Coppers, excepting John Wilkie, a lad belonging to our Regiment of Highlanders, who hadn't a Copper to give her. The woman was vex'd at this, and she went and sought out an officer, to whom she made a complaint against a drummer lad, dress'd in the Highland Uniform. This Officer happen'd to be no less than General Amherst, who afterwards, mentioned the matter to the lad's Colonel, our Colonel Fraser, not in the way of a Complaint, but merely as a boyish trick. The Colonel's pride was however nettled to think that the drummers of the other Regiments should be considered more honourable than his own, and he order'd a Drum-head Court Marshal [sic] on the lad, who was tied-up, and punish'd with two hundred lashes on his bare back, and then drum'd out of the Regiment, and I was order'd to give him his pay, up to the day![134]

The poor devil, with his knapsack, went away about his business! Some days afterwards, General Amherst was going along the road with his Orderly Sergeant, and he observes a soldier before him, whom he consider'd to be a De-

---

133. Remembered by Thompson as "Green Wood," it was actually Green Bush, a small settlement across the Hudson River from Albany, New York. Thompson's regiment stopped here as they marched cross country from Boston to Fort Stanwix. Today Greenbush is a suburb of Albany.
134. A drumhead court-martial is a court-martial held in the field to hear urgent charges of offences committed in action. The term is said to originate from the use of a drumhead as an improvised writing table.

serter. He sends the Sergeant to call after him, and desires him to stop. The poor fellow, having no idea of attempting to escape, very willingly went back with the Sergeant. General Amherst ask'd him where he was going? Wilkie replied that he was going to Newyork [New York]. To Newyork, says the General, what are you going to do there? I am going, says Wilkie, to endeavour to get a passage back to Scotland. Then, I suppose, says the General that you are Discharged? Wilkie said he was. The General ask'd to *see* his discharge. Wilkie began to fumble for it in his pockets, and pretended that he could not find it. (The reason of this was, that it shew'd the *cause* of his having been discharg'd, and that he had not left his Regiment in a creditable way.)

The General told him that if he could shew no discharge, he should be sent back to his Regiment as a Deserter. This soon produced it, and, on looking it over, the General immediately recollected the affair of the two Coppers' worth of milk. And, knowing that the poor fellow had got his punishment through himself having made a slight complaint to Colonel Fraser who had allowed his pride for the regimental character to disgrace the poor lad, he thought he must needs do something to make him amends, so, he ask'd him first, if he wouldn't prefer to remain in New England, rather than go back to his native country? Wilkie seem'd to prefer going Home. Well then, my lad, says the General, what would you think of living in my Service, where you would have nothing to do with the Army, and be well fed, and dressed in a handsome livery? Wilkie very readily agreed to this, and the General sent him, with a Note, to his Steward. Wilkie soon afterwards appeared in livery, and continued to behave himself much to the General's satisfaction. (Indeed he was a well-principled lad, and had a very decent appearance.)

In a little time the General made him put away the livery, and dress in plain clothes, and made him his Confidential body-Servant. In this way he had continued with the General, who was very fond of him.

Anecdote No. 6
Another adventure of Kanavan [the master tailor of the 78th] is when we got to Albany in New England. The Duty was rather slack for a time, and Kanavan bethought himself to put on his Officer's Coat again, that is when the Officers [were out] of the way – in this way he went strolling about and met a Lieutenant of another Regiment. They exchang'd bows, and presently became a little better acquainted. Kanavan was not long about proposing to go to the nearest Tavern, and, as the weather was very warm, that they should take a nip of Punch together. The Lieutenant said, "with all my heart," and to it they went, and nip after nip was order'd on the table until they both became well prim'd. Some subject or other led to argument, and the Lieutenant said something that

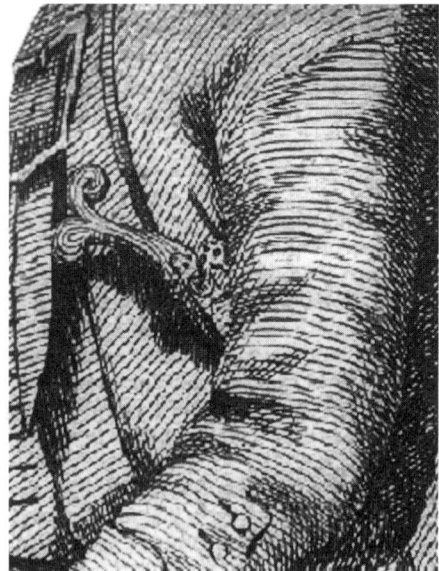

Highland pistols. Two close-ups from 18th-century prints illustrate how the Highland pistol was worn by Scottish soldiers. Suspended on a single strap from the right shoulder, the weapon itself usually hung under the left armpit. Most officers, and some NCOs, carried their own finely crafted pistols while those issued to the men were typically of poorer or inferior quality. (Editor's Collection)

nettled Kanavan, when he seizes hold of his pistol (the Highlanders all wore Pistols in their belts in those days)[135] by the muzzle, and with the cock of it, he gives the Lieutenant such a gash on the head, that he fell on the floor, and was bleeding at a great rate! This alarm'd the people of the house, and Kanavan was supposed to have mortally wounded the Lieutenant, and was accordingly put into confinement.

This affair coming to the Colonel's ear's, he went to see Kanavan, and after list'ning to his story, he told him it was a very serious affair, and that he must remain in confinement until he was tried by a General Court Martial, which would in all probability go hard with him. This he did in order to cure him of his capers for he was always in some hobble or another.

The Colonel then goes to see the Lieutenant, who also told his story, and thought that it would be a matter of Civil Law, by which he could recover heavy damages. No, no, Sir, said the Colonel (wishing to get Kanavan out of

---

135. Thompson's son James Jr. is mistaken in his "helpful" parenthesized footnote. His account of a Highland pistol worn "in" a belt should more properly read "on" a belt, for in the 18th century the Highland pistol was slung on a narrow shoulder belt or strap suspended from the right shoulder and hanging slung by its hook just under the left armpit for easy access as shown in contemporary close-up drawings.

the scrape) it will become a matter for the consideration of a General Court Martial by which it will be prov'd Sir, that you, as an Officer, were keeping company with a private Soldier of my Regiment, and you may depend on it Sir, that you will be cashier'd. The Lieutenant protested that he thought himself to have been in company with an Officer and a gentleman, but as it prov'd to be to the contrary, he was very ready to think no more about it, and was very thankful to the Colonel for his advice. By this means Kanavan got scot free once more.

Anecdote No. 13

On our arrival at Fort Stanwix,[136] the Colonel halted us just outside the town of Skenectady [Schenectady, New York], and as it was late in the afternoon he did not wish to trouble the inhabitants for billets to quarter the men, but order'd them to pitch their tents – which was accordingly done although there was about six inches depth of snow upon the ground. The Colonel waited to see the tents pitch'd, and then went into the Town, and he took me along with him, and we went to the principal Coffeehouse where he expected to find lodgings, but devil a nose of him could get in, for it was already cram'd with people in every part. He however met with the Barrackmaster[137] of the place, who was polite enough to offer him part of his own lodgings for that night. The Colonel sent me out in the meantime to look out for a lodging for myself, and away I went from tavern to tavern, all over the town, and was oblig'd at last to give up the pursuit, and return to where Col. Fraser was lodg'd, about eleven o'clock at night and to report the bad success of my enquiries. The Colonel said, well James, I'll tell you what to do. There is a large room in the house doing nothing, and you and I shall fold up the carpet together. We did so, and 'afaith when we had brought it to the proper size, it made a bed of about fifteen inches thick! I made my plaid serve as a blanket, and the Colonel gave me his own for a second one, and I soon became as comfortable as a bug in a rug. On bidding me goodnight the Colonel told me that I must wake him at five o'clock next morning, but instead of my waking him, he it was that awoke me. Up I started, and as soon as we had re-fix'd the Barrackmaster's carpet, away we went to the Camp. On

---

136. Fort Stanwix was built in the fall of 1758 by British forces to protect the Oneida Carrying Place, a three mile trail connecting the Mohawk and Hudson River watershed flowing east to Albany and the Wood Creek–Lake Oneida–Oswego watershed draining west into Lake Ontario. The fort was actually 100 miles to the west of Schenectady and not co-located as implied here in Thompson's oral history. The 78th Foot provided the fort's very first garrison, consisting of four companies under the command of Major James Clephane.
137. A barrack master of a town or city was responsible for the housing and accommodation of the troops whether the structures used were barracks, private homes, public buildings or tenting. He could be a serving or retired military officer or a civilian appointee.

enquiry the Colonel found that notwithstanding the snow, the men had passed a tolerably good night.

Anecdote No. 14
The same Corporal McPherson that snatch'd the blazing fuze out of a Shell that fell in our Trenches when we were laying Siege to Louisbourg, was a most capital Swordsman. When we were in Cantonments[138] in "Skeneccaty" in New England, it happen'd that the conversation among the Officers turn'd upon the Sword Exercise, and Quartermaster Campbell[139] of our's set himself up as the best swordsman in the Regiment.

He was taken up by Major Cameron[140] who stated that there was a Corporal in the Regiment that was as good as *he* was, if not better. This nettled the Quartermaster and he offer'd to take a bet of any money that he would beat him. After a long talk about the matter they at last agreed to a bet of a hundred guineas, the best of five cuts to win. The Major now sends for McPherson, and tells him that he had made a considerable bet upon him, and that he must prepare himself for a Battle. McPherson told the Major that he was ready to fight for him with the greatest pleasure, and wanted only to know who was to be his man?

The Major told him it was our Quartermaster. Oh, then, says McPherson, I must withdraw my words, for as I am only a Non-Commission'd Officer I might get into the Colonel's bad books for my presumption. The Major assur'd him *he* would settle that matter, and accordingly a day was fix'd upon for the Fight.

Instead of real Swords they were to use Cudgels with Broadsword handles. McPherson knowing that I had a knack that way, ask'd me to make the Cudgels. I said with all my heart, so I set to work and soon made the Cudgels, but was at some loss how to provide the Baskethandles. I got the leather, but not a Shoemaker in the place would undertake to make them, so I thought I could perhaps do that part too, and after settling nightly to work 'afaith I contriv'd to make a capital pair, which pleas'd McPherson very much.

At last the day came for the fight, and the place chosen was a large Barn, which was prepar'd with seats for the Company, among which was a number of the Ladies of the place. The Combatants were to fight on the threshing floor,

---

138. Cantonment. An army's temporary resting place, where the men are placed in people's homes in adjacent towns and villages, as opposed to being placed under canvas in camps.
139. Thompson's memory has failed him. The Quartermaster of the 78th at this time was Lieutenant John Fraser of Culbokie. See Part Three for Biographical Note.
140. Actually, Captain Alexander Cameron, 4th of Dungallon (see Part Three for Biographical Note). As the 78th was entitled to two majors and the only major that had come to North America, James Clephane, was the designated commandant of Fort Stanwix up-river for the duration of the winter, *Dungallon* may have been acting as regimental major or as the "town major" in the Schenectady garrison.

and the collar beam and all the rafters of the barn were crowded with people to witness the novel scene. The Champions, who were both dress'd in a light Jacket and Trousers having step'd up upon the Stage, McPherson said in a loud voice that he had some reluctance in coming forward from the difference of situation that existed between himself and that gentleman who was now before him. Several voices call'd out that there was to be no distinction on the occasion, and not to let *that* damp his Spirits. This eas'd his mind.

He then told Mr. Campbell [Fraser] that it was his intention to play lightly, and not to hurt him, but merely enough to let him feel that he was touch'd, so as to get him to acknowledge it as *a Cut*, but that the respect he had for him forbid his treating him severely. This was so far so good. Then to work they went and after a good deal of sparring, McPherson suddenly drops the point of his Cudgel and rests it on the floor, calling out "a cut," but which Quartermaster Campbell [Fraser] would not acknowledge, and "a Cut" and "no Cut" was repeated through the whole Company, just as they happen'd to have made their bets. When silence had been restor'd, they at it again, and presently McPherson drops his Cudgel. After getting the first two cuts, he again calls "a Cut" which Mr. Campbell [Fraser] positively denied. Then, says McPherson (whose blood was up) as you will not acknowledge this one, you must look sharp for the next, for I'll give you one that shall shew blood, and accordingly he gives him such a devil of a gash across the left cheek, that he bled immediately, and gave up.

This caus'd a great deal of fuss amongst the crowd. There was a good deal of money lost and won. Besides what McPherson may have got from the Major, a number of persons put money into his hands to the amount of fourteen guineas. While sauntering about the Streets some days after, I met the Major, who thank'd me for having help'd him to win the hundred guineas, and he gave me three dollars for my trouble in making the Baskethandles to the Cudgels.

Chapter 5 | The Siege and Battle for Quebec, 1759

After a long and relatively uneventful winter, Thompson's regiment was relieved by Colonel Eyre Massey's 46th Foot and sent down to New York, bound for Louisbourg. There, they were delighted to learn that there would be Danger, Glory and "plentiful War" for all concerned as they were ordered on service once again with the "Red-haired Corporal" – JAMES WOLFE. On 23 April 1759 they were reviewed in New York by the new Commander-in-Chief, Major General Jeffery Amherst, and by early morning 27 June 1759 were landing on the Île d'Orléans across from Quebec. Wolfe decided over the next two days he would send Brigadier General ROBERT MONCKTON's brigade, including Fraser's

The view from Pointe Lévy. This is the view James Thompson and the rest of the Fraser Highlanders saw for most of the 1759 siege of Quebec. In the foreground, grenadier soldiers and a sailor talk to a female sutler while below, at the water's edge, a company of soldiers embark in flat-bottomed boats. Farther out, more boats of the same type and fully loaded form up behind a British man o'war in the Quebec Basin. Engraving from sketch by Richard Short. (LAC A/N 1989-283-1)

Highlanders, across the southern channel of the river to the village of Beaumont on the high ground and have them march northwest to seize the heights at Pointe Lévy opposite Quebec. From there he could then bombard the Lower and Upper Towns.

On Saturday, 30 June 1759, the 78th and 43rd Regiments of Foot crossed over the south channel to join and support the 15th Foot, light infantry and rangers who had already established a bridgehead in the village of Beaumont. By midday Monckton's brigade was marching "through the wood along a good road to Pointe Lévy for about three or four miles, when the rangers in front were fired on from the woods, they skirmished for some time, and the troops were ordered to halt. Some of the rangers were wounded, but the Enemy was obliged to Retire." Lieutenant MALCOLM FRASER of the 78th observed that they:

> … marched on till we came to the Church of St Joseph at Point Levy, when we were again attacked in front. Brigadier Monckton ordered the troops to march to the open field by the River side and the Rangers, Light Infantry and the advanced parties continued popping with the enemy most part of the evening, till

Captain Campbell who was posted with his Company in the church, ordered part of his company to fire a volley at them, when the firing almost ceased, and I suppose most part of the enemy retired as we hear but few shots thereafter...[141]

Grenadier Sergeant James Thompson also remembered this first night of action at Quebec. Apparently the Highlanders of Campbell's company, on entering the church and driving the enemy out, discovered that the high shuttered windows in the church on the left side were level with the hilltop outside being used by the Indians and Canadians to snipe at the brigade below. The story of what happened next is told by Thompson with great relish in the first anecdote of this chapter.

The incident at the church was followed a few days later, Sunday, 1 July 1759, with an incredible display of Robert Monckton's poor generalship. French floating batteries appeared on the river and appeared to be approaching the camp, which had been sited a little too close to the shore.

"I was ordered with Ensign [James] Mackenzie [4th Ardloch] to the colours, and they cannonaded us for about half an hour," remembered Ensign Malcolm Fraser. "There were four of our Regiment killed and eight wounded; and one sergeant of the 15th Regiment and eight of the Colonel's Company were knocked down with one ball, behind the Colour's and all wounded, two I believe mortally."[142]

Contrast this officer's account, which sticks to the facts and underlines the regiment's steadfastness in the face of death, with Sergeant Thompson's memory of the affair later in this chapter. It leaves one in no doubt as to what the men's feelings were on the occasion. Wolfe was furious when he heard that fourteen soldiers had been needlessly killed.

The urbane aide de camp to the commander, Captain Hervey Smythe, noted in his private journal that "it was matter of conversation in the army" as to Monckton's "reason for exposing the soldiers in that manner. 'Twas said that it cou'd not be from apprehension that the Enemy wou'd land to attack his Brigade, as there were not above Eight or ten men in each of the four floating Batteries." Wolfe and his staff now realized that Monckton was "of a dull capacity and may be properly call'd Fat headed, Timid and utterly unqualify'd."[143] (One

---

141. Entry for 30 June 1759 in Malcolm Fraser, *Extract from a Manuscript Journal [vol 2], Relating to the Siege of Quebec in 1759, Kept by Colonel Malcolm Fraser, then Lieutenant of the 78th (Fraser's Highlanders) and Serving in that Campaign*, LHSQ, Historical Documents, Series 2, vol 6 (1867) (hereafter Fraser, *Journal*).
142. 1 July 1759, *Ibid.*
143. Anonymous journal, LAC, MG18-D4, Microfilm A-652. The most likely author (as Charles Stacey posits in "Quebec, 1759: Some New Documents" reprinted in *Quebec, 1759: The Siege and the Battle*, D. E. Graves, ed. (Toronto, 1959. Revised edition, 2002), 219–27) of this particular journal with insider knowledge is one of the two aides de camp

of James Thompson's anecdotes goes one step further and implies the "timid" brigadier lost his nerve.)

Monckton would have to be supervised closely and Wolfe personally crossed over to re-site Monckton's camp further up on the heights closer to where he intended to site his main siege batteries. These gun emplacements were dug with Fraser's Highlanders and other regiments providing large work parties, and were finally finished on the night of 12 July 1759, despite the French subjecting the place to their largest counter-battery barrage since the landing.

Thompson's next recollection is the fierce action at Montmorency Falls, 31 July 1758, where General Wolfe resolved to assault a French redoubt built right at the high-tide waterline, well forward of the entrenched Beauport Heights. Unbeknownst to the Highlanders, the "Red-haired Corporal's" plan was to seize this isolated shore redoubt and hold it, hoping to lure Montcalm's well entrenched infantry down from their nearly impregnable positions to fight with his three brigades. Two of those brigades had to march across the lower ford of the Montmorency River from the British camp east of the Falls, while 200 Royal Americans, the remaining companies of Fraser's Highlanders and the 15th Foot of Monckton's brigade would land to support the grenadiers once they were in possession of the redoubt.

The whole attack, however, was based on the flawed assumption that Montcalm, "the old fox," would seriously consider joining the fight. That Montcalm would abandon the advantage of an excellent entrenched position on the heights was, as most military historians have been wont to say, wishful thinking on Wolfe's part. On the day, the "Red-haired Corporal," standing on the shot-torn deck of the armed transport *Russell*, clearly saw for himself that the so-called isolated French redoubt was in fact much closer to the French entrenchments along the heights than it had first appeared to be when viewed from the Falls camp. Not only that, it was well covered by both musket and artillery fire and thus thoroughly untenable. Yet Wolfe would still order the assault forward.

All grenadiers had been kept in the dark as to their actual purpose once at the redoubt (essentially they were bait), so most officers and men simply assumed that their role was a routine frontal assault up and over the beach. In hindsight, this miscommunication was a serious oversight on Wolfe's part, for the zeal and

---

to Wolfe: either Captain Hervey Smythe or Captain Thomas Bell, Marines. Both officers accompanied the body of Wolfe home after the battle. The LAC erroneously attributes the journal to Major Paulus Æmilius Irving (see Part Three for Biographical Note), but this cannot be, as existing copies of Irving's handwriting do not match that of the unidentified staff officer. Besides, Irving was too preoccupied during the campaign commanding the 15th Foot to have written such an intimate journal which, as Stacey points out, must have been written by someone in Wolfe's inner circle or "family."

The battle of Montmorency, 1759. This is a composite depiction of the events that occurred during the British assault launched against the Beauport Flats and Heights on 31 July 1759, which ended in failure. The French occupy defensive positions on the high ground to the right. Left, the *Centurion*, 50 guns, provides naval gunfire support while two smaller transports fitted out as floating batteries do likewise further up the beach. Two brigades have crossed the ford at the foot of the Falls at low tide and are marching to the support of the Grenadiers of the army, who have assaulted a French battery and are attempting to climb the Heights. Engraving from watercolour by Hervey Smythe. (LAC C-000782)

morale of his soldiers was at fever-pitch and most were over-confident to the point of reckless ardour. When they finally landed on the afternoon of 31 July, discipline, the watchword of Wolfe's army, was forgotten as first platoons, then whole companies, of grenadiers moved forward without orders. The men strove to outrace one another to the French redoubt some one hundred yards away. As the grenadiers closed the distance, the French colonial regulars and seamen manning the guns hastily abandoned the redoubt and scrambled up to the entrenched heights to their rear.

The entire sky had darkened by this time, and the French watching on the heights above now saw Townshend's Brigade, a dark scarlet column crossing the lower Montmorency ford at low tide, marching quickly to effect a link-up with the disorderly attack in progress to their front. A wave of some 1,000 grenadiers, regiments irreconcilably intermixed, laboured up the steep shale slopes after the retreating French only to be repulsed twice with heavy losses. Grenadier Sergeant James Thompson claims to have got so near the top trenches that he "distinctly saw Montcalm on horseback riding backwards and forwards," though this sector was the responsibility of General Lévis. In any event he was close enough to see a senior French officer give the command to fire.

As many neared the top for a third attempt, Mother Nature violently intervened and a flash thunderstorm broke overhead. One officer described it as "the dreadfullest thunder-storm and fall of rain that can be conceived" and all small arms and artillery on both sides fell silent, powder soaked. The slopes running with water and mud virtually washed away what little momentum the final British attempt had and the soaked survivors slid back to the abandoned redoubt at the foot of the hill.[144]

A helpless and angry General Wolfe stood on the beach with Monckton's two battalions, Fraser's Highlanders and the 15th Foot, trying to impose order on disorder, a chore of some magnitude. He ordered the Frasers, freshly landed and spoiling for a fight, to stand fast alongside their sister battalion and cover the broken grenadier companies withdrawal to the shore, a difficult order no doubt for some of the more eager Highlanders. What made the task doubly excruciating for many of the men standing there, brick-red kilts now sodden black and plastered against their knees, was that many of their kinsmen and colleagues were in Captain Macdonell's grenadiers still forward around the captured redoubt. From this bloody, rain-soaked battle comes one of Thompson's more colourful accounts – the story of the rescue of Lieutenant Henry Peyton of the Royal Americans by a sergeant of Fraser's Highlanders.

James Thompson is strangely silent on the climactic battle fought on the Plains of Abraham where his hero, James Wolfe, fell in his moment of glory, 13 September 1759. While there are interesting stories regarding the regimental piper, and his work as a "hospital sergeant" at Pointe Lévy, the lack of any specific personal experiences "on the battlefield" have led us to conclude that he was not present during the actual fighting. The editors believe Thompson was left out of battle, attending to casualty evacuation down at the Anse au Foulon, a task supported by his own anecdotal evidence, as the reader will see.

Anecdote No. 16

There were four Regiments[145] order'd by General Wolfe from the Island of Orleans to cross over to the South side, three to the Point Levi to take up a position

---

144. *An Historical Journal of the Campaigns in North America for the Years 1757, 1758, 1759, and 1760, by Captain John Knox*, A.G. Doughty, ed., 3 vols (Toronto, 1914), I, 453 (hereafter Knox, *Journals*).

145. There were three regiments involved. On Saturday, 30 June 1759, the 78th and 43rd

on the highground opposite the town of Quebec, and the fourth to land lower down, and collect all the cattle they could. After the whole had landed and been form'd into a Column under the Command of General M[onckton],[146] a strong party was sent in advance under the orders of Lieutenant Hayley of the 15th Regiment.[147]

We receiv'd no molestation whatever on our march as far the church.[148] The houses were all deserted by the *young* people, and there remain'd only some very *old* people to take care of the houses. We could not get a sup of milk for love or money. The poor old people gave us to understand that all their cows and other cattle had been kill'd for the French army, and indeed I believ'd it for the only animals we could discover were here and there a dog or a cat, but however, there was plenty of cattle brought up by the 4th Division from below.

Nothing remarkable happen'd on our march, until Lieutenant Hayley and his party had got a little way above the Church of Pointe Levi where they were fir'd upon by some Savages that lay conceal'd on the top of the rock just close by on the left and they kill'd five of his party. No sooner had they fir'd than Lieutenant Hayley comes running back towards the Column (and I observ'd that he was holding his Sword, which was a scymater,[149] by the middle of the blade) and bawling out as loud as he could, "We are surrounded by Savages! There are thirty thousand of them just behind that rock"!

The Column immediately receiv'd Orders to Halt, and there was a consultation what was best to be done. Presently, the word was pass'd for the General and it went all thro' the Column that the General was not to be found! As there was no General to give directions, the troops began to fall out of their places, and 'afaith they soon were no better than a mob. During the confusion, I myself 'spied the General going down along the Fence, in a line towards the River, but I said nothing about the matter as I suppos'd I was the only one that saw him going.

    Regiments of Foot crossed over the south channel from the Île d'Orléans to join and support the 15th Foot, the light infantry and the rangers, who had already established a bridgehead in the village of Beaumont.

146. In the original manuscript, Thompson is silent on this general officer's name, identifying only the first initial of the surname, followed by a series of dots. However, we must assume he is referring to Brigadier General Robert Monckton, who was ordered to seize the heights at Pointe Lévy opposite Quebec to establish siege batteries.

147. There was no officer by the name of Hayley in the 15th Foot. However, there was one Lieutenant Vernon Hawley of the 43rd Foot who made the march serving in Monckton's Brigade and who may have been detached to the light infantry.

148. The church at Pointe Lévy built in 1675 (known to the British as St. Joseph's Church and known today as Église Saint-Joseph-de-la-Pointe-Lévy) was converted into a temporary hospital for use by the British on 5 July 1758.

149. Thompson is referring to a scimitar – a curved sword of oriental origin popular amongst cavalry officers.

As the General could not be found any where, a Lieutenant Colonel (I forget his name)[150] of our Regiment calls for Major Paulus Emilius Irvin[151] [*sic*] of the 15th and says to him, "Major Irvin, in the absence of the General I am next in rank and the Command should fall on me, but as I got my rank without my seeing any active service" (you see, observes my Father, by way of accounting for the propriety of the Colonel's motives, he got his Commission for raising the regular complement of Men, and he was made Lieutenant Colonel at once) – "I should be afraid to take upon myself the responsibility at this very critical moment, I have therefore to request of you, Major Irvin, to assume the Command, and all I can say is, that I shall obey your Orders to the best of my judgement."

Immediately upon this the Major takes off his wig and crams it into his Coat-pocket, and, drawing his Sword, he orders all of the troops to pass over the fences, into the meadow adjoining the church, on the water side. Here they were pell-mell, all jumbled up together, without any order or regularity whatsoever. The first thing the Major does, is to call out the Grenadiers of each Regiment and to post them in each corner of the meadow to watch the approach of the French or the Savages, and to prevent their taking us by surprise. After he had this done, he then mark'd off the ground for each Regiment, and in a little time there was order once more restored. As the day was getting advanc'd, the men stood in need of their dinners, and we encamp'd and Dined on the meadow.

Meeting with SAUNDERS SIMPSON,[152] my Cousin, who was acting as our Provost marshal,[153] he says to me, "Jim, Did you observe the General crossing down along the fence when the Savages were said to be coming upon us"? I told Saunders that I did, but that I thought myself the only one that had seen him, and I didn't like to take notice of it to any body. "Then," says Saunders, "we had better say no more about it." So soon as order was a little restored, the Major orders two Companies into the Church, and nobody suspected what this was for.

He sets the men to work to carry all the forms (there were no Pews) and place them one on top of another under the windows next the land side, and

---

150. Thompson is stating this with tongue in cheek, knowing full well who the untested colonel in this particular anecdote is, for it is his own commanding officer, Lieutenant Colonel Simon Fraser. Fraser had never commanded a battalion in action before except for the few months of siege warfare at Louisbourg.
151. Major Paulus Æmilius Irving (see Part Three for Biographical Note) was commanding the 15th Foot in the absence of its lieutenant colonel, James Murray, then acting as one of Wolfe's three brigadier generals.
152. Sergeant Alexander Simpson *aka* "Saunders" or "Sanders" Simpson.
153. The provost marshal is the officer in charge of the provost, or military police. On 4 July 1759 Wolfe issued the following general order: "The commanding officers of regiments are to enquire in their respective regiments for some sergeant who is well qualified for a Provost, and send his name and character to the Adjutant-General." Presumably Sergeant "Sanders" Simpson was the one submitted by the 78th Foot.

he orders the men on top of them so as to bring them breast high with the windows – this was to get a shot at the rascals of Savages that were still on the look-out on the top of the rock, and as they didn't suspect what was preparing for them, they crowded towards the edge a-watching our motions. When the Major got all his men ready, he told them they were to fire with a good aim at those Savages on the rock just above, and right thro' the sashes, and to wait the signal from him.

When he saw the favorable moment, he gave the word to Fire! and we brought down about a dozen of them, upon which all the others gave a great yell, and away they scamper'd into the woods, carrying their kill'd and wounded along with them. There wasn't anything like 30 thousand, as Lieutenant Hayley had reported in his fright. No, not even *one* thousand, but only about fifty Savages, and the remainder were French Canadians!

Not knowing what might happen during the night, the Major establish'd a Patrole, to keep moving around the Camp all night, and order'd Saunders Simpson to be on the alert. There was, besides, out Sentries to prevent a surprise. While going his rounds, with a small party of Grenadiers, Saunders tho't he saw a faint light on a Point near the waterside and could not think what it could be, but he was determin'd to find out, and after advancing some distance in a line with it, he discovers it to be an old Windmill. Not satisfied with *that* he insists upon getting in, and there, to his astonishment he sees the General sitting in one corner, and a "leetle" end of Candle burning beside him![154] However, he said nothing to him, and withdrew, and at day-break he makes his report to the Commanding Officer that there was nothing extraordinary. It wasn't known for what purpose the General went to the windmill but it was whispered throughout the Division that General Wolfe was highly displeas'd at it – still there was nothing appear'd in General Orders. The next morning he was at the Camp, and resumed his Command of the Division.

The French General, Montcalm, having got intelligence that we had taken up a position at Point Levi, sent over four gunboats from the Falls for the purpose of annoying us, or of drawing off our attention from the object of our movement. As they moved forward, the General 'spied them, and nothing less would do, but he orders the whole Column down to the beach where he form'd us along the edge of the water, altho' there was a ridge of rocks where we could have been form'd under shelter from the effect of the enemy's shot. We had been

---

154. Leetle. A vulgar or humorous variant of little, as in "she may be a *leetle* spoilt by circumstances" in Charles Dickens, *Our Mutual Friend*, iv. 13 (New York, 1865). The editors believe that Thompson is expressing surprise that a general should have only a *little* stub end of a candle to illuminate his temporary quarters rather than something more substantial or indeed several candles.

some length of time form'd in this way before the Boats came near enough to act, for the tide had carried them rather too low, and they had therefore to work up again.

They at last came opposite to us, and the very first shot they let drive at us, kill'd a Sergeant of the 15th and as it passed to the rear, it carried away part of the men's dinner that was cooking in a large Iron pot hung between three poles. On our picking up some of their shot, they prov'd to be 24 pounders! Now, if they had only the sense to have fired *Cannister* [*sic*][155] at us, they would have mow'd us down like grass, for our brave General had paraded us in the best manner possible for that purpose. As good-luck would have it, the tide was fast making, and as the boats were heavy, they were carried away by the Tide and seem'd to drift towards the Town of Quebec. Having got rid of these troublesome visitors we broke up our Camp, and we were again put in motion, and we took post on the high ridges at Point Levi, just between the two Ferry-places.

Unnumbered Anecdote[156]

We were encamp'd at Point Levi when there came an order for a Division from each Regiment to rendezvous at the point of the Isle of Orleans, and when all the troops were collected there, that were to form the storming party, we receiv'd orders to embark in flat bottom'd boats that were collected for the purpose, and cross over, so as to arrive at the Falls at high water, and try to take some Batteries, by storm, that were erected along the brow of the hill at Beauport. From some delay or other the tide had fallen about one fourth, and the men had to form and to march in the mud about ankle deep, which was very harassing to them – instead of forming the whole of the companies into one Division, the Commanding Officer was to attempt to make up the time lost by the falling of the tide, that he march'd them up to the attack singly. As our company of Grenadiers approached, I distinctly saw Montcalm on horseback riding backwards and forwards[157] and

---

155. Canister shot is a type of anti-personnel ammunition used in cannons. It consists of a hollow tin cylinder filled with cast iron or lead balls. When fired, the cylinder disintegrates and its projectiles spread out in a conical formation, causing a wide swath of destruction.
156. This unnumbered anecdote cannot be found in the original Manuscript copy. However, it was published in the *Star and Commercial Advertiser*, Quebec, on 16 April 1828 under the title "Anecdote of Wolfe's Army – History of Sergeant Allan Cameron." While attributed only to "a Companion in Arms," it is clearly one of Sergeant James Thompson's anecdotes which had been missed by James Jr. when he was transcribing his rough notes into a permanent letter-book. It was also published by Alfred Hawkins in his *Picture of Quebec: with Historical Recollections* (Quebec, 1834), 396–98. As the version published in the *Star and Commercial Advertiser* is more complete, it has been selected for inclusion here.
157. Thompson most likely saw Major General François Gaston de Lévis, the actual general officer commanding this sector of the French defensive line.

seem'd very busy giving directions to his men, and I heard him give the word to fire! Immediately they open'd upon us, and kill'd a good many of our men, I don't recollect how many. We did not fire, for it would have been of no use, as they were completely entrench'd and we could only see the crown of their heads.

A Sergeant of another regiment who had strayed away from his Company, came towards our's and seeing some handy fascines lying on the beach, he plac'd one near where I stood and put a second on top of the first, and then laid himself down alongside them, putting the fascines between him and the French as a kind of abbatis, but by my faith he had not been there three minutes when he was kill'd by a musket ball! We were soon order'd to retreat to our boats, that had been kept afloat to receive us, and by this time it was low water, so that we had a long way to wade through the mud.

A Sergeant Allan Cameron,[158] of our Company, seeing a small battery[159] on our left with two guns mount'd, and apparently no person near it, thought he would prevent its doing us any mischief on our retreat, so he picks up a couple of bayonets that lay on the beach, and went alone to the battery, when he drives the points of them into the vents as hard as he could, and then snapp'd them off short.

When the French saw us far enough on the retreat, they sent their Savages to scalp and tomahawk our poor fellows that lay wounded on the beach – among the number was Lieutenant Peyton[160] of the Royal American Regiment, who was severely wounded, and had crawl'd away as far as the pains he endur'd would

---

158. Thompson's memory is hazy. Only one 78th sergeant was commissioned an officer for his acts of bravery before and after the siege of Quebec and this was Archibald (not Allan) Cameron (c.1738–c.1795). A gentleman volunteer like Thompson himself, Archibald Cameron not only saved Peyton but also distinguished himself during the fighting at the battle of Sillery, 28 April 1760. He was thus promoted ensign into the 15th Foot (Amherst's) on the recommendation of Brigadier General James Murray while the 78th were at Montreal in September 1760. He subsequently exchanged into the 28th Foot (Bragg's) the following year and went with that regiment to fight in the Caribbean. He then transferred to the 42nd on promotion to lieutenant at Havana "in room of Alexander Farquharson, died discharged" and went out on half-pay at the 1763 peace. He returned to active duty as a lieutenant in December 1770 with the 2nd / 1st Foot but went out two years later on Irish half-pay, 3 March 1772.
159. Known as Johnstone's Redoubt by the French as it was laid out and its construction supervised by Chevalier James Johnstone, a Jacobite officer serving in the *compagnies franches de la marine*.
160. Lieutenant Henry Peyton, 60th Foot (Royal Americans). Joined the 2nd Battalion, 60th Foot, as an ensign (25 April 1757) and was promoted lieutenant (4 September 1759). He returned to Britain and raised his own independent company (28 October 1760). His company was one of four sent to Jamaica that year and used to reinforce the 74th Foot commanded by Sir John Irwin. He went on half-pay (6 December 1763) as a captain of the 74th when that regiment was disbanded at the peace. He died on half-pay, 28 April 1768.

allow. After the Savages had done their business with the poor fellows that lay nearest the French batteries, they went back, except two who 'spied Lieutenant Peyton, and thought to make a good prize of him. He happen'd to have a double-barrelled fuzee, and ready loaded, and as he had seen how the Savages had treated all the others that came into their clutches, he was sure that if they got the better of him, they would butcher him also.

Fortunately his presence of mind did not forsake him, and he wait'd until the first Savage came near enough, when he levell'd his fuzee, and brought him to the ground; the other Savage thinking that the Lieutenant would not have time to re-load, rush'd in upon him boldly with his tomahawk ready to strike, when Lieutenant Peyton discharg'd his fuzee right into his chest, and he fell dead at his feet! We saw no more of the Savages after that, at least on that occasion, but we saw enough of them afterwards.

While poor Lieutenant Peyton lay upon the ground almost exhaust'd from his exertions and loss of blood, he was accost'd by Sergeant Cameron, who had no other means of helping him than carrying him away, and faith he was well able to do it, for he was a stout, strong, tall fellow. He slings the Lieutenant's fuzee over his shoulder along with his own, and takes him on his back, telling him to hold fast round his neck. As he had a long way to carry him, he was oblig'd every now and then to lay him down to take breath, and to give the Lieutenant some ease, as his wound was exceedingly painful. In this way he got him at last to one of the boats, and laying him down, said, "Now Sir, I have done as much for you as lay in my power, and I wish you may recover." It so happen'd, that in returning to Camp, the Lieutenant was taken to the Isle of Orleans, and Cameron to Point Levi.

After some time Lieutenant Peyton was considerably recover'd from his wounds, and he sent an Officer over to Point Levi to Cameron, to say that he wish'd to see him. Cameron told the Officer, that he would not go. "Why?" says the Officer, to Cameron – "why, do you think, Sir, I could leave Camp without Orders?" This, you see, was out of delicacy to his feelings. The Officer then procured a "Pass" and brought it to Cameron, who at last consent'd to go over to the Island, and away then went. Lieutenant Peyton said he was extremely glad to see him, and to thank him for the very great services he had render'd him in preserving his life, and that if ever it was in his power he would give him substantial proof of the obligation under which he lay. Nothing occurred on any consequence respecting Cameron, to my knowledge, until we were order'd to the reduction of Montreal in the spring of the next year, which capitulated without our firing a shot. From Montreal, Cameron was ordered to New York, where he received an Ensigncy in a corps of Rangers through the means of Lieutenant Peyton's friends and the interest he made with Colonel Fraser in his behalf.

Cameron soon after came back to Montreal and still wore his Sergeant's coat, not being able to procure a better. The whole of his old Regiment, officers and men, were exceedingly glad to see him, and he receiv'd an invitation to become a member of their regimental mess, free of expense; he was sadly put to his shifts what to do for a coat, and told me his distress. I happen'd to have a plain scarlet coat of superfine cloth, which I let him have, and he was not satisfied with that, but he borrowed my silver watch along with the coat. He got soon rigg'd out as an officer, and upon my word he looked remarkably well, however, he did not long enjoy this fine kind of life, for the Regiment he belong'd to was reduced.

He set out on his way to Scotland, by way of New York, at which place he remain'd some time, where he made a good deal of money at a game they call "Long Bowles." From New York, he went to England, and having no employment he betook himself to gambling, and was soon involved in debt, and at length arrested by a bailiff for the sum of £40. Being placed in a Spunging house,[161] he addressed a letter to General Murray (who he knew to be in that neighbourhood at the time), setting forth his distress. The General, who had a knowledge of his bravery as a soldier, and who was attached to him, immediately sent his aide-de-camp to the Spunging house to make enquiries into the nature of his case, and having brought back to the General all the particulars, he was sent back to Cameron with the means of procuring his release.

Cameron was scarcely liberated from his gambling debts than he was arrested a second time at the writ of his landlord, for Board and Lodging for nearly the same amount. Being a strong, powerful fellow, he contriv'd to shake off the bailiff and away he ran, hoping to make his escape, but the bailiff called out to the mob "stop thief," when he was pursued by every person that he met. Almost exhausted, he 'spied a front door of a store open into which he ran, and call'd upon the master for his protection as he was pursued by the mob. The master very good naturedly put him in a room in rear of his counting-room, where he thought himself safe, but being observed to run in the house under suspicious circumstances, the mob gradually collected in front of the house and indicated to the Sheriff's Officer where his victim had taken refuge. He demands admittance in the King's name, and shew'd the master of the house his warrant for apprehending poor Cameron. The master made no resistance and conducted the bailiff to where his prisoner was concealed. Cameron endeavoured to expostulate with him for breach of promise of protection, – says the master, "Sir, I protected you from the mob, but I dare not protect you from the laws of your country,

---

161. A sponging-house was a one-time place of temporary confinement for debtors. This was not a debtor's prison, as such, but a private house, often the bailiff's own home. The debtor would be held there temporarily in the hope that he could make suitable arrangements with the creditors.

and you must quit my house instantly." The bailiff being afraid to grapple with Cameron, called upon six men out of the mob to assist him in the King's cause, whereupon poor Cameron was dragged along, and safely lodged in Jail!

He bethought himself to write another letter to his friend General Murray, stating his miserable situation. The General always ready to help a companion in arms, had the goodness to despatch his aide-de-camp to him, who made minute inquiries into his present situation, and the prospects he had of getting back to his friends in Scotland, and made his report to the General, who, however, did not release him immediately, as on the first occasion, but sent him word that he would see and do something for him. Poor Cameron was left some days, in a sad state of suspense, and began to think that the General had forgot him.

This, however, proved not to be the case, for the General went to the War Office and told Lord Barrington, then the Secretary at War, that he called on him on behalf of a most noble fellow who was in distress, and whom he wished to procure employment for. After asking a number of questions, Lord Barrington turned to a row of pigeon-holes, expressing at the same time, his fears that there was no vacancy, but at last he came to some papers which shew'd a vacancy to exist in a Regiment serving at Minorca. The General said that was exactly what he wanted, and requested it might be secured for his friend Cameron. Lord B. seemed desirous to put him off, on a plea of very pressing business at that moment, but would not fail to hear the matter in mind, upon this the General (who had some influence, it would appear) protested he would not quit the office until he had effected his purpose. Seeing there was no getting rid of him, Lord B. gave directions to some one in an adjoining room to prepare some papers, with which he himself proceeded to the proper officer, and shortly after rejoin'd the General who had waited his return. This was an appointment to a Lieutenancy in the Regiment at Minorca, which he had mentioned before.

The General now lost no time in sending his aide-de-camp to ascertain if there was a vessel ready to sail for any part of the Mediterranean, who had no difficulty in finding one. Afraid that Cameron might get into new difficulties if liberated, he allowed him to remain in Jail, and after securing a passage for him, and getting him a suit of uniform of the regimental pattern, and a stock of other necessaries, etc., etc., he had him let out of Jail, and sent his own aide-de-camp with him to the vessel. Soon after his arrival at Minorca, Cameron wrote to several of his Highlander friends in this country; it was not long after that I heard of his death, on the Island of Minorca.

Anecdote No. 17

I knew Montgomerie [sic] at the taking of Quebec in 1759. He was there a Captain, and Commanded a Fencible Corps of which I don't recollect the name.

He was posted just on the off-side of the Falls of Montmorenci, and was sent by General Wolfe on some particular business down towards Ange Gardien. As he advanced, some of the people turn'd out and fir'd upon his advanc'd party, and this brought on a more general action. Amongst the number that opposed him in this way, was the Priest of the Parish, as Commanding Officer.

Montgomery defended himself obstinately, and kill'd most of the Canadians, including the Priest himself. This exasperated them so much, that they became frantic and scarcely knew what they were about, and from want of discipline and order, they exposed themselves to Montgomery's mercy.

Montgomery knew how to take advantage of this, and his Party kill'd every one that came in his way, without any mercy. He fell in with one of his Sergeants having under his charge a young Canadian gentleman who had been placed with the Priest for his Education, and who after having lost his Teacher, had placed himself under the protection of this Sergeant, in order to save himself from the butchering work that he had witness'd. Montgomery, after finding out that he was a Canadian, had him shot that instant!

General Wolfe was very much vex'd at Montgomery's conduct. It afterwards appear'd that the cause of his resentment towards the Canadians was, his having lost a Brother who had been kill'd, and his body afterwards cruelly mangled by the Canadians that were in alliance with the Savages.[162]

After the War, Montgomery's Corps was disbanded, and he went back to New England, where he engaged in the Revolutionary War against G: Britain and that from his previous knowledge of Quebec, he was no doubt consider'd the best qualified, to Head the Army that came to the attack of the place in the year 1775, on which occasion He, and many of his Army lost their lives on the night of the 31st of December.

Anecdote No. 24
At the battle of the Plains of Abraham we had but one Piper,[163] and because he

---

162. Here Thompson confuses Captain Alexander Montgomery of the 43rd Foot with his younger brother Captain Richard Montgomery, 17th Foot (see Chapter 9) the latter having served with Thompson at Louisbourg, but Richard was not present at the 1759 siege of Quebec. Richard later became the American Revolutionary War commander who invested Quebec. General Wolfe had banned the "inhuman practice of scalping" during the Quebec 1759 campaign unless the enemy were "Indians, or Canadians dressed like Indians." Older brother Alex, commanding a mixed detachment of light infantry, rangers and Highlanders, invoked this directive to justify the cold-blooded killing.
163. The piper at the Plains battle, and the subsequent spring battle in 1760 forward of Sillery Wood, was probably Piper Archibald Macdonald, born c.1730 near Inverness and wounded in the right arm at the latter battle. He was eventually admitted to Chelsea Hospital on 8 September 1761 and later served as a piper in one of the invalid companies of the British army. NA, WO 120/5, Royal Hospital, Chelsea, Regimental Registers of

was not provided with arms and the usual means of defence like the rest of the men, he was made to keep aloof for safety.[164] When our line advanced to the charge, General Townshend [Murray][165] observing that the Piper was missing, and he knowing well the value of one on such occasions, he sent in all directions for him, and he was heard to say aloud, "Where's the highland Piper!"? and "Five pounds for a piper" but devil a bit did the Piper come forward the sooner. However, the charge by good chance was pretty well effected without him, as all those that escaped could testify. For this business the Piper was disgraced by the whole of the Regiment, and the men would not speak to him, neither would they suffer his rations to be drawn with theirs, but had them served out by the Commissary separately, and he was obliged to shift for himself as well as he could.

Anecdote No. 23
After the Battle of the Plains of Abraham, on the 13th September, fifty-nine, where a great deal of the French lay killed or wounded on the field (we kill'd Seventy-two officers alone) – it was horrid to see the effect of the blood and dust on their white coats! They lay there as thick as a flock of sheep, and just as they had fallen, for the main body had been completely routed off the ground, and had not an opportunity of carrying away their dead and wounded men. I recollect to have lost a new Regimental Coat by their means. There was no place about the town to put the wounded in, and they were carried down the bank, to Wolfe's Cove,[166] and from thence put into boats, and taken across to the lower ferry-place at Pointe Levis for the purpose of placing them under the care of our Surgeons, at the Church,[167] which was converted into a temporary Hospital.

Pensioners, 78th Foot, c.1717–1775.

164. Pipers were important non-combatants, playing stirring tunes while the regiment manoeuvred into battle. After the battle they would compose laments to honour the fallen, or in happier circumstances to commemorate the brave exploits of the clan. But as related by Thompson, they were carefully husbanded during action (i.e., kept away from the firing line). However, soldiers expected their pipers to return to the firing line if the regiment charged.
165. Brigadier General James Murray was the general officer commanding the brigade which included the Frasers (not Townshend as Thompson's original manuscript states). According to the chaplain of the 78th, Parson Robert Macpherson, Murray personally led the Highlanders forward. In a letter home, Macpherson wrote: "Your Countrymen, lay'd [led] on by Brigadier Murray, were interspersed amongst the thick of them __ Cutting and Slashing every where about them __". Macpherson to older brother, Andrew Macpherson of Banchor, 16 September 1759, Quebec, JGP.
166. Wolfe's Cove. Formerly the Anse au Foulon, Wolfe's landing place, a mile and a half above Quebec. It became popularly known as Wolfe's Cove shortly after the battle on the Plains of Abraham.
167. Saint-Joseph-de-la-Pointe-Lévy. This would have been used as a hospital until the capitulation of the city. Another hospital was located on the Île d'Orléans. The surrender

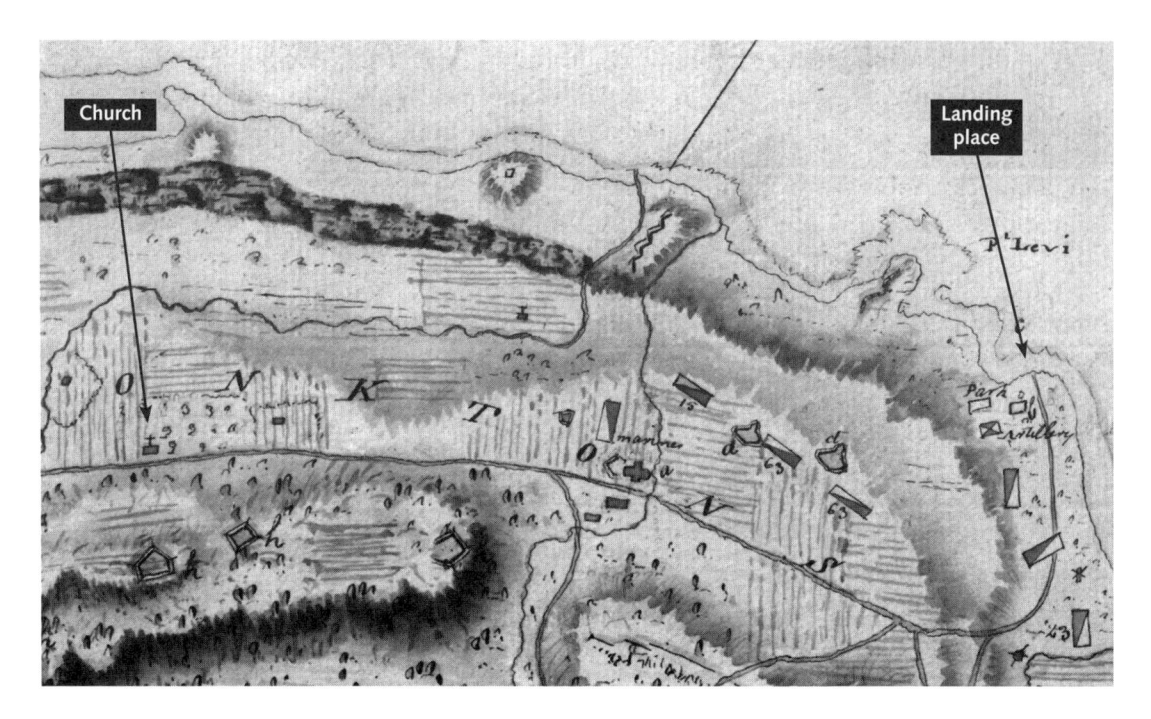

The long haul. A map detail showing General Robert Monckton's camp at Pointe Lévy. Thompson remembered carrying a wounded soldier on his shoulders from the landing place (right) to the British hospital located at the French church of St. Joseph, a distance of nearly a kilometre. (LOC Map Collections, G3454/Q4S26 1759 .P5)

Our men had nothing better to carry them on, than a kind of hand barrow with canvass laid across it. By this means it required two of our men to carry one of them to the top of the Hill at Point Levis.[168] The business going on very slowly, I at last got out of patience looking at them. So, I set to work, and took up a wounded man to my own share, and did not let him down at the top of the hill, but landed him safe at the temporary Hospital. By the time that we had done with them I was fatigued enough, and 'afaith I spoil'd my red coat into the bargain! The poor devils would cry out lustily when they were in an uneasy posi-

---

of Quebec four days after the battle saw the Hôpital Général handed over to the British with all French patients becoming prisoners of war and all British wounded being moved from Lévis and the Île d'Orléans into the comfort and care of that institution.

168. Pointe Lévy, today's Ville de Lévis, is situated on the south shore of the St. Lawrence River, opposite Quebec City. On 30 June 1759 General Wolfe established a large camp at Pointe Lévy and built a number of batteries at nearby Pointe-aux-Pères – the first completed battery opened fire on Quebec 12 July. Assuming Thompson took the existing road from the ferry landing place at Pointe Lévy to get to the temporary hospital, he would have carried the wounded soldier a distance of about 2,400 feet (732 metres). LAC, National Map Collection, No. 21345.

tion, but we could not understand a word of what they said. One of them had one of his cheeks lying flat down upon his shoulder, which he got by attempting to run away, altho' that he had a Highlander at his heels. When the French gave themselves up quietly, they had no harm done to them, but 'afaith if they tried to out-strip a heelandmun, they stood but a bad chance, for *whack* went the Broadsword!

Anecdote No. 7
Oh! he was a noble fellow! and he was so kind and attentive to our men, that they would have gone thro' fire and water to have serv'd him. Poor dear General Wolfe! he was kill'd by the French on Abram's [sic] Plains on the 13th September 1759, at the age of only 33 years, and it fell to my lot to have the direction of the Party that convey'd his Body on board the 64-gun Ship of War, (×) (whose name I now forget) that took it to England.

(×) The Stirling Castle and afterwards, the Royal William.[169]

A remarkable circumstance is, that she struck the ground near the Island of Coudres[170] while going under a brisk gale, and with such violence, that every man on board who was standing on his legs and feet, was thrown down. There was a terrible hullaballoo, under an impression that she would go to the bottom, and the boats were accordingly all lower'd down, to put the people on shore, but, as after repeated trial at the pumps, they found that the vessel was making no water, they at last decided upon going out to the Ocean and take their chances, and they accordingly continued the voyage which was effected, I think, in 27 days. She was laid up in Ordinary, and when afterwards it came to her turn to

---

169. Footnote in the original Manuscript copy, identified with an ×. A matching × indicated where it was to be inserted in the narrative. Believed to have been added by James Jr., this footnote is, in fact, incorrect. Wolfe's body was brought out to the *Lowestoft*, 28 guns, not the *Stirling Castle*, 64. The master's log for *Lowestoft* for 13 September 1759 reads "at 11 was brought on board ye corps of General Wolf...." Wolfe's remains were later transferred to the *Royal William*, 80, under the command of Captain Collins, for transportation to Portsmouth, arriving Saturday, 17 November 1759, when the *Gentleman's Magazine* reported: "This day the remains of General Wolfe were landed at Portsmouth from on board the *Royal William* man-of-war; during the solemnity minute guns were fired from the ships at Spithead, and all the honours that could be paid to the memory of a gallant officer were paid on this occasion."
170. The Island of Coudres, or Île aux Coudres (translation, Hazelnut Island), is situated in the St. Lawrence River, about ten leagues down-river from Quebec. Named by French explorer Jacques Cartier on his second visit to the New World in 1535 and first settled in 1728. Thompson is correct – the *Royal William* did run aground while leaving Quebec. On 13 November 1759 the *London Chronicle* reported that two ships, the *Royal William* and the *Captain*, "were both drove ashore ... but being strong ships, received little damage."

Death of Wolfe. Perhaps the most historically accurate depiction of the circumstances surrounding Wolfe's death on the battlefield. Instead of multitudes of grieving and mourning generals and subordinates, he was actually attended by no more than two members of the Louisbourg Grenadiers and an unknown surgeon's mate. The soldier arriving on the left is reporting that the French are retreating and the battle is won. The uniforms showing anachronistic boots and gaiters indicate that this print is not contemporary and was probably made sometime during the American Revolution. (Anne S. K. Brown Military Collection, Brown University Library)

be taken into Dock at Portsmouth, it was discover'd that there was a stone, as large as "that table," sticking in her bow, half in, and half out, so exactly fitting to the hole, that not a drop of water could come in, and I heard afterwards that the stone was kept at Portsmouth as a curiosity.[171]

---

171. The following paragraph was found in the original Manuscript copy of this anecdote. Added by James Jr., it reads: "I had frequently heard my Father relate the above particulars, and always with the greatest apparent attachment to this friend of the Highland Soldier [General Wolfe]. It invariably brought from him the tribute of an overwhelming heart, an affectionate tear, the quickness of feeling in which he made the recital on the *present* occasion (11 August 1828) in his 95th year, took such a strong hold upon me that I could not deny him the justice, or myself the filial duty of committing the circumstances to writing, in my Fathers' own manner of recital and thus endeavour to rescue from oblivion a trait of character as honorable to the patriotic Volunteer, as it is complimentary to the General, who, at that time held the reins of his future destinies, and whose memory is still so fondly cherished."

Chapter 6 | Winter Garrison and the Battle of Sillery, 1759–60

The British did not regard Quebec as much of a prize. It is "nothing but a shapeless mass of ruins" reported François Bernier, "confusion, disorder, pillage reign even among the inhabitants, each searching for his possessions and, not finding his own, seizes those of other people." Major Patrick Mackellar, Murray's chief engineer, examined the city with a critical eye after its fall and "found the Buildings in general in a most ruinous condition, and infinitely worse than we could have imagined; for besides those burnt, there was hardly a house in the Town that was not injured by either shot or shells nor were they habitable without repairs." The fortifications, in Lieutenant John Knox's opinion, were not much better, "our only defence and dependence six bastions, with their curtains of slight masonry forming a chain from Cape Diamond to Saint Rocque, no foot-bank to the curtains, no embrasures made, no covered-way, nor out-work of any kind and cannon that were on the flanks so indifferent and worm-eaten that they were almost useless."[172]

It was in this ruined, shapeless city that James Thompson and his detail of fascine-making Highlanders found a bombed-out house they could call their home. As one of Thompson's anecdotes relates, they even had one of Ben Franklin's latest inventions, a wood stove. One of General Murray's first moves was to increase the security of the roofless and vulnerable city by establishing a series of outlying fortified posts at Ancienne Lorette, Sainte-Foy, Pointe Lévy and Sillery "to watch the motions of the Enemy's Army, who for some time Lay hovering round bout the Garrison" and to serve as "a check upon their Skulking Parties of Indians and Canadians who during the Winter Season were a great disturbance to the Garrison."[173] Many skirmishes indeed were fought in and around these advanced posts during the winter of 1759–60, the British light infantry and rangers, ever-alert and equipped with snowshoes, usually gaining the upper hand. One of the leaders involved in this bitter fighting was James Thompson's old nemesis, Captain Donald "Donull Gorm" Macdonell.

While James Thompson and his fellow Highlanders tried to stay warm, mounted guards and went on wood-cutting details, the French army was not far off, a strong force supported by Canadian militia left at Jacques-Cartier for the winter. Their general, François-Gaston de Lévis, placed the rest of his regu-

---

172. Bernier to Vaudreuil, September 1759, quoted in Joseph Lister Rutledge, *Century of Conflict: The Struggle between the French and British in Colonial America* (New York, 1956), 504; *A Short Authentic Account of the Expedition against Quebec in the Year 1759 under Command of Major General James Wolfe: By a Volunteer upon That Expedition* (Quebec, 1872), 36; Knox, *Journals*, II, 444.
173. Fraser, *Journal*.

lar battalions in quarters up the St. Lawrence River valley as far as Montreal. During the winter months he worked closely with the governor, the Marquis de Vaudreuil, to develop a strategy for retaking Quebec. Their plan was to use the interior lines of the St. Lawrence River to defeat the invading British armies one at a time – first, retaking Quebec, then shifting the army to the south to counter any enemy thrusts from the Lake Champlain or Lake Ontario frontiers.

The entire strategy, however, depended on recapturing Quebec as the first step and that prize could only be won if strong reinforcements, siege guns, gunpowder and food supplies were dispatched to North America from France, before the Royal Navy could reinforce the British garrison when the river ice broke up. It was a big "if," but Lévis and Vaudreuil believed it was possible and set about preparing the boats, guns, rations and manpower that would be necessary to execute the plan. James Thompson was an eyewitness to the subsequent battle, the second siege of the war and the events that unfolded afterwards to shape the history of Quebec.

Anecdote No. 23
After the conquest of Quebec, the troops had to make shift for quarters wherever they could find a habitable place. I myself made choice of a little house in the lane leading to the Esplanade, where Ginger the Gardner now lives (1828) and which had belonged to Paquet the Schoolmaster, altho' it was scarcely habitable from the number of our Shells that had fallen through it. However, as I had a small party of the Company with me, I contriv'd to get a number of little jobs done towards making it passably comfortable for the men, and for my own part I got Hector Munro, who was a joiner by trade, to knock up a kind of "Cabinet" (as the Canadians call'd it) in one corner of the house for myself.

We had a stove, to-be-sure, but our Highlanders, who knew no better, would not suffer the door to be closed, as they thought that if they could not actually *see* the fire, it was impossible that they could *feel* it. In this way they pass'd the whole of the winter. Three or four would sit up close to the door of the stove, and when these were a little warm'd, three or four others would relieve them and so on. Some days they were almost frozen to death, or suffocated by the smoke, and to mend the matter they had nothing better than green wood!

I contriv'd somehow or other to procure six blankets, so that notwithstanding that I was almost frozen during the day, being the whole winter out on duty, superintending the party of our Highlanders making facines [*sic*] in the woods, still I pass'd the nights pretty comfortably. 'Twas funny enough to see, every morning, the whole surface of the blankets cover'd with ice from the heat of my breath and body. We wore our Kilts the whole of this time but there was no accident, as we were sheltered by the Woods. I bought a pair of Leather Breeches, but I could not walk in them, I laid them aside.

Anecdote No. 21

Captain Donald McDonald,[174] who was appointed to our Grenadier Company, after we lost Captain Baillie at the Landing at Louisbourg, was a surly cross dog as ever was, and I could not manage to please him in anything I could do. After we had taken Quebec he one day sent for me to his Quarters in the lane leading to the esplanade. I accordingly went, and found him sitting at table with another officer. He said that he sent [for] me to taste some liqueur that he had made, and to ask my opinion of it. I thought strange of this, and could not imagine to myself what the deuce could be a-brewing. However, he fills out a glass to me, and one to himself, and drank to my health, which I of course return'd in the same way.

He then says to me, Jim, you have all along thought that I was hard upon you. Aye, Sir, I replied, I did indeed think that you were harsh to me when there was not great necessity for it. I treated you, says the Captain, in that manner, not from any dislike I had to you, but because you were too familiar with the private men. Sir, I replied again, how came you to think that to be wrong in me, when you yourself know that it is impossible to act otherwise? Our men, you know, are not like those of other Regiments – they were all acquaintances before they became Soldiers, and many of the private men are from as good families as the officers themselves. You must recollect well Sir, that McChesney,[175] who ask'd his Captain for some money, and that the Captain told him that he had none, he seiz'd hold of him by the skriff of the neck, and tore the purse out of his pocket, 'afaith he did. I recollect that, says Captain McDonald, and also that McChesney's Captain took it all in joke.

However (continues my father), this was not the cause of Captain McDonald using me so harshly, but he found that I had a friend somewhere,[176] who had got wind of his harsh treatment of me, and he wished, by all means to wipe off old scores with me. There being no more said, I was preparing to be off about my business, when he asks me if I was not a Heelandmun? for, says he, a Heelandmun always wets *both* eyes. You have only wet one eye yet, and now, Jim, you must wet the 'tother one (this was the first time that I had ever heard that

---

174. Captain Donald "Donull Gorm" Macdonell.
175. Probably Corporal James Macky *aka* Mack-Chesney, killed during the dirk fight in Stratford, Connecticut, on 27 December 1759. See Anecdote 12 in Chapter Two.
176. The editors believe that Thompson's "friend" was none other than Lieutenant Colonel Simon Fraser as seen by the familiarity evident in Anecdote 13 where the colonel commandant is addressing Thompson by his Christian name. They were fellow Freemasons in the 78th Lodge.

expression made use of) and he pour'd me out a second glass which I also took, but I had no better opinion of his friendship after all.

Captain McDonald had serv'd in the Rebellion of '45, and he thought that something stood hanging over his head which he ought to wipe away. So he requests General Murray to allow him to have the Command of a Company of Volunteers to go out and annoy the French that were lying at Cap Rouge[177] and St. Augustin.[178]

This the General agreed to, and he accordingly chooses from all the Regiments but his own, and soon had more volunteers than he wanted. He also had four Subalterns allow'd him.[179] With these he sallies out from the Garrison, and finds the French intrench'd behind breastworks of Ice form'd of Snow by scattering water over it. He comes in upon them by surprise and plays the very devil amongst them, and brought in many prisoners.[180] In this way he annoy'd them all the winter of '59, but 'afaith he paid dearly for it at last, for the French swore vengeance against him.[181]

---

177. Cap Rouge, meaning Red Cape, is located in central Quebec on the north shore of the St. Lawrence River within the modern boundaries of Quebec City. During the siege of Quebec it was heavily fortified with entrenchments, batteries and fortified houses to prevent a landing to the west of the city. Jacques Cartier attempted to create the first permanent European settlement in North America at present-day Cap Rouge in 1541 (initially named Charlesbourg-Royal) but it barely survived its first winter and was abandoned in June 1542. Reoccupied with the French colonisation efforts of the latter part of the century, the area was used for agricultural activities until the 1960s when residential developments took over and transformed the area into a residential suburb of Quebec City.
178. Saint-Augustin is situated on the north shore of the St. Lawrence River about 12 miles west of Quebec City. The village (today's Saint-Augustin-de-Desmaures) was founded in 1691 by three families (Desroches, Racette, Couture) at the outlet of the river of the same name. When General James Murray produced his maps of the Province of Canada c.1762, the parish of Saint-Augustin consisted of "96 families," with 155 men "able to bear arms."
179. They were: Lieutenant Allan Grant, 60th Foot (Royal Americans); Lieutenant William Farquhar, 47th Foot (Lascelle's); Lieutenant John Crofton, 48th Foot (Webb's); and, Ensign Crank Maw, 43rd Foot (Kennedy's). Knox, *Journals*, II, 384.
180. This particular attack occurred on 19–20 March 1760 at the advanced post of Le Calvaire near Saint-Augustin, an estate consisting of several corn mills and outbuildings belonging to the nuns of Hôtel-Dieu in Quebec. Macdonell's force, which consisted of 200 light infantry drawn from the various regiments and a company of grenadiers, surprised a French force of some 150 French and Canadians "who were so benummed [sic] with the severity of the cold, that they could scarcely draw their triggers. In this attack of the entrenchment five were killed and thirteen wounded on the part of the enemy: on our side only six were wounded but unluckily we had near a hundred so disabled by the frost that they were obliged to be brought back to the garrison on sleighs." The destruction of Le Calvaire was "executed in view of the prisoners and the miserable inhabitants of the country...." Knox, *Journals*, II, 362.
181. The tone of rebuke in Sergeant Thompson's words is unmistakable and the promise of

Anecdote No. 23

When the spring came round, the French again made their appearance on the high ground[182] between the Town and Abraham's Plains, and General Murray must needs march us out to fight them — indeed did he![183] At this time scarcely a man in the garrison but was afflicted with Colds or Coughs. The day fix'd in orders, for our going out, was the 28th April 1760, at seven in the morning — and cold and raw enough it was!

Before the sortie, I took a biscuit and spread a bit of butter over it, and I set about "cranching" it, and said to Hector Munro for whom I had a great attachment, "you had better do as I am doing, for you cannot know when you may be able to get your next meal." Hector answer'd, "I will not touch anything. I have already taken my last meal, for something tells me that I shall never require another in this world." Toot man, says I, you are talking nonsense, take a biscuit I tell you. No — Hector would have none of it! Well, the hour came for parading, and we were soon after march'd out of the Garrison.

It was my lot to act as Covering-Sergeant[184] to Lieutenant FRASER[185] of our Grenadiers, who had already been wounded at the affair of the Falls,[186] thro' his belly, and out at his back, without his scarcely having felt it. (This Lieutenant Fraser was nephew[187] to my friend Captain Baillie, who was the first man kill'd at the landing at Louisbourg, and who, had he lived, would have been the means of securing to me my Commission, as had been the understanding between him and Colonel Fraser when I volunteer'd in Scotland, for Service in America.) Early in the action with the French, Lieutenant Fraser received a shot in the Temple, which fell'd him to the very spot on which he stood at the

---

retribution and justice at the end of the anecdote classic Gaelic storytelling at its best.
182. Buttes-à-Neveu.
183. For a full account of the 78th Foot at the Battle of Sillery see Ian McCulloch, "'From April battles and Murray generals, good Lord deliver me!': The Battle of Sillery, 28 April 1760," in *More Fighting for Canada: Five Battles, 1760–1944*, Donald E. Graves, ed. (Toronto, 2004). A detailed battle monograph on the second, bloodier battle fought on the Plains of Abraham six months after the one in which Wolfe was killed, it shows how Fraser's Highlanders played a key part. Colonel Simon Fraser commanded the left forward brigade. Detailed maps and orders of battle for the battle and the subsequent siege of Quebec are also available. See also McCulloch, *SOTM*, I, 217–48.
184. Acting as a "covering sergeant" meant that Thompson was busy "closing up" the files in his grenadier company as his Highlanders fell. It does not refer to an official appointment or title — all sergeants performed this duty in battle.
185. Lieutenant Alexander Fraser.
186. The battle of Montmorency, 31 July 1759. For a full account of this battle see McCulloch, *SOTM*, I, 169–96.
187. Several expert genealogists in Canada and Scotland have been unable find any family connection between Fraser and Baillie. The latter officer's only surviving sister married a Sutherland.

Desperate battle. The shouting grenadier (centre) with one foot on his officer is Sergeant James Thompson during a critical moment in the battle of Sillery fought on 28 April 1760 just west of the Plains of Abraham. The supporting British artillery has just run out of ammunition and the British infantry is wavering in the face of overwhelming odds and superior French firepower. The British line eventually broke and retreated back to the city, including the Highlanders, but Thompson recalls that the piper started to play and his regiment turned, reformed again and covered other regiments in getting back through the gates. Detail of modern watercolour by Steve Noon. (Illustration from McCulloch, *Highlander in the French-Indian War, 1755–1763,* Osprey Publishing)

instant, and, as not an inch of ground was to be lost, I had to move up into line, which I could not have done without my resting one foot upon his body![188]

The affair went altogether against us, and we had to retreat back into the town. When I got back to my quarters, I there found poor Hector Munro, who, not being able to walk, had been carried in, owing to a wound he had received in the lower part of the belly, thro' which his bowels were coming out! He had his senses about him, and reminded me of our conversation just before the battle. He was

---

188. Thompson's memory has perhaps failed him as it was Captain Alexander Fraser, 6th Culduthel (see Part Three for Biographical Note) that received a serious head wound at the battle of Sillery, and not Lieutenant Alex Fraser who was lightly wounded but not in the head. Thompson may be excused for this memory lapse (but perhaps not for standing on his captain when he was still alive, and later recovered) as there were twenty-six officers with the surname Fraser in the 78th during his service with the regiment. *Culduthel* was standing in as the grenadier company commander while Captain Donald "Donull Gorm" Macdonell was commanding an *ad hoc* flank company cooperating with the rangers. *Culduthel* was forced to resign his commission because of his injuries.

taken to the Hotel Dieu,[189] where he died the next morning, in great agony. Poor JOHN FRASER[190] too, who afterwards was many years a respectable Schoolmaster in Quebec, and who taught you all (alluding to our own family) your first principles, he caught a musket ball in his skull, and was obliged to quit the ranks.

Having confidence in Doctor Morrison,[191] he applied to him to have his head dress'd, and because he had lately been exchanged out of our Highlanders, to the Surgery of another Corps, he would have nothing to do with him! And poor John Frazer [sic] was obliged to wait until the bustle was over, during which time he suffer'd great pain from the gash that the ball had made. (#)

> (#) but he was at last cared by Doctor BADELARD[192] of the French Army, whom John Fraser had made prisoner on the Plains of Abraham. John Fraser afterwards acquired that property facing the Great Door of the Ursuline Church[193] off the line of Garden Street,[194] and bounded on one side by the rear of Doctor Badelard's which fronts on Saint Louis Street.[195] For many years Dr. Badelard and John

---

189. Founded in 1639 by the Augustines de la miséricorde de Jésus (Augustinian Hospital Sisters of the Mercy of Jesus) as the Hôtel-Dieu du Précieux Sang, it was the first hospital in North America north of Mexico. The original hospital was built in the northeast corner of the Old City of Quebec. Today, the Hôtel-Dieu de Québec hospital is a teaching hospital affiliated with the University of Laval's medical school, but not at its original location (the original location was recognized as a National Historic site).
190. Sergeant John Fraser.
191. The surgeon of the 78th Foot before, during and after the battle of Sillery was Dr. John MacLean (appointed 12 January 1757), who in October 1761 returned to Scotland with General Amherst's permission and never returned to the regiment before its disbandment in December 1763. Thompson was clearly referring to the 78th Foot's surgeon's mate, Donald Morrison, who may have become a doctor in later life.
192. Doctor Philippe-Louis-François Badelard.
193. Thompson means the Ursuline Chapel (Chapelle des Ursulines), part of the Ursuline Convent (Couvent des Ursulines). The Ursulines are a Roman Catholic religious order founded in Italy by Saint Angela de Merici in 1535, primarily for the education of girls and the care of the sick and needy. The convent was founded in 1639 and is the oldest institution of learning for women in North America. The exterior of the chapel was rebuilt in 1902, but its interior contains the original chapel, which took sculptor Pierre-Noël Lavasseur from 1726 to 1736 to complete. After the battle on the Plains of Abraham, Montcalm's remains were buried in the chapel (they were transferred to rest with those of his soldiers at the Hôpital Général de Québec cemetery in 2001).
194. Garden Street (rue des Jardins) interconnects rue Saint-Louis to the south, and rue Sainte-Anne to the north.
195. St. Louis Street was originally a military road running from the fort to the outworks, and then into the forest. It was called the Grande Allée. In Thompson's time it ran northwest from Place d'Armes to the bastion gate and had been renamed St. Louis Street. However, it was still mainly known for its many military offices and buildings. The garrison's engineering office (where Thompson worked in his later years) was located adjacent to the St. Louis Gate, with a yard and workshops in the rear. On 4 January 1776 the remains of Brigadier General Richard Montgomery were interred close to the old powder magazine adjacent to the engineers' workshops. Each morning Thompson would have

Fraser were great friends, and they used to converse together across the fence that divided their properties.[196]

When I first saw the French Soldiers, I thought them a dirty ragged set – their clothing was originally white. Many of them, particularly in the "Régiment de la Reine,"[197] had a bit of blue ribbon to the button hole of their Coat, with a little white shell fixed to it, which they call'd "Pâpâ," and this, it seems, was a mark of honor for having distinguish'd themselves on some former occasion.[198] I, at first, took them for Free Masons!

Anecdote No. 21

Accordingly when General Murray march'd us out on the 28th April 1760 to the highground that crosses the Plains of Abraham, there appear'd a small party of the French at the extremity of the Plains, and General Murray thought if they were immediately attack'd and routed, it would have the effect of intimidating the main body that was known to be at no great distance. He therefore order'd the whole line to advance, about three thousand men,[199] and Captain McDon-

---

left his home on St. Ursula Street, turned right on St. Louis and walked towards the St. Louis Gate to the engineering office. Today, rue Saint-Louis is an eastward extension of the Grande Allée.

196. Footnote in the original Manuscript copy, identified with a letter #. A matching # indicated where it was to be inserted in the narrative. It was likely added by James Jr.

197. One of the eight French regular battalions serving at Quebec in 1760, the 2eme Bataillon, Le Régiment de la Reine, formed part of the six original battalions of French regular infantry that set out for Canada in 1755. During the voyage from France, four companies of the La Reine and four of the 2eme Bataillon, Le Régiment de Languedoc, were captured when their transport, the *Lys,* was intercepted by the Royal Navy off Newfoundland. Shortly after their arrival at Quebec, the remaining men of the La Reine battalion were on their way to Lake Champlain to block the British advance. Two companies of the La Reine and two of the Languedoc were engaged in Dieskau's battle of Lake George. These two regiments shared the distinction of being the first French regulars to be engaged in battle in North America. With the fall of Quebec, the La Reine withdrew to the Montreal area, where the French forces regrouped. The battalion accompanied Lévis on his march back to Quebec in the spring of 1760 and formed part of the French reserve at the battle of Sillery. So, Thompson's first opportunity to see soldiers of this regiment, and to observe their shell and ribbon distinction, would have been on or after 28 April 1760.

198. The shell ornament the soldiers of the 2eme Bataillon, Le Régiment de la Reine, referred to by Sergeant Thompson as "Pâpâ" was likely a personal "battalion" badge of honour rather than some official regimental battle honour, perhaps recognition of being the first French regulars to see action in North America at the battle of Lake George in 1755. French historians and uniform experts we consulted are at a loss as to the significance behind the shell and ribbon.

199. Actual numbers that marched out were 3,362 British troops with twenty-two pieces of artillery. At least 200 of the Highlanders marching behind young Lieutenant Malcolm Fraser, 78th Foot, "had come out of the Hospital on their own accord." Once a proud regiment of some 1,500 men, disease, death and battle over the last two years had now winnowed its ranks down to 400 shivering, sickly men. When the two columns were

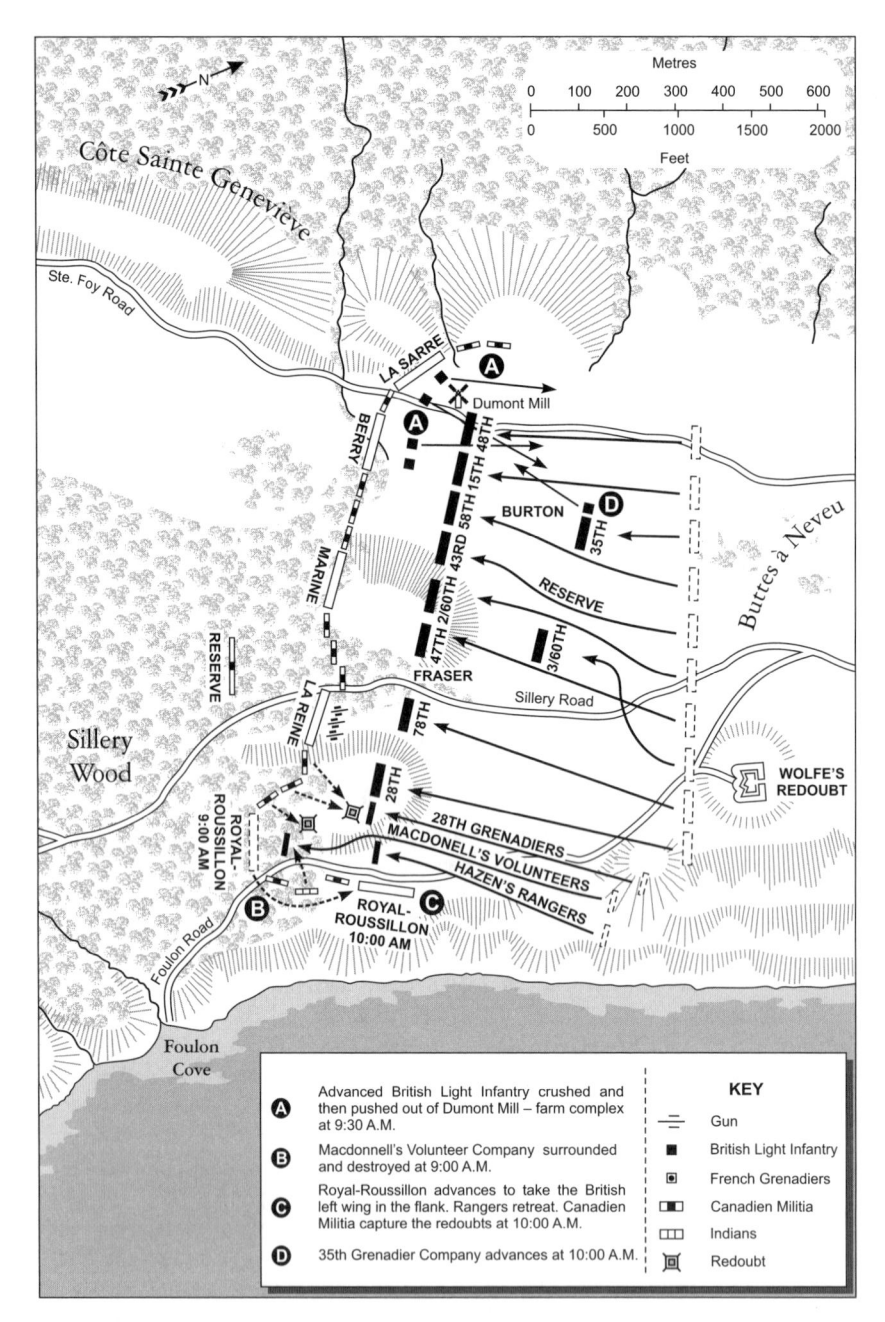

Sillery: the culminating point. This map depicts the height of action during the battle of Sillery, 28 April 1760. Thompson's regiment, the 78th (left forward), bore the brunt of fire from the only three French artillery pieces deployed on the battlefield as well as the accurate fire of two detachments of the *compagnies franches de la marine* firing from cover of the woodline to the regiment's front. Eventually Murray's small sickly army was outflanked and outnumbered and broke around 11:30 a.m. The 58th and 15th Foot retired in good order covering the rest of the army, assisted by the 78th once rallied by their piper. (Map by Chris Johnson from Graves, ed., *More Fighting for Canada: Five Battles, 1760–1944*)

ald [Captain Donald "Donull Gorm" Macdonell], who still commanded his Volunteers, rush'd forward to the attack of a small Redoubt, which he entered, and from which he drove away the French, many of whom were cut to pieces, but there came upon him a stronger body of French that overpower'd and completely butcher'd his whole party, and he himself was found cut and hack'd to pieces in the most shocking manner! There was an end of *him!*[200]

When our main body had mov'd up to this redoubt by-the-law we discover'd the French to be regularly drawn up in Columns in the lower ground, amounting to seven thousand men! We immediately gave them battle, and fought as long as our ammunition lasted, which was thirty rounds a man, and the same for our Field pieces, but 'afaith the French were too many for us, and we were oblig'd to retreat inside of these very walls that we had conquer'd only on the previous 13th September.

Anecdote No. 24
The next spring, in the month of April, when the Garrison of Quebec was so madly march'd out to meet the French, who had come down again to attack us, and while we were on the retreat back to the Town, the Highlanders, who were a raw undisciplin'd set, were got into great disorder, and had become more like a mob than regular soldiers. On the way, I fell in with a Captain Moses Hazen,[201] a Jew, who commanded a Company of Rangers,[202] and who was so badly wounded, that his Servant who had to carry him away, was obliged to rest him on the ground at every twenty or thirty yards, owing to the great pain he endur'd. This intrepid fellow observing that there was a solid column of the French coming on over that high ground where Commissary General CRAIGIE[203] built his house, and headed by an Officer who was some distance in advance of the column, he ask'd his Servant if his fuzee was still loaded? (The Servant opens the pan, and finds that it was still prim'd.) "Do you see," says Captain Hazen, "that rascal there, waving his Sword to encourage those fellows to come forward"? "Yes," says

---

"about three quarters of a mile out of the Town," recalled Fraser, "the General ordered the whole to draw up in Line of Battle two deep, and to take up as much room as possible." Fraser, *Journal*, 164.

200. For a different version of Captain Donald "Donull Gorm" Macdonell's gory end and the personal hatred felt by all ranks toward him, see Essay One in McCulloch, *SOTM*, II, 155–6, which narrates the South Uist tradition that the Devil came for Macdonell.
201. Captain Moses Hazen was a Christian and New Englander.
202. Rogers' Rangers were a colonial militia which fought for Great Britain during the Seven Years' War in North America (the so-called French and Indian War). Commanded by Moses Hazen, they operated primarily in the Lake George and Lake Champlain regions of New York. Although never fully respected by British regulars, Rogers' Rangers were one of the few non-Indian forces able to operate successfully in the region.
203. John Craigie, deputy commissary general in Quebec in 1781.

the Servant, "I do Sir." "Then," says the Captain again, "just place your back against mine for one moment, 'till I see if I can bring him down."

He accordingly stretch'd himself on the ground and, resting the muzzle of his fuzee on his toes, he let drive at the French Officer. I was standing close behind him, and I thought it perfect madness in him to attempt it. However, away went the charge after him, and 'afaith down he was flat in an instant! Both the Captain and myself were watching for some minutes, under an idea that altho' he *had* laid down, he might perhaps take it into his head to get up again. But no, the devil a-get-up did he get, and the moment that he fell, the whole column that he was leading on, turn'd about and decamp'd off, leaving him to follow as well as he might! I couldn't help telling the Captain that he had made a capital shot, and I related to him the affair of the foolish fellow of our Grenadiers who shot the Savage at the landing at Louisbourg, altho' the distance was great, and the rolling of the boat so much against his taking a steady aim. "Oh," says Captain Hazen, "you know that a *chance shot* will kill the devil himself."

But, to return to the Highlanders, as soon as the Piper had discovered that his men had scatter'd and were in disorder, he as soon recollected himself of the disgrace that still hung upon him, and he luckily bethought himself to give them a blast of his pipes. By-the-law-Harry! this had the effect of stopping them short, and they soon allow'd themselves to be form'd into some sort of order. For this opportune blast of his Chaintors, the Piper gain'd back the forgiveness of the Regiment, and was allow'd to take his meals with his old messmates, as if nothing at all had happen'd.

Anecdote No. 21

Upon this, the French came forward and intrench'd themselves on the line of the present Towers,[204] and kept their ground until the 6th May,[205] when we receiv'd

---

204. "Towers" refers to the four Martello towers built by the British between 1808 and 1812 to screen the western approaches to Quebec. Numbered rather than named, the towers were arranged to provide mutual support, being situated along an axis that runs north-south across the Plains of Abraham. Small, round defensive forts standing up to 40 feet (12 metres) high, their conical shape and thick walls of solid masonry made them resistant to cannon fire, while their height made them an idea platform for a single heavy artillery piece, mounted on the upper storey and able to traverse a 360-degree arc. Quebec's towers were never tested in battle and became obsolete in the 1860s with the development of rifled artillery. Tower No. 1 stands on the Plains of Abraham, overlooking the St. Lawrence River. It has been restored as a museum and can be visited during the summer months. Tower No. 2 stands nearby and is available for group activities through the National Battlefields Commission. Tower No. 3 was demolished in the 1900s after being used as a residence. Tower No. 4 is located in a residential area on the north side of the Upper Town overlooking Lower Town and is closed to the public.
205. Thompson is a little off on his dates. In fact, the French withdrew from their siege lines on 15 May 1760 when General de Lévis realized that he would not receive

reinforcements by the Saint Lawrence. They stood only one discharge from our line of Guns, one hundred and one in number, and away they scamper'd never more to return. In this business General Murray was very hasty, and if he did get out of the scrape, it was more by good luck than good guiding.

Anecdote No. 24
On the Sixth of May 1760, which was after we had been drove back into the town by the French, and while they yet lay in the trenches across that high ground where the Towers now stand, there came a Frigate[206] in sight, and she was, for some considerable time, tacking across and across between Pointe Levis and the opposite shore. We were at some loss to know the meaning of all this, when the Commanding Officer of Artillery bethought himself to go and acquaint General Murray (who had taken up his quarters in Saint Louis Street, now the Officer's Barracks) of the circumstance. He found the General sitting before the chimney, his chair somewhat leaning backwards, and one foot resting upon the cheeck [cheek] of the Chimney, thinking of matters and things that had just taken place; not the most pleasant.

On the Officer acquainting him that there was a Ship-of-War in sight, the General was so electrified that he sprang himself over the back of his chair, and stumbled on the floor! He instantly got up, and in the greatest fury order'd the Officer to go to the Citadel, and to have the Colors hoisted immediately! Away he went, but devil a bit could they get the halliards to go free, until at last, they got hold of a Sailor, who soon scrambled up the flagstaff, and put all to rights in a jiffy.

All this time, the Ship-of-War did not shew her own colors, not knowing whether the Town was in the hands of the French or the English. But as soon as she perceiv'd our flag, she hoisted English Colors, and shaped her course towards the town, and was safe at anchor opposite to the King's wharf. Our men had been all the winter in bad spirits from coughs and colds and, their having been obliged to retreat from the French didn't help much to mend the matter, however, when they heard that an English Man of War was come, it was astonishing how soon they became stout-hearted, 'afaith they were like lions, and just as bold!

The Frigate proved to be the "Lowestoffe," [sic] which had been detach'd from the main fleet below, with orders to make the best of her time thro' the ice, and take up the earliest intelligence of the approach of the Fleet. Her sides were very much torn by the floating ice. Our having hoisted colors for the first

---
reinforcements from Europe.
206. Thompson's unidentified frigate is *Lowestoft*, 28 guns, commanded by Captain Joseph Deane, which arrived on the eleventh day of the siege, at 9 a.m. on 9 May 1760.

time since the conquest and a Ship of War having made her appearance, led the French to imagine that there was something strange going on. Indeed they expected a fleet as well as ourselves and this arrival brought them out of their intrenchments as thick as midges;[207] they appear'd to us like so many pigeons upon a roost. While they were gaping at us in this exposed position, they received a salute from the whole line of our Guns, extending from the Cape Diamond down to the Barracks Bastions, in number one hundred and one, and yet they went off almost like one volley – it was funny (fearful) enough to see how they tumbled down off the top of their intrenchments, like so many sacks of wool!

Their seeing soldiers passing a-shore from our Frigate they thought that we had received a powerful reinforcement, and they scamper'd away, taking only their kill'd and wounded men along with them. Our men soon were sent out, and they regal'd themselves upon their soup and pork which they had left cooking on the fire.[208] That single discharge disabled so many of our guns, that we had to get others from the lower town, and our men were so weakly that they could not drag them up, but which was at last done with the help of the Sailors just arriv'd in the Fleet.[209]

In about three days after the arrival of the "Lowestoffe," the remainder of the fleet came up to Quebec,[210] and finding that the French had some ships lying above Wolfe's cove, they went up to look after them. As soon as the French

---

207. Midges are gnat-like two-winged flies in the order *Diptera*, which encompasses a wide range of individual species. Usually found around large bodies of water, they often form thick swarms which are not very enjoyable to look at or walk through.
208. Thompson's memory has combined the withdrawal of General Lévis' besieging forces (15 May 1760) with the arrival of the *Lowestoft* (9 May 1760). In fact, the Franco-Canadien army actually withdrew on the arrival of the remainder of the British fleet six days later.
209. Thompson has characterized the discharge of artillery as a single volley when according to Lieutenant John Knox it was a frenzied hour of firing and jubilation to celebrate the arrival of the British ship. "We had the inconceivable satisfaction to behold the *Leostoffe* frigate sail up into the bason and come to anchor ... the gladness of the troops is not to be expressed: both officers and soldiers mounted the parapets in the face of the enemy and huzzaed, with their hats in the air, for almost an hour the bay and circumjacent country for several miles resounded with our shouts and the thunder of our artillery; for the gunners were so elated that they did nothing but fire and load for a considerable time." No wonder some of the garrison guns were, according to Thompson, disabled. British artillery and batteries incidentally had been engaging the besieging army for several days prior to this incident, disrupting their siegeworks and harassing their camp behind the Buttes-à-Neveu. Knox, *Journals*, II, 415.
210. The remainder of the fleet, comprising *Vanguard*, *Diana* and *Lawrence* under the command of Commodore Robert Swanton, arrived four days later on the evening of 14 May 1760 and attacked early the following morning. The French "Commodore" referred to here is the same Jean Vauquelin who captained the *Aréthuse* at Louisbourg during the 1758 siege of Louisbourg.

saw them coming on they slip'd their cables and endeavor'd to get out of the way with the help of the flood-tide, but the Commodore's ship got upon a ledge of rocks and there stuck fast, and the crew took to the boats and got ashore, leaving the ship to take care of itself. The French Navy have always been devilishly afraid of our Ships of War![211]

There was found, on board this ship, one Monsieur Cuznet,[212] and an Englishman call'd Davis,[213] both of whom had their hands tied behind their backs, and a rope about their neck, and they inform'd that they were both to be hang'd at the yardarm as soon as the Ship's Company had finish'd their breakfast! Monsieur Cuznet was the person who, at the Island of Orleans, gave General Wolfe the information where would be the best place to get up the bank above the Town, and Davis, who had been taken prisoner by the French some years before, had given some other kind of information, and they both were about to be punish'd as Spies. However, they not only got off with their lives, but were afterwards well rewarded by our Government. The former was appointed French translator to the Government Offices and something more, which enabled him to live respectably; and Davis who had been a grenadier soldier, got a pension of twenty-five pounds a year, and they both liv'd a long time in the enjoyment of it.

Anecdote No. 28[214]
After the battle of the 13th September 1759 on the Plains of Abraham, we pick'd up a good many wounded men, and brought them into the Garrison, and many of them were put into the Hôtel-Dieu Convent to receive medical treatment. One of these was a Sergeant John Wilson of Fraser's Highlanders, a fine, likely-looking fellow, and one of the nuns, (the mère St. Gabriel)[215] was allotted to

---

211. Contrary to Thompson's memory of the event, the French were not "devilishly afraid" in this particular naval battle. In fact, Jean Vauquelin's spirited rear guard actions on the river at Quebec 15 May 1760 elicited the British commodore's highest admiration. The *Atalante,* commanded by Vauquelin, fought back fiercely, shielding a large fleet of bateaux as far as Cap Rouge, where they could be safe from an immediate attack. Then he began to fight a running rearguard battle with the frigates *Diana* and *Lowestoft* for almost three hours, buying much-needed time for the French army to get their bateaux at Saint-Augustin safely up-river to Jacques-Cartier.
212. Monsieur "Cuznet." François Joseph Cugnet. See Part Three for Biographical Note.
213. Davis. First name unknown.
214. James Jr. added the following footnote to this anecdote: "The above is an anecdote which my father would relate in all its minuteness of detail. It was a great favourite at Lord Dalhousie's table, when His Lordship had a select party, where I witness'd the pleasure it afforded."
215. The editors have confirmed with the Hôtel-Dieu archives that there was indeed a nun known by the religious name of Saint-Gabriel during the time frame mentioned in Thompson's anecdote.

attend upon him and some others. He lingered a long time, but gradually grew better, and in the course of the winter he was enabled to go about the alleys and passages on crutches, and at length he was able to throw them aside, and do without. This nun was exceedingly attentive, and it was chiefly to her attentions to him, that he got better of his wounds.

Towards the spring, accounts were received that the French were collecting in large bodies in front of the town, and it was generally expected that if they made an attack before the arrival of any reinforcements from England, they would stand a great chance of getting it back from us, as the Garrison was very sickly. However, as good luck would have it, it happened that in this they were, a little, disappointed, for altho' they obliged us on the 28th April to retire into our holes for a time, they were glad to decamp on the 6th of May following.

By order of General Murray (and a mad piece of business it was) we march'd out of the Town of Quebec, on the 28th April 1760, at seven in the morning. On such an occasion, Sergeant Wilson, altho' not quite reinstated in his health, thought himself bound to go out with his Company, in order to avoid being considered as a skulker, a stain which he would not, on any account, allow to rest upon his character, and accordingly he mentioned his wish of returning to duty. He was examin'd and he passed muster.

The instant he mention'd the matter to his nurse and fav'rite nun (a fine, comely-looking, young woman as I'd wish to see) she became very much distress'd, and was taken with violent fits, which was observ'd by the other nuns of the Convent; but no particular notice was taken of the circumstances, because, as she had had the particular care of him her uneasiness of mind was considered as the natural consequence of his having recover'd through her means – however, at last, away he goes.

And, although he faithfully promis'd to come back in the evening, the mère St. Gabriel immediately became inconsolable! This I myself had occasion to witness, from my having frequent business with the wounded men. As the luck-o'-war would have it, we were drove back by the French but still, we had no reason to be asham'd of ourselves, for we were opposed by very considerable numbers. Of course we had a good many men kill'd or wounded, and poor Wilson was amongst the former! The news soon found its way to the Convent, and there was the devil to pay!

Saint Gabriel was again taken with fits and convulsions, and it became necessary to attend to her in particular. She was undress'd and put to bed, when, what in the name of wonder did not the nuns discover? Why, that the Highland Sergeant, whose death had just been reported, was the only cause of her illness. Not satisfied with seeing her to all appearances very sick, they proceeded to look closer into the possible cause, when lo-and-behold, they discover'd that she had

Home of Sister Saint-Gabriel, 1886. Founded in 1639 by the Augustinian Hospital Sisters of the Mercy of Jesus, the Hôtel-Dieu hospital was filled to overflowing after the battles of the Plains of Abraham, 1759, and Sillery, 1760, and its specially trained sisters saved many wounded men's lives on both sides. This hospital was the first established in North America north of Mexico. Detail of painting by Henry Richard S. Bunnett (1845–1910). (McCord Museum, Montreal)

her weame up![216] and they were very ready to imagine that it was by the Highland Sergeant!

The mother-Abbess was now sent for who began by accusing poor Saint Gabriel of vile conduct, and threaten'd to have her put to the torture if she did not immediately acknowledge her apparent guilts, but devil-a-word did the Abbess get out of her, but merely sobs & sighs. At length the Abbess calls a Council of Nuns, and they had the poor unfortunate Gabriel brought before them, but all they could get from her was *"Ah! Nous sommes toutes mortelles!"* ["Oh! We are all mortal!"]

After the Council was closed, there was a paper drawn up condemning poor Gabriel to be smother'd, and to which was obtained the signature of the Bishop. It was next sent by a priest in due form, for the confirmation of General Murray, it having been the rule for the "Intendants" to ratify these judgements during the French time – however, in General Murray they held the wrong sow by the ear, for instead of putting his name to it, he sent the nuns a written message, acquainting them that they had no right to sit in judgement upon the life of any of the subjects of His Majesty the King of England, and declared that if the nun in question was accused of any crime against the laws, she must be brought to trial by a lawfully constituted court, and not by one of their own forming.

---

216. *Weame* means womb or belly, and in this case is Thompson's way of stating the nun was great with child.

And he declared further, that if they did not desist from their present purpose, he would order two field-pieces of artillery to be planted opposite the door of their Convent, and batter down the walls about their ears, and, moreover, would report home to England the shameful transgression that they had committed against the existing laws.

Whether this had the effect of immediately liberating mère St. Gabriel, was not publicly known; but this *I* know to the contrary, and had it repeatedly confirmed to me by the nuns themselves, that for such a high offense (surely not against the laws of *nature*, but) against the Institutions of their own Convent, which did not admit of their even *conversing* with a man, except upon charitable subjects, they were bound, on conscience, to have her smother'd between feather beds, or imprison'd between four walls, and kept upon bread and water!

However, I saw her frequently, and for many years afterwards. I have often thought that poor Saint Gabriel was not much worse than most of the Sisterhood, and perhaps not half so bad, for, having somehow or another, got acquainted at the Nunnery myself, while we had sick men there, and being, by degrees, freely admitted at all hours of the day, I had occasion to witness enough of their capers.

One day, I stroll'd into the eating-room (*Réfectaire*) and from that into the kitchen, where I found the nun who was presiding cook for the week quite alone. She told me, in a joking kind of way, that they made it a rule not to admit *idlers* into the convent, and she handed me a mortar and pestle, and set me to work pounding away at some kind of spice. Whilst I was in the midst of the job, who the deuce should chance to pop in, but the Mother Abbess (Miss Wheelwright) and she immediately took the nun to task (I afterwards was given to understand, that altho' her ladyship appeared to be highly incensed with the cook-nun, that a better reason could be giv'n for it) and I must suppose that the said nun was duly punish'd accordingly, but I am sure of one thing, that she did no more harm with me than the Mother Abbess herself had done before that. I myself have seen her ladyship as full of frolic as the best of them.

One little matter I could mention that several times occurred *after* dinner at which ceremony I have seen them engaged, when each nun seem'd to me to acquit herself with tolerable relish of the duty of emptying down her throat, the contents of a quarter-jug, which, whatever it might have been, had at all events the effect of making them quite frisky! In this humour, I have seen them play at their favourite game of *leap-frog*, by jumping or rather tumbling over each other, through the long passages. At this amusement they thought nothing of showing their legs, for they used to pin their petticoats up between them, as high as was convenient for the purposes of the game, and I assure you that some of them had very good understandings of their own. And it has often occurred in my presence that they have torn off their veils and other parts of their dress, but this, you see, was all in the way of fun.

What brought me more particularly acquainted with them was my attendance at a Court Martial that sat upon a Captain of Artillery (I forget his name) for disobedience, and the Court sat about a month in their Eating-room, there being no other suitable apartment to be had at that time. I continued, for many years, to be acquainted at this nunnery, and had it in my power to be useful to them in giving directions about the repairs of their building. On my tour to the several Garrison works, I would now and then step in, and I was sure to get a glass of liqueur and a sweet cake of some kind or other.

Poor Saint Gabriel at first look'd somewhat shy at my presence, but she gradually became more familiar, and we were very great friends. She afterwards was elected to some office or other, the name of which I now forget, but it seem'd to give her something to say to the money-matters of the house, and she used to consult with me a good deal, regarding the repairs required now and then.

In the year 1774, I was order'd by General Carleton to proceed to the Chambly River to inspect the Fort at that place, and to report on the repairs that were necessary to be performed, to render it secure against the Americans that were then expected to pay us a visit. While there, I was accosted by a young lad who told me that he had heard I was from Quebec, and he begg'd of me to stop at his grandmother's house, which he said was close to the waterside at the lower end of the River, as she was particularly anxious to send a letter by a careful hand, to one of the nuns of the Hôtel Dieu. I promised the lad that I would call.

Accordingly, after I had finished the business that I had gone upon, I set out on my return to Quebec, and stop'd at the house of the old lady in question. It happen'd to be as early as five in the morning, and not yet daylight. I knock'd lustily at the door, and it was the old lady herself who came to unbolt it, having nothing on but her chemise; I stood back, from delicacy, but she bade me to step in, and she told me that she would soon have her letter ready, and in the meantime desired that I should sit down and rest myself. The old lady retired into a closet, where she set about writing, and she was so long about it, that she made me quite fidgetty. However, out came the letter at last, and to mend the matter, she insisted upon my staying to take a dish of coffee with her. I endeavor'd all I could to excuse myself, but it would not do.

So, we had our coffee together, and with it a little chat about the people of Quebec, after which I rose to proceed on my journey, when the young man appear'd to be quite unhappy, and shew'd a great interest respecting me, so much so, that it made me feel quite uncomfortable. It was quite evident to me, that both the grandmother and her grandson had been speaking of me before I call'd, from the frequent allusions they made. In placing the letter into my charge, the old lady made me read the address, but would not allow me to take it into my hands. She insisted upon putting it *herself* into my coat pocket, and then sew'd the lining together to prevent the letter slipping out. Then recommended me to take particular good care of it, and to be sure to deliver it to the nun herself, *En particulier*, and concluded by wishing me a bon voyage.

Notwithstanding the time thus lost, I could not feel displeas'd with the old lady, for she was a good decent body, and she really appear'd to be under the greatest obligations to me. But this was not all; I felt a secret kind of pleasure in having been entrusted with a confidential message to my friend, the mère Saint Gabriel, and I was now convinc'd from the strong resemblance, that the child who claim'd John Wilson for his father, had not been strangled at its birth, as I had been led to believe, but had been convey'd by some means, to the charge of its grandmother, and had become the clever looking lad whom I had just left behind me.

I then started for Sorel-ferry, where I hired a canoe to take me across to Berthier. This was, to my mind, a tedious business, as there was but one Canadian to paddle, and I had to work as hard as himself to make headway of it. We however got across at last, and I took him to my friend Janet McKenzies' house, who kept *"la poste"* according to the Canadian fashion of that time, where I got the man something to eat, and Janet gave him a loaf of bread to take home to his family who, I dare say, were much in want of it. I paid him three dollars, and away he went back as happy as a prince, and singing quite gayly as he paddled himself over.

Janet would have me take something to eat, but I told her that I was not hungry, and could very well wait until we reached the next posthouse. She then ordered the horse to be put to the calash,[217] and a couple of roasted fowls in the box, when she desired me to step in, and she lost no time in jumping in beside me, and afaith she drove the horse herself, and so well did she do it that we got to the next posthouse much quicker than I expected. Here we halted and got out, and she was about taking the two fowls into the house, when, on my observing to her that she had drove the horse so well, that with it she had drove away my appetite for eating, she immediately put the fowls back into the box; desir'd me to jump in, got in herself, and away we started to the second posthouse, and all this time with the same horse! Oh! she was an active body!

Being again halted, she had the fowls put on table, with a few nic-nacks she had roll'd up in a napkin, and we dined together most lustily. Immediately after dinner Janet took her leave for Berthier, and I towards Quebec.

For several days after my return to Quebec, my bones were so sore from the

---

217. *Calash* is the English word for *calèche*, a two-wheeled, single-horse carriage still in use for transporting sightseers around the old streets of Quebec.

badness of the roads, and the confounded jolting of the post calashes, that I had difficulty to walk, and could scarcely get a wink of sleep. However, that was a matter of little consequence. I had now to perform my promise of delivering the letter to mère St. Gabriel, and as my duty frequently led me round the ramparts, I call'd in as usual, but for several days I fail'd in seeing her, which I thought curious, and it led me to have rather strange suspicions, yet I didn't venture to express any uneasiness about the matter, as it might tend to make things still worse.

At last however, I saw her going up a scaffolding that had been erected to perform some repairs to the gable ends of the Church! which was an odd place for a woman to be at. I immediately went up after her, when on turning her face towards me, she exclaim'd with a great degree of emotion *"Ah! Monsr: Tommesonne!"* ["Ah! Mr. Thompson!"] Seeing her so agitated I thought it was best to make my visit as short as possible. I therefore watch'd an opportunity and put the letter into her own hand without any body else knowing anything of the matter.

Although she knew me very well, yet she was struck with some certain recollections at sight of me, and perhaps also from the cautious manner of my accosting her, as if she suspected something mysterious in what I was about to communicate. But the poor body had had her nerves so much shaken, that the least thing would startle her. When she got a sight of the letter, she was very much agitated indeed, and I was afraid that she would faint away, and perhaps tumble down from the scaffolding! I was almost as uncomfortable as herself, and was cursing my stars that I had been so imprudent as to have chosen that dangerous place for the delivery of my message, knowing, as I did, that it was of a very delicate nature. She took the letter from me in a kind of snatching-way, and cram'd it hastily & clumsily into her pocket, and seem'd quite unable to say whether she felt thankful for the trouble I had been at, or whether it had displeas'd her.

I got away as fast as I decently could, and was very glad that no accident had happen'd. However, poor Saint Gabriel took the first opportunity when we were alone together, of returning me thousands of thanks, and I felt quite proud at it. She used always to receive me with a good deal of kindness, but I could observe that she was somewhat under restraint when any of the other nuns were in the way. I very well knew how to account for this, and I felt pity for her, and only that she was so extremely kind, and happy to see me, I would not have been the cause, on any account, of her feelings being hurt. Poor Saint Gabriel and myself were good friends, and indeed I was a kind of a pet throughout the whole *communautée*, for they all were fond of me nothing could be like it. Poor Gabriel died[218] without my having a knowledge of it at the time it happen'd, and as to the young lad at Chambly, I never heard what became of him.

---

218. Sister Saint-Gabriel died in June 1787, aged forty-six years.

Chapter 7 | The Reduction of Montreal, 1760

After the second siege of Quebec was raised, thoughts turned to the final conquest of Canada in June 1760 and General James Murray's much-suffering army prepared to leave the battered walls of Quebec for its offensive up-river. The ambitious Scottish general realized that none of his regiments were truly fit for service so he would be forced to improvise. The Quebec regiments were scarce healed from the ravages of the severe winter, their bloody April defeat on the battlefield, and a three-week-long siege that had merely prolonged the scourge of scurvy that culled their ranks daily. Murray thus issued orders at the end of June to each regiment, including the 78th Foot, to provide a company of grenadiers "completed to one Captain, three subalterns, three Sergeants, three Corporals, two Drummers and sixty privates."[219]

The Frasers were also ordered to provide a picquet company of able-bodied men numbering 147 private men commanded by "Nine Officers, Seven Serjeants and Seven Corporals,"[220] as were the other nine battalions. A detachment of 50 rangers would round out Murray's small strike force to 2,500 men, and the whole would be supported on the water by the *Porcupine* sloop of war. The remnants of Wolfe's once-proud army now numbered only 5,200 all ranks, one half of whom were listed in mid-June as either sick or wounded, for a total of some 2,300 incapacitated men in all. Of the junior regimental officers and NCOs still living, one third of the sergeants were still sick or wounded as well as a good quarter of the officers' corps. That meant whoever was left in charge at Quebec would have some 400 fit men and 2,300 invalids to defend the capital of New France.

Fraser's grenadiers, badly mauled at the battle of Sillery, underwent a complete overhaul, – new officers, new NCOs and new soldiers – but one old face remained, Sergeant James Thompson, the veteran. The Highland grenadiers were allocated to one of two grenadier battalions formed for the expedition, the 2nd Grenadier Battalion under the command of Major Thomas Addison of the 35th Foot (Otway's). It consisted of five companies and was assigned to the Left Brigade of the army under the command of the recently returned Colonel "Billy" Howe, 58th Foot. The 1st Grenadier Battalion with the other five companies was commanded by Major James Agnew, 28th Foot, and assigned to the Right Brigade of the army under Colonel Ralph Burton, 48th Foot.[221]

Howe and Burton's brigades were formed from the ten regimental detach-

---

219. Knox, *Journals*, II, 459–60.
220. *Ibid.*, 463.
221. *Ibid.*, 463. See Table of Forces.

The final prize, 1760. A southern view of the last French city in New France to fall during the Seven Years' War. Mount Royal can be seen looming at the rear of the lightly fortified town, which served as the colony's main commercial trading entrepot. Etching published in 1765. (LOC LC-USZ62-46311)

ments of "able-bodied" men, each organized into five small provisional battalions commanded by majors and consisting of two "draughts" of 170 all ranks apiece. The "draught" from the 78th Foot was allocated to the 5th Battalion under the command of Major John Spittal, 47th Foot, and, along with the 1st and 3rd Battalions, formed the Right Brigade; the remaining two battalions, the 2nd and 4th were assigned to the Left. The Fraser Highlanders told off for the Montreal expedition marched out from their Quebec billets on 5 July and encamped about a quarter of a mile from the city. Two days later many of their comrades "surprisingly recovered and fit for duty" arrived from the Île d'Orléans, some of the same die-hards that had hobbled out of the hospitals after the army on the morning of 28 April 1760.[222]

"I thought it absolutely necessary to leave an Officer of distinguish'd Address and Abilities with so important a command," James Murray wrote to William Pitt on 13 July 1760. His candidate for the post would be the commandant of the 78th Foot, Lieutenant Colonel Simon Fraser. "Col Frazer, [sic] Eager for the Glory that may be acquired in the field, stays with great reluctance to command there," he wrote, but if the truth be told it was the governor, still smarting from the bloody nose he had been dealt in April, who was the more eager of the two "for the Glory that may be acquired in the field."[223]

---

222. *Ibid.*, 464.
223. Murray to Pitt, 13 July 1760, Quebec, quoted in *Ibid.*, II, 466n.

The former Master of Lovat, wounded twice on the field at Sillery, was probably quite content to be excused the rigours of further campaigning and to serve as Quebec's acting governor. Fraser was more interested in seeing his long-suffering regiment recoup its strength and character after the stresses and strains of the previous year. His Highlanders had sustained the highest casualty rates of any regiment in the last two Quebec battles, and, with the final addition of their much-needed fourteenth company the year before, his under-strength battalion had no further prospects of replacements until the war's end.

Admitting that he "had no directions from General Amherst," Murray announced to the Secretary of War, William Pitt, that he was sailing up-river to Montreal on the morrow's tide anyway, having taken the liberty "to press Vessels for the conveyance of the troops." He did so, he claimed, at the head of 2,200 "chosen men" when in fact he was taking 2,500 men with him. He also claimed to have left 1,700 men "fit for duty" back in Quebec, which along "with the sick and Convalescent" would "make more than three thousand men in that Garrison."[224]

Murray went on to reassure Pitt that, if his special force of 2,200 "chosen men" might seem inadequate for the task at hand, he had left orders for two more reinforcement battalions on their way from the Louisbourg garrison, the 22nd and the 40th Foot, to join his force up-river as soon as possible. By Murray's optimistic calculations, this would bring his strike force up to 3,500 men and he confidently predicted that "the moment I arrive at Montreal I shall be probably master of the whole country."[225]

The men of Fraser's grenadiers went on board their transports at five o'clock in the morning of 13 July with the Right Brigade while the Left was finally aboard by five that afternoon. At 3:00 p.m. the following day, they weighed anchor on the flood tide, and the fleet carrying Murray's tiny army ran before the wind for the next four hours, coming to anchor for the first night between Saint-Croix on the south shore and Pointe-aux-Trembles on the north. There, the river was approximately four miles wide, "the land high on each side, with a tolerably clear country, interspersed with a few coppices."[226] In a routine that would be repeated for the next several weeks, the smaller boats clustered around the larger ships like chicks to a mother hen, the latter dropping their anchors mid-channel, where they were safe from cannon and musket shot. James Thompson would remember only pleasant details of the up-river cruise.

---

224. *Ibid.*
225. *Ibid.*
226. *Ibid.*, 467.

With the surrender of Montreal nine weeks later on 8 September 1760, almost one year to the day after the battle of the Plains of Abraham, James Thompson had fought his last campaign as a Highland soldier but would experience at least two more wars.

Unnumbered Anecdote[227]

General Murray, being in want of funds to carry on his Government during the winter, summon'd all the officers and enquir'd if they had any money, and if their soldiers had any money that they could lend to the Governor until the supplies arriv'd from England in the spring. We were told of the wants of the Governor, and the next day we were paraded every man, and told that we should receive our money back with interest, as soon as possible; and in order to prevent any mistake, every man receiv'd his receipt for his amount, and for fear he should lose it, the Adjutant went along the ranks, and enter'd in a book the name and sum opposite to every man, and, by-the-law-Harry! when they came to count it up, they found that our regiment alone, Fraser's Highlanders, had muster'd six thousand guineas![228]

---

227. This unnumbered anecdote, attributed to Sergeant James Thompson, cannot be found in the original Manuscript copy. However, it was published by Alfred Hawkins in his *Picture of Quebec: with Historical Recollections* (Quebec, 1834), 395–6, four years after the death of Sergeant James Thompson, and some years before the anecdotes (in letter-book form) were handed over to the LHSQ. It would appear that Hawkins had obtained a number of anecdotes from the Thompson family when they were still a collection of loose notes, and for some reason he never returned them to the Thompson family, or if he did, they somehow became separated from the rest of the collection. Thus they were not available to James Jr. in 1830 when he started to transcribe his loose notes into the private letter-books.

228. Thompson has exaggerated threefold. Brigadier James Murray recorded in his *Journal* that he published a "kind of proclamation" on 25 November 1759 at Quebec "to encourage the well-wishers of His Majesty to lend what they could afford, for which Colonel [Ralph] Burton (the next officer in command to me) and I gave our Bills, to be repaid in six months, with interest at five percent. This in a short time produced us so considerable a sum as £8000, which without having Recourse to further Expedients, will enable us to await the arrival of the ships, and be it remembered to the Honour of the Highland or 63rd Regiment Commanded by Colonel Fraser, that the non-commissioned officers and private men of that single Regiment contributed of that sum £2000." Seven months later Murray still owed the Highlanders their £2,000 plus 5 per cent interest, as well as owing the entire army their pay and forage money which they had been without since April 1760. He assured them in "Orders, 10 July 1760" that he had been informed by the Royal Treasury that "a large sum was to be sent here" and would shortly, he imagined, "arrive with the Sutherland man of war." He promised "all Officers and men, in whom he has the utmost confidence, they shall be cleared the last shilling, so soon as money comes to hand." According to Lieutenant John Knox, Murray could have saved his breath for "there was not the least distrust, grumbling or appearance of discontent upon this occasion, from any individual whatsoever." Knox, *Journals*, II, 298–9, 465, 465n.

It was not long after we had lent our money, that one morning a frigate was seen coming round Pointe Levi with supplies. We were soon afterwards muster'd, and every man received back his money with twelve months interest, besides the thanks of the General.

Anecdote No. 14
The next year, when we were on our way from Quebec to lay Siege to Montreal, we had a great deal of contrary winds which made the time pass tediously. We had liberty however to go on shore on the South Side of the Saint Lawrence to pass away the day. The *habitans* [sic] were very friendly disposed, and we made it a rule not to molest them in any way, and to pay a reasonable price for any thing we wanted of them. They, notwithstanding, offer'd us any thing they had, without recompense.

While wind-bound somewhere near Sorel, we went ashore upon an Island[229] just by, which had been abandon'd. As we saunter'd about we came to an old barn, and had the curiosity to look in when we found a French Grenadier Deserter, with his knapsack on his back, and on top of that, he had a pair of Fencing files. Our men took a good deal of notice of him, and gave him plenty to eat, and something to drink, and when he became a little familiar, he, with a very polite bow, held out the handle of his files for one of us to accept. Several refus'd, but at last, one accepted, and they had a spar together, and in this way he was beating all hands of us.

McPherson and myself were standing near to each other all this while, and I observ'd that he was in the fidgets to be at him. He says to me, "what d'ye think? this Frenchman is beating us in such a way that he will crow over us – don't you think I had better take a trial at him?" Aye, do so, says I, or he will crow sure enough. McPherson then steps up and makes a signal for one of the files, and to-it they set, and in less than five minutes the Frenchman was disarm'd! He pick'd up his file very composedly, and with a profound bow presented it to McPherson with the handle foremost in token of his defeat. McPherson took it

---

229. Most likely the island of Saint-Ignace near Sorel. On 13 August 1760, whilst his riverine army was becalmed near Sorel, Murray learned that the male inhabitants of Saint-Ignace, despite several warnings not to put up resistance, had left their homes to serve as militia in Sorel. In his *Journal* he recorded: "I resolv'd to make an Example of the inhabitants of this Island who had all left their houses & orderr'd [sic] Major Agnew to collect all the cattle, sheep and greens, to be distributed to the entire army." The following day the grenadiers landed again along with an additional 500 men tasked to cut and make fascines, a specialty of Sergeant James Thompson during the long winter in garrison at Quebec. Two days later, General Murray "order'd the entire Army to land on the Isle St Ignace leaving a few on board each ship to clean & sweeten them." It was probably on this day, with time to kill, that Thompson and his men encountered the French deserter. Knox, *Journals*, III, 322–3.

for a moment, and presently, in the same style, he puts them both together and presents them back to the French Grenadier, who after putting them under his arm, withdrew, making another of his very best bows.

Anecdote No. 25

After we had taken Quebec on the 13th September 1759, we went up to the reduction of Montreal. We were accompanied by eight gunboats[230] for the purpose of covering our landing. We went very slowly indeed, but we got at last to the place where we were to land. On landing at the lower end of Montreal,[231] the gunboats were placed in a position to defend the troops from any opposition which the French might make. T'was funny enough in an enemy, to see one man coming with a horse and cart, another with a Saddle Horse, and a third with a Horse and Caleche, and so on. These were all taken by the Officers as fast as they chose to come forward.[232]

General Murray, seeing this, must have thought to himself, these people are more like friends than Enemies, and he accordingly gave orders to the men to club their firelocks, that is, to carry the Butts upwards, in token of friendship. There was a highroad at some short distance from the river road, and nearly parallel to it, and General Murray divided his little Army into two divisions and ordered a division to move up by each of these roads. We march'd slowly along, and were overtaken by the darkness, when we were order'd to halt for the night.[233] We remain'd by our arms for some time, when there came down a flag

---

230. Murray's force was conveyed primarily in transports and schooners to Montreal and was accompanied by more than just eight gunboats or "floating batteries." Escorts totalled five ships and nine boats: the frigate *Diana*, 32 guns; the frigate *Penzance*, 24; the *Porcupine* sloop, 16; the schooner *Racehorse*, 12; the armed merchantman *True Britain*, 22; and nine (vice eight) "floating batteries" or gunboats. In addition, twenty-two flat-bottomed boats were sent up from Quebec and the *Sutherland*, 50 guns, with its shallow draft accompanied the force up-river as far as Deschambault. *Ibid.*, II, 468.
231. Murray's army landed at Pointe-aux-Trembles on the eastern end of the island of Montreal, 7 September 1760. Samuel Holland's map describes it thusly: "This Parish is of much the same extent as that of la Chine [Lachine]; upon it is a village picketed in, and forming a kind of fortification. It takes its name from the great quantity of Wood upon it before it was cleared." *Ibid.*, 521.
232. Lieutenant John Knox described a similar scene in his *Journal*: "… between one and two we embarked, and soon after landed, without opposition, at the lower end of the Parish of Point au Tremble [*sic*], on the island of Montreal. The place where we disembarked is about three and a half leagues from the city. The country-people brought horses to draw our Artillery, and others saddled, for the Officers to ride, besides carts for our baggage … the roads were lined with men and women, who brought pitchers and pails of milk and water for the refreshment of the soldiers, with many courteous expressions of concern, that they had not better liquor for the Officers." *Ibid.*
233. Thompson's memory is accurate in that Murray's army marched in two divisions towards Montreal (Thompson's brigade was commanded by Brigadier Ralph Burton and

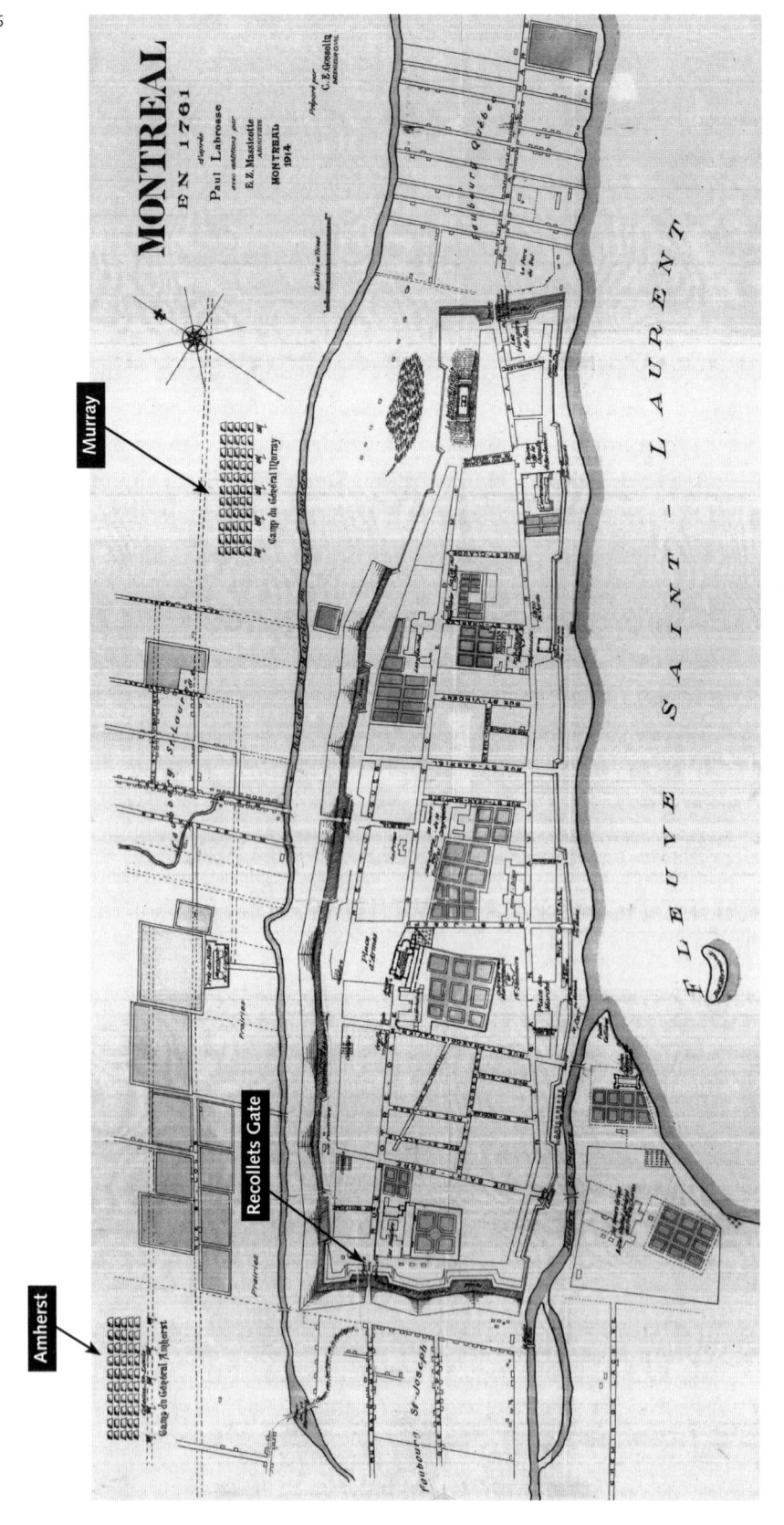

Bird's eye view. A map of Montreal as it looked in 1761 showing where Amherst's and Murray's armies encamped outside the walls of the town. Thompson relates how after the town had capitulated he had "a great curiosity to go and see" the Black Watch. Walking westward from his camp he met the "old Highlanders," whom he pronounced to be "fine, decent, portly men." Map produced in 1914 after Paul Labrosse with additions by archivist E.Z. Massicotte. (BAnQ 105734)

of truce in charge of a French Officer and escort.[234]

The French Officer presented a certain paper to General Murray, which he seem'd to read very attentively, and made some notes upon it with his own hand, and return'd it to the French Officer who went back to the Town. By-and-bye, there comes down a second flag of truce which prov'd to be by the same Officer that came at first, and he brought back, as I then supposed, new proposals more to the General's mind, which he signed, and away went the Officer back to Montreal, and all this was done before the return of daylight. Well, daylight came at last, and we got our breakfast and soon went forward.

When we had got up to the walls of Montreal, we expected, as a matter of course that, at least, we should have the pleasure of *seeing* a place that had *quietly* surrendered to us, but no; the devil a nose of us was permitted to get with inside the town, no more than we had been after the taking of Louisbourg, where we had earn'd it in right-good-earnest, after a Siege of seven weeks and three days, and, to mend the matter (after enduring all kinds of hardships) there came orders from General Amherst to stop our gill of rum! We were order'd to take up a position on a high-ground, somewhat like a platform, near the foot of the large mountain behind the Town, and here we form'd our Camp. We continued there some days, during which the time being heavy on our hands, for we had nothing to occupy us.

Presently comes down the Commander-in-Chief, General Amherst, from the upper Country, after his taking or destroying all the little Posts in his way, and he halts his Army about three miles above our Camp towards Lachine.[235] What with General Murray below them; General Amherst coming down upon them; and General Carleton[236] being over-against them at Laprairie; the French

---

moved forward on the road mentioned as the high ground). However, the reason the army advanced slowly (not explained by Thompson) was that the French regulars had "destroyed all the bridges before us," wrote Lieutenant John Knox, "which retarded our motions, insomuch that, by nine o'clock, we got no farther than Longue Pointe, where, the night being dark, we received orders to take up our quarters in the houses and barns along the road, which are numerous, resembling a long straggling vilage...." *Ibid*.

234. According to Lieutenant John Knox, the French officer was Colonel Louis Antoine de Bougainville (1729–1811). *Ibid.*, 559.

235. The parish of "La Chine" was located on the Island of Montreal. In the early 1760s the parish consisted of seventy-two families with ninety-eight men "able to bear arms." Today, Lachine is a borough of the City of Montreal. When separate British armies advanced on Montreal in 1760, Amherst's army (which included the 42nd Highlanders) first encamped between Lachine and Montreal, but later moved closer to Montreal. Murray's army (which included Fraser's Highlanders) encamped further to the east. When he visited the 42nd Highlanders, Thompson would have walked to and from the two encampments.

236. A red pencil (**X**) appears over the word "Carleton" in the original Manuscript copy. In the right margin, also in red pencil, is the word "Haviland." Obviously, some later editor

had reason enough to offer the Town of Montreal to the first-comer, in order not to have it knock'd down about their ears as Louisburg [*sic*] and Quebec had been, and they therefore thought to do things with the best grace.

After some days, General Amherst must needs see *us*, and when he *did* see us, he saw clever follows, not like *his* Army both ragg'd and dirty. We were all turn'd out to him and form'd in front of the Camp, but without arms. He, with his staff, came on our right, and as he passed along the line, there was a voice call'd out, loud enough to be heard by the General, "a gill o' Rum," and presently another, and another; and, as he passed round the left of the line and between the ranks, many voices were heard to say "a gill of Rum" – "a gill o' Rum," and, in this manner, it went along the whole line.[237]

Now, if it had been only one man, the General would have had him taken up and punished, but, as it was so general, he thought it more prudent to take no notice of it, and 'afaith, in doing that he did well. In talking over this matter with his Royal Highness Prince *Ned* (Duke of Kent)[238] when in Quebec, I mentioned this circumstance, and he told me that somebody or another, had wrote home to England about it, and that the General got very little thanks for his great economy.

Anecdote No. 26

While we were encamp'd before Montreal, which capitulated to us in 1760, General Amherst's Division of the Army moved down from the Lakes, and halted somewhere about Lachine, a few miles above our Camp. One morning, very early, before I had awoke, a person came to my tent, and started me out of a sound sleep, and, who the deuce should this prove to be but John Wilkie! He was now a tall, well-looking man, and very genteely dress'd in plain blue. He said

---

(possibly James Jr.) learned that it was Brigadier General William Haviland who was approaching Montreal from the Richelieu River, and not Guy Carleton.
237. According to Thompson, Jeffery Amherst stopped the army's rum allowance on 8 September 1760. Originally, the rum issue was intended to revive the men after strenuous duty or when they were wet and cold. It had become so regular by this time, at least in Murray's army, that the men considered it a right rather than a privilege granted by a commander. This incident as related by Thompson must have been disconcerting to Amherst as it was a blatant display of petty disobedience by the rank and file. No doubt, Amherst's decision not to order a free issue for his army was based on the fact that many of his regiments had drunk themselves into a stupor at Boston in 1758, celebrating their successful siege of Louisbourg. While Thompson attributes the stoppage to an economy-saving exercise on Amherst's part, the Boston incident may actually be the true reason why Amherst shut down the army's rum allowance so quickly after the surrender of Montreal.
238. Prince Edward Augustus, later Duke of Kent and Strathearn, the father of the future Queen Victoria. The prince was stationed in Quebec with his regiment, the 7th Foot (Royal Fusiliers), over the period 1791–93. See Part Three for Biographical Note.

to me (calling me by my name), I suppose you don't know me? No Sir, I replied, I have not the pleasure of your acquaintance. Why, don't you know John Wilkie the Drumbeater? Bless me! I replied, is it possible? I certainly should not have known you again. And, where have you been, and what have you been about?

So, he related to me all his adventures as I have just told you. Perhaps you will recollect, he says to me, that I got two hundred lashes? 'Afaith, said I, I recollect it well, and I recollect also, that 'twas myself that gave you the last money you received from His Majesty The King. Those 200 lashes, says Wilkie, were as good to me as £200 Pounds, for they were the cause that I left the Army, and had the chance of coming in the way of General Amherst, who has been very kind to me, and couldn't be more so if I was his own child. He was often vexed with himself for having said anything to Colonel Fraser about that drink of milk that cost me so dear, and he seemed to think that he can't do too much to make up for it.

Wilkie went all over the Camp in quest of his old friends the Highlanders, just to have a look at them, but not one of them could have told who he was. He then told me that he had slip'd away before the General was up, his purpose to see me, and that now he must hasten back to the Town, from the fear that he should be wanted. I never saw a sight of poor Wilkie from that day to this, but suppose he must have gone home with General Amherst after the War was over.

Anecdote No. 25
Hearing that the Old Highlanders – the 42nd, were in General Amherst's Camp, I had a great curiosity to go and see them, and after getting leave, I went up accordingly, and I was highly delighted with them. The greater part of the men's heads were nearly the color of my wig, nearly white, but still, they were fine, decent, portly men. I observ'd that almost every man of them wore his silver watch, and that the Officers as well as the private men had silver shoe-buckles, all of the same pattern. Now, our men wore only leather thongs in their shoes.

It was here that I got the history of Colonel Ross,[239] my Townsman (Tain, Ross-shire), who commanded a French Regiment at Quebec, from several of the men of the 42nd that were made prisoners of war at Crown Point,[240] and that were

---

239. The mysterious "Colonel Ross." See footnote 99.
240. Prisoners of the 42nd Foot were taken at Ticonderoga, not Crown Point, in July 1758. The only regiment to get inside the French lines, a number of the 42nd Highlanders were captured when the French counterattacked and cut off their retreat. According to J. Murray Gibbon in his book *Scots in Canada* (Toronto, 1971), 78, "Some Highlanders taken prisoner ... and expecting to be cruelly treated looked on in mournful silence. Presently a gigantic French officer walked up to them and whilst exchanging in a severe tone some remarks in French with some of his men suddenly addressed them in Gaelic. Surprise in the Highlanders soon turned to positive horror. Firmly believing that no Frenchman could ever speak Gaelic, they concluded his Satanic Majesty in person was

detain'd at Quebec the year before we took it from the French. You see, (says my Father) he had serv'd in the Rebellion of "forty-five," and was obliged to fly to France, to save his head. There he met with great encouragement in their Army, and was sent out to the then French colonies. He had shewn a great attachment to the Highland Prisoners and had it in his power to make their situation easy to them. On his getting the news of the Capture of Louisburg [*sic*], which came to him by a French Frigate that escaped from the place and arriv'd safe at Quebec, he set off in her on his way back to France, in order to prevent his falling into the hands of the English.

I pass'd a very quiet time of it with the old Highlanders, and for a very good reason – we could not procure, either for love or money, the means of making merry together, whilst we lay before Montreal, as the mischief was, that our gill of Rum was stop'd the very day that we took the Town! As Prince Edward said, we ought to have had *double* allowance that day.

Chapter 8 | Garrisoning the St. Lawrence, 1760–63

For the 78th Highlanders, the years 1760–63 passed uneventfully, the companies of the regiment parcelled out piecemeal to act as garrisons along the south shore from Lévis and the Île d'Orléans across from Quebec as far as Rivière-du-Loup, where the St. Lawrence River turns into the Gulf. While other regiments in North America were fighting Indians or storming Spanish fortresses in Havana, the Fraser Highlanders mounted guard duty in or near Quebec, or were out in the fields helping *Canadien* families get in the harvest. Sergeant James Thompson lived with several families as the following anecdotes will bear out.

One of his favourite extra-regimental activities was Freemasonry and, in 1761, he was the Senior Warden of Canada Lodge No. 6 in the 78th Foot. He recorded that on St. John's Day, 27 December 1761, the members of his lodge "Walked in procession in due form at one o'clock attended by the Reverend Brother Robert Macpherson, Member of the Select Lodge at Quebec from whom we had

---

before them." If this unsubstantiated anecdote is true, then the Jacobite officer in question was probably either John Douglas *aka* the Chevalier Jean Douglass de Bassignac, or his brother, Francis Douglas, *aka* Captain François-Prosper Douglass, both Jacobite officers serving in the French regulars. Neither, however, fits the description of James Thompson's townsman, a "Colonel Ross" commanding a regiment. Both officers commanded companies *vice* a regiment but both would have taken pains to ensure the comfort of their fellow Highlanders. François-Prosper de Douglass and his wife went to France after the capitulation, taking with them their two sons, Louis-Archambault de Douglass and Charles-Luc de Douglass.

a sermon on the Occasion in the Church of St. Valier." Solemnities over, the *Caipal Mhor* left the small stone church located on the southern shore of the St. Lawrence River, directly across from the Île d'Orléans, to join Thompson and the rest of his brethren Masons at a special dinner. He then helped install new lodge officers and afterwards "Spent the Evening in True Harmony & Brotherly Love." When the lodge closed at 10 o'clock, the records showed that "all Brothers [were] sober and everything in good order and Decorum."[241]

A "return" taken in June 1762, shows the 78th Foot with 61 commissioned officers, 70 non-commissioned officers and 903 rank and file "fit for duty," with another 77 on the sick list, for a total of 1,111 all ranks.[242]

In 1763 orders came for the regiment to be disbanded in Glasgow.[243] Several of the officers wished to remain in the colony. Captain JOHN NAIRNE and Lieutenants Malcolm Fraser and ALEXANDER FRASER agreed to manage seigneuries on General James Murray's behalf, investment properties he had purchased from *Canadien* owners at bargain prices. All three officers would later purchase them and become prosperous landowners. One hundred and seventy sergeants, corporals, drummers and rank and file of the 78th also opted to stay behind in the New World,[244] some of whom would act as tacksmen on Murray's seigneuries, serving under their former company officers. Others were already engaged as tradesmen or interested in acquiring their own farms. Many had already married into *Canadien* families.

Most Canadian historians have assumed that the 170 Fraser Highlanders who remained behind in North America settled in Quebec. In fact, of this number, eighty Highlanders went south to New York, where they had spent the autumn and winter of 1758–59 along the beautiful Mohawk River and had vowed to return. Parson Robert Macpherson had praised it in his letters home, remarking

---

241. A.J.B. Milborne, "The Lodge in the 78th Regiment (Fraser's Highlanders)," *Quatuor Coronati Lodge*, vol. LXV, 19–33.
242. "Returns of His Majesty's Forces," 2 June 1762. Manuscript ledger, private collection.
243. The 78th Foot was disbanded in Glasgow, Scotland, on 14 December 1763. See *Gazetteer & London Daily Advertiser*, Monday, 26 December 1763: "The 14th inst. Frazer's Highland regiment was broke at Glasgow: most of them had learned French during their residence at Quebec." A recent discovery of a soldier's discharge certificate (John Fraser, a "soldier in Major Abercrombie's Company") also confirms this date and location. NAS, E769–139: Forfeited Estates: Lovat.
244. The "discharged in America" list was found in the 1950s by A.J.H. Richardson, Public Archives of Canada, and given to W.S. Wallace. Wallace appended it to his article "The First Scots Settlers in Canada" published in *Bulletin des recherches historiques*, V.56, Levis, January–March, #1–3, 52–62. Here, Wallace writes "this list was found … in one of the Provincial Secretary's letter-books in the S. series of the Canadian Archives (formerly files of the Secretary of State Department) containing letters and warrants from General Murray to Deputy Paymaster John Powell." LAC, RG4, A1, V.2, Microfilm C-2994.

on "the finest Sown Clover you ever saw" and the vacant "land clear'd for hundreds of miles, as plain as isle of Banchor [with] the mold finer than any garden, but now waste and uncultivated."[245]

While still in Quebec, a number of officers and men who wished to "soldier on" were drafted into other regiments which remained on the establishment in North America. "Subsistence rolls," in effect the disbandment muster roll for the 78th Foot, were taken in Quebec in August 1763.[246] These rolls show that the regiment was still an effective fighting machine after six years of campaigning in North America: 736 other ranks, 20 drummers, 95 non-commissioned officers and 36 commissioned officers.[247] Allowing for those who remained behind in North America, and for those who were drafted into other regiments, the 78th Foot numbered well over 500 all ranks when they left Quebec on 12 October 1763.[248] Many of these veteran soldiers would later emigrate to British North America with their families and friends, and some would once again serve the British crown during the American Revolutionary War (1775–83).

Petitions for land grants for those soldiers discharged in Quebec began to show up in 1765. Grenadier Sergeant James Thompson, now clerk of works for the city of Quebec, along with several of his fellow ex-sergeants, submitted a petition for land "in and about the Bays of Gaspey or Chaleurs" on 15 March 1765. The literate Thompson would also help former private soldiers petition for land rightfully due to them and his neat, copperplate script appears on at least two submissions dated 19 and 31 May 1765 respectively for a corporal and twenty-two Highlanders formerly of the 78th, also requesting lands in and around the bays of Gaspé and Chaleur.[249]

---

245. Reverend Robert Macpherson to William Macpherson, 18 November 1758, Schenectady, JGP.
246. Treasury Board Papers, "Subsistence rolls of Fraser's Highlanders (the 78th) 1763." LAC, MG15, T1, V.422, ff 329-340, Microfilm C-15642. These rolls are dated 16, 23 and 30 August 1763.
247. Interestingly, this muster roll includes the names of twenty-seven women, the majority of whom appear to be wives of enlisted men. It was normal practice for each company to carry up to a maximum of six women on rations, the expectation being that they would do laundry, cooking, tailoring and act as nurses, etc., but it is rare to see their names on an official list. In this instance their names were probably captured to ensure that the naval ships/transports responsible for their voyage home were adequately provisioned to the point of disbandment and that there was a formal document authorizing their ration entitlement.
248. "Embarkation returns of the 47th and 78th Regiments, Quebec, 12 October 1763," Centre for Kentish Studies, CKS-U1350/9/1/2/32/6.
249. See "Discharged Sergeants of the 78th Regiment" and "Discharged Soldiers of the 78th Regiment" Petition Rolls in McCulloch, SOTM, II, 173–78.

Highland seigneur. Captain John Nairne (1731–1802) was one of the company commanders of the 78th Foot and, on its disbandment in 1763, took several of his soldiers to be tenants on the seigneury at Malbaie which he leased (and eventually bought) from Governor James Murray. He built a manor house overlooking the village of La Malbaie. During the American Revolution, he joined the Royal Highland Emigrants and helped to defend Quebec against the American rebels under Generals Richard Montgomery and Benedict Arnold. A modern watercolour by C.W. Jefferys. Artist's sketch of mural formerly at Manoir Richelieu and now at LAC. (Editor's Collection)

Anecdote No. 22

Our Regiment had not received a Shilling of Subsistence[250] since they left Cork in 1758, and I was order'd up in the month of December [1760] from St. Valier, where our Grenadiers were in Cantonments, to take money down from Quebec to pay them. It was told out to me by Captain [Ranald] MacDonald,[251] in half-joe's,[252] and amounted to seven hundred Pounds and coper'ards. These I put into my Silk handkerchief, and away I went trudging it along, and now-and-then

---

250. Subsistence was that fraction of every man's pay which remained after all stoppages. Stoppages were deductions for "necessaries" such as clothing, washing and tailoring.
251. By process of elimination, this is Ranald "Raonall Oig" Macdonell, 18th of Keppoch (see Part Three for Biographical Note) one of three "Macdonald" captains still serving in 1760–1. The other two, Captains John Macdonell of Lochgarry and Charles Macdonell, brother of Glengarry, were both badly wounded at the battle of Sillery in April 1760 and both returned to Scotland to recover from their wounds in October 1760.
252. Slang for a Portuguese coin.

I would change hands, so as to relieve me a bit from the weight of carrying it. By-and-by I was thrown into such a fright, nothing could be like it! It was no less than the bursting of the handkerchief and all my money tumbled into the highway, and it being a night as dark as pitch, into the bargain!

What to do I knew not, and I did not like to say a word to any person about the matter. After some little reflection, I bethought myself to scrape with my hands for whatever should come in my way, and then to go as far as my quarters, and bring back a light. I accordingly set about raking and scraping together as many of the half-joe's as I could feel, and I put them into my pockets, and after marking the spot as well as I could by means of the shape of the fence, I went to my lodgings, at Captain JOSÉ BLAIS,'[253] and quietly put the half-joe's into my Chest, and then got me a bit of Candle, and put it into a Lanthorn, and so, without pretending anything to the people of the house, I went back to the spot where I had drop'd my money, and I then saw the marks of my fingers in every direction, on the ground, which was partly frozen, but deuce a piece of money could I discover! I couldn't help thinking that it would be a bad job for me, after all. However, away I went back again to the house, and immediately set to work to find out the extent of my misfortune. It turn'd out, as great good luck would have it, that I had really scraped together, in the dark, every piece of my money, and, by the law, I was as pleas'd as punch!

The next thing was, how was I to pay the Company with half-joe's alone? That was impossible, so I ask'd Mademoiselle Blais (her Father, the Captain being out of the way) if her Father had any Dollars in the house? She shrugged up her shoulders saying *"Je crois que oui"* ["I think that, yes"]. And has he many? To this she said, *"Je ne sais pas, au sûr, mais la dernière fois qu'il les a comptés, il y en avait cinq torrinées!"* ["I don't really know, but the last time they counted them, there were five coins!"][254] Oh, thinks I, it would appear from this that the Capitaine is unable to *count* so many. Presently, in comes the Capitaine himself, and I ask'd him if he had not some dollars which he would let me have in exchange for *"des portuguises?"* ["the portugueses?"]. *"Des portuguises,"* said he, *"Qu'est-ce est que ça"?* ["What is this?"] So, I told him that they were gold coins of eight dollars value each. *"Eh bien, montrez-moi,"* ["Well right, show me,"] said he. I then shew'd him one when he exclaimed *"Sacré-dieu, Je n'en donnerais pas un écu"!* ["Bloody hell, I wouldn't even give a crown!"] These people did not, at that time, know the value

---

253. Captain Michel "José" Blais.
254. The *livre tournois* was the money of account in Quebec, but it was not known in Canada or even in France during this period as a coin. There was however a coin known as *"des sols tournois"* and it is thought that the term *"torrinées"* was a local corruption for this coin. See J. Stevenson, "Currency, with Reference to Card Money in Canada during the French domination," LHSQ, *Transactions,* New Series, No. 11 (1875).

of the gold coins, but egad before long they got to know them well enough.

I was now in another hobble: what was I to do with my half-joe's? So, I took a certain number of them, and away I went immediately back to Quebec, where I procured as many Dollars as I thought would answer my purpose, and I then paid every man his Subsistence, which was the first they got since leaving Cork. And, I made every man of them sign my Book. (#)

I learn'd from the Pay Sergeants of the Companies that they charg'd their men a penny a man, every time that they paid the Subsistence, which I did not do; and this I mention'd to Captain McDonald,[255] who said that he approv'd very much of my not having made any charge against the men, and he made me an offer of one of his four Contingent men,[256] which was much better to me, as it gave me eight pence per day. When the Regiment was near being broken up after the War, the men made a very great Complaint against their Sergeants for the charge in question, and there was a Court of Enquiry order'd, of which Captain Mukin[257] of the 15th Regiment was the President, and the Pay Sergeants of Companies were order'd to attend with their Books.

As I was acting Sergeant of Grenadiers, I was call'd upon first to exhibit my book, which was narrowly examined by the Officers of the Court, and when it was declared that no charge of the kind complain'd of could be found, I was not a little proud. In handing back the book to me, Captain Mukin said, "here, take back your Book, and you need not be asham'd of it," and indeed I had taken great pains to keep it fair, and free of mistakes. Not so the rest of them, for 'afaith they all shew'd charges against the Men's Pay for distributing to them the Pay which they were lawfully entitled to receive in full, and the Court order'd that every penny should be refunded to the men before the Regiment was reduced.

> (#) I forgot to mention that on getting into the Canoe at Quebec, I fell into the Water, which was very cold and that a fine, jolly Canadian Woman, seeing that my legs were bare, she clap'd them under her petticoats, and kept them there 'till we got across to Point Levi, when she stood up in the Canoe, and by the law, my legs smok'd as if they had just come out of boiling water![258]

---

255. Captain Ranald "Raonall Oig" Macdonell, 18th of Keppoch. See footnote 251.
256. Technically known as non-effectives, contingent men (and warrant men) were fictitious names placed on the muster rolls and whose resulting pay would be used to generate extra internal funding within a regiment. In times of war, each Company of Foot was permitted to carry three or four contingent men. Another class of non-effectives was the rank and file left vacant between musters due to death or assigned to other extra-regimental duties, etc. As an example, at a "return" taken on 2 June 1762, Fraser's Highlanders carried forty-two contingent men.
257. Captain Francis Mukins, 15th Foot (Amherst's).
258. Footnote in the original Manuscript copy, identified with a #. A matching # indicated where it was to be inserted in the narrative. It appears to be part of Sergeant Thompson's oral history, which his son, James Jr., had missed when he transcribed his rough notes

Anecdote No. 18

Myself and Sergeant FERGUSON[259] were Billeted upon one Captaine Jacques Leclerc, at Saint Valier below Quebec. We lived pretty well until Lent came on, when the good woman of the house was constantly complaining of the fare which she said *"la religion"* obliged her to lay before us, which was chiefly Salt Fish, milk and eggs, and she said that if she had the "moyen" that she would apply to Mons. [Monseigneur] Parant[260] the Curé, and obtain an order of Indulgence to have *gras* [fat] at her table for the messieurs Anglais.

It was quite clear, however, that our landlady was quite as fond of a bit of *gras* as ourselves, although for my own part I felt very well satisfied to eat *maigre* [lean], but I thought I would try the experiment with the Priest. So, I went to M. [Monseigneur] Parant, in her name, and ask'd him if it was contrary to the rules of the Church to make use of meat during Lent, as my Landlord and Landlady were very old. *"A, point du tout,"* ["Not in the least"] says M. Parant, and he wrote some few words on a scrap of paper, which he desir'd me to give to madame Leclerc. I don't know what it was that he wrote. I then ask'd him if there was not something to pay for the indulgence which he had granted? Oh, said he, shrugging up his shoulders, *"rien qu'une couple de Piastres pour l'Eglise"!* ["nothing more than a couple of dollars for the Church!"] Confound the fellow! I gave him the two dollars, and away I went. Now, I am sure that the Eglise never got a Copper of the money, for the priest was a sad fellow for the bottle, and a dirty dog into the bargain.

The moment I gave madame Leclerc the bit of paper she, without considering whether it was breakfast, dinner or supper-time, instantly put down the *marmitte*[261] on the fire, with a chunk of fat Pork, and Pease and Cabbage, and kept a wacking fire under it, and the moment it was cook'd, she turn'd it out

---

into the letter-book.
259. Sergeant Alexander Ferguson.
260. Monseigneur Parant was the parish priest of Saint-Vallier in 1760. The parish of Saint-Vallier dates back to 1713 and was situated on the south shore of the St. Lawrence River, opposite Île d'Orléans. In Anecdote 27, he appears as the parish priest for Saint-Michel (today's Saint-Michel-de-Bellechasse), which was situated just west of Saint-Vallier. It is not known why he changed parishes, but Anecdote 27 provides some clues. The title "Monsieur le Curé" was used for all Catholic parish priests in France and New France. As well as being the parish's spiritual leader, confessor, teacher, counsellor and social worker, the Curé was also responsible for the administration of the monies and goods belonging to his church. As indicated by Sergeant Thompson, Monseigneur Parant had no qualms about asking Thompson for a "donation" in return for his granting the dispensation to the Leclerc family to eat meat during Lent. While dispensations were normally free of all charges, it was common in poorer parishes for priests to demand payment for any expenses incurred.
261. A French term (actually spelled *marmite*) for a large, covered earthenware or metal cooking pot.

upon the bare table, and we all hands set to it. Our good landlady and her family play'd their parts well, and seem'd to me to have taken enough to serve them a whole week.

Whether Indulgence was meant to include the Capitaine or not, I never could learn, but as I made use of the wife's name, I rather suppose it was not, and consequently attribute the high offense which the Captaine committed against the Church, to be owing to this cause. Immediately adjoining the house, there was a large Field, picketted on all sides, and the penitence which the priest made him undergo was, to put himself on his bare knees at one corner, and, in that position to crawl all along the fences, and back to the same spot! And I myself saw him do it.

While at St. Valier, we received our share of the Grey Cloth which the Quakers of England (hearing that the Highlanders were gone to serve in America, and likely to suffer from the severity of the climate) had subscribed for, and sent out to us at Quebec, at their own expense, calculated at a Great Coat and a pair of Leggins each, for fourteen hundred men!

This present was in consequence of the great rejoicings that took place in England on account of the Capture of Louisbourg and Quebec, in effecting which, as the Quakers are forbid by their religious principles from taking an active part, they thought they were call'd upon to do something or other to shew their Loyalty, and accordingly decided upon clothing the naked limbs of the Highlanders, in approbation of the readiness with which they volunteer'd for the Canada Service, and 'afaith they could not have bestow'd their gift upon a more noble-looking set of fellows!

However, the cloth came to us at the beginning of summer, and was therefore of little use, and before the cold weather came on again, most of the men had parted with such a cumbersome article. For my own part, I gave my share to my Landlord, Capitaine Leclerc, who was delighted with it, and said that he would get a Coat made out of it, which should be worn on Sundays and Holidays only, and I should not be surprised that the coat has been preserv'd in the family to the present day.

Anecdote No. 27
When our Regiment was in Cantonments at Saint Michel below Point Levi, there was a young woman to be married to a tall clever-looking young man of Beauport, and I was ask'd to the Wedding. The Priest of the Parish, Monsr: Parant came there, and by my faith he play'd *his* part at the table *well;* particularly in the drinking way. He got as full as a tick, and after he could swallow no more, he calls for his horse (and a beautiful animal it was, black as jet) – and when he was got cleverly into the saddle, he starts away at full gallop towards his

presbytère bawling out, at the same time swaggering his arm, "*Vive le Roi! Vive le Roi!!*"

As there was a number of matters against him, the people of the parish took this opportunity of shewing in an open manner that they were highly displeased with his conduct, and they accordingly made an *assemblée,* and made a formal complaint against him, and he was removed to the Parish of St. Pierre, where some of our regiment were also in Cantonments.[262] One Sunday afternoon, a party of eight of our men, went strolling along the fields at the lower end of the parish, and, what do they see just within the edge of a Wood, but Monsr: Parant! .... married woman!

He was in terrible fidgets what to do to prevent the men talking about the matter, and he bethought himself to take the whole eight of them to a Tavern, where he order'd them something to drink – this, you see, was in hopes that they would get drunk and forget what they had seen. They all partook of the liquor, but the priest was sadly mistaken if he thought to tempt any of our Highlanders to get drunk. No, the devil a nose of them would take more than they thought would do them no harm, notwithstanding all the coaxing that the priest tried upon them.

The affair somehow, or other got wind, and the parishioners made some fuss about it, and got a letter wrote to the Bishop (I think it was Monseigneur Brilliant) – who order'd him up to Quebec, and there he had his gown taken away from him. From Quebec he went down to the Labrador coast, and I heard that he served as cook to the fishermen there for two years, after which time he again return'd to Quebec, and made some kind of penitence to redeem his character. He succeeded in getting back his gown, and was permitted to serve as Vicaire at Beauport, but upon condition that he was only to say masses, but not to marry, bury, or Confess. For his masses he was entitled to demand a shilling each.

Well, he couldn't be off his old tricks, for no sooner had he muster'd a few shillings than he would find his way into town, and spent them in some ..... house or another at Saint Rocs [*sic*]![263] His conduct was now so publickly known in Quebec, that the Bishop had no chance of keeping it secret, he therefore *himself* accused him, and deprived him of ever exercising the functions of the priesthood. After this last disgrace, he went down to the North shore Fisheries, where he died the year following in great distress.

---

262. Thompson is correct. It was not unusual for parishioners to petition to have a curate replaced. See Cornelius J. Jaenen, *The Role of the Church in New France* (Toronto, 1976), 16.
263. Saint-Roch, a suburb outside the walls of Quebec.

Anecdote No. 18

After having been eleven months at Saint Valier, there came orders for our Company to remove to Saint Pierre on the River du Sud. This was sad news to the family Leclerc for they had become so fond of us nothing could be like it. When we quit the house they all cried like children, and the old couple were as childish as any of them.

Anecdote No. 19

When we got to Saint Pierre, Ferguson[264] and myself had the good-luck to get a billet upon another *Capitaine*, and his name was José Blais.[265] Here we were treated with the greatest civility, and almost adopted as children of the family. I now had pick'd up as much of the French language as to understand almost everything that was said to me, and I myself could manage to gabble tolerably.

Anecdote No. 20

When we were in Cantonments at St. Pierre, my Comrade, Sergeant JAMES SINCLAIR[266] and myself were invited down to Saint Thomas by Ballinagagg[267] to dine with him. We accordingly went down, on a Sunday, and when arriv'd at Ballinagagg's quarters we found that he was gone out. After waiting some time, and our appetites getting somewhat keen, and seeing two pots on the fire, we thought that we might as well see what was cooking and take our dinner by ourselves. Accordingly we took the cover off one of the pots and found in it nothing but Water, and in the other was a huge billet of Wood, and both pots boiling away at a terrible rate! We immediately discover'd that Ballinagagg had play'd one of his usual pranks upon us, and we were satisfied to make the best of it, and go away home, for it was useless to be vex'd about it.

Another time he invited Sergeant Sutherland from the Parish below St. Thomas, to dine with him and to pass the night. After amusing themselves as well as they could, the time for going to bed came round, when (there being but one bed for both) Ballinagagg would not suffer his guest to come to bed until he had taken off his shirt! and to convince him that he was in earnest, he takes off his

---

264. Sergeant Alexander Ferguson.
265. Captain of Militia Michel "José" Blais.
266. Sergeant James Sinclair.
267. Sergeant "Ballinagagg," the regimental practical joker. After extensively consulting records and rolls we have been unable to positively identify any non-commissioned officer by this name serving in the 78th Foot. This is a strong indication that "Ballina-gagg" was probably a Gaelic nickname given to him by other sergeants based on his place of origin. In Gaelic, Ballina is rendered *Baile-na* meaning "town of" and *gag* means a "pass" or "cleft" in the mountains. There is a prominence of place names in Ross-shire beginning Ballina, Balna and Baile-na, though none end with "gagg."

own shirt first. Sutherland was therefore obliged to comply. Sometime before daybreak Ballinagagg slyly creeps out of bed, and after putting on his own shirt, he puts Sutherland's on over it, and away he goes to the next parish above St. Thomas, leaving his guest to provide himself with a shirt as well as he could.

Having been sent up to Quebec upon some business or other, Ballinagagg meets with our Quarter Master Sergeant (LEITH)[268] and ask'd him if he did not feel it cold? Leith said that it was very cold indeed. Well, says Ballinagagg, suppose we step into *"N'entends pas"* (which was the nickname of a Canadian Tavernkeeper in the lower town, owing to his frequent use of that term) – and take a bottle of mull'd wine, it will do us no harm this cold weather? Leith said he had no objection, and in they went. The mull'd wine was order'd in and soon disposed of. Ballinagagg meeting with a favorable opportunity, slips away, leaving Leith to pay the reck'ning, and he proceeds to the upper town.

By some chance he meets with Mrs. Leith, and he made the very same observation about the weather, and as she was shivering with the cold, she readily agreed to Ballinagagg's opinions. He therefore recommended her to take a little mull'd Wine as the very best means of making herself feel comfortable. She very goodnaturedly agreed with him and they both go to a Tavern just at hand – I forget the man's name who kept it. After her taking a little of the Wine, and he making sure of the remainder, he contriv'd to attract her notice to something at the other end of the room, and plays her the same trick as, he just before that, had play'd upon her husband. She got so furious about it nothing could be like it, and called Ballinagagg all the rascally names she could think of. Soon after she got back to her quarters, her husband came in, to whom she related all that had pass'd, and wish'd Leith to get him punish'd for his behaviour to her. He very coolly replied, you had better not make a fuss about the matter, for he has, this very morning, pass'd the very same joke upon myself, and if we say anything about it, we shall only get made game of, so we had better let Ballinagagg have the enjoyment of only one half of the joke.

Chapter 9 | The American Revolution and Siege of Quebec, 1775–76

In 1775 momentous events were happening south of the border. Following skirmishes with the British army at Lexington and Concord in Massachusetts, a rebel army had been formed with George Washington appointed as its commander. Brigadier Generals BENEDICT ARNOLD and RICHARD MONTGOMERY were ordered to march against Quebec and this period of James Thompson's

---

268. Sergeant Alexander Leith.

life is well covered in the essay the reader will find in Part One: A "Brother Soldier…" – James Thompson and the Wolfe Legacy.

Anecdote No. 29
General Montgomery was killed on the occasion of his Heading a Division of American troops while moving up to the assault of Quebec, on the night of the 31st December 1775, or rather the morning of the 1st of January 1776, during a heavy snow storm from the north-east; under the favour of which, as also to avoid the exposed situation to which his men would have been subjected, had the attack been made on the land side where there were Lanthorns [lanterns] and Composition Pots kept burning every night during the absence of the moon, he expected the better to carry his point.[269]

The path leading round the bottom of the Rock on which the Garrison stands, and called Près-de-Ville, was then quite narrow, so that the front of the line of march could present only a few files of men. The sergeant who had charge of the Barrier-Guard (now Cape Diamond, or Raury's Brewery), HUGH McQUARTERS,[270] where there was a gun kept loaded with grape and musket-balls, and levell'd every evening in the direction of the said footpath, had orders to be vigilant, and when assur'd of an approach by any body of men, to fire the gun. It was General Montgomery's fate to be amongst the leading files of the storming-party, and the precision with which McQuarters acquitted himself of the orders he had received resulted in the death of the General, two of his Aides-de-camp,[271] and a sergeant; at least, these were all that could be found after the search made at dawn of day the next morning. There was but one discharge of the gun, from which the General had received a grape-shot in his chin, one in the groin, and one through the thigh which shattered the bone.

I never could ascertain whether the defection of Montgomery's followers was in consequence of the fall of their Leader, or whether owing to their being panic-struck, a consequence so peculiar to an unlook'd-for shock in the dead of night, and when almost on the point of coming into action; added to which, the meeting with an obstruction (in the Barrier) where one was not suspected to exist. Be that as it may, he, or rather the cause in which he had engaged was deserted by his followers at the instant that their perseverance and intrepidity were the most needed. I afterwards learnt that the men's engagements was to terminate on 31st December.

---

269. These illumination pots, lit every night in good weather to prevent the ramparts being surprised, were the brainchild of James Thompson. See details in Part One: A "Brother Soldier…" – James Thompson and the Wolfe Legacy.
270. Sergeant Hugh McQuarters, Royal Artillery.
271. Captains John Macpherson and Jacob Cheeseman.

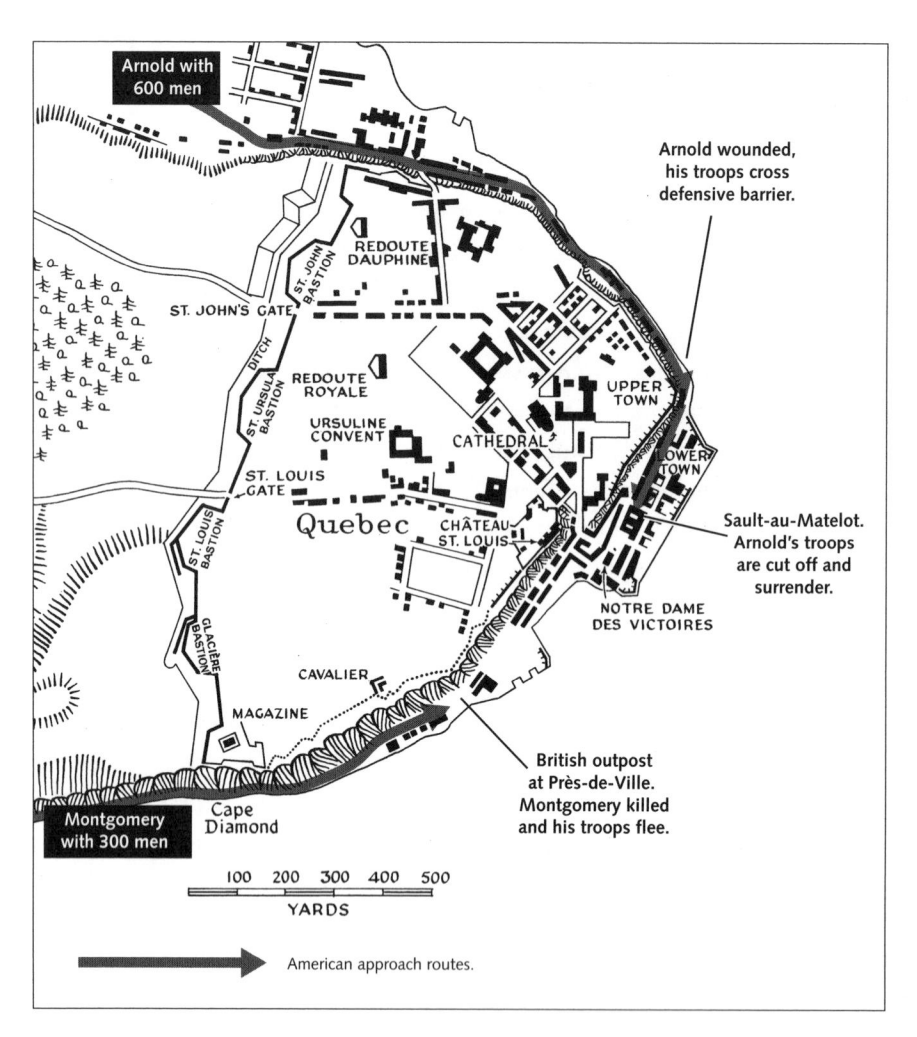

Assault on Quebec. This map shows the two approach routes used by Generals Montgomery and Arnold to assault Quebec on 31 December 1775. It also shows the two British outposts at Près-de-Ville and Sault-au-Matelot where the British stopped the Americans in their tracks. (Adapted detail of map by C. C. J. Bond from Stacey, *Quebec, 1759: The Siege and the Battle*)

Considering the then weak state of the Garrison of Quebec, it is hard to say how much further the enterprise might have been carried, had Montgomery effected a junction with Arnold,[272] whose Division of the storming-party, then simultaneously approaching by the "Sault-au-Matelot" extremity, was left to carry on the contest alone, un-aided, & which was left to sustain the whole brunt of the battle. But, as I do not undertake to give a detailed history of the whole of the events, I return to the *General* and the *Sword*.

---

272. Brigadier General Benedict Arnold.

Holding the situation of Overseer of Military Works in the Engineer Department at Quebec, I had the superintendence of the defences to be erected throughout the place, which brought to my notice almost every incident connected with the military operations of the Blockade of 1775; and from the part I had performed in the affair generally, I considered that I had some right to withhold the General's Sword, particularly as it had been obtained on the battle ground.

On its having been ascertained that Montgomery's Division had withdrawn, a party went out to view the effects of the shot, when, as the snow had fallen on the previous night about knee deep, the only part of a body that appeared *above* the level of the snow was that of the General himself, whose hand (and part of the left arm) was in an erect position, but the body itself much distorted, the knees being drawn up towards the head; the other bodies that were found at the moment, were those of his Aides-de-camp, Cheeseman and McPherson, and one sergeant. The whole were hard frozen.

Montgomery's sword, (and he was the only officer of that Army who wore a Sword that I ever perceived) was close by his side, and as soon as it was discovered, which was first by a Drum-boy, who made a snatch at it on the spur of the moment, and no doubt considered it as his lawful prize, but I immediately made him deliver it up to me, and some little time afterwards, I made him a present of seven shillings and sixpence, by way of prize money.

The Sword has been in my possession to the present day (the 16th August 1828). It has a head at the top of the hilt, somewhat resembling a lion's or bull dog's, with crop'd ears, the edges indented, with a ring passing through the chin or under-jaw, from which is suspended a double silver chain communicating with the front tip of the guard, by a second ring; at the lower end of the handle there is, on each side, the figure of a spread eagle. The whole of the metal part of the hilt is of silver. About half an inch of the back part of the guard was broken off, while in my possession. The handle itself is of ivory, and undulated obliquely from top to bottom. The blade which is twenty-two inches long, and fluted near the back, is single-edged, with a slight curve towards the point, about six inches of which, however, is sharp on both edges, and the word "Harvey" is imprinted on it, five and a half inches from the top, in Roman capitals in a direction upwards. The whole length of the blade is two feet, four inches (when found, it had no scabbard or sheath, but I soon had the present one made, and mounted in silver to correspond).

As it was lighter and shorter than my own Sword, I adopted it, and wore it in lieu. Having some business at the "Séminaire,"[273] where there was a number

---

273. The Seminary of Quebec was founded in 1663 by Bishop François de Laval, first bishop of New France. Its role was to prepare young men to the priesthood.

of American officers, prisoners of war of General Arnold's Division, I had occasion to be much vexed with myself for having it with me, for the instant they observed it, they knew it to have been their General's; and they were very much affected by the recollections that it seemed to bring back to their minds, indeed, several of them wept audibly! I took care however, in mercy to the feelings of those ill-fated gentlemen, that whenever I had to go to the Seminary afterwards, to leave the Sword behind me.

To return to the General; the body on its being brought within the Garrison walls, was identified by Mrs. Widow Prentice,[274] a relation of mine, who then kept the hotel known by the name of "Free Masons' Hall,"[275] by a scar on one of his cheeks, supposed to be a sabre-cut, and by the General having frequently lodged at her house on previous occasions of his coming to Quebec on business. General Carleton, the then Governor General, being satisfied as to his identity, ordered that the body should be decently buried, in the most private manner, and His Excellency entrusted the business to me.

I accordingly had the body conveyed to a small log house in St. Lewis [sic] Street, (opposite to the residence of Judge DUNN)[276] the second from the corner of St. Ursule Street, owned by one François Gaubert, a cooper; and I order'd Henry Dunn,[277] joiner, to prepare a suitable coffin; in this he complied with in every respect becoming the rank of the deceased, having covered it with fine black cloth and lined it with flannel. After the job was completed, there was nobody to indemnify six dollars that Dunn gave to the six men who bore the body to the grave; he wished to insist upon *my* paying his account, as the orders for the other work had been given and paid by me; but, as I could not have required his men (having enough soldiers on my own)[278] I continued to put him off from

---

274. Wife of Lieutenant Miles Prentice, provost marshal of Quebec during the siege. She was not styled widow at the time of the incident as her husband was still very much alive, but had been widowed by 1828 when James Thompson Jr. transcribed this story for his father. See Part Three for Biographical Note on Miles Prentice.
275. Free Mason's Hall. The hall was built on the old site of the famous Chien d'Or (or Golden Dog) to which so much of Quebec's romantic history is attached. Sometime after 1771, the property was acquired by Miles Prentice and converted to a hotel and boarding house known as Free Mason's Hall. The hotel was patronized by Quebec's leading citizens and Freemasons, as well as the British officers of the garrison (including Captain Richard Montgomery of the 17th Regiment, the same Richard Montgomery who was killed at Près-de-Ville in 1775). After Prentice died in 1787, his wife continued to operate the hotel for some years. Eventually, the Freemasons purchased the property.
276. Judge Thomas Dunn.
277. Henry Dunn, a joiner or carpenter, a fellow Freemason and member of the Order of the Gâteau. See Chapter Ten.
278. For the duration of the siege Thompson had command of the 200 artificers who were also a *corps de reserve* for the Quebec Militia. See Part One: A "Brother Soldier…" – James Thompson and the Wolfe Legacy.

Free Mason's Hall. The large stone building strategically located on the left at the top of the stairs connecting the Lower Town with Upper Town was known as Free Mason's Hall. Originally the site of Le Chien d'Or, a famous French tavern, it was acquired by Provost Marshal Miles Prentice c.1771 and converted into a hotel and boarding house. (Editor's Collection)

Montgomery cairn. The final resting place of American General Richard Montgomery in Quebec is commemorated by a small stone cairn and plaque a few yards away from the St. Louis Gate. James Thompson, who was responsible for the general's first burial, also oversaw his exhumation in 1818 and subsequent repatriation back to the United States. (Photos by Louise Gunn)

time to time, and I really believe that it remains unpaid to this day. However, Dunn is long since dead, and as he could well afford to be at the loss, it was perhaps after all, only compelling him to a generous action towards a fallen foe. He deserved, in some measure to sustain the loss, for I gave him no directions about the six men, as I had a party of my own in waiting at the Château, to carry the corpse to the grave at the moment that General Carleton conceived proper; and when I did ascertain his wishes to that effect, I proceeded to Gaubert's, where I was told that Mr. Dunn had just taken away the corpse; this was about the setting of the sun on the 4th January 1776.

I accordingly posted up to the place where I had ordered the grave to be dug, (just along side of that of my first Wife, within, and near the surrounding wall of the powder magazine, in the gorge of the St. Lewis [sic] Bastion), and found, in addition to the six men & Dunn the undertaker, that the Reverend Mr. DE MONTMOLLIN,[279] the military chaplain was in attendance, and the business thus finished before I got there.

---

279. The Reverend David-François de Montmollin.

On satisfying myself that the grave was properly covered up, I went and reported the circumstances to General Carleton, who expressed himself not too well pleased with Dunn's officiousness. It having afterwards been decided to demolish the powder magazine and to erect a Casemated-Barrack in its stead, I took care to mark the spot where Montgomery was buried (not so much perhaps on *his* account, as from the interest I felt in it on *another* score) by having a small cut stone inserted in the pavement within the barrack square; & this precaution enabled me afterwards to point out the place to a nephew of the General, Mr. Lewis,[280] who, hearing that the person who had had the direction of the burial of his uncle's corpse was still living, came to Quebec about the year 1818, for the laudable purpose of obtaining the permission of the military commander, General SHERBROOKE,[281] to take away the remains.

I, of course, was called upon for the purpose of pointing out the spot; and having repaired thither with young Mr. Lewis and several officers of the garrison, together with Chief Justice SEWELL[282] and some friends of the deceased, I directed the workmen at once where to dig, and they accordingly took up the pavement exactly in the direction of the grave. The skeleton was found complete, and when removed a musket ball fell from the skull; the coffin was nearly decayed. No part of the black cloth of the outside, nor of the flannel of the inside were visible; a leather thong with which the hair had been tied, was still in a state of preservation, after a lapse of 43 years; there is a spring of water near the place, which may have had the effect of hastening the decay of the contents of the grave.

The particulars attending the removal of the remains through the several towns in the United States to their ultimate place of deposit (Broadway, New York,) were published in all the Public Papers on that line of Communication.[283]

---

280. Lewis Livingston. Thompson is only partially correct. Montgomery's widow, Janet Livingston, sent her brother Edward's young son, Lewis, to collect her husband's body for reburial in the United States. The body was accorded honours as it travelled south via Lake Champlain and the Hudson River down to New York. The story is told that as the funeral cortege moved down the Hudson, nearing the Livingston estate, Mrs. Montgomery took her place on the broad veranda of the family home and requested that she might be left alone as the body passed. She was found unconscious stretched upon the floor where she had fallen, overcome with emotion. After this solemn duty, Lewis drowned at the age of twenty-three on a return voyage from France.
281. Sir John Coape Sherbrooke.
282. Chief Justice Jonathan Sewell.
283. On 8 July 1818 General Richard Montgomery's remains were re-interred next to his monument in St. Paul's Chapel in New York City.

Additional:[284]

While engaged in giving directions respecting the burial of the General's two Aids (who were both put into the same grave, just as they had been found, a little in advance of the spot where the General was interred), there were sent seventeen dead soldiers of General Arnold's Division brought up from Sault-au-Matelot, for the purpose of being buried. These were all put into one pit dug in the slope of the Rampart, just in the rear of the Powder Magazine, also without coffins as is the practice on the Battlefield, but no particular mark was left to shew the place. Many of the American soldiers that were killed in their attempt to force the Barrier at Sault-au-Matelot, were buried on the beach, in front of the property now Mr. Wilson's and Mr. Racey's, "both brewers."

Anecdote No. 17

It was I who found [General Montgomery's] body in the snow, and afterwards had the direction of Burying it privately by order of General Carleton.[285] The remains were, about the year 1820, taken to the States by his Nephew, Mr. Lewis [Lewis Livingston], who obtain'd the permission of the Governor to that effect. He was the only Officer of that Army that wore a Sword that ever I discover'd and that self same Sword is in my possession to this very day.[286] It is Silver-mounted, but altogether but a poor looking thing. It has however been the means of my receiving the visits of a great number of American Ladies and Gentlemen, who put so many questions to me, that I am heartily tired of answering them now that old-age has got the better of me.

---

284. The contents of this "additional" note were related by James Thompson to his son on the evening of 19 December 1828. James Jr. then added the following words: "The foregoing particulars were committed to writing, in consequence of the frequent visits of American Ladies and Gentlemen, to obtain a view of Montgomery's sword, and a recital of the circumstances attending his death and burial; and in the view also of averting the fatigue occasioned by the repeated recital at my father's advanced age – ninety five years."
285. Governor General Guy Carleton, Lord Dorchester.
286. James Jr. added a footnote to this anecdote: "This sword is now (the 18th March 1831) in my possession, at the Cedars, together with a detailed account of the manner in which Montgomery met his Death; the particulars of his Burial, and of his dis-internment, the whole certified by Father's own Signature." The sword was passed down through the Thompson family until it was purchased by Governor General the Marquis of Lorne in 1878. He subsequently gave it to the chargé d'affaires of the British Legation in Washington in 1881. It was presented to Montgomery descendant Louise Livingston Hunt, whose sister Julia Barton Hunt presented it to the United States. The U.S. Congress deposited it in the Smithsonian Institution, Washington, D.C. (the Smithsonian repaired the sword's quillon in 1977).

Anecdote No. 32

CHARLES GRANT was [during the siege of Quebec, 1775] Captain of Hope Gate[287] Guard, and he had THOMAS AYLWIN (both of them Merchants) for his Lieutenant. I had a party of twenty men under my orders to perform any duty requiring immediate attention. As myself & party wanted accommodation for the night (it being severe winter weather) I ask'd Captain Grant if he would take us under shelter, to which he readily agreed.

In the course of our talk over a bowl of Sangris,[288] I observed a Horn[289] lying on the table and, taking it up, said that it was a very handsome one. Indeed, says Charles Grant? well James, if you think so, I and Thomas Aylwin intend to go together to England next year, if we can get leave, and I promise that you shall have a Horn, mounted in gold, as it will be less "cumbersome" for the pocket, and, says Thomas Aylwin, I'll take good care to put him in mind of it.

Well, as it happen'd, the Yankees broke up the blockade in the course of the winter, and Charles Grant & Thomas Aylwin went to England, on business as they had intended. One day, while in London, and walking along a street together, Thomas Aylwin says to Charles Grant, you seem to have forgot Thompson's Mull? Oh, says Charles Grant, I had not forgot him, but having something else to attend to, I had not time. But, continues Charles Grant, as we happen only five or six doors past the silver smith's who mounted my own Horn, we will just step back to the shop.

Horn snuff mull. A sketch of the snuff mull presented to James Thompson in 1776 by Captain Charles Grant, a friend and fellow Freemason. The artist, son James Junior, received it as a gift in 1784 from his father, who readily confessed "by degrees I got to take so much [snuff] I found the Mull too small." Pen and ink sketch scanned from the manuscript letter-book. (Photo by Earl John Chapman)

---

287. Hope Gate. Located on the northern face of Quebec's ramparts, it was one the first of the two purely British gates of Quebec. Erected in 1786 by Colonel Henry Hope, Commandant of the Forces and Administrator of the Province, from which it took its name, it was demolished in 1874. See Part Three for Biographical Note.
288. Sangria. Mulled wine.
289. A horn snuff mull. Taking snuff, or powdered tobacco, was widespread throughout the Highlands from the 17th century and was not overtaken in popularity by smoking until the end of the 19th. The most important item of equipment for a snuff-taker was an airtight container in which to keep the snuff, and these snuff boxes or snuff mulls were made in large numbers in a wide variety of materials, including silver, horn, pewter and porcelain.

When there, Charles Grant takes a *second* horn out of his pocket, and desires the silver smith to mount it for him, in *silver*. Oh! says Thomas Aylwin, that's not the bargain you promised Thompson, in my presence, that it should be mounted in *gold*. That's very true, replies Charles Grant, but my purse has become so low just now, that I cannot well afford it, and I am sure that Thompson will be quite satisfied with silver. He accordingly had it mounted in that way, and when he returned to Quebec, made me a present of it, with his own initials handsomely engraved on the lid.

This is the very box that taught me to take snuff. At first, I merely smell'd at it, but by degrees I got to take so much, that I found the Mull too small. The lid having become much worn, I took it to Smillie,[290] in 1821, (the silver smith on the Lower-town Hill) & got it remounted, and a Scotch pebble set in the lid, which cost me five Dollars. Now, there it is for you, [James Thompson Jr.] and see that you take as good care of it as I have done.[291]

Chapter 10 | Miscellanea

When storm clouds were gathering over North America in 1773, five old soldiers and Freemasons of Wolfe's army sat down to celebrate the festival of Epiphany and the Light from the East in the house of James Thompson. Just two years later, all would see action in service of the King at the siege of Quebec related in the previous chapter. Below is one of James Thompson's anecdotes, a humorous account of the founding of "The Order of the Gâteau," a quasi-official dining club which lasted in its first embodiment from 1773 until its disbandment in 1785. Then, it was re-constituted as a select group of thirteen Knights and a Sovereign.

Interestingly, James Thompson and his close friends were celebrating a medieval French custom practised by fellow Quebeckers. They gathered to eat a "king cake," a type of cake associated with the festival of Epiphany and still

---

290. James Smillie. An Edinburgh silversmith who emigrated with his family to Quebec in 1821. There he established himself as a manufacturing jeweller, his son James Jr. doing the engravings and making ambitious attempts to do pictorial engraving. In 1827, George Ramsay, 9th Earl of Dalhousie, the Governor General of Canada, became interested in the son James and gave him free passage on a government ship from Quebec to Portsmouth to take up studies in London.
291. As described in this anecdote, Thompson's snuff mull was originally "mounted" by a London silversmith in 1776. In 1821 Thompson had the silver lid replaced by Quebec silversmith James Smillie. When the mull was eventually passed down to James Jr., the words "James Thompson, 1733, to his son James, 1784" were engraved across the edge. Thompson's horn snuff mull was acquired in 1972 by the McCord Museum, Montreal.

enjoyed in the Christmas season in Quebec, France, Belgium and Switzerland, where it is called a *galette* or *gâteau des Rois*. The *galette des Rois* (favoured in the north of France and Belgium) is made with puff pastry and frangipane while the *gâteau des Rois* (from the south and Switzerland) is made with brioche and candied fruits. A little bean was traditionally hidden in it, a custom taken from the Saturnalia in the Roman Empire: the one who stumbled upon the bean was called "King of the Feast."

The remainder of the stories below are timeless and do not chronologically "fit" anywhere and have therefore been collected into this last chapter.

Anecdote No. 40
Be it remembered that, on the evening of the 6th day of January, which was in the year of Our Lord 1773; LAUCHLAN SMITH Esquire, one of His Majesty's Justices of the Peace, and Seigneur of the Seigneurie of Ste. Anne, on the south side of the River St. Lawrence below the Point of Levi, passed the evening with Mr. John Chisholm, Mr. Francis Smith, and Mr. John McLane of this City (all of them now dead)[292] at the House of Mr. James Thompson, Overseer of Works for the Garrison of Quebec, And being the Festival of Epiphany, in commemoration of the Wise Men of the East, who were conducted by the luminous appearance of a Star in the lower regions of the Air, to the place where Our Saviour was Born, a Gâteau was provided which, being cut into as many parts as there were persons in Company, and each one having received his part, Behold! that of the said Lauchlan Smith Esquire contain a Bean, which according to ancient custom constituted him King. He returned thanks, and said, in his facetious way: "Since you, my friends, acknowledge me as your King, I cannot do less than bestow on you some distinguishing mark of my sovereignty;" then, taking hold of a Sword he found hanging in the room, ordered the said James Thompson to kneel down before him, and having put the point of the Sword on his head, said, arise Sir James, and did the same to John Chisholm, Francis Smith, and John McLane, and the evening was spent in great glee.

---

292. Two of these three men were former members of the 78th Foot as well as Freemasons like Thompson. John Maclane was a former sergeant of the 78th who had transferred to the 60th Foot before taking his discharge in 1765. In his earlier years he had been a boarder in Thompson's house. John Chisholm (c.1740–1807) was a former lieutenant of the 78th, commissioned initially as an ensign (17 January 1757) and subsequently lieutenant (4 September 1759) after the death of Captain Alexander Cameron, 4th of Dungallon and "in room of" Simon Fraser. He was wounded at the battle of Sillery, 28 April 1760, and was the sole lieutenant serving in Major James Abercrombie's company on disbandment.

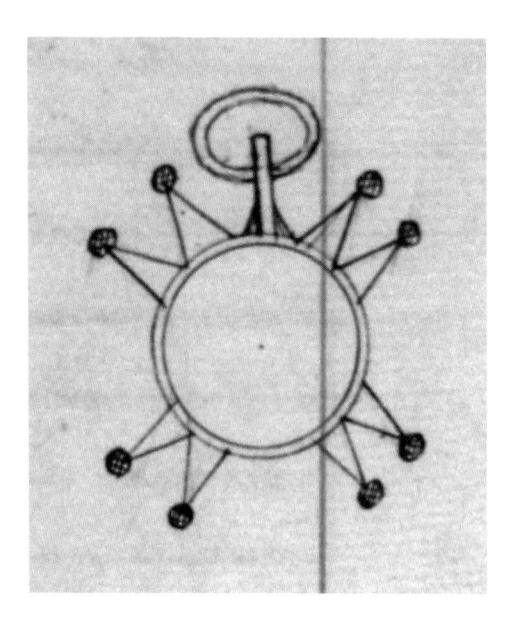

Badge of the Order. The eight-pointed star pendant shown here, designed by James Thompson, was to be worn exclusively by members of a quasi-official dining club known as the Order of the Gâteau which consisted of thirteen "Knights" and a "Sovereign." Made of gilt and enamel, it was worn suspended from the third button of the vest by a mazarine blue ribbon "as a distinguishing Badge of the Order of the Gâteau." Pen and ink sketch scanned from the manuscript letter-book. (Photo by Earl John Chapman)

That on the evening of the 4th of January following, the gentlemen thus Knighted, waited on their Sovereign with a formal Address of Thanks for his great goodness on Knighting them on the evening of last Epiphany day, and praying that he would be pleased to confer the same honor, on three gentlemen who accompanied them with the Address: viz. Hugh Fraser, Henry Dunn and Francis Anderson.[293] This prayer was readily granted, the Sovereign having immediately Knighted them also.

The Sovereign having ordered a sumptuous entertainment, proposed that the Knights be incorporated into an Order, to be henceforth and for ever called by the name and title of The Knights of the Honorable Order of the Gâteau. That Articles of By-Laws be immediately drawn out for the good-government of the same. The Knights having thanked the Sovereign for this additional mark of his goodness, Mr. McLane was directed to make out these articles, and a day was fixed for the Knights to assemble for the purpose of signing the same. The By-Laws required that the Chapter of the Order should be held monthly, and in conformity thereto the Chapters have been regularly held from the above period, to some time in 1788, when the members became so numerous that some of them could not be kept to that order required by the Laws, which caused discontent, consequently many had withdrawn and soon after the Chapter tumbled into a dormant state.

The Sovereign, with deep regret, contemplated much on the foregoing circumstances, and ever since the discontinuance of the Chapter, it was his intention to revive and new model the same into such form and on such principles as may effectually prevent any future discord, but, the Sovereign's removal from Quebec to his Seigniory at Saint Anne's, has hitherto been the cause of his not having carried his design into execution, and now, considering his advanced years, that by any further delay his Order of the Gâteau (in which he greatly de-

---

293. Likewise, these men were fellow Freemasons.

lighted) might fall into eternal oblivion. He doth therefore, and by the authority vested in him as Sovereign of the Order of the Gâteau first Revoke and Annul all Laws and usages heretofore observed, in the late Chapter of this Order, and do hereby and by the Authority aforesaid, Revive and Re-constitute the same in ample form, and being thus constituted, to consist of The Sovereign, and, in its fullest extent, of Thirteen Knights, and no more, on any pretense whatever, well knowing that the downfall of the former Chapter proceeded entirely from the number of Knights being unlimited, and for which cause this is made essential, perpetual and unalterable.

That a Chapter will be held on the evening of the 6th of January in every year, to celebrate the Festival of Epiphany according to the ancient custom. That the Knights shall wear a Star pendant to a mazarine blue Ribbon, from the 3rd button of the vest, as a distinguishing Badge of the Order of the Gâteau. This Badge to be made according to the design hereto annexed, in gold, or in gilt, or, as it may be hereafter agreed upon by the Knights when duly convened in Chapter.

That in the absence of the Sovereign, the Chapter shall be governed by a President, who shall be elected and installed in that office on the evening of a Festival of Epiphany in every year, and shall be invested with Sovereign Authority, in as much as if the Sovereign himself were personally present.

The Laws for the good Government of the Order of the Gâteau shall be framed by the Knights in Chapter, and when the same is made out and agreed to by unanimous consent, the Sovereign will approve and confirm that Law by his Sign Manual.

Anecdote No. 11

My Father having seen the following verses in the "Star" Gazette publish'd at Quebec,[294] by the Rev'd Daniel Wilkie, he desir'd me to take a copy of them, at the same time expressing his admiration of the subject, and particularly the last line, as underscored, in order to denote the *emphasis:*

> WOLFE
>
> Descend ye chaste Nine, and assist me to sing,
> Not to Venus or Bacchus an off'ring I bring;
> Far loftier visions my fancy pourtrays,
> A Hero cut off in the bloom of his days!

---

294. The poem was published in the *Star and Commercial Advertiser* on 15 April 1829, under the title "Poetry – For the Star." At this time, the paper's proprietor and editor was Daniel Wilkie (c.1777–1851). The editors have been unable to track down the poet (initials "J.M.") but he/she could be a local talent as the following words appear at the end of the poem: "Quebec, March 1829."

A Hero whose mem'ry shall ever impart,
A sensation of grief to each true British heart;
And whose deeds 'midst the annals of Glory shall shine,
Whilst the records of Histr'y, Britannia, are thine.

'Tis to thee, valiant Wolfe, whom my muse would aspire,
And thy gallant deeds that all nations admire;
And for which, near the spot where thy fates were appeas'd,
A lasting memento has Canada rais'd.

On the Plains of Quebec, thy pure life blood was drain'd,
Where the rights of old England you bravely maintain'd;
And, when mortally wounded, and gasping for breath,
When told that the Victr'y was her's, smil'd in death.

May Britain ne'er want such a Spirit as thine!
May She never the conquering laurel resign!
And though War, with its terrors, her Sons should surround,
May *the Heart of a Wolfe* in each bosom be found!

(signed) J: M.)

Anecdote No. 19

I obtain'd from Captain Blais[295] a long account of the hardships that he underwent during the American Revolutionary War in having had all his property plunder'd, and himself and his sons cruelly treated while in the hands of the Rebels before Quebec, and also at Montreal to which place they had been drag'd on Sleds, in the cold winter, and almost starv'd to death for their Loyalty and exertions in raising men to beat off the Enemy while cannonading Quebec from Point Levi.

I form'd a strong attachment to Captain Blais and so did he for me. He thought himself entitled to some reward for his losses and Services, and ask'd my opinion about petitioning The Government to obtain some waste-lands adjoining his Property. I thought the idea a good one, and I myself took the hint and join'd with him in a Petition for some Waste-lands in that part now called the Township of Armagh. We met with a great many put-offs by the Council. Poor Captain Blais died before we could effect anything, and I afterwards, in 1784, associated myself to the children of the deceased in other petition to General HALDIMAND and after some perseverance, I at last got the lands which I now hold, but as yet they have been but of little value to me.

---

295. Captain of Militia Michel "José" Blais.

Anecdote No. 31
The first or second Sunday after the arrival of His Grace the late DUKE OF RICHMOND[296] at Quebec, there was the usual parade of the troops in Garrison, and I must needs go to the Esplanade and see what sort of a looking man the Duke was. It was not until the troops had march'd off that I could get a sight of him, and then the Band of Music began to play, when there was a broad circle formed by a party of soldiers around them, and the Duke and all the great folks walked round and round the musicians. I got a squint of him several times as he pass'd round, and I thought him a good sort of a looking body enough. Having satisfied myself in this way, I was about going away about my business, for I didn't care a copper for all the music.

As I was sauntering away homewards, there comes an Officer after me (Colonel COCKBURN,[297] the Quarter Master General) and he taps me on the shoulder, saying that His Grace the Duke of Richmond wanted to speak to me. 'Faith I started at the idea, and thought to myself what the deuce can the Duke of Richmond have to say to *me?* I had scarcely time to bethink myself however, when, who did I see coming towards me thro' the crowd, but The Duke himself! and several of his young ladies and staff.

His Grace ask'd me if my name wasn't Thompson? I replied that it was, and took off my hat to him as if he had been His Majesty himself (now, how the deuce, thinks I to myself, does he come to know anything about *me?*) – Mr. Thompson, says The Duke, did you know General Wolfe? Yes, may it please your Grace, I replied, I knew him to my sorrow! Aye, says His Grace, how is that? Why, your Grace, only because he was a good friend lost to me!

Were you not in Fraser's Highlanders? Yes, I was. What kind of a Regiment was it? Why, your Grace, they were a most honorable Corps. To-be-sure they knew nothing about parade-exercise, and figuring away with their fuzees, and they could not bear to be *taught* to "Prime & load," for every mother's son of them knew that from his infancy, and the only difficult matter to teach them was to "form the Line," and then, it was just as difficult to make them keep it, that is to say, when they had an enemy in sight. As for all the rest of the business, they could do just as well as other soldiers.

Aye, Aye, says the Duke, I understand that they were a fine set of men. By this time, we were completely mobb'd with people gathering around us, and, I assure *you,* I felt within myself that it was no small matter to become acquainted with me.

---

296. Charles Lennox, Duke of Richmond and Lennox. When the Duke arrived in Quebec in July 1818, James Thompson was eighty-five years old.
297. Colonel James Pattison Cockburn, Royal Artillery.

"The front face is no likeness at all." This was how James Thompson described the efforts of Quebec sculptors Thomas-Hyacinthe and Ives Chaulette in 1780 (see facing page), adding "the profile is all that they could hit upon and which is good." In Anecdote 8, Thompson implies that the Chaulette brothers used his sketches to carve the wood statue of General Wolfe that would adorn George Hipps' corner niche for many years. However, it would appear that the sculptors had another source for Wolfe's appearance, other than Thompson's memory. When the old Hipps house was demolished in 1846, workers found this hand-coloured mezzotint which corresponded exactly to the coloured statue. Mezzotint by Richard Houston after a 1760 painting by J.S.C. Schaak. (New Brunswick Museum)

While I yet stood with my hat in my hand, His Grace walk'd away saying that he was glad to see me looking so well, and he wish'd me a "good morning," altho' it was not far from six in the afternoon. I had some difficulty in getting out of the crowd, for the people were all staring at me as a matter of great curiosity.

Anecdote No. 8
We had a loyal fellow in Quebec, one George Hipps,[298] a Butcher, who own'd that House at the corner of Palace and John Streets, still call'd "Wolfes' Corner," and, as it happen'd to have a Niche probably intended for the Figure of some Saint, he was very anxious to fill it up, and he thought he could have nothing better than a Statue of General Wolfe, but he did not know how to set about getting one. At last he finds out two French Sculptors, who were brothers of the name of Charlotte,[299] and he asks me if I thought I could direct them how to

---

298. George Hipps served in Wolfe's army, and at the peace in 1763 he turned his bayonet into a butchers' knife. He became quite successful and invested his earnings in real estate, purchasing the lot and house on the corner of Palace and John streets on 20 April 1780. See also Part One: "Brother Soldier…" – James Thompson and the Wolfe Legacy.
299. The sculptors were the Chaulette brothers, Thomas-Hyacinthe and Ives. The wood statue was executed around 1780 and remained at the old Hipps residence for many years.

General James Wolfe. The "Red-haired Corporal" points the way for visitors at the library of the Morrin Centre, home of the Literary and Historical Society of Quebec, first established in 1824 by Lord Dalhousie. The statue once stood in a corner niche at Wolfe's Corner (see "A Colour Album," page 106) and was carved by the Chaulette brothers c.1780. (Private Collection)

make a likeness of the General in Wood? I said I would, at all events, have no objections to undertake it, and accordingly they, the Charlottes, tried to imitate several sketches I gave them but they made but a poor job of it after all, for the front-face is no likeness at all, and the profile is all that they could hit upon and which is good.

Yet the body gives but a poor idea of the General, who was tall and straight as a Rush, so that after my best endeavours to describe his person, and I knew it well, and for which purpose I attended every day at their Workshop which was in that house in St. Louis Street, where the Miss Napiers are now residing [1828], and which is somewhat retired from the line of the Street, the shop itself being in the projecting wing. I say we made but a poor General Wolfe of it!

Since 1899, the statue has been part of the collection at the Morrin Centre in Quebec (the Literary and Historical Society of Quebec, now part of the Quebec Anglophone Heritage Network).

It has been several times, the House being then only one Story high, pulled down by mischievous persons, and broken, and as often repair'd by the several owners of the house and much to their credit be it spoken, and it still keeps its ground, and I hope it may do so until the Monument (×) is finished. I suppose that the original parts of the Statue must now be as rotten as a pear, and would be moulder'd away, if it was not for their being kept so bedaub'd with paint.

> (×) Wolfe and Montcalm's Monument erected in the upper Garden of the Castle of Saint Louis, was, at the time the above was last related, in a state of progress (it was completed on the 8th of September following the very day on which the Earl of Dalhousie, under whose auspices it was erected, embark'd for England) and it is a singular coincidence that my now late Father, who felt a peculiar anxiety to witness the completion of this work (at the laying of the foundation Stone of which he had as the last survivor of Wolfe's Army in Canada been called upon to assist) should, as it were, have reserv'd his last pedestrian effort to view the same, which he effected, assisted by the help of my arm on the 21st September 1828 (Sunday) in his 96th year. His enfeebled state, made it a serious undertaking, he having been obliged to rest himself frequently, by sitting on the steps of street doors. So also was he very much exhausted on his return home. So also, as a remarkable occurrence was it the last time he walk'd from his house in St. Ursula Street, and equally so that he should have been the last Survivor of Wolfe's Army, in Canada. He died at the age of 98.[300]

Anecdote No. 30 [301]

This is one of the Cups which each of my grand mother's children received, and it was a rule with her to make them take a small dram of whiskey on New Year's morning. My own Father was eighty three years of age at the time of his death, which was occasioned by his falling into his cellar. I, myself, am now nearly ninety seven, which makes 180 years, and supposing my mother to have arrived at a middle-age when her son, my father, received the cup from her, which may be reckoned about 35, the cup must now be about Two hundred and fifteen years old. The initials are those of Jeannot McKulloch. I left home

---

300. Footnote in the original Manuscript copy, identified with an ×. A matching × indicated where it was to be inserted in the narrative. The monument's foundation stone was laid on 15 November 1827, with James Thompson an integral part of the ceremonies. It was completed 8 September 1828, just one day before the Earl of Dalhousie left Canada. See also Part One: A "Brother Soldier…" – James Thompson and the Wolfe Legacy.
301. Thompson's silver cup was made by Tain silversmith Hugh Ross (c.1680–1732), probably between about 1700 and 1720. Made of heavy-gauge silver, the words "I MK – Tain, Ross-shire, 1637" ("I MK" would be shorthand for Jeannot McKulloch, Thompson's grandmother) are engraved above the girdle. Thompson's silver "thistle" cup is extremely rare, one of only three known examples. The cup was acquired in 1972 by the McCord Museum, Montreal.

in the year 1757, to volunteer with Fraser's Highlanders, and I forgot to take the cup along with me, but upon my applying for it after my coming to Canada, it was sent out to me by my oldest sister,[302] and I knew it again the very instant I saw it. In order not to break the family-rule, I have made it a point to take a drop of whiskey out of it every New Year's morning since it has been in my possession.

    Jeannot McKulloch, was born in 1637

    Her son, James Thomson 1672

(x) His son, James Thompson 1733

    His son, James Thompson 1784

(x) The letter "P" was introduced into the family name at the instance of my Father's Captain (Baillie) at sea in 1758, who considered it the more correct mode of spelling it, but none of his relations, in Scotland, have ever adopted it.[303]

Thistle cup. Crafted by Tain silversmith Hugh Ross between 1700 and 1720, this exquisite thistle cup was passed down in the Thompson family from James's grandmother, Jeannot McKulloch, the original owner. James Thompson maintained the family tradition of taking a "drop of whiskey out of it every New Year's morning." Pen and ink sketch scanned from the manuscript letter-book. (Photo by Earl John Chapman)

---

302. Name not known, but one of three sisters.
303. Footnote in the original Manuscript copy, identified with an x. A matching x indicated where it was to be inserted in the narrative. This footnote was added by James Jr. to clarify when and why the letter "P" was added to his father's surname.

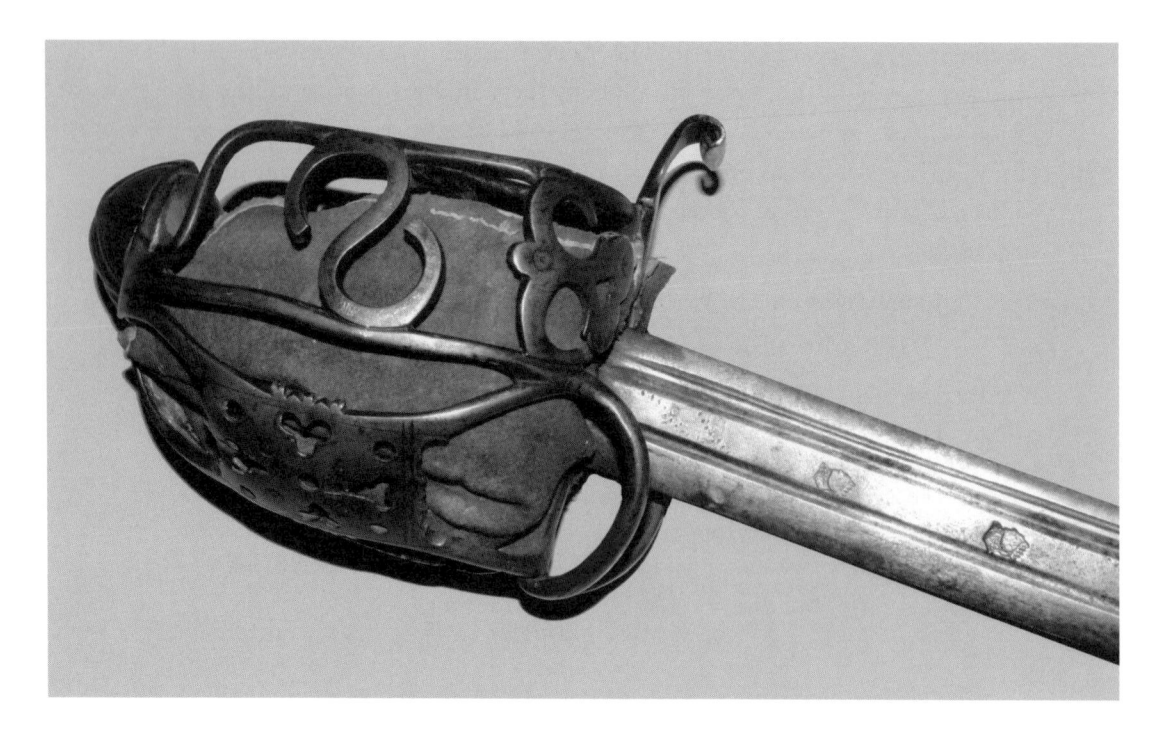

"**Whack went the Broadsword!**" So James Thompson described the pursuit of the French army at the battle on the Plains of Abraham (see Anecdote 23, page 188). Thompson's basket-hilted broadsword shown here is of unknown origin, the blade likely imported from Germany. Certain features of the ornate hilt (one being the reverse "S" figure imprint) suggest that it was made by Stirling hammersmiths. It is a sturdy, fighting man's weapon, and likely a family sword given to him when he volunteered for service in Fraser's Highlanders. It is certainly a cut above the inexpensive, patterned swords manufactured by London sword maker Nathaniel Jefferys which were used by the enlisted men of the Highland regiments during the Seven Years' War. The sword was passed down through the Thompson family in Quebec and later acquired by the Canadian War Museum. (Image detail, Editor's Collection)

(Facing page, lower)
Maison historique James Thompson. This photograph, taken in 2008, shows the combined dining and living room on the lower floor of the old Thompson house at the corner of rue Sainte-Ursule and ruette des Ursulines. Construction started in 1792 and was finally completed in late 1800 when Thompson had the windows glazed. However, it would appear that Thompson and his family was living in the partially completed house by 1798 or even earlier. The exterior stone work was completed on 3 August 1807 when Walter Stewart was paid for "rough casting the house in the manner as it is done in Scotland." Remaining in the family until June 1957, Maison historique James Thompson is now a popular "bed and breakfast" in the historic part of Quebec City. (Photo by Earl John Chapman)

The modern city. Viewed from the Basin, the modern city of Quebec is dominated by the Citadel. Built by British engineers between 1820 and 1831, the star-shaped fortifications were intended to secure the strategic heights of Cap Diamant against the Americans and to serve as a final refuge for the British garrison in the event of attack or rebellion. The preservation of much of the fortifications and defences of Quebec is due to the intervention of Lord Dufferin, Governor General of Canada 1872–78, who also established the Citadel as a vice-regal residence. The Citadel has been the home station of the Royal 22nd Regiment since 1920. (Photo by Earl John Chapman)

St. John Street Gate, 2009. The upper photograph shows the exterior façade of the St. John Street Gate. On 27 August 1830 Thompson's funeral procession would have passed this way on its journey to the St. John Street Cemetery. The lower photograph, taken from the top of the western rampart, looks towards the St. John Street Gate and its *guérite* or watchtower. The top portion of the rampart seen here, termed the parapet, was a mass of earth typically 15 to 20 feet thick. In Quebec's fortifications, this mass of earth was sandwiched between two masonry walls called revetments, thus forming a *revetted parapet*. Three gun platforms can be seen along with their embrasures – openings cut in the parapet through which the guns could be fired. In military terms, Quebec's fortifications had become obsolete by the mid-19th century – rifled artillery, more powerful and precise than smooth-bore cannon, had seen to that. Following the departure of the British in 1871, the walls of the *enceinte* were gradually abandoned and many sections demolished, including most of the traffic-restricting gates. Despite the earlier efforts of Governor General Dufferin to preserve and restore the fortifications, the old St. John Street Gate was finally demolished in 1897. However, carrying the romantic spirit of the Dufferin project into the 20th century, major restoration work was carried out by the Department of National Defence, culminating in the construction of a new St. John Gate in 1939, on the site of the one demolished in 1897. Completed the following year, it borrowed the pseudo-historical style of the St. Louis and Kent gates erected at the end of the preceding century. (Photos by Earl John Chapman)

PART THREE

BIOGRAPHICAL NOTES

The many people listed in these biographical notes, from governors general down to private soldiers, are those whom James Thompson encountered over his sixty-eight years of service to the Crown in North America. They are presented alphabetically and all officer entries are accorded their rank at the time of their *first* appearance in Thompson's anecdotes.

The 78th Regiment of Foot, commonly known as Fraser's Highlanders, was originally styled the 2nd Highland Battalion of Foot, and then entered into the order of battle as the 63rd Regiment of Foot. This number was short-lived as they were adjusted upwards to the 78th when fourteen second battalions of existing senior regiments in the British army were established as regiments in their own right. For easy reference and clarity in these biographies, we have used their final number designator, the 78th Foot, throughout.

If descendants of any of the officers or civilians listed herein have any additional information or corrections they wish to bring to our attention, they are strongly encouraged to contact the editors via the publisher so that their biographical data can be revised and updated for future editions.

Major General Jeffery Amherst (1717–97), *British army officer.*
Gazetted an ensign in the prestigious Guards in 1731, Jeffery Amherst's rise was swift due to the patronage of the Duke of Dorset and his lifelong friend and first commanding officer,

Major General Jeffery Amherst. A cautious and deliberate general, Amherst was a former aide to the captain general of the British army, Field Marshal Ligonier. He would eventually win the war in North America for the British, earning himself the title Lord Amherst of Montreal. (Private Collection)

General John Ligonier. He served in the War of the Austrian Succession on the staffs of Ligonier and the Duke of Cumberland and in 1756 became colonel of the 15th Foot. In 1758 he was sent to America as a major general to command the attack upon the crucial French stronghold of Louisbourg on Cape Breton Island. The capture of the French fortress gave Britain her first important victory in the war and the victorious Amherst, on hearing of the reversal of arms at Ticonderoga, marched across Massachusetts into New York colony to reinforce the unfortunate General James Abercromby.

The advanced cold weather precluded another attempt against the French on the Lake Champlain corridor, and Amherst's force, including the 78th Foot, went into winter quarters in upstate New York. Amherst soon replaced Abercromby as the commander-in-chief in North America and in the late summer of 1759 pushed northwards from Albany and took Ticonderoga and Crown Point after minimal resistance from the French. He then halted cautiously to consolidate his gains by building a massive fort at Crown Point. Unable to push on to Montreal and thereby relieve pressure on General JAMES WOLFE's army besieging Quebec, he dispatched Robert Rogers and a force of chosen men to penetrate into French territory and destroy the Abenaki village of St. Francis near present-day Drummondville, Quebec.

The next year, 1760, he led one of three forces against Montreal, the other two being JAMES MURRAY's force coming up-river from Quebec while Brigadier William Haviland pushed north from Crown Point. Launching from Oswego, where he had ordered Fort Ontario rebuilt, Amherst's force crossed Lake Ontario, descended the St. Lawrence River, captured Oswegatchie (La Galette) and besieged Fort Lévis on an island at the head of the Long Sault Rapids.

Amherst arrived at Montreal 6 September 1760, as did his other two armies, and accepted its surrender on 8 September 1760. He dispatched Rogers and some of his rangers westward to take possession of French forts on the Great Lakes. From his headquarters in New York, Amherst's next mission was to deal with a series of Indian uprisings and rebellions in the Carolinas and western Pennsylvania while simultaneously supplying regiments of his experienced "American Army" for the campaigns to wrest the West Indian sugar islands and the port of Havana from French and Spanish control.

The so-called Pontiac uprising of 1763–64 saw the western frontiers of Virginia and Pennsylvania go up in flames when Amherst failed to realize that the western Indians needed careful diplomatic handling, including the distribution of gifts and material. Most of the French forts ceded to the British in 1763 were captured and their tiny British garrisons butchered, the only exceptions being Fort Pitt and Fort Detroit. Amherst was recalled for his misreading of Indian affairs in late 1763 and he gladly handed over his responsibilities to Brigadier General Thomas Gage. He never returned to North America, despite being asked twice by King George III to reprise his role as C-in-C in North America. He agreed however to be C-in-C of forces in Britain and thus was responsible for the bloody suppression of the Gordon Riots. Amherst was created baron in 1776 and died a field marshal in 1797.

DCB; J.C. Long, *Lord Jeffery Amherst: A Soldier of the King* (New York, 1933); J.C. Webster, ed., *Journal of Jeffery Amherst. Recording the Military Career of General Amherst in America from 1758 to 1763* (Toronto, 1931); R. Whitworth, "Field Marshal Lord Amherst, a Military Enigma," *History Today,* IX (1959), 132–7.

Brigadier General Benedict Arnold (1741–1801), *merchant sea captain, entrepreneur, American and British army officer.*

Benedict Arnold Jr. was born on 14 January 1741 in the river town of Norwich, Connecticut, the elder of two surviving children of six born to Benedict Arnold, a cooper and merchant, and Hannah Waterman King. From 1752 to 1755 Arnold attended grammar school at nearby Canterbury, and after the deaths of his mother in 1759 and his father in 1761, the young Benedict was dependent on charitable cousins, who accepted him as an apprentice in the apothecary trade, then aided him in 1762 in establishing a business as a sea captain in the coastal town of New Haven. In 1766 he led the New Haven "Sons of Liberty" against a former crewman who had informed against him for smuggling.

At the outbreak of the Revolutionary War,

Arnold cooperated with Ethan Allen and his Green Mountain Boys from Vermont to capture the weakly defended Ticonderoga and its sister fort at Crown Point. When his wife died unexpectedly at age thirty, he returned to Boston and offered to command a force in the proposed attack on Canada under the command of Brigadier General RICHARD MONTGOMERY. In eleven weeks Arnold led more than a thousand men from Boston in a gruelling march up the Kennebec River, through the Maine wilderness, then down the Chaudière to the St Lawrence River opposite Quebec. He lost a third of his men to death, desertion and disease on the march of some 500 miles. The exhausted Americans, in rags and suffering from exposure, were offered shelter by sympathetic *Canadiens* before they joined Montgomery's force from Montreal.

Arnold and Montgomery's combined force was scarcely larger than the British garrison in Quebec under the command of Governor GUY CARLETON, who declined their hopeful summons to surrender. Facing more desertion from low morale, an outbreak of smallpox and dwindling supplies, Arnold and Montgomery were forced to mount a desperate night assault on New Year's Eve, 1775. Their independent attacks, mounted under the cover of a snowstorm, both failed. Montgomery was killed and Arnold was wounded in the left leg. From that point on, the siege lasted only until melting ice in the river allowed a British fleet with substantial reinforcements to arrive in early May 1776, forcing the Americans to retreat to Montreal.

Back in Philadelphia, the American Congress promoted Arnold a brigadier general for his services in Canada. With operations in the north stymied and the potential of British forces going over to the offensive, the recuperating Arnold worked feverishly throughout the summer to build a fleet of gunboats to oppose any British thrust southwards on Lake Champlain. Early in October 1776 Arnold's fleet was met

Brigadier General Benedict Arnold. This ¾-length mezzotint portrait entitled "Colonel Arnold – Who commanded the Provincial Troops sent against Quebec, through the Wilderness of Canada, and was Wounded in Storming that city, under General Montgomery" was published in 1776 by an artist who had never seen Arnold nor the city of Quebec, a fanciful version of which appears in the background. (LOC LC-USZ62-39570)

by a much larger British fleet at Valcour Island near present-day Plattsburgh. Outgunned and outmanoeuvred, Arnold withdrew his battered naval force to Crown Point, satisfied in the knowledge that the British had been contained in the north for 1776.

Congress promoted him major general but would not give him the seniority he desired, and thus, on this point of honour, Arnold submitted his resignation. Washington did not accept his resignation and sent him north for the Saratoga campaign of 1777, which ended with the capitulation of a British field army and France joining the war. On arrival, Arnold had pushed with his superior officer for an aggressive harassing campaign against the leading elements of Lieutenant General "Gentleman Johnny" Burgoyne's army. In the last of these engagements he sustained a severe leg wound and was evacuated to Albany, missing the final American victory over Burgoyne. His timid commander, Horatio Gates, took all the credit for defeating the British, a large factor in subsequently alienating the already disgruntled Arnold from the patriot cause.

A bitter Arnold was subsequently posted to Philadelphia as the military governor, a city recently under British occupation. He led an active social life and married Margaret (Peggy) Shippen (1760–1804) from a Loyalist family. When he was severely criticized for using his new position of power to line his own pockets and those of his friends, the exasperated Arnold secretly contacted British authorities about switching sides. For more than a year he supplied intelligence to the British and in late summer 1780, on request, he was given the key command of West Point on the Hudson River. He offered to hand the fort over to the British for a price but his plans were discovered and thwarted, Arnold escaping to the British forces. Given a minor command of Loyalist forces, Arnold's remaining exploits of the war were looked upon by both British and Loyalist society as somewhat repugnant and he and his wife were shunned as pariahs.

After the British surrender at Yorktown in October 1781, the Arnolds sailed for England, where he was paid more than £6,000 for his defection, including small pensions for his wife and children and military commissions for his sons. He would press the British government frequently for more financial compensation as the last twenty years of his life were marked by financial mishaps and an inability to gain the preferment he believed he deserved. He died at his residence in Gloucester Place, London, on 14 June 1801, his reputation ruined and his family impoverished. Though many Americans changed sides during the American Revolution, it is Arnold's name, unsurprisingly, that has become synonymous with treason for time immemorial.

DAB; DNB.

Lieutenant Thomas Aylwin (c. 1729–91), *British merchant, militia officer, justice of the peace.*

Thomas Aylwin was born in Romsey, Hampshire, England, and was probably one of the first merchants to establish himself at Quebec after its capture in 1760 (his name appears on a list of Protestant "house keepers" contained in a certificate given by General JAMES MURRAY in 1764). Aylwin specialized in the retail sale of imported products including dry goods, foodstuffs, wine, hardware, stationery and other merchandise and pursued his commercial activities at Quebec until 1769, when he seems to have removed to Massachusetts for about six years. In 1771 he married Lucy Cushing of Boston and he returned to Quebec at the beginning of the American Revolution, setting up business on St. John Street (rue Saint-Jean). During the siege of Quebec 1775–76, he served as a lieutenant of militia under Colonel Henry Caldwell.

Along with his activities as an entrepreneur, Aylwin also held office as justice of the peace from 1765 until his departure for Massachusetts. Reappointed in 1785, he retained the post until his death. By 1764 he was an active member of the Quebec grand jury chaired by merchant James Johnston which opposed Murray's administration. A member of the Quebec grand jury again in 1787, Aylwin took the government of the day to task for the taxation of public buildings, poor road maintenance, and the lack of assistance for the poor and those affected by famine.

Aylwin was an active Freemason, well known to James Thompson. In 1769, Aylwin was treasurer of the Provincial Grand Lodge and a member of the committee set up to obtain a Grand Lodge seal. In October 1775 he undertook to be secretary to St Andrew's Lodge, No. 2, at Quebec and the following year became its master, again for a one-year period. Deputy provincial grand master by the end of 1776, he retained this post until at least 1781 (he shows up in this post in the *Quebec Almanac* for 1780); as such he signed the commissions authorizing the creation of St. Peter's Lodge, No. 4, Quebec, at Montreal, and Unity Lodge, No. 13, Quebec, at Sorel. Thomas Aylwin died in April 1791 leaving his wife, who survived him by only a month, and three sons who were still minors.

DCB; Quebec Almanac; "List of Protestant House Keepers in Quebec," quoted in A.G. Doughty & N.E. Dionne, *Quebec Under Two Flags: A Brief History of the City...* (Quebec, 1903), 188–91.

Surgeon Major Philippe-Louis-François Badelard (1728–1802), *French army officer and surgeon, military and civilian doctor under the British regime.*

Philippe-Louis-François was born on 25 May 1728 in France and early in his career practised medicine and surgery in a hospital at Metz. Badelard came to North America as the surgeon major to the régiment de Berry and was present at the battle of the Plains of Abraham, despite his unit being stationed at Île aux Noix south of Montreal. During the French retreat he encountered JOHN FRASER, a wounded Highlander, and after dressing Fraser's wound, surrendered to his patient, turning over his weapons, which included a small, double-barrelled pistol, handsomely mounted in silver, with the initials "P.B." on the butt. After the war Badelard took up residence in Quebec and was appointed surgeon to the Canadian militia. In this capacity he took part in the defence of Quebec against American forces during the invasion of Canada.

On 15 May 1776 he was officially commissioned as surgeon to the Quebec garrison (in 1795 he shows up as surgeon's mate, under Surgeon James Fisher). In addition to his army duties, Badelard had a sizeable civilian practice and resided on St. Louis Street (rue Saint-Louis) for many years, close to John Fraser and James Thompson. In the parish census taken in 1792 he was simply enumerated as "Louis Bedelard, 30 St. Louis Street, Chirurgien," the household comprising three parishioners. Badelard was a "person of gentlemanly aspect" and constantly wore a sword, as was customary with the *bourgeoisie de Paris*. Although he was one of the most respected specialists of the Francophone medical community, Badelard was also well known for his argumentative nature and sometimes violent behaviour. His wife left him about 1770 and when he died thirty-two years later on 7 February 1802 in Quebec, the parish priest of Notre-Dame-de-l'Annonciation at L'Ancienne-Lorette tried to prevent his burial in the parish cemetery.

JTC; *DCB;* J.-M. Lemoine, *Maple Leaves* (Quebec, 1894); Parish census, 1792, BAnQ.

Captain Charles Baillie, yr of Rosehall (c.1725–58), *British army officer.*

Charles Baillie was born in Ross and Cromarty, the eldest of the six sons of William Baillie of Rosehall, the factor to Ross of Balnagowan. He was probably schooled in the Royal Burgh of Tain, the nearest town, and the editors believe it is here that he first met James Thompson and formed a close friendship. Charles married Janet Mackay, granddaughter of the 3rd Lord Reay and widow of Colin Campbell of Glenure, infamously murdered by a Stewart of Ardshiel in 1752. His military career started as a second lieutenant in the 21st Foot and he transferred to SIMON FRASER's newly-raised 78th Foot in 1757 to become one of its original company commanders. Gazetted the battalion's grenadier captain on 10 January 1757, he encouraged his friend James Thompson to join Fraser's Highlanders. Baillie promised to try to secure Thompson a commission but was unfortunately killed the following year at the Louisbourg landings, 8 June 1758.

CBs; BALs; SBs; Col. David Stewart, *Sketches of the Character, Manners and Present State of the Highlanders of Scotland, with Details of the Military Service of the Highland Regiments*, 2 vols. (Edinburgh, 1822), II, 20–1 (hereafter, Stewart *Sketches*); J.C. Webster, ed., *Journal of Jeffery Amherst. Recording the Military Career of General Amherst in America from 1758 to 1763* (Toronto, 1931); NA WO 64/12.

Captain Michel "José" Blais (1709–83), *landowner and co-seigneur, militia captain (French regime).*

Born in 1709, Michel Blais was the head of the Blais family, consisting of his wife, Marie-Françoise (née Lizot), and his aging mother, Françoise (née Baudoin). Michel's father, Pierre, had died in 1733. While the original Blais farm was on the Île d'Orléans, Michel and his brother Joseph ran highly successful farms in nearby Saint-Pierre. Michel had obtained a captain's commission in the militia under the French regime, but he lost this commission when the British abolished the Canadian militia in 1764. Thompson became very friendly with Michel and this friendship continued until Michel's death in 1783.

During the American Revolutionary War, the Blais family was cruelly treated by the Americans and Michel's property was plundered and burnt, "the only persons in that parish who have been plundered by both Bostonians and rebel Canadians." In spite of his extensive property holdings, Michel believed that he was entitled to some compensation for the losses he had suffered and he elicited the support of Thompson, then in a civilian position of authority. They decided to make a joint application for land, but Michel died before it was approved. In 1784 Thompson re-applied for the land, this time with Michel's eldest son (also named Michel). This application was processed through FREDERICK HALDIMAND and both Thompson and Blais were awarded joint ownership of a parcel of waste-land in the township of Armagh.

DCB; JTC.

Captain Ralph Henry Bruyères (c. 1765–1814), *British army officer.*

Ralph Henry Bruyères was born in Montreal, the son of Ensign John Dèsbruyères of the 15th Foot. His father, John, was a Huguenot and a gentleman volunteer, as was James Thompson, and had been commissioned 27 July 1759 before the battle of the Plains of Abraham. Because of his language skills in reading and writing French, the father John was named secretary in charge of vetting all prisoners' letters and captured enemy documents, then served post-war as the secretary to the governor of Trois-Rivières, Colonel Ralph Burton. John then accompanied Burton when he was transferred to the governorship of Montreal and Ralph, named for his father's patron, was born in 1765.

Raised in a bilingual environment, Ralph was sent to England on his acceptance as a cadet into the Royal Military Academy at Woolwich and graduated in 1781 as a second lieutenant in the Engineers (22 December 1781). He returned to Quebec to work as a supernumerary engineer. A month before being promoted first lieutenant (24 May 1790), Ralph married Janet Dunbar on 16 April 1790, the daughter of Captain William Dunbar. By 1793 he had returned to Europe and was campaigning in Flanders. He was promoted captain lieutenant on 31 December 1795 and, while fighting in the Netherlands, he was promoted to the rank of captain (1 July 1799).

He was ordered back to Canada the same year and arrived for duty at Montreal in July 1800, but was soon re-assigned down-river to Quebec. In the spring of 1802 Bruyères was dispatched on a tour of inspection to Upper Canada by the senior engineer in the Canadas,

Colonel GOTHER MANN. His "Report of the state of the public works and buildings at the several military posts in Upper Canada" presented many thoughtful recommendations for remedial action, which were not acted on due to insufficient funds.

On his promotion to lieutenant colonel on 1 July 1806, Bruyères then became the commanding engineer for Upper and Lower Canada, his superior, Major General Mann, having left for England in 1804. Like Mann, he was frustrated by a lack of funds, but by 1807 the deterioration in Anglo-American relations convinced him that at least the first phase of Mann's plan for Quebec, a line of four mutually supporting Martello towers, be placed across the Buttes-à-Neveu, a ridgeline that dominated the walls of the fortified city from the west and had been used advantageously by the French during their 1760 siege.

The four towers were completed early in 1812 just before the outbreak of war with the United States, a conflict which forced Bruyères to focus on strengthening the frontier posts as quickly as possible, especially Kingston, the principal shipyard and dockyard for Lake Ontario. By January 1813 he suggested to General Prevost, the British commander-in-chief in North America, that British forces should conduct a pre-emptive attack on the rival American base at Sackets Harbor, New York, to buy time.

On 1 March 1813 Bruyères was granted the acting rank of colonel in Upper Canada but fell seriously ill there in the autumn and was evacuated to Quebec. On the news that British forces had captured the American fort at Niagara in December 1813 by a *coup de main*, he felt compelled to travel back to that frontier to supervise the repairs to the damaged fort. Not fully recovered, Bruyères quickly succumbed to his previous complaint and was evacuated back to Quebec, where he died on 15 May 1814. His obituary in the *Quebec Mercury* described him as a meritorious officer "fallen victim to professional zeal" and a "good citizen of Quebec."

BALs; *DCB;* W.C.H. Wood, *Select British documents of the Canadian War of 1812*, vol.2. (Champlain Society Digital Collection, 1920); *Quebec Mercury*, 17 May 1814; R.F. Edwards, *Roll of Officers of the Corps of Royal Engineers from 1660 to 1898...* (Chatham, 1898); André Charbonneau et al., *Quebec The Fortified City: From the 17th to the 19th Century* (Parks Canada, 1982); Whitworth Porter et al., *History of the Corps of Royal Engineers* (Chatham, 1889).

Captain Alexander Cameron, 4th of Dungallon (c. 1730–59), *British army officer.*
A former Jacobite officer whose father, Alexander (3rd Dungallon), had been a major in Cameron of Lochiel's regiment and standard bearer to the Prince. Alexander Jr. served as an ensign in his father's regiment. In 1758 he was selected to command one of three newly-authorized additional companies that joined the 78th Foot while in Connecticut winter quarters April 1758, and he was chosen by Colonel SIMON FRASER to command a 100-man light infantry company in Halifax for the 1758 Louisbourg expedition. His command, drawn from the best and most fit men of the three additional companies left at Halifax, was temporarily assigned to Major George Scott's Provisional Light Infantry Battalion. His company was kept together for the march across Massachusetts later that year and Cameron was one of four field officers initially assigned to the garrison of Fort Stanwix during the winter of 1758–59.

He features in one of Thompson's anecdotes concerning the champion sword contest that took place at Schenectady the same winter. He died the following year of a fever on 3 September 1759, ten days before the battle of the Plains of Abraham. He was buried at the Lévy camp but his body was later removed and re-interred at Quebec, a monument to his memory erected by JOHN NAIRNE and MALCOLM FRASER, brother officers who had served with him in the 78th Foot's light infantry company.

Cameron's last will and testament bequeathed his "whole estate heritable and movable to Allan, brother of John Cameron, 3rd of Glendessary." Young Lieutenant Donald Cameron, a cousin with the newly-arrived 14th Additional Company commanded by ALEXANDER FRASER of Culduthel wrote to his brother Ewan back in Scotland that he arrived just in time for his funeral: "I came time Enouch to see him Interd and that was all. Hew Cameron who is now Capt took care of all his things and saw every thing Roped but his Silver hulted Sword and Goold Wach [sic, gold watch] and Ring. I have his Ring at Present till such time as Glendesry calls for it but I hop I will get from Glendeseray which if I do I will send it home to you."

CBs; BALs; JTC; SBs; Somerled Macmillan, *Bygone Lochaber: Historical & Traditional* (Glasgow, 1971, privately printed), 137; Stewart, *Sketches*, II, 20–1.

Colonel Sir Guy Carleton, later first Baron Dorchester (1724–1808), *British army officer, colonial governor.*

Guy Carleton was born on 3 September 1724 at Strabane, Ireland, the third son of Christopher Carleton and his wife, Catherine, daughter of Henry Ball. Carleton was commissioned ensign in the 25th Foot (Rothes's) on 21 May 1742. He purchased a lieutenancy in the prestigious 1st Foot Guards in 1745 and was promoted captain 22 July 1751. By 1757 he had become lieutenant colonel and he took command of the newly raised 72nd Foot in 1758. On 30 December 1758 he was made a "colonel in America," a brevet rank granted to British field officers to ensure they could command provincial officers of the same rank.

He served as JAMES WOLFE's deputy quartermaster general during the siege of Quebec and was wounded during the battle of the Plains of Abraham while at the head of the Louisbourg Grenadiers. He returned to England to recover and took part in other Seven Years' War campaigns, including the amphibious assault on Belle-Isle off the coast of France in April 1761 and the siege of Havana in 1762. Carleton suffered life-threatening wounds in both campaigns and was promoted colonel on 19 February 1762.

In 1766 he was promoted "brigadier in North America" and was appointed lieutenant governor in Quebec after JAMES MURRAY's recall. When Murray did not return, he assumed the titles of captain general and governor-in-chief on 12 April 1768. Carleton's term of office lasted ten years until his departure 27 June 1778. During this period he successfully defended Quebec from the American invasion of 1775–76. Carleton resigned his military post

Sir Guy Carleton, later first Baron Dorchester. Wolfe's right hand man during the siege of Quebec in 1759, Carleton was wounded at the head of the Louisbourg Grenadiers on the Plains of Abraham. He subsequently did two tours as Governor of British North America. Unknown artist. Copied by Mabel B. Messer in 1923. (LAC A/N 1997-8-1)

on 27 June 1778 after continual disagreements with Lord Germain over the conduct of the war and his governance style and left Canada a month later. However, on 2 March 1782 he received the posting of commander-in-chief in North America and returned to supervise the orderly withdrawal of British forces and Loyalists from the former Thirteen Colonies. On 9 July 1796 Carleton returned once more to England, where his reward was an annual pension of £1,000 for life.

He was soon asked to return and implement a centralized system of government for the surviving colonies (Quebec, New Brunswick and Nova Scotia), but was initially reluctant until offered a peerage and the office of commander-in-chief, which sealed the deal. During this second tenure, the Constitutional Act of 1791 split Quebec into Upper and Lower Canada and each was assigned a lieutenant governor reporting to Carleton. When mildly rebuked in 1794 by the Duke of Portland for criticizing American policy in the west, Dorchester asked in September of the same year to be relieved of his governorship. Although his request was granted, it was to be two more years before his successor, Lieutenant General Robert Prescott, arrived to take over. Lord Dorchester returned to England and retired to his country estates. Carleton died suddenly on 10 November 1808, aged eighty-four.

DNB; DCB; JTC; A.G. Bradley, *Sir Guy Carleton* (Toronto, 1907).

Colonel James Pattison Cockburn (1779–1847), *British army officer, watercolourist.*
James Pattison was the son of Colonel John Cockburn and Mary Cockburn, daughter of Colonel Sir James Cockburn (a veteran of the Plains of Abraham and Sillery, like Thompson), born on 18 March 1779 in New York City at the height of the American Revolution. He came from a long family tradition of soldiering, and thus, at the tender age of fourteen, entered the Royal Military Academy at Woolwich as a gentleman cadet. There, like many other future artillery and engineer officers, he flourished under the tutelage of the famous Paul Sandby, learning all aspects of topography and the intricacies of landscape painting and survey.

Cockburn was commissioned in the Royal Regiment of Artillery as a lieutenant and participated in the taking of Cape Colony in September 1795 and in an expedition against Manila via India in 1798. By 1803 he was back in England and on 1 June 1806 was promoted to the rank of captain. His company was first stationed at Colchester, and then in September 1807 was shipped over to Denmark to participate in the siege of Copenhagen. Succumbing to sickness, he returned to Norwich to recuperate from September 1807 until late November 1808. He was back on active service at the siege of Antwerp by August 1809, where he distinguished himself in conducting the bomb flotilla and thus was given the reward and honour of negotiating the terms of surrender.

It was during his time in East Anglia that Cockburn, an accomplished artist, first began to exhibit watercolours he painted in his spare time, scenes that included his tours to Cape Colony and Bengal. Cockburn was promoted to brevet major in June 1814 and posted to Colchester in December of the same year, remaining in that garrison for the next two years. With the Napoleonic Wars over, Cockburn visited the Continent frequently to pursue his artistic bent, producing a wealth of landscapes and topographical views from his travels through the Italian and Swiss Alps.

His first posting to Canada was brief, his artillery company arriving in November 1822 and departing by August the following year. On his return to Woolwich, he was promoted major, 29 July 1825, and at the same time lieutenant colonel "in the army." The following year he was posted back to Canada, this time entrusted with the command of all Royal Artillery in both Upper and Lower Canada. Most of his many Canadian watercolours were made during this second posting, during which he made several inspection tours of Ontario and Quebec. Cockburn's streetscapes of Quebec City and Montreal are particularly valuable records of the architecture and daily life characteristic of these cities. Several of his Canadian scenes were published as engravings.

From 1826 to 1832 he was a frequent guest and visitor at Lord Dalhousie's dinner parties, which featured the old Highlander James Thompson. In 1831 Cockburn brought out anonymously a small tour book of the town of Quebec with seven plates entitled *Quebec and its Environs: Being a Picturesque Guide to a Stranger* (Quebec, 1831). In it Cockburn gave Thompson one of the most glowing tributes when he observed that "As a soldier he was intrepid; as a servant of the King he was strictly faithful." When Cockburn returned to England with his family in 1832, he settled in Woolwich, where he owned a house, and on 10 October 1838 he became the director of the Royal Laboratory of the Royal Arsenal. He held that post until retiring in November 1846 with the rank of major general. He died the following year at his residence in Woolwich, 18 March 1847.

BALs; DCB.

Marie-Anne Aubert de Courserac (c. 1715–62), *wife of Governor de Drucour.*
Madame de Drucour was the daughter of Charles Aubert, Seigneur de Courserac, and Dame Anne-Marie de Longueville. She was the second wife of the Governor of Louisburg, AUGUSTIN DE BOSCHENRY DE DRUCOUR. The Drucours arrived at Louisbourg on 15 August 1754. A campfire tale, or perhaps a piece of propaganda, suggests that Madame de Drucour attempted to escape the 1758 siege of Louisbourg on 13 June in the frigate *Echo*

along with other high officials. However, the *Echo* was intercepted by British warships, and if Madame de Drucour was on board, she was returned to her husband and the matter kept confidential.

Another unsubstantiated story is that Madame de Drucour helped to fire three guns every day from the ramparts against the British siege works to encourage the French garrison and their families. During the siege, AMHERST paid her compliments at parleys by sending gifts of food, and after the capitulation Admiral Boscawen granted every favour she asked with regard to her repatriation to France. The Drucours sailed from Louisbourg for France on 15 August 1758, exactly four years after their arrival. Impoverished by their posting to Louisbourg, the Drucours were forced to live on the charity of their relations. Her husband died in 1762, and she was dead two months later.

DCB; JTC; *Armorial général de France,* VI; M. Vergé-Franceschi, *Les Officiers généraux de la marine royale: 1715–1774...,* III (Paris, 1990).

Sir James Henry Craig (1748–1812), *British army officer, colonial administrator.*
James Henry Craig was born in 1748 at Gibraltar, son of Hew Craig, a judge of the civil and military courts in the British fortress. In 1763, at age fifteen, he was commissioned an ensign by purchase in the 30th Foot (1 June 1763). He purchased his lieutenancy 19 July 1769 in the 30th Foot, then transferred to the 47th Foot on purchasing a captaincy 14 March 1771. He went with his regiment to North America to fight the American rebels and was badly wounded at the Battle of Bunker Hill (Breed's Hill), but refused to leave his regiment and participated in the defence of Quebec in 1776. During the 1777 campaign he fought at Fort Ticonderoga, Hubbardton and Freeman's Farm as a member of General John Burgoyne's army and was wounded twice in action. Burgoyne, who held

Sir James Henry Craig. A professional soldier of the Revolutionary and Napoleonic Wars, the sickly Craig spent most of his time in bed as the governor of British North America. Reproduction of a painting by Dutch artist Gerrit Schipper. (LAC A/N 1990-317-1)

him in high regard, recommended him for the rank of a major in the new-raising 82nd Regiment of Foot (Prince of Wales's Volunteers) in recognition of his merit and experience. From 1778 to 1781 Craig served with the 82nd Foot, which garrisoned Halifax in Nova Scotia and fought at Penobscot, Maine, and later in North Carolina.

Having attained the rank of lieutenant colonel on 31 December 1781, Craig transferred to the lieutenant colonelcy of the 16th Foot on 30 June 1783 and was promoted brevet colonel in 1790. His next significant post was that of adjutant general to the Duke of York's army in the Netherlands in 1794, and he was promoted major general in 1794. In 1795 he collaborated with Vice Admiral Viscount Keith and Major General Alured Clarke in operations against the Dutch in the Cape Colony (South Africa) and after a successful campaign remained as its first governor until 1797. He then went to Bengal and Madras in India, where he actively campaigned with Sir Arthur Wellesley, the future Duke of Wellington, returning to England in January 1801. Promoted to lieutenant general, he served for the next three years as the commander of the Eastern District.

In 1805, despite his poor health, the British government sent Craig to command in Italy, but he was forced the following year to return to England, suffering from chronic dropsy. Seemingly recovered the following year but not keen to endure the rigours of active service, again he accepted the post of Governor-in-Chief of British North America in 1807, succeeding Robert Shore Milnes. On his arrival in October 1807, despite being seriously ill from his passage, Craig devoted much energy and money to rebuilding fortifications in the province, particularly at Quebec. A better soldier than politician, he antagonized the French-Canadian members of the Assembly. Plagued with recurring bouts of ill heath, Craig from 1810 onwards repeatedly asked British authorities in London to be replaced. Finally, in June 1811, feeling himself fading fast, he sailed for England without authorization. Dying as he reached London, he passed away there 12 January 1812.

BALs; *DCB;* Robert Christie, *Memoirs of the Administration of the Colonial Government of Lower-Canada, by Sir James Henry Craig, and Sir George Prevost; from the year 1807 until the year 1815...* (Quebec, 1818).

Deputy Commissary General John Craigie (c. 1757–1813), *British commissary officer.*

Born in Scotland, John Craigie first came to Quebec in 1781 as deputy commissary general for the British army. He was appointed commissary general in 1784, replacing Nathaniel

Day and the following year became private secretary to Lieutenant Governor HENRY HOPE. He married Susannah Coffin in 1792. Along with other commercial business concerns, Craigie pursued a political career, representing the riding of Buckingham in the Legislative Assembly of Lower Canada from 1796 to 1804. By 1792 he was living on St. Anne Street (rue Sainte-Anne) in the most fashionable quarter of Upper Town, and in 1804 he purchased a larger house on St. Louis Street (rue Saint-Louis). In 1801 he was named to the Executive Council but was dismissed in 1808 as commissary general for misappropriation of funds. Craigie retained his seat however on the Executive Council and died in Quebec City in 1813 at fifty-six years.

DCB.

François-Joseph Cugnet (1720–89), *lawyer under the French regime, spy, seigneur, judge, attorney general, chief road commissioner (grand voyer)*.
Referred to simply as "Cuznet" in James Thompson's anecdotes, François-Joseph Cugnet was born at Quebec on 26 June 1720, eldest son of François-Étienne Cugnet and Louise-Madeleine Dusautoy. He came from a long line of Parisian lawyers and trained under Attorney General Louis-Guillaume Verrier at Quebec from 1739 to 1741. He worked as a scrivener in the French Caribbean for several years then reappeared in Quebec in 1752 looking for work. Refused a commission as an assessor to the *Conseil supérieur*, a job his brother had held, he worked as a scrivener in the head office of the *Domaine d'Occident* from 1755 to 1758 at Quebec. On 14 February 1757, at the age of thirty-six, Cugnet married Marie-Josephte de Lafontaine de Belcour, one of the heirs of the Bissot estate at Notre-Dame in Quebec. At some point during the siege of Quebec, 1759, he came under suspicion of espionage and by 1760 was placed under guard by orders of Major General François de Lévis on board the frigate *Atalante*. Thompson claims that when the British navy captured the ship after a running gun battle, they found Cugnet on board the ship with another prisoner, both prepared for hanging from the yardarm as spies.

In January 1760, possibly as a reward for his espionage services, Governor JAMES MURRAY appointed Cugnet judge for the parishes of Charlesbourg, Beauport and Petite-Rivière. On 2 November 1760 he became attorney general for the North Shore in the District of Quebec before becoming the chief road commissioner for the district on 20 November 1765, an office he retained for three years. On 24 February 1768 Cugnet was awarded the post of French translator and French secretary to Governor GUY CARLETON and the Council of Quebec. Carleton had Cugnet draw up an abstract of the laws during the French regime, which was published in four volumes.

Cugnet took part in the controversy over the framing of the Quebec Act and was the object

François-Joseph Cugnet. A spy for the British cause during the Seven Years' War, he was saved from execution by the timely intervention of the Royal Navy. Unknown artist. (BAnQ P266, S4, P34)

of a verbal attack by Francis Maseres (*Mémoire à la défence d'un plan de l'acte de parlement … contre les objections de M. François Joseph Cugnet*, London, 1773). One of the last favours Cugnet was able to obtain from Carleton before he was replaced by Sir FREDERICK HALDIMAND was a commission as a lawyer; he received it on 1 May 1777 at the same time as his son, Jacques-François, who was less than twenty years of age. It constituted official recognition of the title of "lawyer in the parlement" that Cugnet had assumed six years earlier.

After a busy and public life, Cugnet died at Quebec on 16 November 1789. His funeral was held in the Church of Notre-Dame in Quebec, where he had been both baptized and married. In keeping with custom, Cugnet as the seigneur of Saint-Étienne, received the honour of being buried under his pew on 18 November 1789.

DCB; JTC; *Quebec History Encyclopedia.*

James Cuthbert of Berthier (c. 1719–98),
British army officer, seigneur, justice of the peace, merchant, legislative councillor.
James Cuthbert was born c. 1719 at Farness in Sutherland, Scotland, the son of Alexander and Beatrix Cuthbert. He began his military career in the Royal Navy but soon switched to the army, becoming a captain commanding an independent company by October 1760 which was then joined with other companies to form the 101st Foot. In December 1762 he exchanged into the 15th Foot and, at the conclusion of the war, became a member of General JAMES MURRAY's staff. In 1765 he left the army and by the following year had been appointed to the Council of Quebec (14 June 1766) and made a justice of the peace.

On 7 March 1765 Cuthbert bought the seigneury of Berthier, where he had a manor house built, and between 1770 and 1781 he acquired the seigneury of Du Sablé, known as Nouvelle-York, and part of Lanoraie, Dautré and Maskinongé seigneuries. In June 1776 the Americans burned down his manor house and sent him as a prisoner to Albany, New York. After his release, he spent some time in England in 1777, then returned to rebuild his manor house at Berthier on a more imposing scale. His return also saw him take his seat on the Legislative Council set up by the Quebec Act, to which he had been appointed in 1775.

A thoroughly obnoxious and arrogant individual who alienated most people he came into contact with, Cuthbert clashed often with Governor FREDERICK HALDIMAND. Subsequently, when Cuthbert spent the years 1781 to 1784 in England on business, Haldimand complained of his prolonged absence and in 1786 Cuthbert was arbitrarily barred from the Council and dismissed from his post as justice of the peace without explanation. From 1786 onwards Cuthbert made repeated protests to the authorities against his exclusion and dismissal as well as vainly seeking compensation for the alleged

James Cuthbert of Berthier, c. 1820. A retired British officer turned seigneur, Cuthbert rankled all he met, including Governor Haldimand. After the Revolutionary War, Thompson was assigned to investigate the alleged damage Cuthbert's estates had sustained at the hands of American rebels and methodically determined his claims were highly exaggerated. Unknown artist. (BAnQ P560, S2, D1, P212)

damages his seigniorial lands had suffered during the American Revolution. James Thompson was instrumental in determining the exact scope of damages on behalf of the British government, the majority of which he determined to be inflated or nonexistent.

In 1792 Cuthbert ran as a candidate for the House of Assembly and was defeated in the county of Warwick, where the vast majority of voters were his own *censitaires*. The argumentative Scot disputed the election results, not only with the authorities in the colony but with the Colonial Office in London, but without success. Enraged, he returned to England in 1795 in a final effort to obtain satisfaction for his disallowed war damages and political claims, as well as to lobby for a colonelcy in the militia and a baronetcy in recognition of his services during the American Revolution. He was unsuccessful on all counts and given the cold shoulder by all. After his sudden death at Berthier in September 1798, his sons divided his landed property among themselves.

BALs; *DCB*; JTC; F.-J. Audet, "James Cuthbert de Berthier et sa famille; notes généalogiques et biographiques," *Transactions, Royal Society of Canada*, Ser. III (1935); D.R. McCord, "An Historic Canadian family, the Cuthberts of Berthier," *Dominion Illustrated*, VII (Montreal, 1891), 110–12, 123–25.

Lieutenant François Dambourgès (1742–98), *entrepreneur, militia officer, politician*.
François Dambourgès was born in Salies, Béarn, a province of France, in 1742 and was educated at Bayonne. He emigrated to Canada in 1763 and settled in the parish of Saint-Thomas in Montmagny, Quebec, where he set himself up in business. During the American siege of Quebec in 1775–76 he helped defend the town as a lieutenant in the *Canadien* militia and, for his gallantry, was granted a lieutenancy in the 1st Battalion of the Royal Highland Emigrants. Taken prisoner in 1777, he retired on half-pay in 1784. He was subsequently named a justice

Lieutenant François Dambourgès. A hero of the siege of Quebec, this French-born militia officer received a lieutenancy in the Royal Highland Emigrants (84th Foot) as a reward for his gallantry in repulsing Arnold's assault on the Lower Town. Unknown artist. (BAnQ P1000, S4, D83, PD7)

of the peace and served again in the local militia, becoming colonel in 1790. In 1792 he was elected to the 1st Parliament of Lower Canada as the member for Devon. In 1795 Dambourgès became a captain in the Royal Canadian Volunteer Regiment and moved to Montreal. He died there of pleurisy on 13 December 1798.

BALs; JTC; Francis-Joseph Audet, *Les Députés au premier Parlement du Bas-Canada* (1792–1796), 85–94.

Private Davis (dates unknown), *British army soldier, spy*.
According to James Thompson, Davis (first name unknown) was a former grenadier soldier in the British army who had been taken prisoner by the French early during the Quebec campaign. When the Royal Navy returned to Quebec in the spring of 1760, they found Davis tied up on board the grounded French frigate *Atalante* (with FRANÇOIS-JOSEPH CUGNET)

prepared to be to be hanged from the yardarm as a spy. Davis had given "some kind of information" to the British and after the war he had been rewarded for his services, receiving a pension of "twenty-five pounds a year ... liv'd a long time in the enjoyment of it" according to Thompson (Anecdote 24).

In his journal, John Knox claims Davis was actually a boy who had been taken captive by the Indians on the "back settlements of New England" and afterwards had been sold to the French. When Quebec fell, Davis offered his services to the governor and, as he was fluently bilingual, proved a useful informant. This version of Davis's antecedents is more plausible than that offered by Thompson.

Again, according to Knox, in late April 1760 Davis was sent down-river in anticipation of the arrival of the British fleet but was taken prisoner by the French and accused of spying. Knox adds that the enterprising Davis was cleared, released and "came back to us," providing the British with details on French losses at the battle of Sillery, as well as French plans to storm the garrison. Davis also told the British that every man fit to bear arms had joined M. de Lévis except for the citizens of Quebec. So, Knox's recollections seem to corroborate some elements of Thompson's memories. The one inconsistency is that Davis at the time of his pending execution was a civilian and not a soldier, as Thompson claims. Davis, however, may have become a grenadier after the fact, and therefore was remembered by Thompson in his dotage as a soldier *vice* a captured settler.

JTC; A.G. Doughty, ed., *An Historical Journal of the Campaigns in North America for the Years 1757, 1758, 1759, and 1760, by Captain John Knox*, 3 vols (Toronto, 1914), II, 441–3 (hereafter Knox, *Journal*).

Governor Augustin de Boschenry de Drucour (1703–62), *French naval officer, governor of Île Royale.*

Augustin de Boschenry was baptized 27 March 1703 in Drucourt, France, son of Jean-Louis de Boschenry, Baron de Drucourt, and Marie-Louise Godard. He entered the French navy as a sixteen-year-old midshipman in 1719 and had risen to the rank of captain by 1751. In the late 1740s he was appointed commandant of the *"gardes du pavillon amiral"* at Brest. After several years in this post he was offered the governorship of Île Royale (Cape Breton) but declined the office because of his lack of wealth and the expenses he would invariably incur in such an overseas appointment. However, he was persuaded to change his mind and appointed governor effective 1 February 1754, arriving in Louisbourg on 15 August 1754 accompanied by his second wife, Marie-Anne Aubert de Courserac.

Drucour was an adequate administrator, despite problems resulting from insufficient funds, ill-disciplined troops and infrequent supplies and he endeavoured to the best of his abilities to carry out his instructions to prepare the town for the coming war. In 1758 Louisbourg was besieged by a joint naval and military expedition under the commands of Major General Jeffery Amherst and Admiral Edward Boscawen. Drucour's instructions "to resist and postpone our end as long as possible" were followed and to that extent he was relatively successful.

On 26 July 1758 Drucour accepted the British terms of surrender and his garrison marched out as prisoners denied the honours of war. Personally, Drucour received "all the honors which a person of his rank deserved" and he and his wife sailed for France on 15 August exactly four years after the day of their arrival. Drucour's health had suffered at Louisbourg, and he had been obliged to borrow heavily to maintain himself in office. Having lost nearly all his possessions in the siege, he and his wife were destitute on their return home. He returned to the naval service briefly in 1759 and then retired to Le Havre with his wife, where they existed on the charity of his brother. He died on 28 August 1762, too soon to receive the war pension he richly deserved. Mme Drucour died two months later.

DCB.

Thomas Dunn (1729–1818), *businessman, seigneur, office holder, politician, judge, colonial administrator.*

Thomas Dunn was born in Durham, England, in 1729 and nothing is known about his early life before he arrived in Canada. One of the first entrepreneurs to set up in Quebec after the conquest, he quickly became one of the most powerful men in the colony. First he obtained the trading lease to the king's posts with his partners, John Gray and William Grant, ensuring them a monopoly of the fur trade and the fisheries throughout the crown's domain. Their immense territory of operations stretched from the eastern limits of the seigneury of La Malbaie to Sept-Îles.

When civil government was instituted in August 1764, Dunn obtained a commission as justice of the peace for the districts of Quebec and Montreal, an office he retained until 1815. Eventually, Dunn saw his judicial mandate extended to all the districts of Lower Canada, including Gaspé. He also became a member of the Quebec Council, which was created by Governor Murray in 1764, and also served as a master in the Court of Chancery. He became the acting receiver general on 31 July with the redistribution of offices on the departure of Governor CARLETON, as well as judge of the Court of Common Pleas for the districts of Quebec and Three Rivers, a post he held until the judicial system was reorganized in 1794. In addition he sat on the Circuit Court in 1771 and 1772, the Prerogative Court in 1779, and the Court of Appeal in 1788.

Dunn started his massive acquisitions of land in 1764 by purchasing the seigneury of Mille-Vaches in 1764 and by 1788 had acquired several properties in Quebec as well as building his own wharf for commercial purposes. From 1767 to 1783 he also rented the seigneury of Saint-Étienne with some associates and in December 1788 he bought the seigneury of Saint-Armand on the shores of Lake Champlain. The following year, with partners William Grant and Peter Stuart, Dunn succeeded in buying almost all of the seigneuries of Mingan (the mainland and the islands) and Île d'Anticosti. The Quebec Act consolidated Dunn's well established position within the administration of the colony. His name headed the list of members of the new Legislative Council, and he was called to serve on the Privy Council instituted by Governor Carleton. Dunn remained focused on his personal business interests and avoided being drawn into political factions.

In 1794 at the time the judicial system was being reorganized, he became a judge of the Quebec Court of King's Bench. In 1801, shortly before he left for London, where he spent a year, he was appointed presiding judge of the Court of Appeal. As president of the Executive Council Dunn was civil administrator of Lower Canada from the departure of Lieutenant Governor Milnes in August 1805 until the arrival of Governor JAMES CRAIG in October 1807. Once more he managed to avoid taking sides during a time of fierce conflict between the Canadian and British parties in the House of Assembly. Thomas Dunn passed away at Quebec on 15 April 1818 at eighty-eight years of age.

DCB; "List of Protestant House Keepers in Quebec"; quoted in A.G. Doughty & N.E. Dionne, *Quebec Under Two Flags: A Brief History of the City…* (Quebec, 1903), 188–91.

Lieutenant Colonel Elias Walker Durnford
(1774–1850), *British army officer, colonial administrator.*

Elias Walker was born 28 July 1774 in Lowestoft, England, son of Elias Durnford and Rebecca Walker. He spent his childhood in North America as his father was commanding engineer in Pensacola, Florida, then lieutenant governor of the British colony of West Florida. He returned to England at the age of four, and at age fourteen was admitted as a cadet to the Royal Military Academy in Woolwich (October 1788). Initially commissioned into the Royal Regiment of Artillery in April 1793 at eighteen years of age, he was subsequently promoted second lieutenant in the Royal Engineers in October of the same year. He was posted to the West Indies to serve alongside his father. In 1794 he was responsible for the construction of defensive works at Pointe-à-Pitre in Guadeloupe, where he was subsequently taken prisoner by the French. After seventeen months of captivity, Durnford was exchanged (July 1796) and resumed engineering duties in England, and then in Ireland.

In 1808 Durnford was appointed commanding engineer in Newfoundland, where he directed the building of coastal batteries and erected a blockhouse on Signal Hill, St John's. In 1813 he was promoted major "in the army" and a lieutenant colonel in the Royal Engineers. From 1816 to 1831 Durnford was the senior commanding officer of the Royal Engineers in the Canadas and was headquartered at Quebec, where he no doubt came into contact with James Thompson. The construction of the Quebec Citadel was undoubtedly his major accomplishment in British North America.

Durnford also coordinated the reorganization of the colonies' defences to fit a new plan developed after the War of 1812 by the governor, the Duke of Richmond (CHARLES LENNOX). In addition, Durnford coordinated the construction of canal systems on the Rideau and Ottawa rivers as well, although the construction of Rideau Canal was the special purview of his friend John By in the period 1826–31. In March 1825 Durnford was promoted colonel in the Royal Engineers and given command of all troops in Lower Canada in addition to his engineering duties.

Durnford finally returned to England in 1831 and six years later retired from active service. In 1846 he was promoted lieutenant general and appointed colonel commandant of the Royal Engineers. He died 8 March 1850 in Tunbridge Wells, Kent.

Elias Walker Durnford. This 1841 sketch portrays Durnford in retirement in England. Executed by his daughter, Jane Durnford, it is now proudly displayed in the regimental headquarters of the Royal 22nd Regiment (the famous "Vandoos") inside the Citadel he built. (Courtesy: La Citadelle de Québec)

BALs; *DCB;* Mary Durnford, ed., *Family recollections of Lieut. General Elias Walker Durnford, a colonel commandant of the Corps of Royal Engineers* (Montreal, 1863); John Kane and W. H. Askwith, eds., *List of Officers of the Royal Regiment of Artillery from the year 1716 to the year 1899* (London, 1900); André Charbonneau et al., *Québec The Fortified City: From the 17th to the 19th Century* (Parks Canada, 1982); Whitworth Porter et al., *History of the Corps of Royal Engineers* (Chatham, 1889).

Prince Edward Augustus, later Duke of Kent and Strathearn (1767–1820), *British army officer, member of Royal Family.*

Edward was born 2 November 1767, the fourth son of George III (1738–1820) and Queen Charlotte (1744–1818), at Buckingham House, London. Best known as the father of Queen Victoria, he spent a chequered career in the British army. In 1785 Edward was sent to study in his father's electorate of Hanover, where he became a cadet in the Hanoverian Foot Guards. Under his governor, Lieutenant Colonel George von Wangenheim, he studied military sciences, the classics, German, law, history and religion. Gazetted a brevet colonel in the British army in 1786, he moved to Geneva, where, from 1788 to 1790, he concluded his education before being appointed colonel of the 7th Foot (Royal Fusiliers) in April 1789.

In January 1790 he returned home from Europe without leave and after a brief meeting with his furious father was virtually banished to Gibraltar, where he served in the garrison as an ordinary officer. While at Gibraltar, he sent for Thérèse-Bernardine Mongenet from Marseilles to be his mistress. She devoted herself to Edward for nearly twenty-eight years before she was cast aside. Posted in 1791 to Canada, Prince Edward arrived there with his regiment and mistress and they promptly became firm fixtures in Quebec society, where he no doubt came into contact with James Thompson. Promoted major general on 2 October 1793, the prince served with distinction in the West Indian campaigns. While in transit from Quebec to the Caribbean, travelling via Boston and New York, Prince Edward became a celebrity – the first prince to visit the United States since that fledgling country's Declaration of Independence.

After his service in the West Indies, the unrepentant prince's request to return home was denied by his father, and instead he was posted to Halifax, Nova Scotia. There he attempted

Prince Edward Augustus. Painted by Sir William Beechey in 1818, Prince Edward, the fourth son of George III, is shown here as the colonel of the 1st Foot (Royal Scots). Around his neck he wears the Badge of St. Patrick and on his chest the Ribbon and Star of the Order of the Garter. (National Portrait Gallery NPG 647)

to maintain the standards of social life he had established in Quebec and entertained himself by designing and building Halifax's prominent Town Clock Tower and making alterations to the house and grounds he rented from Sir John Wentworth, the governor of Nova Scotia.

Prince Edward was promoted lieutenant general on 12 January 1796, but it was only when he suffered a fall from his horse that he was permitted to leave Nova Scotia and return to Britain for medical care. He landed at Plymouth on 15 November 1798, his North American sojourn remembered by the renaming of Isle St. John to Prince Edward Island in 1799.

Edward's career peaked in 1799 when, in addition to being created Duke of Kent and Strathearn on 24 April, he was gazetted general on 10 May and in July was appointed commander-in-chief of British forces in North America. In response to a petition from James Thompson seeking a pay increase, Edward's subsequent approval prompted Thompson to send off a letter of appreciation to the duke "for his great goodness and attention to an old servant of His Majesty...." Edward was subsequently appointed governor of Gibraltar on 27 March 1802 and promoted field marshal on 5 September 1805. Three days after his thirty-eighth birthday (5 November 1805), the duke retired from active military service.

He married at Coburg in Saxony, Germany, on 29 May 1818 (Lutheran rite), and then at Kew Palace on 13 July 1818. His daughter, the future queen of England, was born on 24 May 1819. The following year, Edward died of pneumonia at Sidmouth, Devonshire, on 23 January 1820 and was buried in St George's Chapel, Windsor, on 11 February.

DCB; DNB; Burke's Peerage.

Sergeant Alexander Ferguson (dates unknown), *British army soldier.*

Paymaster sergeant in the 78th Foot, Ferguson was billeted with Sergeant James Thompson in the home of Jacques Leclerc in St. Vallier, Quebec (Thompson refers to this town as St. Valier) over the winter of 1760–61. On 22 October 1760, Ferguson shows up as a warden in the Lodge of Free & Accepted Masons in the 78th Foot, designated as "No. 6 Canada." The proceedings covering this appointment show that Brother James Thompson was a fellow warden. A Sergeant Alexander Ferguson shows up on a list of non-commissioned officers and men of the 78th Foot who received their discharge in Quebec in 1763 (Captain Ranald McDonell's Company). He is also one of twelve former sergeants that appear on a land petition to Governor JAMES MURRAY dated 15 March 1765, requesting 200 acres each "in and about the Bays of Chaleur and Gaspey."

JTC; Col. R.J. Harper, *The Fraser Highlanders* (Montreal, 1979); A.J.B. Milborne, "The Lodge in the 78th Regiment (Fraser's Highlanders), *Quatuor Coronati Lodge*, vol LXV (1952).

Lieutenant Alexander Fraser (c. 1735–98), *British army officer, Indian agent.*

Gazetted a lieutenant in the 78th Foot on 22 July 1757, Alexander Fraser fought at Louisbourg in 1758 under JEFFERY AMHERST and at Quebec under JAMES WOLFE in 1759. He was wounded at the battle of Sillery on 28 April 1760. On disbandment of his regiment in 1763, he was placed on half-pay and by 1765 was employed by General Gage as his special emissary to cooperate with Sir William Johnson's deputy, George Croghan. Both men had the common goal of paving the way for Stirling's expedition to the Illinois country. Stirling noted that General Gage was "determined to send an Indian agent by way of Fort Pitt & the Ohio to prepare the way for reception of troops coming up the Mississippi." The French-speaking Scot's specific task was to ensure the inhabitants of the Illinois were fully informed on the terms of the Treaty of Paris and how it would affect them. For this purpose, Fraser carried copies of Gage's proclamation for widest distribution to ensure no rumours or misinformation came up-river from the French governor at New Orleans.

Fraser's reception in the Illinois country was hostile to say the least and his entire party were made prisoner several times and roughed up. Only the firm intercession of the war chieftain Pontiac, who was in the Illinois country at this time, saved their lives, and Fraser soon had his men slip away to New Orleans and followed shortly afterwards. He returned with the 34th Foot in December 1765 to complete his mission of issuing General Gage's proclamation, and then returned to New York to make his personal report to Gage. As a reward for his singular efforts and hardships in the Illinois country, Fraser was taken off half-pay and gazetted a lieutenant (25 October 1766) in the 9th Foot, stationed at St Augustine, Florida, and the Bahamas. This safe billet on the peacetime establishment of one of the army's most senior regiments ensured Fraser would never go on half-pay again.

Eventually, the 9th Foot rotated back to Ireland, and Fraser was promoted to captain lieutenant (20 May 1776) on the eve of the American Revolution. In a paper shuffle he was transferred immediately to the 20th Foot, and then transferred again to the 34th Foot as a full captain (11 November 1776). No doubt the 34th Foot were pleased to secure such a battle-hardened veteran of Louisbourg, Quebec and Sillery to command their light infantry company and to train the battalion for North American conditions. Fraser's talents (and reputation as the officer who had met the great Pontiac face-to-face) were quickly noticed on his arrival by Governor GUY CARLETON, who had soldiered with Fraser at Quebec. Fraser was detached from his regiment "on command" in 1776–77 to command Indians and light troops as assistant superintendent of Indian Affairs in Canada. Governor Carleton personally directed that each company of every British regiment in Canada provide Fraser two men to form an elite company of skirmishers. Fraser was directed to choose the best shots from each company and to secure the army's most accurate weapons.

Long after the war, Captain Alexander Fraser of fourteen years seniority was gazetted major of his regiment on 18 November 1790, and then lieutenant colonel on 1 March 1794. He transferred to the 45th Foot in 1795, then stationed in the sickly West Indies, far removed from the Napoleonic wars in Europe. According to the 45th regimental history "in 1797 and 1798 no less than 13 officers died, namely, Lieut. Col. Colonel Frazer; Captains Morrison and Hutchinson...."

BALs; James M. Hadden, *Hadden's Journal and Orderly Books: A Journal Kept in Canada and Upon Burgoyne's Campaign in 1776 and 1777* (Albany, 1884), 473–76; Col. P. H. Dalbiac, *History of the 45th: 1st Nottinghamshire Regiment (Sherwood Foresters)* (Nottingham, 1902), 18; "Croghan's Journal," Gage Papers, WLCL, vol II, 3.

Captain Alexander Fraser, 6th of Culduthel (1729–78), *British army officer.*

Son of Alexander Fraser, 5th Culduthel, and Grizel Abercromby of Birkenbog. Alexander was the heir of his older half-brother, Malcolm Fraser, a captain in the 42nd Foot who was killed while serving as a volunteer at the siege and capture of Bergen-op-Zoom in 1747. Gazetted captain of the 14th Additional Company of the 78th Foot in September 1758, Culduthel and his men spent the next five months aboard ship trying to join their regiment in North America. According to Lieutenant Donald Cameron, son of Fassifern, and one of the company's new subalterns, they "arrived at Virginia the twentieth of June 1759 after a long and tedious Pasage and from Virginia we ware Ordered for York, and from York up the River to Albonay, where we parted with Captain [Mungo] Campbe[ll]s Componay, [14th Company, 77th Foot] then we ware Ordered Down that same River to York again and from York to Luisbrough, and up the River Sant Lawrence to the Sage of Quebeck. We arrived in Camp before Quebeck September the 3..." just in time to take part in the battle of the Plains of Abraham, 13 September 1759.

The following spring, while commanding the grenadier company at the battle of Sillery, 28 April 1760, Culduthel was wounded in the head and Sergeant James Thompson took temporary command of the company during the battle. Fraser resigned his commission, 23 October 1761, and returned to Scotland to recover from his wounds. Culduthel was considered one of the finest singers, huntsmen and sportsmen of his day. He died at Beaulieside, near Inverness, 17 November 1778.

BALs; CBs; JTC; SBs; Amherst Family Papers, O36/15; NA WO 34/87: f. 220.

Sergeant Alexander Fraser (dates unknown), *British army soldier.*
A sergeant in the grenadier company of the 78th Foot. During the march through Ireland, Fraser was the recipient of money raised by grateful citizens following a house fire which Fraser's Highlanders helped to extinguish (the money was intended to have the "men refresh'd at the nearest tavern"). On 27 December 1757, while the regiment was in winter quarters in Stratford, Connecticut, Fraser stopped at the guard house after first borrowing James Thompson's dirk. Corporal James Macky, the acting sergeant of the guard, was intoxicated and asleep on the guard room bed. Woken by Fraser and reminded of his duties, he lunged at Fraser with his sword drawn, wounding him on the head. In the ensuing scuffle, Fraser, blinded with blood, struck back at Macky with Thompson's dirk, killing him. A military court of inquiry was convened 3 January 1758 to gather the facts, with Captain CHARLES BAILLIE presiding. A verdict of manslaughter in self defence was rendered. But Fraser was subsequently charged by a civilian court of law with willful murder, the civil trial taking place in Stratford. Fraser was duly acquitted on the murder charge, the jury agreeing with the regiment's initial finding that Fraser had acted in self defence. A Sergeant Alexander Fraser shows up on a list of non-commissioned officers and men of the 78th Foot who received their discharge in Quebec in 1763 (Captain Wood's Company).

JTC; Col. R.J. Harper, *The Fraser Highlanders* (Montreal, 1979); Proceedings, Military Court of Inquiry, 3 January 1758, NAS GD45/2/29/2b.

Lieutenant Hugh Fraser (1730–1814), *British army officer, gentleman farmer.*
Hugh Fraser was the original regimental adjutant of the 78th Foot, appointed 12 January 1757, and served in that capacity until 24 July 1760. Fraser is not mentioned by name in James Thompson's reminiscences, but appears several times in his "Anecdotes of Wolfe's Army" simply as "the adjutant." Gazetted ensign 9 June 1758, the day after the Louisbourg landings, Fraser was promoted lieutenant the day after the battle of Sillery, 29 April 1760. Exchanged to half-pay in 1763. Hugh Fraser returned to Scotland and married Elizabeth MacTavish, daughter of a fellow 78th officer, Lieutenant John MacTavish of Garthbeg, and brought her back to Albany, New York, by September 1764. He also brought with him his younger brother-in-law, Simon McTavish (1750–1804), who would become the driving force behind the highly successful North West Company fur trading enterprise and subsequently the richest man in Montreal. Fraser apparently had an agreement with Sir William Johnson to settle lands in the Mohawk Valley and brought with him an undisclosed number of settlers. By November 1780, disenchanted with the ongoing Revolutionary War, Fraser returned to Scotland with his family and settled on a farm called Brightmony, near Auldean, Nairnshire. He died at Perth 21 January 1814, aged eighty-three.

BALs; CBs; SBs.

Lieutenant John Fraser (c. 1727–95), *British army officer, judge.*
The younger son of William Fraser of Culbokie and 8th Guisachan, and Margaret Macdonald of Ardnable, John was the older brother of Archibald, also serving in the 78th Foot. Gazetted a lieutenant 24 January 1757 in Captain Simon Fraser's company (original parchment is in the Château de Ramezay Mu-

seum, Montreal), he was later appointed regimental quartermaster 27 September 1758 after the successful siege of Louisbourg. Sergeant James Thompson mentions that he was an accomplished swordsman and fought in a special regimental contest at Schenectady the winter of 1758–59, losing to one Corporal Macpherson of Captain ALEXANDER CAMERON of Dungallon's company. He resigned his appointment as quartermaster 22 April 1759 and was promoted captain 15 April 1760 just prior to the battle of Sillery, 28 April 1760. He was appointed paymaster of troops in Montreal in 1763 and was commanding one of the companies when the regiment was disbanded. John retired on half-pay and stayed in Canada.

In 1764 he was appointed a judge of the Court of Common Pleas for Montreal District and the following year he married Marie-Claire Fleury Deschambault. In 1775 he resigned his commission as a half-pay officer and became a member of the Legislative Council of Quebec.

Fraser was briefly imprisoned by the Americans during the occupation of Montreal in 1777. At the end of the American Revolution, he helped to relocate his widowed sister-in-law and her young family and provided financial assistance and guidance to his youngest nephew, Simon Fraser, born 1776 near Bennington, Vermont, who joined the North West Company of Montreal as an apprentice clerk. Simon later became the fur trader and explorer after whom the Fraser River in British Columbia is named.

In 1784 John Fraser became a member of the Executive Council of Lower Canada and a judge of the Court of the King's Bench in 1792. His Worship, aged sixty-eight, died in Montreal on 5 December 1795 and was buried three days later, 8 December 1795, in the Saint-Amable crypt of the Church of Our Lady.

BALs; CBs; SBs; Stewart *Sketches*, II, 20–1.

Sergeant John Fraser (1734–1803), *British army soldier, schoolmaster.*

Born in Scotland in 1734, John Fraser must have received an excellent education. A giant of a man, he served as a sergeant in the grenadier company of the 78th Foot and during the battle on the Plains of Abraham sustained a severe sabre cut on the forehead. He was discovered leaning his back against a fence by a retreating French surgeon, PHILIPPE-LOUIS-FRANÇOIS BADELARD, who dressed his wound. Soon afterwards, Badelard surrendered to Fraser and they became good friends. Whenever Fraser met the doctor in later years, it would begin with the friendly greeting "Good day, my prisoner."

When the regiment was ordered back to Scotland to be disbanded in 1763, Fraser took his discharge and remained in Quebec, and his name appears on a list of Protestant "house keepers" contained in a certificate given by General JAMES MURRAY in 1764. He became a member of Quebec's "Scotch Congregation," likely attending early Presbyterian services at the Ursuline Convent led by regimental pastor ROBERT MACPHERSON (the *Caipal Mhor*). In Quebec, as elsewhere in the colony, a shortage of schools existed in the aftermath of the conquest, particularly schools for the small British community. Fraser first started to teach boys privately in his home but by 1769 was officially appointed as schoolmaster by Governor CARLETON, although his previous petitions for government certification had been refused. On 26 October 1784 Governor FREDERICK HALDIMAND authorized the acting receiver general, Henry Caldwell, to pay Fraser £15 to cover his "salary and allowance for school house rent" for the period 11 April to 10 October 1784.

In his bachelorhood, Fraser, better known as "Long John Fraser," boarded with Joseph Trahan, a former militiaman of the French regime. Like many former soldiers of the 78th Foot, Fraser was a Freemason, and by 1764 he was the Master of the Lodge of the 78th Foot, then known as "Canada No. 6." Fraser appears as one of twelve former sergeants on a land petition to Governor James Murray dated 15 March 1765, each requesting 200 acres "in and about the Bays of Chaleur and Gaspey."

Prior to 1778, Fraser lived on St. Anne Street (rue Sainte-Anne), but in that year he bought a single-storey stone house at 3 Garden Street (rue des Jardins) and moved there with his wife, Agnes Maxwell, and daughter. Interestingly, Fraser's home was close to the home of Dr. Badelard, the former French army doctor who tended to his injuries on the Plains of Abraham (the two lots adjoined each other in the rear).

In 1801 the Royal Institution for the Advancement of Learning was formed and John Fraser's School immediately became part of this system. Contrary to some accounts, he was not the first to teach English in Quebec, although his school became the forerunner of the High School of Quebec. Fraser died on 13 February 1803 at sixty-nine years of age. He was survived by his second wife, Ann Hudson, two daughters (one by each marriage) and a stepson; to them Fraser left a modest succession, including a library of approximately 180 volumes and a grant of 400 acres in Granby Township, patented one month earlier. The *Quebec Gazette* noted that "a large number of respectable citizens of Quebec" were indebted to the "old and respected" schoolmaster for their education, including all of the children of James Thompson.

DCB; JTC; *The Old Gentlemen Stood to Pray* (St. Andrew's Church, Quebec, 1828); *Tales of Remembrances,* and *Historical Sketch* (St. Andrew's Church, Quebec, 1984); J.-M. Lemoine, *Maple Leaves* (Quebec, 1894); J.-M. Lemoine, "The Scot in New France," LHSQ, *Transactions*, New Series, No. 15 (1881); "List of Protestant House Keepers in Quebec," quoted in A.G. Doughty & N.E. Dionne, *Quebec Under Two Flags: A Brief History of the City…* (Quebec, 1903), 188–91; Haldimand to Henry Caldwell, Quebec, 26 October 1784, BAnQ P1000 S3 D2135.

Lieutenant Malcolm Fraser (1733–1815),
British army officer, seigneur.

Malcolm Fraser was born 26 May 1733 in Abernethy, Scotland, son of Donald Fraser (c. 1712–46) and Janet McIntosh. His father was killed fighting with the Fraser of Lovat regiment at the battle of Culloden, 16 April 1746. He received a good education and is reported to have spoken Gaelic, English, French and Latin. Gazetted an ensign on 18 July 1757, the twenty-four-year-old Fraser came to America with one of the three additional companies sent to America to augment the 78th Foot in spring 1758. Wounded at the battle of the Plains of Abraham 13 September 1759, he was promoted lieutenant 25 September 1759, then wounded again at Sillery on 28 April 1760. He was appointed adjutant 24 July 1760 and resigned this appointment 9 April 1763.

On exchanging to half-pay in 1763, he took up the management of the seigneury of Mount Murray belonging to JAMES MURRAY, which he later purchased, building a manor house overlooking the village of La Malbaie. (The previous year, 1762, Murray had divided his newly purchased seigneury at La Malbaie in two portions, Mount Murray and Murray Bay — Mount Murray was granted to Fraser while Murray Bay was granted to Captain JOHN NAIRNE, Fraser's best friend.) On the outbreak of the American Revolution, Fraser helped recruit former Fraser Highlanders for the 1st Battalion, 84th Foot (Royal Highland Emigrants), in which he was gazetted a captain on 24 June 1775. In 1797 he was brevetted major "in the army." After the American Revolution he continued to acquire landed property across the colony, including houses in Quebec's Upper Town. In May 1794 Governor Lord Dorchester (GUY CARLETON) promoted him colonel in the Kamouraska battalion of militia, and in 1805 he was colonel of the Baie-Saint-Paul battalion of militia. One of his biographers, William Stewart Wallace, asserts that he had numerous illegitimate children, five of them with Marie Allaire of Beaumont. Three other children were born later of his liaison with Marguerite Ducros *dit* Laterreur of Murray Bay. He died on 16 June 1815 at Point Fraser, Murray Bay, aged eighty-two years. His obituary in the *Quebec Mercury* reads: "Colonel Malcolm Fraser ... an officer in the victorious army of the immortal Wolfe, and resided in the country from the conquest to the period of his death; where he was at all times honored and respected as one of its principal worthies." In his will (4 November 1811) Fraser bequeathed an annual pension to his partner and divided his Canadian estate among all his children.

BALs; CBs; *DCB;* SBs; 3 August 1798, Military Papers C931, 106–7; 109–9a; *JSAHR*, Vol. 18 (1939), 9–22; *Quebec Mercury*, 20 June 1815.

Lieutenant Colonel Simon Fraser, formerly Master of Lovat (1726–82), *British army officer, Member of Parliament, office holder.*
Born at Kiltarity, Scotland, 19 October 1726, Simon was the eldest son and heir of the 11th Lord Lovat. During the '45, the eighteen-year-old Master of Lovat, though designated the colonel of the Frasers of Lovat regiment, wisely stayed out of the fray so that command devolved upon Lieutenant Colonel Charles Fraser, younger of Inverallochy. The latter officer, while lying wounded on the battlefield, was killed on the orders of General Henry Hawley. Simon was imprisoned briefly in Edinburgh Castle, pardoned, and took up work as a solicitor, passing the Scottish Bar 25 July 1750. He became advocate depute and assisted in the prosecution of James Stewart of Aucharn in Appin, who was executed for the murder of Colin Campbell of Glenure. Gazetted lieutenant colonel commandant of the 78th Foot on 5 January 1757, Fraser quickly raised over 1,000 men, which he confessed "could not have been procured so speedily by any sum of money, without the

Lieutenant Colonel Simon Fraser, former Master of Lovat. Now believed to be the only extant image of Simon Fraser, this detail from Benjamin West's *The Death of General James Wolfe* shows him wearing a full belted plaid in a brownish-red sett. As Fraser was neither at the battle nor present at Wolfe's death, he reportedly paid the required £100 to be added to the group of mourning officers. (Editor's Collection)

concurrence and aid of friends, Gentlemen of the country with proper connections."

He initially took his regiment to Ireland and then to Halifax, Nova Scotia. They were too late to participate in any 1757 campaigning and his regiment was rerouted to winter quarters in Connecticut. Fraser's regiment featured prominently at the Louisbourg landings the following year and, after the successful conclusion of the siege under General JEFFERY AMHERST's command, he took his regiment into winter quarters in upstate New York for 1758–59.

At the 1759 siege of Quebec, Colonel Fraser was wounded in an ambush while leading a raiding force of some 300 Highlanders sent to St. Michel parish on the south shore, 26 July 1759. He missed the actions at Montmorency at the end of July, as well as the victory on the Plains of Abraham three months later. An unidentified staff officer (probably the urbane Captain Hervey Smythe, one of Wolfe's personal aides de camp) wrote: "Col. Fraser has a good deal of the Low Highland cunning. Penurious and not held in esteem in the army, nor did we think him very enterprising."

Fraser was wounded a second time the following year at the battle of Sillery near Sainte-Foy on 28 April 1760, where he commanded the left wing of General MURRAY's army. He was left in command at Quebec as the acting governor in June 1760 by Murray, who led the healthier elements of his army up-river to effect a union with Amherst and Haviland's armies converging on Montreal. During this period, Fraser was installed as a Grand Master of the first Grand Lodge of Ancient & Accepted Freemasons in Canada.

The absent officers list of 1760 recorded Colonel Simon Fraser had "gone to England 23rd Octbr. 1760 by General Amherst's leave," and he never returned. Daily command of the regiment passed to the first major, James Abercrombie. Fraser went to London from Scotland in the spring of 1761 to take up his seat in the House of Commons as an elected Member of Parliament for Inverness and was appointed a brigadier general on Lord Loudoun's 1762 expedition to Portugal to help defend against a Spanish invasion. He was promoted major general in 1772 and two years later saw the Lovat estates fully restored for his loyal service to the Crown (on payment of £20,983!).

In 1775 as war in North America loomed, Major General Simon Fraser was asked to raise another regiment, and accordingly was gazetted colonel of the 71st Foot (Frasers' Highlanders), 25 October 1775. It was a two-battalion regiment totalling 2,340 officers and men. Fraser died in London on 8 February 1782, aged fifty-five, having reached the rank of lieutenant general in the British army.

BALs; CBs; JTC; SBs; Stewart, *Sketches*, II, 20–1; *Muster Roll of Prince Charles Edward Stuart's Army 1745–46*, A. Livingstone et al, eds. (Aberdeen, 1985); Fraser to Amherst, 25 October 1759, NA WO 34/78: f. 103 and Amherst to Fraser, 24 March 1760, WO 34/4: f. 135; PRO Northern Ireland, *Dobbs Collection*; DOD 162/77; Fraser's MSS in *JSAHR*, XVIII (1939), 9.

Sergeant John Gawler (c. 1740–1805), *British army soldier, civilian clerk, brewmaster.*

John Gawler was born in London, England. He served as a sergeant in the Royal Artillery during the siege of Quebec in 1759, where he later became acquainted with James Thompson through their respective duties as Freemasons (Gawler was a member of Lodge No. 11, P.G.L., Quebec, held in the Royal Artillery; while Thompson was a member of St. Andrew's Lodge). Gawler, known to Thompson as "a fine, sensible person," returned with his regiment to England in 1764, and thereafter acted as unofficial Masonic representative of the Quebec brethren in England. On leaving the army, Gawler established a small shop in London with his wife, later accepting a clerical position in a London brewery. After a short stint as clerk he accepted the position of brewery master at a competing firm.

Gawler and his wife had two sons, William and Felix, who were both sent to Quebec under the care of James Thompson to complete their "mercantile education." It is from his correspondence with his old friend James Thompson and with the Grand Secretary of the Grand Lodge in England that much of the early Masonic history of Quebec has been reconstructed. The close relationship between Gawler and Thompson is evidenced by the fact that Thompson named one of his sons John Gawler Thompson. Unfortunately Thompson's good friend had an addiction for porter beer which in later life "caused him to become so fat and full habit, that he was struck with apoplexy." Gawler died in London in 1805.

JTC; A.J.B. Milborne, "Freemasonry at the Siege of Quebec 1759–60," *The Papers of the Canadian Masonic Research Association*, vol 1.

Lieutenant Colonel William Gordon, 18th Earl of Sutherland (1735–66), *British army officer.*

William Gordon was born in Scotland on 28 May 1735 to William Gordon, 17th Earl of Sutherland (1708–50), and Lady Elizabeth Wemyss (1721–47). Young William began his military career during the Jacobite Uprising of 1745, with the purchase by his father of an ensign's commission in the 2nd Battalion, 1st Regiment of Foot (29 November 1745). As William was only ten years old it is doubtful he soldiered with the regiment until he had finished his schooling. William would transfer to the 1st Battalion, 1st Foot in 1748 and on his father, the 17th Earl's, death on 7 December 1750, Ensign Sutherland inherited both the former's title and estates.

The 18th Earl of Sutherland was promoted to lieutenant in the 2nd Battalion, 1st Foot (22 January 1755). He took his next step upward in rank by leaving the 1st Foot to become a captain in the new-raising 58th Regiment of Foot (later renumbered as the 56th Foot), 30 December 1755. Captain Sutherland resigned his commission on 1 January 1758. Oddly enough, Sutherland's records specify that he became a brevet lieutenant colonel on 4 July 1759, but they do not reveal in what capacity he served. This brevet lieutenant colonelcy could actually be a backdated commission granted on his return to service. That occurred on 11 August 1759, when he was appointed lieutenant colonel commandant of the new-raising Sutherland Regiment of Fencible Men, which he recruited himself. This home-defence unit contained two grenadier companies and it was reported that 260 of the Fencible men stood five foot eleven or taller.

Lieutenant Colonel Sutherland did not devote all his thoughts during the Seven Years'

"**William Earl of Sutherland, Aide de Camp to his Majesty & Colonel of a Highland Regiment.**" William Gordon stands in his full dress uniform as the lieutenant colonel commandant of the Sutherland Regiment of Fencible Men, a unit raised in 1759 for home defence during the Seven Years' War and disbanded in 1763. Mezzotint by J. McIntosh after the painting by Allan Ramsay. (Anne S.K. Brown Military Collection, Brown University Library)

War to military matters. He married Mary Maxwell, the daughter of William Maxwell of Preston and Elizabeth Hairstanes, on 14 April 1761. Mary bore him two children. The first was Catherine Gordon, who was born on 24 May 1764 only to die tragically less than two years later on 3 January 1766. The couple's second daughter, Elizabeth Gordon, lived a much longer life, from 24 May 1765 to 25 January 1839, and eventually became the notorious Countess of Sutherland.

Sutherland lost his lieutenant colonelcy

when the Sutherland Fencible Regiment was disbanded on 3 March 1763. He found considerable consolation, however, on 20 April 1763 when he received an appointment as aide de camp to King George III with the rank of brevet colonel. Three years later, Sutherland's life came to an intensely sad end. As noted above, Sutherland's first daughter died on 3 January 1766. On 1 June 1766, he lost his wife at Bath. Fifteen days later, the Earl died. He was only thirty-one years old.

BALs; *DNB*.

Captain Charles Grant (c. 1730–84), *merchant, British militia officer.*
Charles Grant was one of the first merchants to establish himself at Quebec immediately after its capture in 1760 and by 1763 was providing room and board for the children of a fellow business associate, Samuel Jacobs, and his name appears on a list of Protestant "house keepers" contained in a certificate given by General JAMES MURRAY in 1764. By 1773 he was one of the most prominent Quebec merchants and was part of a citizens committee headed by William Grant requesting their own House of Assembly at Quebec. His holdings included wharves, warehouses and a store, located near St. Peter Street (rue Saint-Pierre) at Quebec.

He took an active part in the defence of Quebec at the time of the American invasion in 1775–76, serving as a captain of militia. Grant was an active Freemason, serving as Grand Treasurer in Quebec in 1780, and was well known to James Thompson. In 1783 he was in business at Quebec with John Blackwood under the company name of Grant and Blackwood. Grant died on 7 January 1784, leaving a wife and five small children. Upon his death, his partner bought part of his buildings and fixtures for the sum of £2,000. In 1793 Blackwood succeeded in getting hold of Grant's other assets by marrying Jane Holmes, his widow.

DCB; JTC; *Quebec Almanac*, 1780; "List of Protestant House Keepers in Quebec," quoted in A.G. Doughty & N.E. Dionne, *Quebec Under Two Flags: A Brief History of the City…* (Quebec, 1903), 188–91.

Governor Frederick Haldimand (1718–91), *army officer, colonial governor.*
Frederick Haldimand was born in 1718 at Yverdon, Switzerland, the second of four children of François-Louis Haldimand, an administrator in Yverdon, and his wife, Marie-Madeleine de Treytorrens. Haldimand sought a career in the Prussian army and first saw action at the battles of Mollwitz, Hohenfriedberg and Kesseldorf during the War of the Austrian Succession. Ever on the alert for promotion, he accepted a position in the regiment of Swiss guards serving in the Dutch army. By 1748 he had risen to the position of 1st lieutenant.

Haldimand was part of a group of foreign officers recruited by Colonel Jacques Prévost, a fellow Swiss, to serve in the Royal American Regiment, a new-raising unit recruiting the German and Swiss inhabitants of Pennsylvania. In January 1756 Haldimand was commissioned the lieutenant colonel of the 2nd Battalion, 60th Foot. Despite army regulations that only permitted foreign officers to serve with British forces in Europe, Haldimand benefited from special dispensation that permitted up to fifty non-British officers to hold commissions in units serving in America. However, throughout his career he would encounter the animosity of some British-born officers who resented the presence of foreigners in their ranks.

During the Seven Years' War, Haldimand acquitted himself well fighting at Ticonderoga, 1758, Oswego, 1759, and Montreal, 1760. Haldimand's language skills made him invaluable to his respective commanders, and in 1760 he was chosen by General JEFFERY AMHERST to liaise with Governor Vaudreuil and Major General François de Lévis and negotiate the terms of surrender of New France. Later, he was made mili-

Sir Frederick Haldimand, c. 1778. A Swiss-born officer who came to North America as one of the Royal American (60th Foot) battalion commanders during the Seven Years' War, the bilingual Haldimand was well liked by the inhabitants of Quebec. Painting by Sir Joshua Reynolds. (National Portrait Gallery NPG 4874)

tary governor for the district of Trois-Rivières, where he provided competent administration of the district but was removed in September 1765. While making plans to return to Europe, he was notified of the death of his best friend and fellow Swiss officer Henry Bouquet at Pensacola, Florida, and was immediately promoted brigadier general and commander of the Southern Department in Bouquet's place. His experience as a military commander in East and West Florida would stand him in good stead when he was appointed governor of Quebec. In May 1772 he was promoted colonel commandant of the 60th Foot and later raised to the rank of major general the same year. During the absence of Thomas Gage in England from June 1773 to May 1774, Haldimand served as acting commander-in-chief of North America

On Gage's return, Haldimand departed for England in August 1774 and on arrival was given the lucrative sinecure of inspector general of the West Indian forces as well as being indemnified £3,000 for expenses incurred while he was commander-in-chief.

In 1777 Haldimand was appointed as replacement to Sir GUY CARLETON, the former governor of Quebec and arrived to take up his new post on 26 June 1778, just as the rebellion flared to the south. He adroitly managed the needs of various conflicting groups and ensured the loyalties of French Canadians and allied Indian tribes, returning to England in November 1784. The King recognized Haldimand's loyal and valuable service by appointing him to the Order of the Bath in September 1785. He died at the age of seventy-three in his birthplace, Yverdon, Switzerland, on June 1791.

BALs; *DCB; DNB;* Jean N. McIlwraith, *Sir Frederick Haldimand* (Toronto, 1911).

Captain Moses Hazen (1733–1803), *British army officer, office holder, landowner, seigneur, merchant.*

Moses Hazen was born 1 June 1733 in Haverhill, Massachusetts, the third child of Moses Hazen, merchant, and Abigail White. He started his military career in a provincial regiment, serving in Nova Scotia in 1755 as a lieutenant in Governor William Shirley's Massachusetts Regiment, commanded by John Winslow. He participated in the capture of Fort Beauséjour under Colonel ROBERT MONCKTON, and the following year re-enlisted in another provincial regiment, this time Colonel Richard Saltonstall's regiment raised for service on Lake George. He took a year off from soldiering in 1757 and turned to more lucrative ventures, such as shipping provisions and supplies for the projected British attack on Louisbourg to Halifax. In 1758 he was offered a 2nd lieutenancy with Rogers' Rangers but refused on the grounds that he had already held the rank of lieutenant on two previous campaigns. On 7 April 1758 Hazen accepted a counter-offer as 1st lieutenant of Captain John McCurdy's Company of Rogers' Rangers and subsequently fought with this company at the siege of Louisbourg, 1758.

In January 1759 his company was assigned as part of a force under Brigadier General Robert Monckton to clear the enemy from the St. John River valley in what is now New Brunswick. On a raid north from Fort Frederick at the mouth of the St. John River, his captain, John McCurdy, was killed by a falling tree. Hazen took command of the company and destroyed St. Anne's (Fredericton) burning it to the ground in February 1759. Although AMHERST confirmed Hazen's captaincy of McCurdy's Company in April 1759, he was later to comment that Hazen had sullied his merit and the honour of British arms because of the cold-blooded killing of women and children at St. Anne's and Grimross (Gagetown, N.B.).

On 5 June 1759 Hazen's Company embarked for Quebec as part of Wolfe's army and, on its capture, remained at Quebec. During the winter, his ranger company was active in the many skirmishes and small engagements fought in the countryside outside the city. In one such engagement at Lorette in April 1760, Hazen's rangers drove off a much larger French force, killing six and capturing seven. At the battle of Sillery, 28 April 1760, his company fought on the left flank of the army and Hazen was wounded in the thigh (as reported by James Thompson), and was forced to remain at Quebec recuperating during the summer campaign against Montreal.

His company, under the command of Captain Jonathan Brewer, was present at the capture of Montreal and his men then accompanied Robert Rogers to Detroit. When Hazen's company was disbanded in March 1761, Hazen was allowed to purchase, for 800 guineas, a lieutenant's commission in the 44th Foot with the recommendation of JAMES MURRAY, who attributed to him "so much ... Bravery and good Conduct as would Justly Entitle him to Every military Reward he Could ask or Demand." From 1761 to 1763 Hazen's regiment performed garrison duty at Montreal.

When the 15th Foot was reduced to nine companies in 1763, Hazen as one of the most junior officers, was forced to go on half-pay at Montreal. He eventually settled along the Richelieu River at Iberville across from St. Johns (Saint-Jean) and for a time was a partner of Lieutenant Colonel Gabriel Christie, whom he eventually fell out with over money.

When the War for Independence broke out, Hazen was initially neutral, waiting to see which side would prevail, but he eventually threw his lot in with the Americans and raised troops for service with Continental forces. He rose to the rank of brigadier general by brevet and retired from the American services in 1783. Ironically, he remained on the half-pay rolls of the British army until 1781. A stroke in 1786 disabled him for life. In 1787 he settled at New York, but then moved to Troy.

In the last twenty years of his life Hazen was arrested fourteen times in debtors suits, and he instituted as many suits against others. A court found him of unsound mind in 1802; nevertheless, he was arrested twice more for debt only weeks before his death on 5 February 1803. He was buried 8 February 1803 in Albany, N.Y.

DCB; JTC; *New England Historical & Genealogical Register*, XXXIII, 231 ff.; Allan S. Everest, *Moses Hazen and the Canadian Refugees in the American Revolution* (Syracuse, 1970).

Colonel Henry Hope (1742–89), *British army officer, colonial administrator.*

Henry Hope was born 1742 in Linlithgowshire, Scotland. He was the second son of Charles Hope-Weir, the second son of Charles Hope, 1st Earl of Hopetoun, from his second marriage to Lady Anne Vane, daughter of the 1st Earl of Darlington.

As the Seven Years' War came to a close, Henry Hope, then twenty, was commissioned a lieutenant (9 January 1762) in the newly raised 103rd Foot and participated in the Belle-Isle expedition. He went out at the peace a year later on half-pay (10 June 1763) but returned to active service the following year with the purchase of a captaincy in the 27th Foot (Inniskillens) (14 March 1764) while it was garrisoned in Quebec.

After his first North American tour of duty he returned with his regiment to Ireland in 1767, where it remained in garrison until the outbreak of the American Revolution. While stationed in Northern Ireland he met and married Sarah Jones of Mullaghbrack from Armagh. On 3 May 1775 he left the Inniskillens by purchasing his majority in the 44th Foot and went with it to Halifax, Nova Scotia, the same year. He participated in campaigns in New York, New Jersey and Pennsylvania and took part in the battles of Brandywine, Germantown and Monmouth Court House. On 5 October 1777 he was promoted lieutenant colonel of the 44th Foot, taking a leave of absence from the regiment in 1779 to return to England to settle his affairs and see his wife. He took another leave of absence from 1780 to 1781 while the 44th was stationed in Quebec. In 1782 he was made a colonel "in America" and visited Fort Michilimackinac as a member of a board of inquiry investigating excessive construction costs at that post. Hope was appointed quartermaster general in the Canadas in 1783 and by 1785 was "double-hatted" as commandant at Quebec since the commander-in-chief, Barrimore Matthew St. Leger, chose to reside at Montreal. In October 1785 Hope succeeded St. Leger as commander-in-chief in Canada and was also sworn in on 2 November 1785 as the interim lieutenant governor of Quebec, succeeding Henry Hamilton, who had been administrator of the colony since Governor FREDERICK HALDIMAND's departure.

Hope, despite a hot temper, was considered by most "a very polite Man" and an efficient administrator. His regiment returned to England in 1786 without him while Hope remained on hand to greet the new governor general, Lord Dorchester (Sir GUY CARLETON). Hope retained "the management of all business, both civil and military" but was allowed by Dorchester to visit Britain in 1788 on private business as well as to collect his wife. On the voyage back to Canada, Hope fell ill with what doctors mistakenly diagnosed as consumption but which proved to be venereal disease. In April 1789 he died from "his improper Gallantries ... the most shocking object that can be imagined — his Features & the greatest part of his Face entirely destroy'd."

BALs; *DCB, DNB*; JTC; A.L. Burt, *The Old Province of Quebec* (Minneapolis, 1933); W.C. Trimble, *The Historical Record of the 27th Inniskilling Regiment...* (London, 1876).

Major Paulus Æmilius Irving (1714–96), *British army officer, colonial administrator.*
Paulus Æmilius Irving was born on 23 September 1714 in Bonshaw, Dumfries, Scotland, the 4th and youngest son of William Irving (1663–98), Laird of Bonshaw. The somewhat unusual name of Æmilius was derived from his mother, the Honourable Æmilia Rollo, eldest daughter of Andrew, 3rd Lord Rollo. He was commissioned an ensign in the 15th Foot and had risen to the rank of major in the same regiment by 1758. He served at Louisbourg and commanded the 15th Foot during the Quebec campaign as his lieutenant colonel, JAMES MURRAY, was doing duty as one of Wolfe's three appointed brigadiers.

According to James Thompson, Major Irving was instrumental in securing Pointe Lévy on 30–31 June 1759. Slightly wounded in a subsequent engagement on 8 August 1759, Irving was fit enough to participate in the battle of the

"Damn the old wig!" The nickname given to Major Paulus Æmilius Irving, the feisty Lowland Scot who commanded the 15th Foot (Amherst's) during the Quebec campaign of 1759-60 by his soldiers after the battle of Sillery. When his trademark wig kept falling off during combat he was heard to exclaim repeatedly "Damn the old wig" and finally crammed it into his pocket. Print after oil pastel. (Editor's Collection)

Plains of Abraham on 13 September, where he was once again wounded. After the surrender of Quebec on 18 September, he continued in his role as acting commanding officer of the 15th Foot as Murray was made governor of Quebec. In October 1759 Murray appointed Irving deputy quartermaster general to succeed Colonel GUY CARLETON, who had been wounded during the battle and evacuated to New York for recovery. As deputy quartermaster general, Irving sat on the Military Council.

On 28 April 1760 he was again required to lead his regiment on the field of battle, this time at the battle of Sillery outside the walls of Quebec. The feisty Lowland Scot was known for cramming his trademark wig into his pocket during combat and his coolness under fire at Sillery became legendary in his regiment, one veteran remembering his commander calmly ordering men to right about turn and fire disciplined volleys at pursuing Frenchmen. In the heat of action Irving risked losing his trusty wig: "He however put it under his arm, with great Sang froid, and said 'damn the old wig,' a name by which he is known, to this day, by the old souldiers."

Later the same year his cousin, Lieutenant Colonel Andrew Rollo, the 5th Lord Rollo, arrived in command of the 22nd Foot and served as one of Murray's brigadiers during the capture of Montreal. Promoted lieutenant colonel in January 1762, Irving was chosen by Murray to occupy a post of councillor in the civilian government established August 1764. Two weeks later Murray commissioned him lieutenant governor for the District of Montreal but his post was disallowed by a parsimonious British government eager to recoup some of its heavy losses incurred by the war.

In 1764, when Murray was recalled to Britain over the political and civilian unrest after an attack on the merchant Thomas Walker by British troops, Irving, as the senior member of the council, became the interim council president and principal administrator of the colony. He filled the post for four months until the arrival from New York of Lieutenant Governor Guy Carleton in late September 1764. During the Revolutionary War he served as lieutenant governor of Guernsey (1770–84), one of the Channel Islands, and died 22 April 1796 while acting as the lieutenant governor of Upnor Castle in Kent, England.

DCB; DNB; JTC; Knox, *Journal,* II; *Quebec Gazette,* 21 July 1768; A.L. Burt, *The Old Province of Quebec* (Minneapolis, 1933); A.L. Burt, "Sir Guy Carleton and his first council," *Canadian Historical Review,* IV (1923), 321–32.

Thomas Ivers (c. 1724–1808), *American citizen, ropemaker, United States army officer.*
Thomas Ivers was born c. 1724 in the colony of Connecticut. He was working as a ropemaker living in the coastal port of Stratford when the grenadier company of the 78th Foot arrived and was billeted upon the townsfolk over the winter of 1758–59. Assigned to the Ivers household, James Thompson claimed he "liv'd here like a fighting cock, without its costing … a copper." Ivers and his wife, Hannah, became quite attached to Thompson, eventually offering him their twelve-year-old daughter's hand in marriage, if Thompson should quit the army, the marriage to take place only when the daughter reached "a proper age." As a further incentive, Thompson was offered partnership in Ivers' rope-making business. Thompson reluctantly turned the offer down but promised Ivers that he would return to Stratford when the war was over.

A rope-maker named Thomas Ivers, husband of Hannah, shows up in New York City some time before the American Revolution, having moved there from Stratford. While Ivers was a common name in 18th-century America, it is likely that the Thomas Ivers of Stratford and of pre- and post-revolutionary New York City are one and the same person. An unsubstantiated family record shows Thomas Ivers taking part in one of the most flamboyant episodes of the early Revolution, being "one of those who threw overboard the tea in Boston Harbour."

A daughter, Elizabeth, was born mid-1756 and could be the daughter offered to James Thompson, although there is a large discrepancy in the age remembered by Thompson. There is also a record of a Thomas Ivers who served as a captain lieutenant in John Lamb's Company, New York Artillery, raised in New York in 1776 for Continental service. Ordered to the Northern Army, it served under General RICHARD MONTGOMERY at the siege of Quebec, where they did excellent service but suffered severely from a lack of winter clothing and provisions. After the siege of Quebec, Thompson tried to locate his old friend "in consideration of the very great kindness he had shewn for me" but was unsuccessful.

After the war, Ivers returned to New York City and is found in the 1787 New York City directory listed as a rope-maker with no fixed address. By the 1800 census Thomas Ivers was listed as the sole male over forty-five in a household of thirteen, including five slaves. Although the last directory listing for Thomas Ivers is 1803, he remained active until at least 1805. The *New York Evening Post* reported the death of Thomas Ivers, eighty-four years, on 15 February 1808, in New York City. His wife, Hannah, predeceased him in 1801.

JTC; *Manual of the Corporation of the City of New York,* 1869, 793; *Genealogical and Biographical Notes on the Haring-Herring, Clark, Denton, White, Griggs, Judd, and related families,* compiled/published by P. H. Judd (New York, 2005).

James Johnstone, *aka* the Chevalier de Johnstone (1719–91), *Jacobite army officer, French army officer.*
James Johnstone was born 25 July 1719 in Edinburgh, Scotland, the son of James Johnstone, a merchant. He appears to have had a misspent youth and while residing in London was forced by his father to return to Scotland in 1740. When news reached Edinburgh in 1745 that Prince Charles, the Young Pretender, had landed in Scotland, Johnstone sped to join his army. Through his Douglas relatives, he was introduced to Lord George Murray, second-in-command of the rebels, who appointed him to be an aide de camp. Johnstone served throughout the Jacobite uprising and occasionally served as aide de camp to the Prince. After the battle of Prestonpans, September 1745, Charles granted Johnstone a captain's commission and he was assigned to the Duke of Perth's Regiment. Following the rout at Culloden in 1746, he escaped

north and was concealed by Lady Jane Douglas, wife of Colonel John Roy Stewart.

Johnstone eventually escaped to Paris, where he was introduced to the Marquis de Puysieux, minister of foreign affairs, and was granted a pension from special funds allocated by the king for Scottish gentlemen exiled in France. Despite promises from Puysieux, his captain's commission was not recognized in France, and a mortified Johnstone received only an ensigncy in the colonial regular troops of Île Royale (Cape Breton Island). He went to Louisbourg in 1750 and was promoted lieutenant in 1754.

During the 1758 siege of Louisbourg, Johnstone was stationed on Île Saint-Jean (Prince Edward Island), whence he made his way to Quebec, arriving there in September 1758. He became an aide de camp to Lévis and also served as interpreter and engineer. With credentials as an officially appointed interpreter, and acting on the general's behalf, he probably also acted unofficially as an intelligence officer, tasked to hold conversations with prisoners to see if they revealed any information. He may be the mysterious "Colonel Ross" mentioned by James Thompson in his anecdotes. When Lévis was dispatched to Montreal to counter AMHERST's northwards thrust up Lake Champlain, Johnstone remained at Quebec as aide de camp to Montcalm. Following the 1759 siege and capture of Quebec, he retreated with the army. Stationed at Île aux Noix from April to August 1760, he escaped to Montreal when the French were forced to abandon the Champlain–Richelieu front. When the British finally approached Montreal, Lieutenant John Knox noted in his journal that there "the [British] deserters were commanded by one Johnston, a proscribed rebel, who is a Lieutenant in the French service."

After the capitulation of the city, he returned to Quebec with other French officers and sailed for France on 16 October 1760. He was retired from the Marine service with a pension of 300 livres in 1761 and the following year was made a knight of the order of Saint-Louis. He lived in Paris, but visited Scotland in 1779 to settle personal matters. By 1790 his pension had been increased to 1,485 livres, and in 1791 he successfully petitioned the assembly for 500 livres for losses incurred during the Jacobite rebellion. He died shortly thereafter.

DCB; Knox, *Journal,* II, 507; "A Dialogue in Hades: A Parallel of military errors, of which the French and English armies were guilty during the Campaign of 1759 in Canada," a narrative attributed to Chevalier James Johnstone, LHSQ, *Historical Documents,* Series 2, Vol 2 (1867); "The Campaign of 1760 in Canada," a narrative attributed to Chevalier James Johnstone, LHSQ, *Historical Documents,* Second Series (1887).

Colonel Valentine Jones (1723–79), *British army officer.*

Valentine Jones was born 1723 in Wales, and little is known of his parents or early schooling. He joined the army on 26 March 1744 when he "purchased his colours" as an ensign in the 33rd Foot (Johnson's). A veteran of the famed battles of Dettingen (1743) and Fontenoy (1745), Jones was promoted lieutenant 1 May 1745 and captain lieutenant 26 September 1754 in the 33rd Foot. On promotion to captain 13 October 1755, he subsequently transferred to a company in the newly-raised 54th Foot in December 1755. In 1758 his regiment was renumbered downwards as the 52nd Foot and he became its major 14 October 1758. Two years later he was promoted lieutenant colonel (4 March 1760) and was given a brevet promotion to the rank of colonel "in the army" on 25 May 1772.

After lengthy garrison duties in Ireland throughout the 1760s, the 52nd Foot was transferred to the Province of Canada, where it garrisoned the fortified city of Quebec. In his capacity of commander-in-chief of the forces in Canada, Jones came into contact with the overseer of works, James Thompson. In the spring of 1774, Jones and the two regiments under his care (the 10th Foot and his own 52nd) were ordered to Boston during the period of growing unrest in that city. By the year end, Jones had been appointed to the command of the 3rd Brigade and received the local rank of major general (in America only) on 1 January 1776.

Only weeks later, on 15 January 1776, he learned that he was appointed colonel of the 62nd Foot on the death of its elderly founding colonel, Lieutenant General William Strode (1698–1776), and was subsequently made a substantive major general in the British army on 29 August 1777. As commander of the 3rd Brigade of General Sir William Howe's army, Jones and his regiments participated throughout the lengthy campaign of 1776, assisting in the subjugation of Long Island, Manhattan, lower New York and New Jersey.

Writing to Lord George Germain in December 1776, Howe expressed his opinion that Major General Valentine Jones was "too inactive and infirm" for active duty. Major James Wemyss, a British officer who served with the main army in America, remembered Jones as an "honest hotheaded Welchman, altogether destitute of abilities; but hospitable and friendly, and [on] all occasions did the best he could." Due to failing health, Valentine Jones returned home and was in England by early November 1778.

After a fall from a horse, his health deteriorated further and he died at Llanidloes, in Montgomeryshire, Wales, at the age of fifty-six. His obituary in the November 1779 *Gentleman's Gazette* reads: "He had been in the army thirty-eight years, and during that period had served his country on many important and trying occasions.... At the close of last year [1778] he returned from America, where he had served fourteen years, and where he had been employed on many services, both civil and military, and distinguished for his bravery, humanity, and every other virtue which can adorn the soldier and the man."

BALs; *DCB;* JTC; *Gentleman's Gazette*, 15–17 November 1779.

Private David Kanavan (dates unknown),
tailor, British army soldier.
Possibly this individual remembered by James Thompson is one Corporal Donald McKenivan whose name appears on a petition of discharged men of the 78th Foot requesting land grants in Quebec, 19 and 31 May 1765. According to Thompson, Kanavan was a native of Ireland and had served a seven-year apprenticeship to his brother, then a master tailor in Paris, France. During this time, Kanavan became fluently bilingual but got into some unknown difficulties and, according to Thompson, was "obliged to leave the country." Returning to Ireland, Kanavan enlisted in the newly raised 78th Foot then on the march to Cork for embarkation to North America, and took on the duties of master tailor for the regiment. Characterized as a "funny dog" and "continually in hobbles" by Thompson, Kanavan liked to impersonate field grade officers by wearing their uniform (presumably left in his care for mending, alterations, etc.). During one episode, he fell in with a lieutenant from another regiment, got drunk and assaulted the officer. Only the personal intervention of the regiment's colonel commandant, SIMON FRASER, kept Kanavan from a general court marshal and probably the gallows.

JTC; "An account of H.M. Royal Bounty of 14 days subsistence, also the sword money paid the following men of the 78th Regiment Discharged in America," August 1763, LAC RG4-C2, vol 1, Microfilm C-10462; Col. R.J. Harper, *The Fraser Highlanders* (Montreal, 1979).

Governor Sir James Kempt (c. 1765–1854),
British army officer, colonial governor.
James Kempt was born in Edinburgh c. 1765, the son of Gavin Kempt and Miss Walker, the daughter of Alexander Walker of Edinburgh. Nothing is known of his early life, but he was

Sir James Kempt. Painted by William Salter about 1836, Kempt was governor of British North America from 1828 to 1830, replacing George Ramsay, the Earl of Dalhousie. (National Portrait Gallery NPG 3728)

commissioned as an ensign in the 101st Foot in March 1783 and promoted to lieutenant in August 1784. When the junior regiment was disbanded the following year, Kempt was placed on half-pay and remained so until 1794, when he was gazetted captain and then major in the newly raised 113th Foot. Following that regiment's disbandment, he served for a while as inspecting field officer of recruiting at Glasgow but was reduced to half-pay in 1796. Three years later, as lieutenant colonel unattached, he was appointed aide de camp to Sir Ralph Abercromby, then commanding the troops in Scotland, whom he accompanied with expeditionary forces to Holland and subsequently to the Mediterranean. On Abercromby's death in 1801 in Alexandria, Kempt was attached to the staff of Lord Hutchinson and was present throughout the Egyptian campaign.

In 1803 he became aide de camp to General David Dundas, commander-in-chief of the Southern District in England, and later that year obtained the lieutenant colonelcy of the 81st Foot, which he took to the Mediterranean in 1805 under the command of Sir JAMES HENRY CRAIG. Between 1807 and 1811 Kempt served as quartermaster general in British North America and in 1809 was promoted colonel. He returned to Spain in 1811 to serve on the staff of the Duke of Wellington with the rank of major general.

Severely wounded in the assault on Badajoz, he returned after his recovery to command of a brigade in the famous Light Division (comprising the 43rd Foot, 52nd Foot and the 95th Rifles), which he led to victories at Vera, the Nivelle (where he was again wounded), Bayonne, Orthez and Toulouse. Kempt was sent back to North America to fight in the ongoing War of 1812, commanding a brigade allocated to an expedition to attack the vital American post of Sackets Harbor, New York. Delayed by winter weather and logistical problems, news of peace between Britain and America reached Canada early in 1815 and Kempt returned to Europe with his troops.

At the battle of Waterloo, he led a brigade consisting of the 1/28th, 1/32nd, 79th and 1/95th Rifles in the division of Sir Thomas Picton, and on the latter's death succeeded to the command. Early in 1815 he was made KCB, and in July for his services at Waterloo, GCB. He was promoted lieutenant general in 1825, and from 1828 to 1830 he was governor of British North America, replacing the Earl of Dalhousie (GEORGE RAMSAY). He was afterwards master general of the Ordnance. At the time of his death, 23 December 1854, he had been a full general for thirteen years.

BALs; *DCB; DNB;* RGO.

Surgeon Major Louis-François Lajus (Lajuste) (1721–99), *French army officer and surgeon, civilian doctor.*

Louis-François was born 28 August 1721 in Quebec, the son of Jordain Lajus, a surgeon, and Louise-Élisabeth Moreau, *dit* Lataupine. Referred to as "Dr. Lajuste" by James Thompson in his anecdotes, Lajus learned surgery from his father. On 11 January 1745 Intendant Hocquart granted him a commission to go to Acadia as surgeon major, but he returned to Quebec three years later, where he married Marguerite Audet de Piercotte de Bailleul on 14 November 1747. They had several children but all died in infancy.

By 1758 he had returned to Acadia and was present at the siege of Louisbourg and its capitulation to the British. Accompanied by an Indian guide, he returned overland to Quebec, bringing the first news that the fortress had fallen. During the 1759 siege of Quebec, Lajus treated the many French wounded brought to the Hôpital Général and, after the battle of the Plains of Abraham, soldiers of both armies. After the conquest, he continued in private practice in the town and, although not attached to any particular hospital, was often called into consultation at the Hôtel-Dieu.

Dr. Lajus had a good reputation and a large practice, including the family of James Thompson, who styled him as "very clever." On 11 August 1776 Lajus took Angélique-Jeanne Hubert as his second wife, her brother, Jean-François, being the Father Superior of the Jesuit Seminary and later Bishop of Quebec. In 1788 he was chosen by Governor CARLETON to sit as a member of the first Board of Medical Examiners in Quebec. He died in Quebec on 6 October 1799.

JTC; *DCB;* J.-M. Lemoine, *Maple Leaves* (Quebec, 1894); J.-M. Lemoine, *Picturesque Quebec: A Sequel to Quebec Past and Present* (Montreal, 1882).

Sergeant Alexander Leith (dates unknown), *British army soldier.*

The quartermaster sergeant in the 78th Foot, Alexander Leith first appears in James Thompson's anecdotes as the butt of one of Sergeant Ballinagagg's pranks when the regiment was in cantonments at St. Pierre in 1760. On 22 October 1760 Leith was appointed Master of the Lodge of Free and Accepted Masons in the 78th Foot, known by the name of "No. 6 Canada." The proceedings covering this installation show that Brothers James Thompson and ALEXANDER FERGUSON were officiating wardens. Leith is also one of twelve former sergeants whose names appear on a land petition to Governor JAMES MURRAY dated 15 March 1765, requesting 200 acres each "in and about the Bays of Chaleur and Gaspey." Leith is not shown as discharged on the 1763 disbandment muster rolls of the 78th Foot, which probably indicates he transferred to one of the two infantry regiments left in Quebec that did not disband – the 15th Foot or 60th Foot – then subsequently took his discharge in 1765.

JTC; Col. R.J. Harper, *The Fraser Highlanders* (Montreal, 1979); A.J.B. Milborne, "The Lodge in the 78th Regiment (Fraser's Highlanders)," *Quatuor Coronati Lodge*, vol. LXV (1952).

Governor Charles Lennox, Duke of Richmond and Lennox (1764–1819), *British army officer.*

Charles Lennox was born in Scotland (reportedly in a barn when his mother was on a fishing party) on 9 September 1764, the eldest son of Lieutenant General Lord George Henry Lennox and his wife, Louisa, eldest daughter of William Henry Kerr, 4th Marquess of Lothian. He was privately educated and while in his teens served as secretary to his uncle, the master general of the Ordnance, from 1784 to 1795. He entered the army in 1785 and, while a captain in the Coldstream Guards in 1789, fought a duel with his colonel, the Duke of

"The Most Noble Prince Charles Duke of Richmond, Lennox & Aubigny, etc." Mezzotint by John Faber after the painting by Louis Michel van Loo. Lennox is shown here, c. 1750, with armour and cloak, a fashion in military portraiture of the 18th century. (Anne S.K. Brown Military Collection, Brown University Library)

York. Although no one was hurt in the duel, his fellow guards officers adjudged he had shown poor judgment and he was obliged to transfer out of the prestigious unit. Lennox exchanged his captaincy in the Guards for the command of the 35th Foot, then stationed in Edinburgh.

In 1790, through the influence of his uncle, the Duke of Richmond, he became Member of Parliament for Sussex, in succession to his father, and continued to represent the county until he succeeded to the dukedom of Richmond and Lennox on the death of his uncle on 29 December 1806. In 1794 Lennox and his 35th Foot were sent to the West Indies, where his regiment was severely afflicted by yellow fever, 640 officers and men dying of the disease. In 1795 Lennox obtained the rank of colonel and was appointed aide de camp to the king, and in 1798 he was promoted major general. On 17 March 1803 he was appointed colonel of the 35th Foot, replacing General Harry Fletcher, and two years later was promoted to lieutenant general. On 1 April 1807 he was sworn into the Privy Council and appointed lord lieutenant of Ireland. Colonel Arthur Wellesley (afterwards the Duke of Wellington) acted as his chief secretary.

Richmond was unofficially present at the battle of Waterloo in 1815, despite several attempts by his former secretary to send him home. Richmond was subsequently appointed governor-in-chief of British North America in 1818 and reached Quebec in July 1818. The House of Assembly, then dominated by Louis-Joseph Papineau's party, was a hotbed of dissent, which soon led to the prorogement of the governing body. While on an extensive tour of Upper and Lower Canada in the summer of 1819, Lennox was bitten by a fox and died in agony from hydrophobia (rabies) a few miles from Richmond, Upper Canada, 20 August 1819. He was buried on 4 September in the cathedral of the Holy Trinity, Quebec.

DCB; DNB; JTC; RGO.

Captain Donald (Donull Gorm) Macdonell, of Benbecula (c. 1728–60), *British army officer.*

"Donull Gorm" was the second and natural son of Ranald Macdonell, 17th "Old" Clanranald, and half-brother to the 18th "Young" Clanranald. His younger half-brother, William, served at the same time in the 78th Foot. Donull Gorm joined the French army as a regular officer before the Jacobite rebellion in 1745. In his own words, written at Edinburgh Castle, 15 December 1746: "I went to France in year 1742 and served as Cadet in Booth's Regmt. till I got a Company in Drummond's

Regmt. [Royal Ecossais] the year 44 and came along with it to Scotland in Novr 45, and being wounded before Sterling, I returned to my father's country, where I remained till hearing that all my Reg^mt. surrender'd themselves prisoners of War at Inverness, after the Battle of Culloden, I was desirous of doing the same, and I surrendered myself to Capt. John Mackdonald [yr of Glenlyon, 43rd Foot, and brother of Archie Roy MacDonald] as soon as he came to the Country I was in, in July last...."

In 1756 the Duke of Argyll said of him: "brother to Clanranald was sent into the French Service when a boy, & had a Company several years, which he quitted some months ago upon the late Act of Parliament & took the Oaths to the Government; for these facts, as well as for his Character, he appeals to My Lord Holderness & undertakes on this occasion to raise 100 men." Accepted as one of the original company commanders of the newly raised 78th Foot, Macdonell replaced CHARLES BAILLIE as captain of grenadiers at Louisbourg, June 1758, and was wounded on the night of 21 July 1760 in the siege trenches. Macdonell was universally disliked by the Highlander rank and file, Grenadier Sergeant James Thompson unabashedly styling him "a surly cross dog," and in his anecdotes hinting that Macdonell was intentionally wounded or "fragged" by his own men at the siege.

Markedly, at the battle of Sillery, 28 April 1760, none of the volunteers of Macdonell's elite company were drawn from the 78th Foot and he died on that day amongst strangers. Oral traditions in the Highlands of Cape Breton, where several Fraser soldiers returned to settle on the eastern Bras Dor Lakes of Cape Breton (Barra MacNeils, MacEacherns, and Clanranald Macdonells), maintain that it was at this 1760 battle that "the de'il finally got him." Harper, in his book *The Fraser Highlanders*, did not include Thompson's somewhat satisfied description of his nemesis's gory death – "a stronger body of French overpowered and completely butchered his whole party, and he himself was found cut and hack'd to pieces in a most shocking manner. There was an end of him!" This was, no doubt, Canadian retaliation for "Donull Gorm's" ruthless winter raids against the outlying countryside of Quebec, where he kept the *Canadien* militiamen and French regulars constantly off balance.

CBs; BALs; JTC; SBs; Stewart, *Sketches*, II, 20–1; "Donald McDonald" NA WO 64/12; Cumberland Papers, Windsor Castle, 49/5; NAS GD201/4/81; *Muster Roll of Prince Charles Edward Stuart's Army 1745–46*, A. Livingstone et al, eds. (Aberdeen, 1985); Col. R.J. Harper, 78th *Fighting Frasers in Canada: A short history of the old 78th Regiment or Fraser's Highlanders, 1757–1763* (Laval, 1966), 101–2.

Captain Ranald "Raonall Oig" Macdonell, 18th of Keppoch (c. 1732–88), *British army officer.*

Oldest legitimate son of Alexander Macdonell, 17th Keppoch, and Jessie Stewart. He styled himself "Son of Keppoch" when gazetted a lieutenant in the 78th Foot on 14 January 1757, despite his father having been dead for ten years, a clear indication that he felt that his older "natural" brother, Angus Ban, in exile, was the rightful chieftain and not he. Served at Louisbourg, 1758, and was wounded "thro' the knee" at the battle on the Plains of Abraham on 13 September 1759. Promoted to captain lieutenant on 25 September 1759 and captain on 17 October 1759. The monthly returns of November 1759 list him as having gone "to continent for recovery." The hereditary piper of *Clann Dhomhanuill na Ceapaich, Padraig Cambeuil* (Patrick Campbell), was not happy with Keppoch's decision to serve the British king and his wounding was seen partially as a punishment for renouncing his Catholic religion.

After his promotion to captain, his older stepbrother, Angus Ban, formally wrote out a resignation of the chieftainship in order that

Ranald could start the process to reclaim the Keppoch lands. He was back with his regiment by 1762, General Orders dated 3 June 1762 stating that "Capt Ron^d. McDon^d. is appointed to command the Grenadier Company." When the regiment was disbanded in 1763, he exchanged onto half-pay. He returned to active service in December 1766 as a captain in the 66th Foot, was made major "by brevet" in 1772 and retired in June 1775. In December 1777 he was persuaded to come out of retirement and raise a company of Keppoch Macdonells for the new-raising 74th Foot (Argyll Highlanders) commanded by his old 78th colleague, John Campbell of Barbreck. "Major" Macdonell retired a second time in January 1779 and died nine years later at Keppoch in 1788.

BALs; CBs; SBs; Stewart, *Sketches*, II, 20–1; "Ronald McDonald," NA WO 64/12; NA C5/51.

Sergeant Duncan McPhee

(c. 1713–unknown), *labourer, part-time cattle thief, British army soldier.*

Based on his application to the Royal Hospital, Chelsea, Duncan McPhee was born in Glenelg, Invernesshire, about 1713. According to James Thompson, McPhee was a homeless cattle thief for seven years, carrying off cattle from the Lowlands and selling them in England. Thompson also described him as "the biggest thief in the world ... a wicked rascal as ever lived ... bold as a lion." In 1757, at forty-four years, McPhee volunteered for service in the newly raised 78th Foot as a private soldier "only to save his neck."

During the siege of Louisbourg, McPhee caught the attention of General JAMES WOLFE, who became intrigued by his unusual sense of duty. He was appointed by General Wolfe first as an orderly and later as a "sergeant in the army, never to be broke!" Illiterate and unable to speak English, McPhee could not take orders without the help of other sergeants, including James Thompson. At Louisbourg he chased down a French officer, taking his sword as a "trophy of war." A difficult man to deal with, McPhee reluctantly returned the sword to its owner only after the regiment's commanding officer had personally interceded.

Late in 1763 McPhee appeared at the Royal Hospital at Chelsea, looking for a pension. According to the Chelsea Regimental Registers of Pensioners, McPhee was fifty-one years old, with twenty-nine years of military service, so he must have had military experience before joining the 78th Foot in 1757, perhaps during and prior to the War of the Austrian Succession. Listed as "worn out," McPhee was admitted as a pensioner on 6 January 1764.

JTC; NA WO 40 *Regimental Registers of Pensioners.*

The Reverend Robert "Caipal Mhor" Macpherson (1731–91), *British army chaplain.*

Robert Macpherson was born 19 December 1731, the third of six sons of John Macpherson of Banchor, and the first son of the second marriage to Christian Macpherson. He initially had hoped to get a regular infantry commission in the newly raised 78th Foot (according to correspondence between himself and his cousin William Macpherson) but instead was offered the appointment of chaplain, which he accepted, the date of his seniority 12 January 1757. The twenty-six-year-old chaplain was known affectionately to his men as the *Caipal Mhor* (Big Chaplain) because of his towering physique. According to David Stewart of Garth, Macpherson was not shy soldiering alongside his men and "was indefatigable in the discharge of his clerical duties," so much so that "the men of the regiment were always anxious to conceal their misdemeanors from the *Caipal Mhor*...."

After the conquest of New France in 1760, Macpherson, a Freemason, served as chaplain to the Quebec Select Lodge composed of officers serving in the various regiments then in garrison. Sergeant James Thompson, himself a Freemason and Senior Warden of Canada Lodge No. 6 in the 78th Foot, recorded that on St. John's Day in the winter of 1761, the members of his lodge "walked in procession in due form at one o'clock attended by the Reverend Brother Robert Macpherson, Member of the Select Lodge at Quebec from whom we had a sermon on the Occasion in the Church of St. Valier."

On disbandment of Fraser's Highlanders, Robert Macpherson exchanged to half-pay like many of the 78th officers and returned to Badenoch, where he petitioned the factor of the forfeited estates at Aberarder in 1766, stating he had "served in America for seven years, on reduction put on half-pay. Being a half-pay chaplain, he is prevented by an act of Parliament from holding an ecclesiastical position. He therefore wants to try farming. Seen methods while traveling home and abroad which he thinks will enable him to carry on better than most. Therefore requests Aberarder and Tullochrom comprehending Strachronnachan as possessed by Ronald and Alexander Macdonell."

He took up residence at Aberarder by 1770, where he was known for many years by his neighbours as "Parson Robert." He married Louisa Campbell, daughter of Duncan Campbell of Achlyne, in 1775, and of his five sons three entered the army, Duncan attaining the rank of lieutenant general. His eldest son, John Macpherson of Ness Bank, was factor to both Lord Macdonald in Skye and to the Lovat estates at Inverness. The *Caipal Mhor* died in March 1791 and is buried in Perth.

Stewart, *Sketches;* Robert MacFarlane, "The Macdonells of Aberarder," *Clan Donald Magazine,* No. 12 (1991); Alexander Macpherson, "Sketches of the Old Seats of Families and of Distinguished Soldiers, etc., connected with Badenoch," *Journal of the Clan Macpherson Association (U.S. Branch),* No. 92 (Summer, 1999), 335–36.

Sergeant Hugh McQuarters (c. 1747–1809), *British army soldier.*

During the siege of Quebec on 31 December 1775, Hugh McQuarters, then a twenty-eight-year-old sergeant in the Royal Artillery, was assigned to the gun crew posted at the Près-de-Ville barricade commanded by Captain Barnsfare (the master of a British transport laid up in the harbour for the winter). According to Quebec historian James-MacPherson Lemoine, it was sturdy Hugh McQuarters who "applied the match to the cannon which consigned to a snowy shroud Brigadier General RICHARD MONTGOMERY and his two aides, McPherson and Cheeseman, and his brave, but doomed followers, some eleven in all, the rest having sought safety in flight." McQuarters was an active Freemason and his name appears on a petition before his lodge on 10 July 1781. McQuarters was also a member of Quebec's Presbyterian congregation and his name and that of his son Hugh Jr. appear on a 5 October 1802 petition to George III requesting land to build a Presbyterian church in Quebec. He would have been well known to Thompson and his family. McQuarters lived on Champlain Street (rue Champlain) in Lower Town, Quebec. He died on 13 August 1809, aged sixty-two.

JTC; *Register Book,* St. Andrew's Church; *Quebec Mercury,* 24 August 1809; A.J.B. Milborne, "The Lodge in the 78th Regiment (Fraser's Highlanders), *Quatuor Coronati Lodge,* vol LXV (1952); J.-M. Lemoine, *Picturesque Quebec: A Sequel to Quebec Past and Present* (Montreal, 1882).

Captain Gother Mann (1747–1830), *British army officer, colonial administrator.*

Gother Mann was born 21 December 1747 in Plumstead (near London), the second son of Cornelius Mann and Elizabeth Gother. In 1763 he graduated at the age of sixteen from the Royal Military Academy at Woolwich, and for the next twelve years of his career he was employed on constructing defensive installations along

Captain Gother Mann. With two tours of duty in Canada as commanding engineer (1785–91 and 1794–1804), Gother Mann came into frequent contact with James Thompson. One of Mann's projects was Hope Gate on the northern face of the ramparts, with Thompson in charge of the masons and stone layers. (Royal Engineers Museum, Chatham)

the English coast. He married Anne Wade in 1767 and they had eight children. Commissioned a lieutenant in 1771, he was posted to Dominica in the West Indies late in 1775 and while there was promoted captain (1777). On his return to Britain in 1777 he spent the next six years reporting on defence installations along the eastern coast of England.

In 1785, the thirty-eight-year-old Mann was sent to the province of Quebec on his first tour as a captain and commanding engineer, where he came into contact with James Thompson. His remit during this period was to carry on with the coordination and construction of canals on the St. Lawrence, as well as the construction of fortifications at Quebec. In 1788 the governor, Lord Dorchester (Sir GUY CARLETON) instructed Mann to conduct an extensive inspection of military posts from Kingston to St. Mary's (Sault Ste. Marie) in Upper Canada. His thirty-four page report contained a detailed critique of the posts, harbours and navigable water routes.

After his first tour in Canada, Mann spent 1792–93 in the Netherlands, participating in the sieges of various French-held towns. Promoted lieutenant colonel late in 1793, he was ordered to return to Lower Canada for a second tour to prepare defences at Quebec, since war with the United States was a distinct possibility. Four years later he was promoted colonel. In 1803 Mann was promoted major general and requested he be allowed to return to England, where his family had remained over the past ten years.

Mann departed Quebec in 1804 and, on arrival in Britain, assumed various engineering responsibilities, as well as the post of colonel commandant of the Royal Engineers in 1805. He was promoted lieutenant general in 1810 and appointed inspector general of fortifications the following year. He was responsible for appointing engineer John By to superintend the construction of the Rideau Canal in Upper Canada. In 1821 Mann was promoted general. He died in Lewisham (near London) nine years later on 27 March 1830, the senior officer in his corps.

BALs; *DCB; DNB;* JTC; RGO; André Charbonneau et al., *Quebec The Fortified City: From the 17th to the 19th Century* (Parks Canada, 1982); Whitworth Porter et al., *History of the Corps of Royal Engineers*; R.F. Edwards, *Roll of Officers of the Corps of Royal Engineers from 1660 to 1898* (Chatham, 1898).

Captain John Marr (c. 1740–86), *British army officer.*

Little is known of John Marr's early life except that he was born in Scotland. He entered the British army as a practitioner engineer on 17 March 1759 in the middle of the Seven Years' War. By the end of the war, Marr was a sub engineer (25 February 1763) and working at

Quebec, the superior of James Thompson, then clerk of works. When Marr returned to Scotland in 1772 on extended leave, Governor GUY CARLETON, then stationed in New York, ordered Lieutenant Colonel VALENTINE JONES to appoint an infantry or artillery officer to take over as head of military engineering services in Quebec, the normal practice when an engineer was not available. However, Colonel Jones was reluctant to appoint an officer from the garrison as he considered that such an officer would not be "acquainted with the forms of office, the framing of estimates, and the nature of Works and materials." As the position was of a temporary nature, Colonel Jones offered it to Thompson, presumably after clearing it with Carleton, and Thompson was given the impressive title of overseer of works (25 October 1772).

When Marr returned there is no indication that Thompson gave up this title, and on 24 January 1774 Marr was promoted engineer extraordinary (the equivalent of an infantry captain lieutenant). Two years later, the elderly Marr became jealous of WILLIAM TWISS, the young engineer aide de camp to General William Phillips serving in General John Burgoyne's army. Sir Guy Carleton, commander-in-chief at Quebec, chose Twiss over Marr to be controller of works for the construction of a fleet on Lake Champlain, and to add insult to injury Twiss was appointed senior engineer for Burgoyne's army.

In 1778 Twiss, a gifted engineer, was promoted to engineer extraordinary, the same rank as Marr. Thereafter, for the next three years, Twiss was employed in strengthening the defences of Canada and supervising the construction of a temporary citadel at Quebec, which commenced in 1779. Although Marr was the nominal commanding engineer at Quebec, most command decisions were made by Twiss, causing Marr to complain directly to Governor FREDERICK HALDIMAND that reports were not made to him as commanding engineer and that he was being treated "as a cypher." Furthermore, Marr believed that an injustice was done to him "by the appointment of a junior engineer to the command of the Engineers" and requested permission to return to England "to prevent the effects of such treatment." When Marr left in 1781, Twiss officially assumed the duties of commanding engineer in Canada which he had been performing all along. The sickly Marr was made a brevet major by the end of the war (19 March 1783) and was finally transferred to the Corps of Engineer Invalids in October 1784. He died two years later, 30 October 1784, in Scotland.

BALs; CBs; *DCB; DNB;* JTC; R.F. Edwards, *Roll of Officers of the Corps of Royal Engineers from 1660 to 1898* (Chatham, 1898).

Brigadier General Robert Monckton (1726–82), *British army officer.*
Robert Monckton first came to North America in 1754 as the lieutenant colonel (28 February 1751) commanding the 47th Foot (Lascelles) and captured Fort Beauséjour the following year. He was made lieutenant governor of Nova Scotia in 1758 and remained in Halifax when General JEFFERY AMHERST and Admiral Edward Boscawen took Louisbourg 1758. In 1759 he was the most senior of JAMES WOLFE's three brigadiers at Quebec and was wounded in the lung while commanding the right wing of the army at the battle of the Plains of Abraham.

Sent to New York for recovery, he succeeded Brigadier General John Stanwix in command of the troops at Philadelphia and was actively involved in trying to induce the northern colonies to supply more soldiers on behalf of Amherst. On 20 February 1761 he was promoted to the rank of major general and on 20 March 1761 appointed governor of New York and commander-in-chief of the province.

By the end of 1761 he was placed in command of the expedition to take Martinique and suc-

Brigadier General Robert Monckton. The senior of Wolfe's three brigadiers, Robert Monckton was a professional soldier who had served in North America since 1752, primarily in Nova Scotia, where he was lieutenant governor from 1755 to 1758. He was regarded as "timid" and "unimaginative" by Wolfe, a view supported by Thompson in one of his anecdotes. Mezzotint by James McArdell after a painting by Thomas Hudson, c. 1760. (Anne S.K. Brown Military Collection, Brown University Library)

cessfully captured it in addition to the islands of Grenada, St. Lucia and St. Vincent. On 28 June 1763 he left America for good, later taking up the military governorship of Berwick-upon-Tweed in 1765. In 1770 he was made lieutenant general and in 1778 became governor of Portsmouth. He represented that city in Parliament from 1779 until his death 3 May 1782.

DCB; DNB; JTC.

Major General Louis-Joseph de Montcalm (1712–59), *seigneur of Saint-Veran, Candiac, Tournemine, Vestric, Saint-Julien, and Arpaon, Baron de Gabriac, French army officer.*
Louis-Joseph de Montcalm was born 28 February 1712 at Candiac into an old and established noble family with large estates in southern France. Other Montcalms before him had served their king faithfully, so much so, the local saying went, "War is the tomb of the Montcalms." Louis-Joseph was the son of Louis-Daniel de Montcalm and Marie-Thérèse-Charlotte de Lauris de Castellane, and his parents had him commissioned an ensign in the régiment d'Hainault at the age of nine, but he did not join. After his education, they purchased a captaincy for him on his nineteenth birthday, but his active and extensive military career did not start until the following year (1722) when he turned twenty. Despite his hot temper, sharp tongue and tendency to hold a grudge, the haughty Montcalm did well in the army.

During the War of the Austrian Succession, Montcalm served as the lieutenant colonel of the régiment d'Auxerois and was made a Knight of St. Louis (*Ordre Royal et Militaire de Saint-Louis*) for gallantry. He was badly wounded at the battle of Piacenza, 1746, where his regiment was virtually destroyed and he was taken prisoner. In 1748 peace brought his release and he petitioned the French minister of war for leave to retire on pension to his estates, citing his long service of thirty-one years, eleven campaigns and five wounds.

For the next seven years, Montcalm lived the life of a provincial noblemen, periodically making inspection visits to his regiment in its peacetime garrison. When Baron de Dieskau was captured at Lake George in 1755, Louis XV had to quickly find a replacement. With a major continental war looming, no senior experienced French officer wanted to serve in a country which most viewed as "so many acres of snow." The monarch reached lower and appointed Montcalm a major general (*marechal de camp*) in 1756 and sent him to New France with two battalions of regular infantry to add to the eight already stationed there.

Montcalm won a string of victories in North

Major General Louis-Joseph de Montcalm. A fiery tempered but professional soldier, this native of Provence assumed command of all regular French troops in New France in 1756. Eternally pessimistic about the outcome of the war in New France, his command was not made any easier by his tempestuous relationship with the governor of New France, the Marquis de Vaudreuil. This 19th century copy was made from the original belonging to the Montcalm family in France. The original artist is unknown. (LAC A/N 1991-209-1)

America, commencing with the siege and capture of Oswego in 1756, the siege and destruction of Fort William Henry in 1757 and the bloody repulse of Major General James Abercromby's army at Ticonderoga in 1758. His relations with the Governor of New France, the Marquis de Vaudreuil, were constantly strained, which severely affected the morale and defensive strategy of the French-Canadian forces. During the Quebec campaign in 1759, James Thompson claimed to have seen Montcalm riding along the top of the Beauport Heights at the battle of Montmorency, 31 July 1759, but instead probably saw his second in command, Brigadier General François-Gaston de Lévis, who commanded that sector.

At the battle of the Plains of Abraham, after a lengthy siege of some four months, Montcalm was outmanoeuvred by General JAMES WOLFE, his French regulars outfought by Wolfe's regiments. By attacking Wolfe instead of remaining secure behind the walls of Quebec and manning his entrenchments, Montcalm ensured his own defeat. Wounded by grapeshot from British artillery as he retired from the battlefield with his retreating soldiers, Montcalm died the following day and was buried in a crater outside the convent of the Ursuline nuns. In 2001 Montcalm's body was disinterred and reburied alongside those of his soldiers in the cemetery of the Hôpital Général.

DCB; Canadian Encyclopedia; Guy Frégault, *Canada: the War of the Conquest* (Toronto, 1969); C.P. Stacey, *Quebec, 1759* (Toronto, 1959).

Brigadier General Richard Montgomery (1736–75), *British army officer, United States army officer, member of provincial congress, landowner.*

Richard Montgomery was born 2 December 1736 in Swords, near Dublin, into a respectable family of Irish gentry, the third son of Thomas Montgomery, Member of the Irish Parliament for Lifford, and Mary Franklyn. After his initial schooling, he was sent to Trinity College, Dublin, in 1754, but did not finish his studies. He was commissioned an ensign in the 2nd Battalion, 17th Regiment of Foot, 21 September 1756, and was immediately sent overseas to America during the Seven Years' War. Sometimes confused with his infamous older brother, Alexander, who fought with Wolfe's army as a captain in the 43rd Foot (Kennedy's) and was responsible for some of the more gruesome war atrocities committed during the 1759 campaign, Richard served at the siege of Louisbourg in 1758 at the same time as James Thompson. Montgomery was promoted lieutenant at Louisbourg 10 July 1758 after the death of Lord Dundonald commanding the regimental grenadiers. After the surrender of Louisbourg, the 17th Foot was sent via Boston, Massachusetts, and Albany, New York to reinforce Abercromby's defeated army bivouacked at the southern end of Lake George.

Montgomery spent the 1758–59 winter in garrison at Albany, and in the summer his regiment participated in the successful expeditions against Ticonderoga and Crown Point on Lake Champlain under General JEFFERY AMHERST. The following year, as part of Brigadier William Haviland's force thrusting north up Lake Champlain to converge on Montreal with two other armies, Montgomery was present at the capture of Montreal in 1760 along with James Thompson and soldiers of the 78th Foot. In 1762 Montgomery's regiment participated in the amphibious operations conducted against the French island of Martinique and the port of Havana.

Montgomery rose steadily in rank during these years. In May 1760 he had become the regimental adjutant of the 2nd/17th Foot, and in May 1762, after the capture of Martinique, he secured his captaincy. But peacetime soldiering after 1763 proved frustrating because of his inability to advance. By 1771 he thought he had "the promise of a majority … and had lodged his money for the purchase" but "was overlooked, and another purchased over him." This gave him "a disgust for the service." He therefore sold out in April 1772 and emigrated to America. In January 1773 he arrived at New York and purchased a small farm of 67 acres on the high ground in Westchester County, near Kingsbridge, where he indulged his "violent passion" for farming.

On 24 July 1773 Montgomery married Janet, a daughter of Robert R. Livingston, a local magistrate and wealthy landowner, and moved

Brigadier General Richard Montgomery. A former British officer, General Montgomery remains a tragic figure in the pantheon of American Revolutionary war heroes. Married into the influential Livingstone family in upstate New York, he chose to support his adopted country and fight against his former brother officers. (New York Public Library)

to Rhinebeck in the Manor of Livingston. His marriage into the powerful and strongly pro-colonial Livingston family was, given his social background, unusual, but he was a friend of liberal politicians back in England and had formed a genuine sympathy for the American cause. When the Revolution started, Montgomery's beliefs and views on the whole subject had been sufficiently aired that he had been elected to the New York provincial congress earlier in 1775. On 22 June he was appointed a brigadier general in the newly-formed Continental Army, and though at first somewhat conflicted, accepted the post, convinced that "the will of an oppressed people … must be respected."

Sent to capture Quebec, the 14th colony, Montgomery's small army easily took the forts at Saint-Jean and Chambly in succession and by 11 November had occupied the city of Montreal. Pressing on to Quebec with 300 men on 28 November, he left behind garrisons totalling some 500 men under Brigadier General David Wooster in Montreal, Saint-Jean and Chambly.

His plan was to move down-river to marry up with a second American force led by BENEDICT ARNOLD moving north along the Kennebec River in Maine. Only some 600 militiamen of Arnold's original command of 1,100 men actually made it to Pointe Lévy on 9 November 1755. They crossed over the river to the Plains of Abraham on the night of 13 November, hoping to take the city by surprise, but were forced to retreat upriver to Pointe-aux-Trembles to wait for Montgomery and sorely needed supplies coming down from Montreal.

Montgomery arrived on 3 December 1755 and took Arnold's force under command, then moved forward to start the "siege" of Quebec. Montgomery and Arnold had both optimistically believed that Quebec would capitulate immediately on seeing their forces outside its walls. Both were unaware that morale in the beleaguered city had significantly improved with the arrival of Lieutenant Colonel Allan Maclean and 100 of his newly-raised Royal Highland Emigrants on 11 November as well as the arrival of Governor GUY CARLETON a week later on 19 November. The governor had immediately expelled all those refusing to serve in the militia and had made preparations for a vigorous defence.

Thompson, in command of 200 artificers, was intimately involved in the mounting of guns on the walls as well as the erection of palisades, barricades and blockhouses in the more exposed and vulnerable parts of the city. The garrison of 1,800 men, composed of British regulars, seamen and Canadian militia, was more than a match for Montgomery's tiny army and had sufficient provisions and military stores for themselves and the 3,200 city inhabitants for eight months.

Montgomery soon discovered that the British artillery was considerably superior to his own and that he could not hope to conduct a conventional siege with his starving and virtually untrained mob. Under immense pressure from home to secure Quebec with its artillery and munitions as soon as possible, and facing the looming expiry date of many enlistments in his smallpox-stricken force, Montgomery decided he would have to attack quickly and decisively before Carleton received any more reinforcements, or, more pointedly, his own small force melted away through desertion and disease.

It was finally decided to mount a surprise attack on Lower Town, relying on a dark night, confusion and collaborators to force Carleton to abandon the strongly fortified Upper Town and give battle. During a snowstorm on the night of 31 December at about five o'clock in the morning, Montgomery, at the head of about 200 men, advanced along the river bank from Cape Diamond (Cap Diamant) towards the district of Près-de-Ville. Simultaneously Arnold's 600 men were advancing from the suburb of Saint-Roch towards rue du Sault-au-Matelot to effect an eventual junction with Montgomery in Lower Town. The British defenders, however, had already been warned by deserters and alerted and so were primed and ready. At Près-de-Ville in Lower Town, a gun, mounted by James Thompson and his artificers, loaded with grapeshot and manned by British seamen under Captain Adam Barnsfare and Canadian militia under François Chabot and LOUIS-ALEXANDRE PICARD, watched Montgomery's column approach and then delivered a combined blast of fire which cut down Montgomery, his two aides de camp and several others instantly. The other Americans turned and fled.

On the other front, Arnold was wounded and evacuated, but his men pressed on to overrun a barricade at Sault-au-Matelot and take some prisoners. They were then halted by stiff resistance from regulars and militia under Henry Caldwell, in which JOHN NAIRNE and FRANÇOIS DAMBOURGÈS were prominent. Informed of Montgomery's repulse in Lower Town, Carleton quickly transferred troops to the threatened sector and surrounded Arnold's force, which capitulated at about eight o'clock that morning. One British officer boasted that the Quebec garrison had won "as compleat a little victory as ever was gained." Between 60 and 100 American rebels had been killed or wounded and another 400 captured for the loss of not quite 20 men. Montgomery was mourned by his compatriots, who considered him a promising and popular officer. One officer wrote that Montgomery was "a genteel appearing man, tall and slender of make ... of an agreeable temper, and a virtuous General."

On New Years' Day 1776, the frozen bodies of Montgomery and his two aides de camp, John Cheeseman and John Macpherson, were discovered beneath a snowdrift. Thompson recovered the unfortunate general's sword and then supervised the burial of Montgomery's body at the expense of Montgomery's former friend, Lieutenant Governor Hector Cramahé (Cramahé was a former officer in the 15th Foot who had served with Montgomery in the previous war at Louisbourg and Quebec). Montgomery's body was disinterred, under Thompson's direction, some years later in 1818 and repatriated to the United States. His sword was also returned, but not until 1924, and is now on display at the Smithsonian.

BALs; *DAB; DCB;* JTC; A.L. Todd, *Richard Montgomery: Rebel of 1775* (New York, 1966); F. B. Heitman, *Historical Register of officers of the Continental Army during the War of the Revolution...* (Washington, 1893); T.H. Montgomery, "Ancestry of General Richard Montgomery," *New-York Genealogical & Biographical Record*, Vol. 2 (New York, 1871), 123–30.

The Reverend David-François de Montmollin (1721–1803), *Church of England clergyman, landowner.*

David-François de Montmollin was the fifth of eleven children born into a family of the Swiss rural aristocracy. His father was Louis de Montmollin, a city official in Neuchâtel, and his mother Salomé Gaudot. He entered university at Basel at the age of seventeen to study medicine and completed his studies three years later. In 1744 he went to Leyden in the Netherlands and was ordained a minister the following year. By 1748 he was in London, again studying medicine. There he met Jane Bell and they married 2 June 1762.

In 1761, when Protestants of Quebec petitioned Governor JAMES MURRAY for a French-speaking assistant to John Brooke, the unofficial Anglican missionary in Quebec, Montmollin was sent and arrived at Quebec, probably in June 1768. He soon encountered hostility from Governor GUY CARLETON, who feared that the appointment of French-language Protestant ministers in the colony would offend the Roman Catholic hierarchy.

Carleton's fears were unfounded as Montmollin's congregation remained tiny, since many Protestants were leaving Quebec and most that remained were Presbyterians like James Thompson, who had their own minister, George Henry. Remaining Englishmen like Henry Caldwell ascribed the deplorable state of the Church of England in the colony to the policy of appointing French-speaking clergy, who, he argued, knew little of the English language and less of Anglican rites. In 1785 the Reverend Charles Mongan was sent to Canada to investigate, and he forwarded to the British government an anonymous memorandum in which Montmollin was described as very old and unable to speak a word of plain English.

Worse still, Montmollin's private conduct was considered scandalous. "What opinion must the Canadian's form of our religion," it was asked, "when they daily see the Minister of it degrading the very name, by keeping a little dirty dram shop, and himself so scandalously indecent, as to measure out, & sell rum to the soldiers of the Garrison — And all this too in the Capital of the Province, the Seat of Government, and Residence of the French Bishop, & other dignified Clergy of that Church."

By 1788 the complaints against the Swiss minister had reached the ears of Charles Inglis, newly appointed Bishop of Nova Scotia, which included jurisdiction over the province of Quebec. On a pastoral visit in 1789, Inglis found that Montmollin was totally unsuited to his post and informed him bluntly that he should retire. Although sixty-eight years of age, Montmollin was reluctant to do so and complained bitterly to Lord Dorchester (Guy Carleton's title during his second tenure as governor) that he was being ill treated after his many years of service. The old priest's principal fear was that his superannuation would deprive him of much-needed income, for he was heavily in debt. Retirement meant losing a salary of £200 per annum and fees for his chaplaincy services to the regiments in garrison. Dorchester however supported the forced retirement of Montmollin and on 31 July 1789, after "a disagreeable scene," Montmollin was removed.

Early in his retirement, Montmollin's financial situation deteriorated. By February 1790 his sons, John Frederick and John Samuel, had fled the province, leaving their father guarantor of a debt of £1,550 to the firm of Fraser and Young. In 1794 Montmollin was forced to sell his house and a lot behind it to pay off the debt but his fortunes improved thereafter. In 1796 and 1797 he received appointments as deputy regimental chaplain to the 5th Foot and the 60th Foot, and in November 1796 he began to make small loans, which by September 1803 totalled about £800. He died 17 December 1803 and left his widow £650 in cash as well as debts owed to him and several properties.

DCB; JTC.

Brigadier General James Murray (1721–94), *British army officer, colonial governor.*
James Murray was born in 1721 at his family's seat of Ballencrieff in Lothian, Scotland, the fifth son and fourteenth child of Alexander Murray, Lord Elibank, and his wife, Elizabeth "Bare Betty" Stirling. He was a short man with bright staring eyes, a hawk-like nose and a fiery disposition, who did not suffer fools gladly. Two of his four brothers were avowed Jacobites and Murray's military career was an uphill struggle to prove his loyalty and worth to the British Crown.

He served as the most junior of JAMES WOLFE's brigadiers during the 1759 siege, but was actually the oldest at thirty-nine years of age. He was left in command of a bomb-shattered Quebec for the winter of 1759–60, and it is in this capacity that he features in the majority of Thompson's oral histories. He is perhaps best known in North American history for his six tempestuous years as Quebec's first peacetime British governor and made his greatest impact as one of the first champions of French-Canadian rights. No matter what his failings as a military commander might have been, he was a generous, compassionate man of principle. He was ultimately a victim of New England and British interest groups who engineered a series of false charges against him that resulted in his recall.

Murray's military career started at the age of fifteen when he was enrolled as a cadet in Colyear's 3rd Scot's Regiment of the Dutch army in 1736. Murray considered the three years he spent with these hardened soldiers of fortune to be his true military education and claimed in later life, "I served in all ranks except that as drummer." In February 1740, anxious for

Brigadier General James Murray. The most junior of Wolfe's three brigadiers during the Quebec campaign in 1759, Murray assumed command of the British garrison for the winter of 1759–60 and was narrowly defeated by Lévis at Sillery the following year. Becoming governor of the province and later, of Canada, his conciliatory attitude towards the French *Canadiens* led to his recall in 1765. Artist unknown, but likely painted about 1767. (LAC A/N 1997-227-1).

advancement, Murray obtained a commission in Wynard's 4th Marine Regiment and participated in the 1740 British-American expedition against Cartagena in Central America. Disease-ravaged marching regiments lost officers and men by the hundreds, and on 20 November 1741 Murray transferred from the Marines to become a twenty-year-old captain in the 15th Foot. For the next ten years he soldiered in the West Indies, Flanders and France and participated in the 1746 L'Orient expedition as the captain of the regiment's grenadier company.

In 1749 Murray purchased a majority in the 15th Foot and a year later the lieutenant colonelcy of the same regiment. At the outbreak of the Seven Years' War, Murray met JAMES WOLFE for the first time on the Rochefort expedition in September 1757. The following year he served under Wolfe at Louisbourg, earning the latter's respect for his "infinite spirit," and in 1759 commanded the left wing of the army on the Plains of Abraham. He remained behind as the governor of Quebec after the victory and had the difficult task of holding the prize of Quebec in the face of a very severe winter and limited accommodations to house his troops.

On 28 April 1760 he met a larger Franco-Canadian army under de Lévis on the Plains of Abraham near Sillery, was defeated after a three-hour battle and was forced to retire within the walls of the city. After besieging the city for three weeks, de Lévis' army finally retired on the arrival of the Royal Navy. Later that year, Murray commanded one of the three armies that converged on Montreal and forced its capitulation.

Murray would face one more siege in his lifetime as the governor of the small island of Minorca off the east coast of Spain in 1782. Severely outnumbered, with a garrison smaller than the one he commanded at Quebec, he surrendered after a spirited resistance reminiscent of his 1760 siege. A court of inquiry looking into the loss of the island determined that Murray, now nicknamed "Old Minorca," had acquitted himself honourably and he retired satisfied to his Sussex estate, where he spent his twelve remaining years. During this time he was promoted full general (February 1783) and acquired the appointments of colonel to the 21st Foot and the governor of Hull. He died 18 June 1794 at Beauport House, near Battle, Sussex.

DCB; DNB; JTC; RGO; Maj. Gen. R.H. Mahon, *Life of General the Honourable James Murray* (London, 1921); James Murray, "Journal of the Siege of Quebec, 1760," LHSQ, *Historical Documents,* Series 3, Vol 5 (1871).

Captain John Nairne (1731–1802), *British army officer, seigneur.*

John Nairne was born in Scotland in 1731 and educated at Edinburgh. He enlisted at the age of fourteen with the Dutch Scots Brigade in Holland and served in the 1st Battalion of Stewart's Regiment. He transferred to the British army when he was offered a lieutenancy in one of the three additional companies of the 78th Foot sent over to North America in spring 1758. Selected as one of the light infantry company's subalterns for the Louisbourg campaign, he took command of one half of the company with Ensign MALCOLM FRASER for the landings, while the other half company was commanded by Captain ALEXANDER CAMERON of Dungallon.

After the capture of Louisbourg, Nairne became ill with fever and his regiment sailed for Boston without him. On recovery Nairne was able to catch up with the 78th in Boston, just in time to march across Massachusetts and New York to Fort Stanwix for the winter. He participated in the battle of the Plains of Abraham, September 1759, and was subsequently wounded at the battle of Sillery on 28 April 1760. Nairne purchased his captaincy in the 78th Foot the following year (24 April 1761) after borrowing £400 from his patron, Governor JAMES MURRAY, and was commanding a company at Quebec when his regiment was disbanded in 1763, forcing him out on half-pay.

The previous year, 1762, Murray had divided his newly purchased seigneury of La Malbaie in two portions on 27 April and granted half to Nairne and the other to Nairne's best friend, Lieutenant Malcolm Fraser. While Nairne took Murray Bay, Fraser took Mount Murray and built a manor house overlooking the village of La Malbaie. He also employed some of the Fraser Highlanders who opted to stay behind in Canada on the regiment's disbandment to settle the land, and these Harveys, Warrens, Macleans and Blackburns who accompanied him married local girls and a generation later had been completely assimilated into the local French-Canadian culture. He married Christiana Emery on 20 July 1769 at Quebec.

On the outbreak of the American Revolution, Nairne, the experienced veteran, was immediately gazetted a captain in the 1st Battalion, 84th Foot or Royal Highland Emigrants. Under the command of Henry Caldwell, Nairne played a leading role in the stubborn defence of Quebec against the American army of BENEDICT ARNOLD and RICHARD MONTGOMERY on the night of 31 December 1775. Promoted major "in the army" 29 August 1777, Nairne served at Île aux Noix in 1777 and Carleton Island (now in upstate New York) in 1779. At the latter Nairne supervised the rebuilding of the original fort as well as the guarding of American POWs.

John Nairne. A professional officer who had served with the Dutch Scots Brigade before the Seven Years' War, Nairne was one of several officers who opted to stay in North America after the 78th Foot was disbanded. Portrait is by an unknown artist and shows him as a lieutenant colonel of the Sedentary Militia, c. 1795. The painting once hung in the Manor House at Murray Bay but its whereabouts today are unknown. (BAnQ P560, S2, D1, P945)

He transferred from the Royal Highland Emigrants on 4 October 1780 on promotion to major of the 53rd Foot and was made a lieutenant colonel "in the army" 19 February 1783. At war's end he retired to his seigneury at Murray Bay and died 14 July 1802 at Quebec.

BALs; CBs; *DCB;* SBs; D. Currie, *The Lairds of Glenlyon: Historical Sketches Relations to the Districts of Appin, Glenlyon, and Breadalbane* (Perth, 1886), 281; Captain John Nairne's Orderly Book, 8 May 1762 – 31 December 1762; "A Military Sketch of Colonel John Nairne," 51–52, LAC MG23-GIII 23, Vol. 6; Stewart, *Sketches*, II, 20–1.

***Capitaine* Charles-François Tarieu de la Naudière (1710–76)**, *French naval officer (colonial regulars), seigneur, colonial administrator.*

Born 1710 at La Pérade, Quebec, Charles-François Tarieu de la Naudière (identified as de Lanaudière in James Thompson's anecdotes) was a long-serving officer in the French colonial regulars and descended from one of the original great families of the colony. At the age of twelve, the plucky youngster saved the life of his mother when she was attacked by four Indian women. In 1727 he received his commission as a 2nd ensign in the colony's *Compagnies franches de la marine.* Promoted full ensign in 1734 and lieutenant in 1742, he was appointed adjutant of Quebec in 1743.

On 6 January 1743 he attached himself to the distinguished Acadian family of Henri-Louis Deschamps de Boishébert by marrying the latter's daughter, Louise-Geneviève. His military career was uneventful and by 1749 he had achieved the rank of captain. A report written in 1761–62 described him as a "very mediocre officer" but "rich." He was granted the seigneury of Lac-Maskinongé on 1 March 1750, which soon became known as Lanaudière.

After a brief period as an entrepreneur in Quebec, La Naudière once again assumed military duties on the outbreak of the Seven Years' War. Dispatched to Acadia in the spring of 1756, La Naudière was responsible for distributing provisions to the many habitants who had retired to the forests to wage *"la petite guerre"* against English forces who ascended the St. John River burning Acadian settlements. Two years later he was present at the battle of Fort Carillon (Fort Ticonderoga, July 1758) where his actions were noticed by General MONTCALM. He received the cross of Saint-Louis (*Ordre Royal et Militaire de Saint-Louis*) in January 1759, and then returned to Quebec in June of the following year, where he fought at the battle of the Plains of Abraham.

Sometime in 1759 it is thought, he became the commissary of prisoners, and during this appointment he came into contact with a number of Highland prisoners imprisoned at Quebec from the 42nd Foot (Black Watch) captured at Ticonderoga and 77th Foot (Montgomery's Highlanders) taken at Fort Duquesne. According to Thompson, the humane La Naudière became very attached to the Highlanders, who

"Mediocre... but rich." This sketch by an unknown artist shows a youthful Charles-François Tarieu de la Naudière, likely done when he was serving as an ensign in Quebec's colonial regulars, the *compagnies franches de la marine.* (BAnQ P1000, S4, D83, PL29)

received "every kind of good treatment" from their keeper, even to the point where he would send for spring water, rather than let the prisoners drink the water from the St. Lawrence River.

After the conquest, La Naudière spent some time in France and during his absence his wife died (July 1762). When he returned the following summer, he remarried, this time to Marie-Catherine, the daughter of Charles Le Moyne de Longueuil, second Baron de Longueuil. In 1766 he was one of the seigneurs in the District of Quebec who signed the address to Governor JAMES MURRAY lamenting his departure. When CARLETON asked the British government in 1769 to admit members of the Canadian nobility to the Council of Quebec, La Naudière's was one of the twelve names put forward.

During his last years, La Naudière used part of his fortune to purchase additional seigneuries. In 1775 he became one of the founding members of the Legislative Council created by the Quebec Act, but he scarcely had time to take his seat, dying during the American siege of Quebec on 1 February 1776 at Quebec's Hôpital Général.

DCB; JTC.

Lieutenant Louis-Alexandre Picard (c.1729–99), *jeweller, silversmith, militia lieutenant.*
Louis-Alexandre was born c.1728 in the parish of Saint-Eustache, Paris, the son of Pierre-François Picard and Marie-Jeanne Leger. He is thought to have apprenticed as a silversmith in Paris, but in 1750 went "for a soldier" and enlisted in the cavalry. After two years of army service, he re-settled in the coastal city of Bordeaux, where he remained for two and a half years before emigrating to Quebec in 1755. He established himself initially on rue de l'Escalier working with silversmith Jacques Terroux, but quickly made friends with the town's leading silversmith, Ignace-François Delezenne, and began to work for him from a store on St. Louis Street (rue Saint-Louis).

He appears to have not served in any military capacity during the Seven Years' War and in May 1759 married Françoise Maufils a month before English forces arrived to place the city under siege. When peace was restored, Picard became heavily involved in real estate dealings and through a number of poor transactions ran into financial difficulties. During the American invasion in 1775, which saw the city yet again under siege, Picard was commissioned lieutenant in the Quebec militia (August 1775) and was with the barricade guard in Lower Town on 31 December which repelled a surprise night assault by Brigadier General RICHARD MONTGOMERY and his forces, resulting in the American commander's death.

After the war Picard stubbornly remained in Quebec, though Montreal had become the principal centre for the silver trade. In 1783 he went bankrupt and, unable to pay off 9,380 livres owing in instalments on his residence, was sent to debtors prison. Released in 1785, he slowly re-established himself and by 1795 he and six other Quebec silversmiths were petitioning to be exempt from a law concerning the use of forges within city walls. Unsuccessful, Picard soon made up his mind to move his business to Montreal but he was too late to break into the competitive market and died penniless 27 April 1799 at Montreal's Hôtel-Dieu hospital.

DCB; J.-M. Lemoine, *Maple Leaves* (Quebec, 1894).

Provost Marshal Miles Prentice (c. 1727–87), *British army soldier, tavern-keeper.*
Miles Prentice was an Irishman serving in the ranks of the 43rd Foot (Kennedy's) and in 1758 was listed as one of the Wardens of the Lodge held in the 17th Regiment, No. 136, Grand Lodge of Ireland, when the army was besieging Louisbourg. A non-commissioned officer like James Thompson, Prentice was appointed

provost marshal on 6 July 1759 by General James Wolfe with the honorary rank of lieutenant.

When peace and his discharge came in 1763, Prentice became a tavern-keeper and opened the Sun Tavern on St. John Street (rue Saint-Jean). His name appears on a list of Protestant "house keepers" contained in a certificate signed by Governor James Murray in 1764. About the same time, he helped form the first civilian Masonic Lodge for the inhabitants of the town, known as Merchants Lodge, No. 1, Quebec, and later became its Worshipful Master in 1766. He continued to occupy the Sun Tavern until 1771 when, needing to expand his business, he purchased the first stone house ever erected in Quebec, known as Le Chien d'Or because of a gilded statue of the dog gnawing a bone sitting over its front portal. The enterprising Prentice converted it into a hotel and boarding house known as Free Masons' Hall, where the Grand Lodge of Quebec and several other local lodges met for their monthly meetings and festive occasions. A 1773 census reveals he was forty-seven years old at the time, with a wife, two sons (Samuel, nineteen, and John, thirteen), as well as an eleven-year-old "negro boy" and a servant woman.

In 1775, when Generals Montgomery and Benedict Arnold attacked Quebec, Prentice resumed his old job as provost marshal. An extant orderly book kept by Captain Anthony Vialar reveals that as of 19 September 1775, Miles Prentice Esquire was "appointed Sergeant Major to the British Militia and is to obey and be obeyed as such." A later entry in the same orderly book, dated 20 February 1776, states "Mr. Miles Prentice is appointed Provost Marshal to this Garrison with the rank of lieutenant as given him by General Wolfe in the last war. The guards are to assist him with whatever partys [sic] he may demand from them."

Free Masons' Hall on Buade Street (rue de Buade) became the headquarters of Lieutenant Colonel Allan Maclean's 1st Battalion, Royal Highland Emigrants, and the defence of the city was no doubt planned in its lower room, for the above-mentioned orderly book makes frequent reference to meetings held there by the officers of the garrison. When General Montgomery was killed during a surprise New Years' Eve attack upon the town, his body was later positively identified by Prentice's wife (Montgomery having been a frequent visitor at the Sun Tavern when he served as a captain in the 17th Foot). Miles Prentice died in 1787 at the age of sixty and was buried in the St. Louis Gate Cemetery on 11 June 1787. His widow eventually sold Free Masons' Hall, and as she was the aunt of James Thompson's wife, Fanny Cooper, moved in with the Thompson family, where she lived until her death.

JTC; A.J.B. Milborne, "Miles Prentice: Soldier and Mason," *The Builder*, Vol. XV (1929), 274; *Quebec Gazette*, 1764; A. Vialar and R. Lester, "Orderly Book begun by Capt. Anthony Vialar of the British Militia…," LHSQ, *Historical Documents*, Ser. 7 (1905); G. Gale, *Historic Tales of Old Quebec* (Quebec, 1920); Census of the English population living in Quebec circa 1773 (Recensement de la population Anglais demeurant à Quebec vers 1773), *Archives du Séminaire de Québec*, Polygraphie 37, No. 1; "List of Protestant House Keepers in Quebec," quoted in A.G. Doughty & N.E. Dionne, *Quebec Under Two Flags: A Brief History of the City…* (Quebec, 1903), 188–91; Register Book, St. Louis Gate Cemetery, BAnQ.

Governor George Ramsay, 9th Earl of Dalhousie (1770–1838), *British army officer, governor-in-chief of British North America.*
George Ramsay was born on 22 October 1770 at Dalhousie Castle, Edinburgh, the eldest son of George Ramsay, 8th Earl of Dalhousie, and his wife, Elizabeth, daughter of Andrew Glene. After being educated at the Royal High School and the University of Edinburgh, George was commissioned a cornet in the 3rd Dragoons in July 1788 and had reached the rank of captain

"A man of culture." Historians have not been kind to George Ramsay, the 9th Earl of Dalhousie, styling him as "boring" and possessing "a cold, aloof manner with a touch of aristocratic hauteur, and a prickly personality reinforced by a dour Scottish Presbyterianism." Observed through an artistic lens as a patron of the arts, Lord Dalhousie emerges in a different light: a "passionate," "energetic," "man of culture." Painted about 1816 by William Douglas, Lord Dalhousie is shown here with his dogs, Basto and Yarrow. (Private Collection)

by January 1791. He exchanged the same year as a captain to the 1st Foot (Royal Scots), securing a majority in June 1792, and was promoted to lieutenant colonel in December 1794. In 1795 Ramsay served at Gibraltar and in the West Indies with his regiment, returning in 1798 to help suppress rebellions in Ireland. Brevetted a colonel in January 1800, he accompanied General Ralph Abercrombie to Egypt and on his return to England was appointed a brigadier general on the staff in Scotland. There he met his future wife, Christian Broun, the only child and heir of Charles Broun of Colstoun, East Lothian, and they were married on 14 May 1805.

Promoted major general in April 1808, Dalhousie took part in the Walcheren expedition and in August 1809 was appointed colonel of the 6th Garrison Battalion. In 1812 he was promoted major general and sent to Spain, where he served as one of the Duke of Wellington's division commanders with the local rank of lieutenant general, later confirmed as substantive rank in June 1813. Appointed colonel of the 26th Foot (Cameronians) and made a Knight of the Bath the same year, in 1815 he was made a GCB and created Baron Dalhousie of Dalhousie Castle in the peerage of the United Kingdom.

In July 1816, keen to secure his post-war financial situation, Dalhousie obtained the appointment of lieutenant governor of Nova Scotia. There he championed improved methods of farming and road-building to open up the countryside to the settlement of British immigrants and he helped found Dalhousie University. He subsequently became governor-in-chief of British North America in November 1819 and governed during turbulent political times. During his tenure at Quebec, he would often invite James Thompson, then in his twilight years, to dinner at the "Castle," where he would revel in the company of the old Highlander. Dalhousie would usually record these evenings in his private journal and one entry on 7 January 1827 bears repeating here: "... the old man drank his wine freely, played as usual some hits at backgammon with Lady D., not using spectacles, and walked away to his home at half past 10 PM. I do think him one of the most remarkable instances of long life I have ever met with...."

Dalhousie's Presbyterian upbringing gave him an aversion to priests who meddled in politics and he never really sought the active backing of the influential hierarchy of the Roman Catholic Church. As friction between political parties escalated during the 1820s, Dalhousie was forced to take draconian measures and dissolved the legislatures. The British colonial secretary decided to hasten Dalhousie's transfer to India as commander-in-chief of the army there, and the latter left in 1828. After a short tenure in India dogged by ill health, Dalhousie resigned his command and returned to Britain to spend the remainder of his years at Dalhousie Castle. He passed away on 21 March 1838 and was buried at Cockpen, Scotland, on 29 March.

DCB; DNB; JTC; RGO; Dalhousie fonds, LAC MG24-A12; Marjory Whitelaw, ed., *The Dalhousie Journals*, 3 vols (Ottawa, 1978–82); *Burke's Peerage*.

Captain Henry Rudyerd (c. 1740–1828), *British army officer.*
Henry Rudyerd was born c. 1740, likely near Whitby, North Yorkshire, to Benjamin Rudyerd and his second wife, Mary. His early education is not known, but military records show he started his military career in the Royal Artillery as a lieutenant fireworker (29 November 1769), and then transferred to the Engineers as a practitioner engineer (10 January 1770). He rose in rank and was promoted sub engineer and lieutenant 13 July 1774 (rank title changed to 1st lieutenant in '82). Sent to Quebec about 1783, he became James Thompson's commanding engineer on the departure of WILLIAM TWISS. By 1784 Rudyerd was a captain lieutenant, and when he left Quebec on 15 August 1785, James Thompson entered the following in his journal: "I never yet parted with a Commanding Officer without regret" adding that Rudyerd had been "very civil to me during his Command here." He was promoted full captain 21 September 1787, brevet major 6 May 1795, and promoted lieutenant colonel in the Royal Invalid Engineers 3 March 1997. He was made a brevet colonel (30 June 1805), major general (4 June 1811) and lieutenant general (12 August 1819). He was married (date unknown) to Mary Pryer, daughter of S. Pryer Esquire of Litchfield, Hampshire. He died at Hammersmith, 18 October 1828.

DCB; JTC; RGO; *Notes & Queries: A Medium of Inter-Communication…* (London, 1863), 338.

Justice Jonathan Sewell (1766–1839), *lawyer, musician, office holder, politician, author, judge.*
Jonathan Sewell was born 6 June 1766 in Cambridge, Massachusetts, into a prominent Bay Colony family, son of Jonathan Sewell and Esther Quincy. His Loyalist father, attorney general of the colony, left Massachusetts in 1775 with his family and returned to England because of the rebellion. Educated at Brasenose College, Oxford, Jonathan left England in early 1785 to article in law with an old family friend, Solicitor General Ward Chipman, in New Brunswick.

In 1789 he moved to Quebec, where there was greater scope for his abilities, and in October 1790 he was appointed attorney general of the province of Quebec *pro tempore*. The position eventually went to James Monk, but, boosted by the temporary appointment, Sewell's private practice flourished once he had mastered French civil law. In 1793 Governor Lord Dorchester (Sir GUY CARLETON) and Chief Justice Smith obtained Sewell's appointment as solicitor general and inspector of the king's domain. On 24 September 1796 he married Henrietta Smith (familiarly known as Harriet), a daughter of the late chief justice.

On 22 August 1808, Sewell was appointed chief justice of Lower Canada in succession to Henry Allcock, and the following month took

Justice Jonathan Sewell. Unknown artist. (BAnQ, P1000, S4, D83, PS21)

his seat on the Executive Council, quickly becoming the most powerful official in the colony after the governor. In 1809 he published orders and rules of practice for the Court of King's Bench at Quebec and for the Court of Appeals. A highly competent criminal law judge, he was internationally recognized as a leading jurist of his time. As chief justice, Sewell also enjoyed a prominent place in the social and cultural life of Quebec. In 1824 he won the Royal Institution's prize for service to education, and in 1825–26 acted as president of the institution.

At the Earl of Dalhousie's (GEORGE RAMSAY) urging, he and his brother-in-law, William Smith, were instrumental in founding the Literary and Historical Society of Quebec in 1824. Named a vice-president in March 1824, he gave the society's first paper in May, a study of French law before 1663 as it applied to the colony. He was president of the society from 1830 to 1831. A staunch Anglican, he presided over the Quebec branch of the British and Foreign Bible Society for many years and was a leading member of the Cathedral of the Holy Trinity. Sewell was asked by Dalhousie to chair the committee to erect a monument to JAMES WOLFE and LOUIS-JOSEPH DE MONTCALM, which he did with pleasure. Sewell resigned as chief justice on 20 October 1838 due to health reasons and died the following year at Quebec.

DCB.

Governor Sir John Coape Sherbrooke (1764–1830), *British army officer, governor-in-chief of British North America*

John Sherbrooke was baptized 29 April 1764 in Arnold, Nottinghamshire, son of William Sherbrooke (Coape) and Sarah Sherbrooke. He was commissioned an ensign in the 4th Foot (7 December 1780) and was promoted the following year to lieutenant (22 December 1781). In March 1783 Sherbrooke became a captain in the 85th Foot, but the regiment was disbanded at the end of the American Revolution the same year and he transferred to the command of a company in the 33rd Foot, then stationed in Halifax, Nova Scotia.

Sherbrooke returned to England in 1786 with his regiment and for seven years led a quiet existence in various garrisons. He was promoted major (30 September 1793) with the outbreak of the Napoleonic Wars and promoted lieutenant colonel the following year (24 May 1794). He soldiered with his regiment in Flanders in the Duke of York's army for a few months before returning to England.

In April 1796 Sherbrooke's regiment was ordered overseas to India, where two years later he was promoted to full colonel (1 January 1798). He took part in the Mysore War of 1799, including the siege of Seringapatam under the command of the future Duke of Wellington. Forced to return to England in January 1800 due to ill health, Sherbrooke was placed on half-pay in 1802 but returned to active duty the following year and was promoted major general on 1 January 1805. Sent to Sicily, his energies were largely devoted to diplomatic activities and in May 1807 he was sent on a diplomatic mission to Egypt.

A fellow army officer described him as a "short, square, hardy little man, with a countenance that told at once the determined fortitude of his nature. Without genius, without education, hot as pepper, and rough in his language, but with a warm heart and generous feelings; true, straight forward, scorning finesse and craft and meanness, and giving vent to his detestation with boiling eagerness, and in the plainest terms. As an officer, full of energy, rousing others to exertion, and indefatigable in his own person."

Appointed to the colonelcy of the 68th Foot on 27 May 1809, he served in the Peninsular campaign with the local rank of lieutenant general, second in command to his old battalion commander, Sir Arthur Wellesley (later, the

Duke of Wellington). The duke commented in later life that "Sherbrooke was a very good officer, but the most passionate man I think I ever knew."

As a reward for his actions and service at the battles of Oporto and Talavera he was made a KCB in September 1809, but fell ill and was invalided back to England in May 1810 and recuperated at Cheltenham. Promoted full lieutenant general in 1811, he was appointed in July of the same year to be lieutenant governor of Nova Scotia. Taking time to first get married, he left Portsmouth on 8 September with his new wife and her sister and arrived at Halifax on 16 October 1811, double-hatted as commander of all British and Canadian forces in the Atlantic provinces.

Sherbrooke's administration was dominated by the War of 1812 and continual efforts to improve defences and guard against the ravages of American privateers, though he also proved to be an able and well-liked administrator. Notably he issued proclamations declaring a friendly disposition towards the adjacent New England states, where the war was highly unpopular. He encouraged merchants on both sides to continue trading, a policy that stimulated the free exchange of goods between New England and the Atlantic provinces for the remainder of the war.

Sherbrooke also led a successful military expedition against Castine, Maine, subduing the entire region between the Penobscot and the St. Croix rivers. The eight-month occupation of Castine yielded significant customs revenues, which were subsequently used to finance the establishment of the Cambridge Military Library for the Halifax garrison as well as helping found Dalhousie College, named after his lieutenant governor, GEORGE RAMSAY.

On 10 April 1816 Sherbrooke was commissioned governor-in-chief of British North America and was replaced in Nova Scotia by Lord Dalhousie. Leaving Halifax on 27 June,

Sir John Coape Sherbrooke. Described as a "short, square, hardy little man" by a fellow officer, and as a "very good officer" by the Duke of Wellington, John Coape Sherbrooke had a distinguished military career before becoming a colonial administrator. The apex of his career was his appointment as governor-in-chief of British North America in 1816, holding this post for a short period of time. (BAnQ P560, S2, D1, P1693)

Sherbrooke arrived at Quebec to assume his new responsibilities on 12 July 1816 and through firm and fair dealing, managed to establish a cordial and gracious relationship with all competing parties. Unfortunately on 6 February 1818 he suffered a severe paralytic stroke, promptly resigning and recommending that Lord Dalhousie be his successor. Instead the administration was handed over to the Duke of Richmond (CHARLES LENNOX). The following month Sherbrooke left for England and lived quietly in the English countryside at Calverton until his death on 14 February 1830.

BALs; *DCB; DNB;* RGO; *Gentleman's Magazine;* W.S. MacNutt, *The Atlantic Provinces: the Emergence of Colonial Society, 1712–1857* (Toronto, 1965); A.P. Martin, *Life and Letters of the Right Honourable Robert Lowe, Viscount Sherbrooke ... with a memoir of Sir John Coape Sherbrooke...* (London, 1893).

Sergeant Alexander "Sanders" Simpson (c. 1718–81), *British army soldier, businessman.*
Alexander "Sanders" Simpson was born in Scotland c. 1718, likely in or near the village of Tain, Ross-shire. The name "Sanders" is likely an Anglicization of Sandy, a diminutive of Alexander. Simpson was James Thompson's first cousin, as well as one of his best friends. He likely joined the 78th Foot at the same time as Thompson and like Thompson was appointed as a sergeant in the regiment's grenadier company. Simpson acted as the regimental provost marshal (the modern day equivalent is regimental police sergeant) at Louisbourg, Quebec and Montreal.

When Fraser's Highlanders were disbanded in 1763, Simpson transferred to the 2nd Battalion, Royal Americans (60th Foot). On his discharge in 1765 Alexander was one of twelve former sergeants whose names appear on a land petition to Governor JAMES MURRAY, dated 15 March 1765, requesting 200 acres each "in and about the Bays of Chaleur and Gaspey," the petition stating that Simpson was a "late sergeant in the 2nd Battalion of the 60th Regiment (Royal Americans)." Simpson remained in Quebec, living in an imposing stone house on St. Louis Street (rue Saint-Louis) close to the St. Louis Gate.

He married a girl named Sarah (not known if he married in Scotland or in Quebec) and over the period 1766 to 1778 the couple operated Simpson's Coffee House in Quebec, an alternate meeting place to PRENTICE's Free Masons' Hall for Quebec's Masonic lodges. Their daughter, Mary, was born about 1760. During the American War of Independence, Simpson served as the garrison's provost marshal (chief of police). A 1773 census of English-speaking citizens in Quebec shows Alexander Simpson, fifty-five, with a wife and daughter (unnamed), as well as a step-son named William Robertson, twenty. This would suggest that Saunders' wife Sarah was previously married to a man named Robertson.

Simpson died of a stroke on 27 March 1781, leaving Sarah in serious financial difficulty. James Thompson helped the grieving family make the funeral arrangements, as well as taking on the responsibility to look out for the family, and Simpson's daughter, Mary, began to look upon Thompson "in the light of a parent." It has been claimed that it was Mary who was the famed Quebec beauty that was the object of Captain Horatio Nelson's affections when he visited Quebec as commander of *Albemarle* in 1782. Sarah Simpson died virtually penniless about 1795, leaving what little possessions she had to Mary and William Robertson. In 1798, however, Mary married Robert Mathews in London, the former military secretary to Governor FREDERICK HALDIMAND.

JTC; Col. R.J. Harper, *The Fraser Highlanders* (Montreal, 1979); Land Petition, 15 March 1765; Census of the English population living in Quebec circa 1773 (Recensement de la population anglais demeurant à Québec vers 1773, *Archives du Séminaire de Québec*, Polygraphie 37, No. 1).

Sergeant James Sinclair (1732–1821), *British army soldier, magistrate.*
James Sinclair was born in Inverness in 1732 and fought with the British army at Culloden, 16 April 1746, likely as a drummer boy. A brave and resourceful soldier, Sinclair held the rank of sergeant in the grenadier company of the 78th Foot. According to James Thompson, during the march through Ireland in 1757, Sinclair jumped through the window of a burning house to save the life of a woman with the ceiling "blazing over her head." When the woman ran back into the burning house to recover something of value, Sinclair once again risked his life to save her. Unfortunately this time she perished.

Sinclair shows up on a list of non-commissioned officers and men of the 78th Foot who received their discharge in Quebec in 1763 (Captain Alexander McLeod's Company). He is also one of twelve former sergeants whose names appear on a land petition to Governor James Murray dated 15 March 1765, requesting 200 acres each "in and about the Bays of Chaleur and Gaspey." Sinclair settled on a farm on the north side of the Saint-Charles River. He had one son, George, and a daughter, Elizabeth. On 3 August 1783 Elizabeth married Captain Erskine Hope, a British officer then serving in Quebec with the 26th Foot.

During the Revolutionary War, Sinclair served as a staff officer with the Quebec Battalion of the British Militia. Sometime after the war, he relocated to Trois-Rivières, where he lived out his old age on a "handsome property" where he was known to regularly dress in "the costume of a Highland laird of the 17th century." He died in Trois-Rivières as a district magistrate on 19 March 1821 and his massive tombstone survives today in the old St. James Protestant Cemetery.

JTC; Col. R.J. Harper, *The Fraser Highlanders* (Montreal, 1979); J.-M. Lemoine, *Maple Leaves* (Quebec, 1894); Register, Église protestante de Trois-Rivières, 1767–1875; *The Military Register*, 23 September 1818.

Sergeant Lauchlan Smith (c. 1733–1823), *British army soldier, merchant, landowner, justice of the peace.*

A native of Inverness, Scotland, Lauchlan Smith is one of ten former sergeants of the 78th Foot who names appear on a land petition to Governor JAMES MURRAY dated 15 March 1765, requesting 200 acres each "in and about the Bays of Chaleur and Gaspey." Smith became a Freemason in Quebec's garrison on 5 November 1760 and rose to become an officer in the Provincial Grand Lodge, indicating that he remained in Quebec when the regiment disbanded in 1763, despite his name not appearing on the list of those "discharged in America" found in one of the Provincial Secretary's letter-books c. 1950.

James Thompson doesn't mention Smith in his "Anecdotes of Wolfe's army" but does mention his good friend in later anecdotes as well as in his work journals. Smith kept a store on Palace Street (côte du Palais) just outside Palace Gate, and his name appears on a list of Protestant "house keepers" contained in a certificate given by General JAMES MURRAY in 1764. A 1773 census confirms his address as well as revealing he was forty years old and living with a wife, two daughters and a "negroe woman."

Smith accumulated wealth and in October 1777 purchased the seigneury of St. Ann's (Ste-Anne-de-la-Pocatière) for just over £170. He likely relocated to St. Ann's, returning to Quebec only when business or Lodge duties were pressing. On 22 November 1783, by then a widower, Smith remarried one Barbara Boyton, a cousin of James Thompson's wife, at Quebec's Metropolitan Anglican Church. The marriage was officiated by Reverend DAVID-FRANÇOIS DE MONTMOLLIN and witnessed by James Thompson. On 10 April 1784 Smith was a witness to the baptism of Thompson's son, James Jr. On 15 October 1795 Smith married for the third time, this time to Catherine Mills, a widow living in Quebec. On his death on 29 June 1823 Smith's seigneury passed down to his children. His obituary in the *Quebec Mercury* reads: "In the parish of St. Ann's ... Lauchlan Smith Esquire, Seignior of St. Denis & La Pocatière. Mr. Smith was a native of Inverness (Scotland) and is supposed to be upwards of 100 years of age. He served as a private in General Wolfe's Army at the taking of Quebec."

JTC; J.-M. Lemoine, *Maple Leaves* (Quebec, 1894); "List of Protestant House Keepers in Quebec," quoted in A.G. Doughty & N.E. Dionne, *Quebec Under Two Flags...* (Quebec, 1903), 188–91; J.H. Graham, *Outlines of the History of Freemasonry of the Province of Quebec* (Montreal, 1892); N.-E. Dionne, *Sainte-Anne de la Pocatière, 1672–1900* (Lévis, 1900); Census of the English population living in Quebec circa 1773 (Recensement de la population anglais demeurant à Québec vers 1773, Archives du Séminaire de Québec, Polygraphie 37, No. 1); *Quebec Mercury*, 4 July 1823.

Captain William Spry (1734–1802), *British army officer.*

William Spry was born 1734 in Titchfield, Hampshire, the son of George Spry and Elizabeth Short. Commissioned from the ranks of the Corps of Engineers as a practitioner engineer in December 1755, he was also given the rank of ensign in the 3rd Foot, also known as "the Buffs" (26 February 1756). He served during the Seven Years' War at the siege of Louisbourg as a sub engineer (4 January 1758) and lieutenant, 3rd Foot (27 September 1757). Spry was promoted engineer extraordinary (17 March 1759) and resigned his infantry commission (18 March 1760) and about this same time he shows up in Quebec as James Thompson's first commanding engineer when Thompson was first "attached" to the garrison's engineers. In 1769, while stationed in Halifax, Spry bought a lot of land outside the town above the Northwest Arm. In 1771 Spry acquired adjoining land and his 150-acre farm became known as Spry's Farm and subsequently Spry's Field, the name the entire area is still known by today.

Promoted brevet engineer in ordinary (25 May 1772) and then to substantive engineer in ordinary (24 January 1774), Spry assumed overall command of the Engineers at Halifax in 1775, supervising the building of Fort Needham in Point Pleasant Park as well as making improvements to the fortifications of the Halifax Citadel. In January 1783, when he was promoted lieutenant colonel, he put Spry's Field up for sale and sailed for England. He was promoted full colonel three years later and in 1790 appointed Lieutenant William Bartlett, RE, in Nova Scotia "his attorney to receive money debts, goods, owing payable and belonging to him from his settlers on the River Saint John, the Hillsboro' River or in any part of Nova Scotia."

Spry eventually rose to the rank of major general (1793) and later lieutenant general (1799). His brother was Lieutenant General Horatio Spry (1730–1811) and his son (born 1770 in Halifax) later became Major General William Frederick Spry (1770–1814). Spry died in 1802 at the age of sixty-eight and is supposedly buried under the clock tower of St. Margaret's, Westminster, London. One of his obituaries reads, "Died in Howland Street, age 68, Lt. Gen. William Spry, Commander of the Corps of Royal Engineers. His death was occasioned by a cold caught in attending the ascension of Garnerin's balloon. He was a man of mild and amiable manners and deservedly respected by all who knew him. He lived but a very short time to enjoy his promotion, about which he had expressed more than common anxiety."

BALs; *DCB; DNB;* JTC*;* RGO; R.F. Edwards, *Roll of Officers of the Corps of Royal Engineers, from 1660 to 1898* (Chatham, 1898).

Anne "Nancy" Thompson (1786–1861), *wife of Robert Harrower.*

Anne was born on 9 January 1786 in Quebec, the eldest of two living daughters to James Thompson and Frances "Fanny" Cooper. On 11 September 1815 Anne married Robert Harrower in Quebec. Anne and Robert had five children: Frances, born 13 October 1816, died 30 March 1869; Ann, born 12 April 1818, died 13 December 1873; David, born 19 June 1822, died October 1861; and James Thompson Harrower, born 23 February 1826, died 18 December 1918. When James Thompson died in 1830, his land in Armagh Township was bequeathed to Anne, and sometime after Robert Harrower's death in September 1832, she sold her land to Colonel JOHN NAIRNE. In 1860, then a widow and without any means of support, Anne persuaded her brother, JAMES, to return to Quebec to live with her and her three children (she lived on rue Saint-Louis). Anne contracted cholera during an epidemic in Quebec City and died on 30 April 1861.

JTC

Frances Thompson (1798–1855), *wife of John Whitelaw.*

Frances was born on 11 June 1798 in Quebec, the younger of two living daughters to James Thompson and Frances "Fanny" Cooper. On 6 December 1825 she married John Whitelaw, a Quebec City physician and surgeon. Although well-positioned in Quebec, her husband had a desire to settle in Western Canada, and so they relocated first to Brockville, and then progressively westward to Kingston and Toronto. While living in Toronto, they learned that a grammar school was to be opened in Upper Canada at Niagara, whereupon John applied and obtained the position of headmaster.

Frances and John had eight children: James Thomson, born 29 January 1827, died 1 September 1846; Frances Allison, born 10 June 1828, died 1855; John, born 1 October 1829, died 1857; Margaret Anne, born 4 October 1830, died 1857; Robert Harrower, born 21 June 1832, died after 1855; William, born 26 August 1833, died after 1855; Jane, 13 January 1835, died 1855; and George Thompson, born 19 June 1843, died after 1855. Of their eight children, only Jane had issue. Jane married James Bruce W. Bluntach in 1854 and they had one child, James Bruce W. Bluntach, who died in 1855. Frances died in Niagara, Ontario, in 1855, perhaps giving birth to her child.

JTC.

Lieutenant George Thompson (1780–1817), *British army officer.*

George was born on 5 July 1789 in Quebec, the youngest of the four surviving sons of James Thompson and Frances "Fanny" Cooper. He attended John Fraser's school in Quebec, and later the school of James Tanswell, the latter to learn French. Based on strong recommendations to the master general of the Ordnance from Colonel Robert Mathews, former military secretary to Governor FREDERICK HALDIMAND and Colonel WILLIAM TWISS, both old friends of his father, George was admitted to the prestigious Royal Military Academy at Woolwich near London. He was commissioned as a 1st lieutenant in the Royal Artillery 1 February 1808. George suffered from a serious lung problem throughout his short military career and accepted a post to Canada from Gibraltar in the hopes that a change in locale would improve his health. Unfortunately George's health continued to deteriorate. He passed away in Montreal on 12 February 1817, age thirty-seven.

BALs, JTC.

James Thompson, Jr. (1784–1869), *British commissary officer.*

James Jr. was on born 27 March 1784 in Quebec, the eldest surviving son of James Thompson and Frances "Fanny" Cooper. He attend John Fraser's school in Quebec initially, then transferred to James Tanswell's school to learn French, in which he became proficient, as well as land surveying and mathematics.

On 15 October 1798, when he was thirteen, his father secured him a place in the commissary service as a clerk under Commissary General JOHN CRAIGIE, thus "stamping a professional nature on his character." By 1811 he had become the chief clerk of the Accountancy Branch, in charge of general cash accounts and paid seven shillings, six pence per day. He continued his education by night while his father endeavoured to enroll him in Woolwich's prestigious military academy, but this application was rejected as he did not meet maximum age requirements.

In 1807 he married Anne Ross, the daughter of Alexander Ross and Anne McCulloch. They had no children. He was appointed acting deputy assistant commissary general (10 July 1812) and deputy assistant commissary general (2 November 1812). On 25 October 1819 he was placed in charge of the commissariat was offered a position in the West Indies, but he turned this down to remain close to his aging parents. The same year, while on half-pay and with "time on his hands," he decided to start recording his father's oral anecdotes as loose notes. On his father's death in 1830, he started to transcribe these notes into a set of letter-books.

During the 1837–38 Lower Canada Rebellion, he returned to active duty and full pay in the Eastern Townships. After the troubles he remained in the commissariat service, stationed at Chambly with responsibility for nineteen military stations. While at Chambly, the Thompsons adopted two young children, Caroline "Carry" and Eliza Julia Smith, the daughters of a former commissariat officer who had died in the West Indies. He was promoted to deputy commissary general (23 April 1846) and at the same time he was "discontinued from the strength of the Commissariat Department" and placed on half-pay. In his sixty-second year, this promotion and immediate retirement was a way for his commanding officer to recognize his many years of service (the retirement allowance for a deputy commissary general was considerable more than that for an assistant).

In May 1846 he moved to St. Johns (Saint-Jean-sur-Richelieu). After his wife died in December 1856, he spent some time with friends in Montreal, but he returned to Quebec City to live with his widowed sister, ANNE HARROWER, née THOMPSON, and her children, becoming their only means of support on his meagre fourteen shillings, eight pence daily retirement allowance. They lived in a small house just outside the St. Louis Gate. When Anne Harrower died in August 1861, he continued to support her children. He had been a generous man all of his life, often sending cash to friends and family in need, but eventually his cash resources fell to the point where he was in debt with his local bank.

His last years were difficult, with his on-

James Thompson, Jr. Photographed at a Quebec City studio in his eighty-fourth year, James Junior proudly wears the full dress uniform of a deputy commissary general, a position he had achieved in 1846. A generous and proud man, financial difficulties, failing health and squabbles with his brother John Gawler over the family home made his last years difficult. (LAC C-052167)

service at Cedars (Les Cèdres), with Côteau-du-Lac station added to his area of responsibility in December 1820. On 25 June 1823 he was transferred to Montreal and placed in charge of magazines.

He was promoted to assistant commissary general (23 November 1827) and placed in charge of the garrison's military chest. Without any prior warning, he was relieved from all duties and placed on half-pay (10 June 1828). He going squabbles with his brother John Gawler over the family home on St. Ursula Street (rue Sainte-Ursule), his worsening financial difficulties, his failing health and his deteriorating eyesight. He died on 7 December 1869 "in the 86th year of his age" with funeral services held at St. Andrew's Church, Quebec. The next day, the *Morning Chronicle* gave him a glowing obituary: "One by one our old living landmarks are disappearing from our midst, and this morning we have to record the death of our respected friend, Deputy Commissary General Thompson … we will miss our old friend very much from his familiar haunts. We will miss his kindly smile and cordial greeting and of his interesting details of what he had witnessed during his long residence in Canada…. He has died full of years, being we believe the senior of Quebec, and full of honor, if honor consists in a life spent in unblemished integrity." His remains were moved by Grand Trunk Railway ferry and then by train to St. Johns, where he was buried next to his wife on 9 December 1869.

BALs; JTC; James Thompson letter-book, Stewart Museum; Obituary, *Morning Chronicle*, 8 December 1869; Parish Register, St. James Church, Saint-Jean-sur-Richelieu, 1845–1869.

John Gawler Thompson (1787–1868),
lawyer, judge.
John Gawler, the twin brother of WILLIAM ALEXANDER, was born on 7 January 1787 in Quebec to James Thompson and Frances "Fanny" Cooper. He attended Reverend Daniel Wilkie's school. With his father's upwards progression through the garrison's engineering department (and his rising salary), he was permitted to remain in school much longer than his brothers, JAMES and William. Through the influence of his father, and the assistance of Chief Justice JONATHAN SEWELL, he was recommended to Andrew Stuart, a prominent lawyer in Quebec.

John Gawler Thompson. Appointed as a judge in the District of Gaspé by the Earl of Dalhousie, John Gawler became one of the very few powerful and influential Gaspesians of his day. A heavy drinker, he had a querulous relationship with his older brother, taking control of the family house on St. Ursula Street on the pretext that James Jr., then living in St. Johns, was too distant to properly attend to the needs of the property. Years later, when his brother had returned to Quebec and was providing for his widowed sister and her children on a small government pension, John Gawler refused to allow his brother occupancy of the house. (BAnQ P560, S2, D1, P1189)

He was one of a very few powerful and influential Gaspesians of his day. Admitted to the Bar in 1814, he successfully filled various positions including assistant coroner, chairman of the Quarter-sessions, coroner, and in 1827 he was appointed by the Earl of Dalhousie (GEORGE RAMSAY) as judge of the fledgling District of Gaspé as a special mark of respect to his father, James Thompson. In 1822 he married Margaret Robinson, and they had one child, Fanny, who died from a lung infection in 1832. In 1859 he was appointed judge of the Superior Court for the same district and remained in this position until his death. His rulings, considered to be arbitrary and partial, not to mention his drunkenness while performing his duties, infuriated the regional establishment so much that the member for Bonaventure County, Joseph-François Deblois, demanded his dismissal at the House of Assembly in 1835, but to no avail.

About 1838, John built a large Regency-style house on a 32-acre section of land in New Carlisle, overlooking the Baie des Chaleurs. Restored in recent years, it is now a popular bed and breakfast known as the "Judge Thompson House." When John died in 1868, he was the oldest judge in the Dominion of Canada.

JTC; Mario Mimeault, *Gaspésie* (Laval, 2005).

William Alexander Thompson (1787–1838), *British commissary officer.*
William Alexander, the twin brother of JOHN GAWLER, was born on 7 January 1787 in Quebec to James Thompson and Frances "Fanny" Cooper and educated at Reverend Daniel Wilkie's school in Quebec. His father secured him a job as a clerk in the commissariat department in 1805. Selected for active service during the War of 1812, he was promoted to deputy assistant commissary general (11 May 1813).

After the war, William continued in the commissariat, serving in virtually every station throughout the two Canadas. In 1830 he was serving in Kingston when he received notice to return immediately to Quebec to attend to his dying father. He was promoted to assistant commissary general (23 September 1830) and in January 1831 he was ordered to proceed to England, where he was immediately reposted to the West Indies. During his time there, he had two illegitimate children (Fanny and Mary) with Emile Marseille, born in Dominica. Seven years after his Caribbean posting he succumbed to disease on 18 May 1838. His obituary in the *Bytown Gazette* reads: "At Dominica, on the 18th of May, having landed only on the preceding day, in a state of great debility, Assistant Commissary General WILLIAM A. THOMPSON, in the 52nd year of his age. He was a native of Quebec; brother of Assistant Commissary General JAMES THOMPSON, now in charge of commissariat duties at Chambly, and twin brother of Mr. JUSTICE THOMPSON, at Gaspe."

JTC; *Bytown Gazette,* 8 August 1838.

Brigadier General George Townshend, 4th Viscount and 1st Marquess Townshend (1724–1807), *British army officer, Member of Parliament, office holder.*
George Townshend was born on 28 February 1724, the eldest son of Charles, 3rd Viscount Townshend, and his wife, Audrey Harrison. He was educated at St. John's College, Cambridge. In 1742, at eighteen, he was allowed to serve as a gentleman volunteer on the staff of Lord Dunmore and thus was present at the battle of Dettingen (16 June 1743). Undeniably brave and clever, Townshend is reputed during the battle to have witnessed a drummer boy standing nearby have his head struck off by a cannon ball. An old soldier who had thought to reassure the young officer was told sharply by Townshend: "I'm not afraid, sir! I am only astonished that a fellow with such a quantity of brains should be here!"

In May 1745 he was commissioned a captain in Bligh's Regiment (later the 20th Foot) and on the outbreak of the Jacobite rebellion that same year, returned to his regiment in England, fighting with it at the battle of Culloden (1746), near Inverness. He then accompanied the Duke of Cumberland as an aide de camp back to Europe and was thus present at the battle of Laffeldt (21 June 1747). He was elected *in absentia* as a Member of Parliament for Norfolk, which he continued to represent until succeeding his father, the viscount, in 1764.

He exchanged as a captain into the 1st Foot Guards (25 February 1748), which also carried the rank of lieutenant colonel "in the army."

Brigadier General George Townshend. A wealthy, aristocratic officer with less active service than Wolfe, Townshend was the government's choice to command a brigade in the Quebec expedition, not Wolfe's. An amateur artist, he produced several caricatures of Wolfe, mocking his idiosyncrasies. As a result, relations between the two officers were never cordial. After Wolfe's death and Monckton's wounding, Townshend assumed command of the British army and responsibility for the siege. On the capitulation of the French, some criticized Townshend for trying to steal the dead general's glory. (LAC C-8674)

When the War of the Austrian Succession ended in 1748, he returned to England and, after a falling out with Cumberland, resigned from the army; he then attacked his former commander in Parliament. He became a supporter of militia reform and, largely as a result of his efforts, an effective new militia bill was enacted in 1757. The same year, the Duke of Cumberland retired from active service in disgrace and was replaced as captain general of the army by Sir John Ligonier. Townshend now returned to active service, receiving a commission as colonel "in the army" on 6 May 1758.

In August 1758 he wrote to William Pitt asking for active employment against the French and was appointed to command a brigade in JAMES WOLFE's army sent against Quebec. Wolfe was not thrilled as he had wanted Colonel Ralph Burton, not a pretentious viscount's son, and this may have been the start of the ill-feeling that soon arose between the two officers. Townshend would prove to be a difficult colleague on campaign, a senior officer who, due to his considerable family influence and prestige, had never been afraid of criticizing authority, including the king. He would become Wolfe's most bitter critic during the Quebec campaign and drive his leader to the brink of despair through malicious comments and mischievous caricatures that he drew of Wolfe (which were then widely circulated amongst the staff).

Townshend was junior to ROBERT MONCKTON, but senior to JAMES MURRAY, and thus was third in command of Wolfe's army. On 9–10 July 1759 Townshend's and Murray's brigades crossed from the Île d'Orléans and landed on the north shore of the St. Lawrence River below Montmorency Falls, where they entrenched themselves. Wolfe's relations with his brigadiers, particularly Townshend, were not cordial and Wolfe wrote in his journal on 7 July 1759: "Some difference of opinion upon a point term'd slight & insignificant & the Commander in Chief is threatened w[i]th Parliamentary Inquiry into his Conduct for not consulting an inferior Officer & seeming to disregard his Sentiments!" The "inferior officer" in question was presumably George Townshend. By September 1759 Townshend was writing to his wife: "Genl Wolf's Health is but very bad. His Generalship in my poor opinion – is not a bit better...."

At the battle of the Plains of Abraham, 13 September 1759, Townshend commanded the British left wing. When Wolfe went down, mortally wounded, and Monckton, the next in command, was shot through the lungs, Townshend assumed command of the army. His first task was to deal with French reserves approaching from the rear, which he did effectively, but the major part of the French army escaped while Townshend ordered his men to dig in for the night. Going by the book, he brought up large numbers of guns onto the Plains of Abraham to lay siege to the city but before he could start operations proper, the city capitulated on 18 September 1759.

James Murray was left in command at Quebec and Townshend returned to England before the winter set in. In England he was appointed colonel of the 28th Foot and given the thanks of Parliament. His official reports made little or no mention of the fallen hero, James Wolfe, which resulted in him being sharply and publicly criticized in the press and the House of Commons for his disrespectful behaviour toward the country's dead hero. The controversy, though bitter, was brief and did not impede his advancement.

In March 1761 Townshend was promoted major general and took command of a British brigade serving in the Allied army in Germany which saw fierce action at the battle of Vellinghausen (15–16 July 1761). In 1762 he went to Portugal with the local rank of lieutenant general and took command of a division of the Anglo-Portuguese army protecting that country against Franco-Spanish forces.

On his return to Britain, Townshend was appointed lord lieutenant of Ireland in 1767 and served in this post until 1772. From 1772 to 1782, he served as the master general of the Board of Ordnance. Promoted general in 1782 and a field marshal in 1796, he was created a marquess in 1787, appointed lord lieutenant of Norfolk in 1792, governor of the Royal Hospital Chelsea from 1795–96, and governor of Jersey. Townshend died at Raynham Hall, Norfolk, on 14 September 1807.

BALs; *DCB; DNB;* RGO; George Townshend Collection, LAC MG18-L7; *Burke's Peerage*; Lieut. Col. C.V. F. Townshend, *The Military Life of Field Marshal George First Marquess Townshend, 1724–1807 ... From Family Documents not Hitherto Published* (London, 1902).

Captain William Twiss (1745–1827), *British army officer.*

William Twiss is believed to have been the only son of William Twiss (d. 1766), waterman and victualler of Gravesend, Kent, and his wife, Ann. Baptized at St. Anne's Church, Westminster, on 23 November 1744, not much is known of William's early life. However, at the tender age of sixteen he was appointed to the Ordnance Office at the Tower of London (22 July 1760). Twiss worked there for two years and in July 1763 became overseer of the King's works at Gibraltar at nineteen, which suggests that he was of above-average capacity and probably blessed with the patronage of someone well placed in the Ordnance Department.

Twiss received a commission as practitioner engineer and ensign (19 November 1763) while at Gibraltar, and eight long years later, in April 1771, he was promoted to sub engineer and infantry lieutenant on his return to England. Employed on the defences of Portsmouth dockyard, he went overseas on active duty during the American Revolution in 1776. On arrival at Quebec in June 1776, Twiss was appointed aide de camp to General William Phillips serving in General John Burgoyne's army. Sir GUY CARLETON, commander-in-chief at Quebec, made him controller of works for the construction of a fleet on Lake Champlain, and the following year Twiss was appointed senior engineer for Burgoyne's army. Extensively involved in planning the siege works before Ticonderoga, his manoeuvring of two guns onto Mount Defiance at the rear of the American siege lines caused the Americans' premature abandonment of Fort Ticonderoga (5 July 1777) and

Captain William Twiss. William Twiss arrived in Quebec in 1777, and when Captain Marr left in 1781, he assumed the duties of the commanding engineer in Canada. Directed to construct a temporary citadel in Quebec, he quickly appreciated the loyalty and efficiency of James Thompson, his overseer of works, and later assisted in finding a cadet vacancy at the Royal Military Academy at Woolwich for the latter's son George. (Royal Engineers Library, Chatham, St. Lawrence, 351-77)

their precipitous withdrawal south.

After Burgoyne's army was defeated at Saratoga in October 1777, Twiss temporarily became a prisoner of war but was exchanged a few days later. The following year he was promoted engineer extraordinary (the equivalent of an infantry captain lieutenant). Thereafter, for the next six years, Twiss was employed in strengthening the defences of Canada and supervised the construction of a temporary citadel at Quebec, commencing in 1779. Twiss also made significant improvements to navigation on the St. Lawrence River above Montreal, particularly by his fortified canal at Côteau-du-Lac, and in 1781 was appointed Canada's commanding engineer.

On his return to England in October 1783, Twiss was appointed secretary to the Board of Land and Sea Officers reporting on the defences of Portsmouth and Plymouth dockyards. Promoted captain on 23 March 1786, he served at Portsmouth (1785–92), where he supervised the construction of Fort Cumberland at the entrance of Langston harbour. He was then appointed senior Royal Engineer for the Southern Military District (1792–1809). On promotion to lieutenant colonel, Twiss was appointed lieutenant governor of the Royal Military Academy at Woolwich.

During the Napoleonic Wars Twiss oversaw the strengthening of the eastern defences of Dover Castle. In September 1799 he joined the Duke of York's expedition to the Netherlands as the senior Royal Engineer, and after returning home in November was promoted full colonel (1 January 1800). He subsequently made inspection tours of the Channel Islands (1800) and Ireland (1802) to report upon their defences and, during the heightened threat of a French invasion in 1803, he was again put in charge of the defences of Dover. Appointed brigadier general on 11 February 1804, he spent the next three years overseeing the construction of a chain of seventy-three Martello towers guarding vital landing points along the Kent and Sussex coasts.

Twiss was promoted major general (30 October 1805) and colonel commandant of the Corps of Royal Engineers (24 June 1809). He was promoted lieutenant general in 1812 and full general on 27 May 1825. On his retirement in 1810, Twiss bought a home at Bingley in Yorkshire, where he died on 14 March 1827.

BALs; *DCB; DNB;* JTC; RGO; R.F. Edwards, *Roll of Officers of the Corps of Royal Engineers, from 1660 to 1898* (Chatham, 1898).

Lieutenant Jean Vauquelin (1728–72),
French naval officer.

Jean Vauquelin was born in Dieppe, France, in February 1728, the son of a captain in the merchant marine. Little is known of his early life except that he went to sea with his father at an early age. During the War of Austrian Succession he appears as an officer on a privateering frigate before getting his own command in the merchant marine c. 1750. He was recruited at the beginning of the Seven Years' War to serve as an *officier bleu* and received command on 26 April 1757 of the frigate *Tourterelle* and in February 1758 he was commissioned a lieutenant in the French Royal Navy.

Given command of the 30-gun frigate *Aréthuse*, he was sent to Île Royale (Cape Breton Island) and, despite Admiral Edward Boscawen's blockade, succeeded in entering Louisbourg harbour on 9 June 1758. Moored near Barrachois in Louisbourg harbour, Vauquelin's accurate gunfire significantly hindered British siege operations. He was ordered by Governor DRUCOUR to go to France with dispatches reporting on the situation at Louisbourg. Setting sail on the night of 14–15 July, he ran the British naval blockade once again and reached Europe after a rapid and uneventful crossing.

Vauquelin returned to Canada in 1759 as commander of the frigate *Atalante* though he did not play a major part at the siege of Quebec. In the spring of 1760 Vauquelin formed a small naval division, including the *Atalante*, which left Sorel for Quebec on 20 April to follow and supply Lévis' army. It reached the Anse au Foulon on 28 April, the day of the French victory at Sillery. During the French siege of Quebec, a British frigate arrived on 9 May in the Quebec basin and was soon joined by another frigate and ship of the line. Lévis decided it was time for his besieging army to withdraw to Montreal, but unfortunately the message to retire up the river did not reach *Capitaine* Jean Vauquelin, the flotilla commander, owing to bad weather.

Lieutenant Jean Vauquelin. The bronze statue shown here, sculpted by Paul-Eugène Benet, was inaugurated on 22 June 1930. It shows Vauquelin with arms stretched backwards, defending what remains of his frigate, *Atalante*. Located in Old Montreal at the foot of Place Jacques-Cartier, Vauquelin defiantly glares up the hill towards Admiral Horatio Nelson, perched on top of the column which commemorates his 1805 victory over the French at Trafalgar, at the head of Place Jacques-Cartier. (Editor's Collection)

On the first flood tide at 4:30 p.m. the next morning, 16 May 1760, the Royal Navy moved quickly, cutting their cables and running before the wind up to where Lévis's supply ships were still at anchor. They caught the French by surprise and one of Vauquelin's ships was "run ashore by the Frenche camp under there batterys" according to Andrew Knox, master of the *Vanguard*. The *Atalante*, commanded by Vauquelin, fought back fiercely, shielding a large fleet of bateaux as far as Cap-Rouge, where they could be safe from an immediate attack.

Then Vauquelin began to fight a running rearguard battle with the frigates *Diana* and *Lowestoft* for almost three hours, buying much-needed time for the French army to get their bateaux at Saint Augustin safely up-river to Jacques-Cartier. All of the lesser transports anchored at the Anse au Foulon, however, were destroyed by *Vanguard* except the small sloop of war *La Marie*, which, by throwing her guns overboard, was the only ship of the fleet able to escape up-river.

Vauquelin succeeded in giving his British opponents as good as he got and his gunners, aiming high, did great damage to the rigging of the pursuing British ships. A cheer went up from his sailors when a lucky shot sheared off the foretopmast steering sail of *Diana*. Vauquelin's crippled frigate *Atalante* could get no further than Pointe-aux-Trembles and so he ran it aground, nailed his colours to the mast and fought until his powder ran out. Sword in hand, Vauquelin ordered the mizzen mast chopped down at 11 a.m. so his surviving crew could use it as a raft to get to shore. Then he and his officers waited on board, their colours still flying defiantly.

By 11:30 a.m. boarding parties from *Diana* had "brought the first and second Captn, officers, and sume of the people on board us" the master noted, but "our cutter was bilg'd and lost upon a rock in boarding the enemy." The British naval officers were highly impressed with Vauquelin's fighting spirit and seamanship, so much so that the British naval commander, Commodore Robert Swanton, asked how he could serve the French captain. Vauquelin requested to be sent back to France at the first opportunity, with which the commodore immediately complied. "This noble and generous behaviour of the English," noted the Chevalier de JOHNSTONE, "did honour to their nation, far beyond what De Vauquelin met with from De Berryer, secretary of the navy, on his arrival in France." The returning Vauquelin was thrown into prison and court martialled for losing the fleet.

When he was vindicated, Vauquelin was promoted to the rank of fire-ship captain (5 November 1761) and lieutenant commander (1 October 1764). Given the command of the flute *Bricole* in 1764, he took command of the *Coulisse* the following year for a mission to Guiana, where Choiseul, the minister of marine and the colonies, was endeavouring to found a settlement to make up for the loss of Canada. Vauquelin commanded several more ships in his lifetime and died at Rochefort in October 1772.

DCB; "A Dialogue in Hades: A Parallel of military errors, of which the French and English armies were guilty during the Campaign of 1759 in Canada," a narrative attributed to Chevalier James Johnstone, LHSQ, *Historical Documents,* Ser. 2, Vol 2 (1867); "The Campaign of 1760 in Canada," a narrative attributed to Chevalier James Johnstone, LHSQ, *Historical Documents,* Second Series (1887).

Major General James Wolfe (1727–59),
British army officer.

James Wolfe was born 2 January 1727 at Westerham, Kent, the son of Lieutenant General Edward Wolfe and Henrietta Thompson. Educated in schools at Westerham and Greenwich, he was commissioned in his father's regiment, the 1st Regiment of Marines, (3 November 1741) at the tender age of fourteen. Prone to seasickness, Wolfe never served with the marines; the following year on 27 March 1742 he exchanged into the 12th Foot as an ensign and deployed with it to Flanders. The following year, at sixteen, he underwent his baptism of fire in Bavaria at the battle of Dettingen and thereafter was appointed adjutant and promoted lieutenant.

In 1744 he exchanged to the 4th Foot as a captain and in 1745 he returned to England to serve as a staff officer with the Duke of Cumberland's forces assigned to deal with the Jacobite uprising led by "the Young Pretender," Charles

Edward Stuart. In January 1746 Wolfe was present at the battle of Falkirk and was shortly afterwards made aide de camp to Lieutenant General Henry Hawley. In this latter capacity, he was present at the battle of Culloden on 16 April 1746. One anecdote states that Wolfe, after the battle, was ordered by General Hawley to execute a wounded Highlander found on the battlefield. It just happened to be Lieutenant Colonel Charles Fraser, younger of Inverallochy, who had led the Frasers of Lovat into battle. Wolfe refused to do so and Inverallochy was dispatched by a soldier. Wolfe's behaviour and sense of honour on this occasion may have well been common knowledge to the Frasers later serving in the 78th Foot under his command at Louisbourg and Quebec. Certainly Simon Fraser, the younger brother of the executed Jacobite officer, served as a company commander in the 78th Foot at Louisbourg and was killed at the battle of the Plains of Abraham.

In January 1747 Wolfe returned to the continent, where the 4th Foot was serving, and on 2 July was wounded in the battle of Laffeldt. Following a period of sick leave in England, he was sent back to the Low Countries as a brigade major. When the War of the Austrian Succession ended in 1748, he obtained his majority in the 20th Foot, then stationed in Scotland, and became the acting commanding officer when Edward Cornwallis was appointed to the governorship of Nova Scotia and left to fill that post. Wolfe was promoted lieutenant colonel in 1750 at the age of twenty-three and two years later obtained a six-month leave of absence to study French and military sciences in Paris. Thereafter he rejoined his regiment on garrison duties in Scotland before moving south to England.

His first active service in the Seven Years' War was as quartermaster general to the failed 1757 expedition against Rochefort on the French Biscay coast. On his return, the 2nd Battalion of the 20th Foot was converted into a new regiment, the 67th Foot, and Wolfe was appointed its colonel. In January 1758 Wolfe was given local rank as "brigadier in America" and made one of JEFFERY AMHERST's three brigade commanders. In February he embarked in Admiral Edward Boscawen's flagship, *Princess Amelia*, which reached Halifax only on 9 May and three days later he reported to Lord Sackville that he found "Fraser's and Brigadier Lawrence's Battalions were … in very good condition," adding with some admiration that "the Highlanders are very useful serviceable soldiers and commanded by the most manly corps of officers I ever saw."

On 2 and 3 June Amherst's force appeared off Gabarus Bay but the weather prevented a landing until 8 June. The psychological impact of having warlike Highlanders to use as shock troops was not lost for a minute on commanders like Wolfe and he requested that the remainder of the 78th Foot be transferred from another brigade to beef up his assault force slated to go in at Kennington Cove, as the 78th Foot's light infantry and grenadiers already formed a goodly proportion of it. For this honour of being one of the first regiments to land, the 78th was eternally grateful to Wolfe and this does much to explain his high esteem amongst the Highland officers and rank and file.

The landings were made despite high surf and Wolfe proved to be very active throughout the siege. He was back and forth constantly to confer with Amherst and report on developments around the harbour and was constantly passing through the Highlanders' main camp in the siege lines. His visits were frequent and a source of great pride and excitement among the young Highlanders. James Thompson remembers that "while before Louisbourg, which lasted a period of seven weeks and three days, the Camp where our Regiment lay, was three miles distant from the General's, yet he almost every day came to see Us, when our men would 'turn-out' to him with the greatest alacrity … every Mother's Son of them would … quit his 'porritch' to be in time for the 'turn-out' ... the word would be passed on these occasions, in Gaelic, 'Here comes the red-haired Corporal' from the circumstances he had red hair and because he wore an aiguillette similar to the worsted badge of distinction worn by Corporals of that day."

After the capture of Louisbourg, Wolfe returned to England only to be sent back the following year to command the expedition against Quebec. His exploits are well chronicled in many books, and after a prolonged siege of four months with several setbacks, he finally brought General LOUIS-JOSEPH DE MONTCALM's army to battle outside the city of Quebec on the Plains of Abraham. The beginning of the operation was marked by a difficult night-time descent on the St. Lawrence River by a third of his army in small boats. They successfully landed at dawn and gained the heights of Abraham in darkness while successive waves of solders were brought over from Pointe Lévy. During the beginning of the battle he was wounded three times, the last mortally, and he died on the battlefield before he could see the fruits of his labours. That Wolfe on his final campaign at Quebec in 1759, a commoner and protégé of "the Great Commoner" himself, was argumentative and quarrelsome with his three brigadiers, all sprigs of nobility, is a matter of public record. What is often lost in the stereotypical, and predictable, focus on his command staff's in-house bickering and backstabbing is that the thirty-two-year-old major general, in tandem with his competent naval counterpart, Charles Saunders, mounted and maintained the largest joint operation ever seen in North America to that date, despite his brigadiers' rancour and ill will.

In sum, despite James Wolfe's character flaws and lapses of judgment, he was a man of action and an excellent trainer of men, well known and respected throughout the army long before his public image took wings after his dynamic performance at Louisbourg and Quebec. He was acknowledged by many contemporaries as a progressive and innovative professional soldier whose oft-expressed views on improving the common soldier's welfare, marksmanship, drill, interior economy and logistics, and on replacing obsolete doctrine and tactics, were always sound and practical. His constant search within the 18th-century British army to enhance its war fighting capabilities and to improve the lot of the common soldier were qualities that endeared him to men like James Thompson.

Wolfe's role and influence in the British army as a professional soldier, innovator and trainer have been misunderstood until recently. He was quick to grasp the challenges of the operating environment he faced — the hurdles to be overcome by the mid-18th-century Georgian army transposed to the North American wilderness where it had to, in Darwinian fashion, quickly adapt and evolve to meet the challenges of riverine and amphibious operations; the ruthless savagery of *"la petite guerre"*; and the overwhelming dependence on good logistics to just move, sustain and fight.

On both sides of the Atlantic, Wolfe has been mythologized (1874–1928) or demythologized (1934–2008) by historians to the point that the pendulum swing from one extreme to the other has perpetuated a series of extremely cartoonish and anecdotal vignettes: a young ethical Wolfe refusing to execute a wounded Highlander at Culloden; a courageous Wolfe landing at Louisbourg with his silver-topped cane; a reflective, sensitive Wolfe reciting Thomas Gray's poem "Elegy in a Country Churchyard" as his flotilla of troop-laden boats drifts down the St. Lawrence on the ebb tide; a sickly but dauntless Wolfe climbing a treacherous goat path to surprise an astonished Montcalm; and a tragic Wolfe gasping his last words: "Now I can die in peace, God be praised!" Wolfe certainly died, but it is debatable whether his reputation will ever rest in peace.

Wolfe, warts and all, though not a Great Captain of Antiquity, was undoubtedly a great soldier, albeit blessed with a large store of luck and audacity. Most historians, however, have a single-sided view of Wolfe, primarily the persona of a young priggish British commander at Quebec, killed at the very moment of his singular spectacular victory, then deified as a martyr of the Great War for Empire, an icon of British imperialism and Victorian poster boy for the stiff upper lip school of war fighting.

The bottom line is that James Thompson and the rank-and-file loved him, and many wept tears on the Plains of Abraham upon hearing the news of his death. On reflection, Wolfe would probably modestly agree that he achieved a celebrity in death that he never achieved in life, though his earthly exploits are, in themselves, sufficient to warrant a modest label of being an innovative and progressive soldier of the British army. Wolfe as an individual faced insurmountable odds and managed to persevere to the end.

Wolfe's mission, while not impossible, was a thorny complex tactical problem compounded by prevailing winds, forbidding geography and peevish subordinates. Criticisms that he was a bad strategist are true, but Quebec was but one line of operation within the North American campaign strategy dictated by Pitt, and Wolfe was an executor of the operational plan, not its mastermind. Wolfe's expertise, drive and superior leadership qualities saw him through. To Thompson and his fellow Highlanders, the "Red-haired Corporal" embodied the spirit of the fighting Highlanders' own culture, where "love of honour and dread of shame" went hand in hand.

BALs; *DCB*; *DNB*; JTC; Robert Wright, *The Life of Major General James Wolfe* (London, 1864); Beckles Willson, *The Life and Letters of James Wolfe* (New York, 1909); Robin Reilly, *The Rest to Fortune: The Life of Major General James Wolfe* (London, 1960); Steve Brumwell, *Paths of Glory: The Life and Death of General James Wolfe* (Montreal 2006); D. Peter MacLeod, *Northern Armageddon: The Battle of the Plains of Abraham* (Toronto, 2008); C.P. Stacey, *Quebec, 1759: The Siege and the Battle* (Toronto, 1959).

Captain John Crawford Young (1788–1859), *British army officer, artist.*

Born in Dalkeith, Scotland, in 1788, John Crawford Young was commissioned an ensign in the 91st Foot (16 August 1804) at the age of sixteen and was promoted lieutenant the following year (13 August 1805). He served in the Peninsula from August 1808 to January 1809 and fought at the battles of Roleia, Vimeira, Calcavellas and Corunna under Sir John Moore. He participated in the 1809 Walcheren expedition, and then returned to the Peninsula with his regiment to serve in Wellington's army in October 1812. A year later he was promoted captain (6 October 1813) and fought at the battles of Nivelle, Nive, Orthez, Tarbes and Toulouse.

In October 1817 he exchanged to the 79th Foot (Cameron Highlanders) and went to Canada with his new regiment in October 1825. While in Quebec he served as aide de camp to Lord Dalhousie (GEORGE RAMSAY) from October 1826 to June 1827. In July-August 1826 Young accompanied Dalhousie on an inspection tour of New Brunswick and Nova Scotia. An accomplished watercolourist, Young painted a great number of scenes of Bonaventure Island and Percé Rock as well as Chaleur Bay on the return voyage to Quebec.

In June 1828 the 79th Foot left their quarters in Quebec's Jesuit Barracks and relocated to Montreal, where on 18 June the regiment received new colours. Young, then captain of the regiment's grenadiers, marched the colours to the saluting flag under the watchful eye of Lord Dalhousie, who had travelled to Montreal to attend the ceremony.

On 7 August 1827, Dalhousie wrote in his journal: "Capt. Young has made a large collection of drawings, with which he will certainly tempt Colonel COCKBURN to visit ... Pooley and Denny are both drawing for me, which those of Young will form a valuable collection to illustrate my excursions this year." Captain Young subsequently offered his American Portfolio No. 1 to Lord Dalhousie, prior to Dalhousie's return to Britain in September 1828. The album, which is made up of forty watercolours and washes, constitutes the most important work of Young's career.

Young also designed the 20-foot obelisk to commemorate the deaths of Montcalm and Wolfe at the battle of the Plains of Abraham and had obtained leave from his regiment to attend the ceremonies to lay the foundation stone on 15 November 1827. During these ceremonies, held in the Governor's Garden in Quebec's Upper Town, he supported the aging James Thompson, whose function, as Quebec's senior Mason, was to give the "mystic three taps of the mallet" to officially set the stone. The monument's top-stone was ceremoniously placed and inaugurated by Lord Dalhousie one year later on 8 September 1828, the day before he left Canada. Again, Young had obtained leave from his regiment to attend the ceremony, but this time his compatriot-in-arms, James Thompson, was too weak to attend. However, Young did drop by the Thompson residence the next day and made arrangements to execute a pen and ink sketch of his old friend (likely on the express orders of Lord Dalhousie).

Young was promoted major (6 September 1833) and went out of the army on half-pay (10 May 1839). He was brevetted a lieutenant colonel "in the army" (9 November 1846) and promoted to colonel "in the army" (20 June 1854). He died in Cheltenham, Gloucestershire, early in 1859.

BALs; JTC; Marjory Whitelaw, ed., *The Dalhousie Journals*, 3 vols (Ottawa, 1978–82); Capt. T.A. Mackenzie et al, eds., *Historical Records of the 79th Queen's Own Cameron Highlanders* (London, 1887), 86–80.

APPENDIX A

ANECDOTE 38

"Memorandum of the most arduous Services performed by James Thompson, overseer of works since his joining the Engineer Department at Quebec, in the year 1761."

To,
the Respective Officers,
of His Majesty's Ordnance,
Quebec.

Previously to my joining the Engineer Department I had served His late Majesty George the Second as a volunteer, in a new raised Regiment of Highlanders, consisting of fourteen hundred Rank and File, commanded by the Honourable Simon Fraser of Lovat. In this Corps I served at the harassing siege and conquest of Louisbourg in 1758, and in the year following at the memorable reduction of the Garrison of Quebec, both of which achievements were conducted by the immortal Wolfe. I was also in arms at the reduction of the Garrison of Montreal, which terminated the entire conquest of the British American Colonies as at present subsisting (year 1828).

After these services, I was attached to the Royal Engineers Department, by order of General James Murray then Commander of the Forces. The first employment assigned to me in the Engineer Department was to superintend and direct two hundred men from the garrison in making Fascines (I having acquired that art at the siege of Louisbourg) on the north side of the River Sainte Charles. In this service I continued during the whole of the winter 1759-60 when I experienced all the severities of a Canadian winter, aggravated by the circumstance of my being unprovided with any other clothing than my Regimental Highland dress, nevertheless, I succeeded in getting forty-five thousand & five hundred well-bound Fascines made & brought on the mens' shoulders to the Garrison, which enabled the Engineer in the spring to put an unfinished & extensive Fortification in a state of defence, at which latter service also I was extensively engaged.

From this time & until the Conquest of the Canadas was finally secured, my Services were chiefly in the field, under the denomination of Clerk of Works, under the immediate command of General, then Captain Spry of the Corps of

Royal Engineers, who was relieved in 1762 by Captain John Marr. Under this officer also, I served as Clerk of Works until 1772, when he obtained leave to return to Scotland.

In granting Captain Marr the leave of absence, the Commander-in-Chief authorized Colonel Jones, of the 52nd Regiment, then Commanding the Forces in Canada, to appoint an officer of the Garrison to the charge of the Engineer Department, until the return of Captain Marr or of some other engineer. This the Colonel hesitated to do, supposing an officer of the Line to be unacquainted with the forms of office, the framing of estimates, and the nature of works and materials, and under these considerations he consulted with me, and said that if I would undertake the charge he would suspend the appointment of an officer from the Line, and would state the circumstance to the Commander-in-Chief then at New York. I readily assented to the proposal, and the return of the Post or Express, brought a letter from Head Quarters approving of the arrangement, and I was accordingly ordered to proceed upon the duties required. The same express brought me a letter from the Engineer of Head Quarters requesting an accurate return of all the mathematical instruments in my charge, and directing that I should transmit through him all my vouchers for expenses incurred for the Public Work then carrying on in Canada, after the 25th December, annually, and to include myself for Extra-Pay, at two shillings & six pence per day, under the title of *Overseer of Works*. This service I performed during three years & six months, without any assistance of Clerks or others, & had the satisfaction of obtaining the Commander-in-Chief's approbation and thanks for having carried on the extensive Works and repairs throughout the Province with punctuality and economy.

I was detached to the town of Three Rivers to make arrangements for the immediate erection (year 1773) of large magazines and storehouses for the security of the provisions, etc., for the troops, which Works were performed by contract and in a workman-like manner, & I venture to assert that no person unacquainted with the prices of work & materials, and the peculiar customs of the country, could have completed buildings of the same dimensions for double the sum.

Before I was relieved from my charge, the Americans invaded Canada (year 1775) when I received the orders of General Carleton, afterwards Guy, Lord Dorchester, to put the extensive Fortifications of Quebec in a state of defence at a time when there was not a single article of material in store with which to perform such an undertaking. I was consequently authorized to purchase all that was needful, & to prosecute the work with the greatest dispatch. My first object was to secure stout spar-timber for pallisading a great extent of open ground between the Gates called Palace & Hope, and again from Cape Diamond half-bastion, along the brow of the Cape, towards the Castle Saint Louis. From my thorough knowledge of the first cost of materials of every description, I could not be imposed upon by any Dealer, and I accordingly succeeded in securing from Monsieur Lafleche's Timber Yard, as much spar-timber as I required at three farthings per foot, for which he at first demanded three pence. Having thus established the price of one kind of timber, I took all I required at proportionate rates by which means the whole of my expenses in the article of timber, did not amount to One thousand Pounds. I made a beginning with fourteen Canadian carpenters, at Palace Gate, in pallisading with loop-holes for musketry, and made a projection in the form of a Bastion, as a defence for the line of Pickets, in the gorge of which I erected a Block-house, which made a good defence.

While employed at this station of the works, a company of artificers arrived from Halifax, and another company from Newfoundland joined me soon after. The Halifax men I set to work at pallisading the open ground on Cape Diamond, & framing & erecting a large Block-house on the outside of Port Saint Louis, to serve as a Captain's nightly Guard-house in order to be prepared against a surprise; also a Block-house on the Cape, under Cape Diamond Bastion. At the same time a party was employed in laying platforms and repairing embrazures. I also had a party of the carpenters barricading the extremities of the Lower Town, by blocking up all the windows of the houses next to the River-side and those facing the water, leaving only loop-holes for musketry, as a defence in case the Saint Lawrence should freeze across. Whilst these detached services were in progress I was on horseback from the rising to the setting of the sun in attending the several points where my presence was required, and again owing to the weak state of the troops in Garrison, I had to mount Picket with my artificers, who were armed for that purpose, from nine o'clock at night until daybreak each morning, and again resume our labours at the Fortifications. This I continued during the Blockade, without being enabled, in the interval, to lie down on a bed. After completing the works of defence I, with all my artificers were called upon to do duty as Soldiers & ordered to join Major John Nairn's party as a corps-de-reserve, in case of alarm, the Grand-parade being fixed upon as our rendez-vous.

On the 3rd November 1775, General Arnold with a party of upwards of seven hundred Americans came out of the woods at the settlements on the River Chaudiére, and on the 9th they marched to Point Levy where they showed themselves on the bank immediately opposite the Town of Quebec. On the 14th in the night, they passed across the Saint Lawrence and paraded in front of Port Saint Louis at about three hundred yards distance, where they saluted the town with three cheers, in full expectation no doubt that the Gates would be opened for their reception. At this juncture I was on Cape Diamond Bastion and myself levelled & fired a 24 pounder at them which had the effect of making them disperse hastily, and retire to Pointe aux Trembles.

On the 5th December General Montgomery, their Chief Commander, came with troops from Montreal and joined Arnold, making their Head Quarters at Saint Foy. They sent in a flag of truce which General Carleton utterly disregarded, declaring that he would not have any communication with rebels, unless they came to claim the King's mercy. Montgomery was then induced to try his strength by erecting a six-gun Battery in front of Saint John's Gate; a Battery of two guns on the off-side of River Saint Charles; & one of four guns on the Pointe Levi side, none of which did us any material injury. At this time, the nights being dark, I strongly recommended the use of Lanthorns extended on poles from the salient angles of all the Bastions, the effect of which, as witnessed by Colonel McLean commanding the 84th Regiment, was highly approved. By means of these lights, even a dog could be distinguished if in the great-ditch, in the darkest night. Thus we continued during the absence of the moon, with the exception of a composition burned in iron pots substituted for candles. On the 31st December, before daylight, General Montgomery made an attempt at assault by Près-de-Ville, and Sault-au-Matelot, the southern & northern extremities of the Lower Town. Montgomery moved forward with his Division to the advanced barrier (which he did not expect to meet with) where a stop was put to his further progress, & where he, and two of his officers and a sergeant were shot dead by a single discharge of grape from the second floor of the house now called Cape Diamond Brewery. As soon as these fell, the whole made a precipitate retreat. From the part I had performed in this service, generally, as also for having had the disposal of the body of the General, which I interred with permission, inside the Saint Louis Gate Bastion, along-side the grave of my first wife; I considered myself entitled to withhold the General's sword, and which has remained in my possession to the present day. It bears the imprint of an eagle-head on the hilt, but is, no doubt, made by an English cutler, having "Harvey" on the blade.

General Arnold made his advance by Sault-au-Matelot, and forced a Blind made of one-inch boards & placed in front of two guns at the outside of a Barrier. Here he received a wound, and was carried away to the Hopital Général. All attempts to force the Barrier were fruitless, but the enemy got into the houses & fired from the windows, when a Sally through Palace Gate, attacking them in the rear, succeeded in surrounding them, in number about three hundred and fifty, about sixty more having been killed. During the contest the Garrison sustained a loss of only five killed & thirteen wounded.

On the 6th there arrived three ships of war, bringing two companies of the 29th Regiment, which with Marines, about two hundred in all, immediately landed & were marched out with our small Garrison in pursuit of the enemy, who were found to be in full retreat & having left behind them every thing which they could not carry on their backs.

Now that the enemy had ceased to disturb us, I had leisure to think of my own situation and being excessively worn down with fatigue and anxiety I ventured upon an indulgence which I had not enjoyed for six months before, namely, that of extending my wearied limbs on a bed. It would seem that the luxury had been ill-timed, for I was immediately afflicted with a debility which confined me to my bed for fourteen days, & my ultimate recovery was extremely tedious. Here, I think it worthy of notice, that although the American General had ordered scaling ladders to be made by the inhabitants, & brought & laid down on the ground in parcels, in several places in front of our Works, for the purpose of storming, yet he must have desisted from his original purpose from a consideration that a night attack upon a Rampart thoroughly lighted, was much too hazardous, & that his better chance of success would be in attacking the Lower Town, under the favor of a snow storm, as was indeed the case.

Captain William Twiss, our Commanding Engineer, having been made prisoner in 1777 at Saratoga, where General Bourgoyne surrendered to the Americans, there was a temporary suspension of the public works, but being again liberated from his captivity the following year, he immediately returned to Quebec, & commenced a temporary Fortification on Cape Diamond. In this work I had a Redoubt assigned to my exclusive superintendence, and besides the materials required for this, I had the immediate duty of purchasing all that were required for the various other works then carrying on.

It having been decided that the whole of the state prisoners in our possession should be quartered in some place of security, & the remoteness of Mal Baie, about 90 miles below Quebec, on the north side of the Saint Lawrence, being considered as well adapted to the purpose, I received orders to proceed thither, & to erect suitable buildings for their reception. Accordingly I selected a spot of ground, with the concurrence of the proprietor, Colonel Nairn, & laid down picketing for three buildings contiguous to each other. The workmen, who were selected from among the prisoners themselves, were taken down with me, & I remained with them until the mason work rose about a foot from the surface, including a double stack of chimneys to each building. This service, from the circumstance of the country being unsettled with inhabitants, & the workmen being disaffected, was exceedingly irksome. It was not long after I had left them, under the directions of an Overseer whom I had chosen, that an Express announced their having all deserted by means of two flat-bottom'd boats, across to Kamouraska, where the river is twenty-one miles broad! From the vigilance of the Canadian peasantry, they were all however brought back to Quebec, for which act of loyalty the inhabitants met with a generous reward.

There being some German troops quartered at Saint Thomas & the parishes in that vicinity, under the orders of Brigadier-General Rochanplatt (year 1780) I was ordered down to make arrangements for the construction of magazines, a guardhouse, & sheds for the protection of Field guns. This service I effected by a given day, for which I gave an order of payment on the late Honorable Thomas Dunn, the Paymaster-General, for One hundred & fifty Pounds, the sum agreed upon.

There having been received by an English mail recently arrived (10th July 1782) an Allegation from the Seigneur of the Parish of Berthier in the District of Montreal, through the medium of the Minister of State's Office, to the effect that his property had sustained sundry damages, caused by the Army serving in Canada, during the American Revolutionary War, & particularly by the Engineer Department, the whole amount of which he set forth at the sum of Ten thousand Pounds Sterling, less two shillings & six pence!

In order to ascertain the actual damages sustained, I was entrusted with all the papers connected with the subject, & ordered to proceed forthwith to the spot, being furnished also with instructions, in due form, touching the most essential points to be investigated. After two most minute enquires, in which I was assisted by Conrad Gugy, Esquire, Justice of the Peace, Monsieur Leguay, Notary Public, Monsieur Olivier, Captain of Militia, & some of the most intelligent farmers, I elicited all the information that I conceived necessary to the object of my mission, & returned to Quebec, after an absence of only six days. On delivering back to Captain Twiss the papers which he had entrusted to me, together with the mass of Declarations & Depositions procured at Sorel, Berthier, Lanoraie, and Machiche, I received an intimation to be in attendance at the Chateau Saint Louis, where I met Captain Twiss; His Excellency General Haldimand and Major Mathews, his secretary, then proceeded to a perusal of the particulars which astonished the General exceedingly. A vessel being on the point of sailing for England, and which had been detained for the purpose at £13 per day, Mr. Leguay the Notary was employed to make out copies of the papers & they were immediately sent home to the Minister of State's office. The only loss to which the Seigneur could, with any justice lay claim, was occasioned by the erection of a useful bridge at a place where he had once established a ferry, which yielded about twenty five dollars per annum to himself & possibly to the Ferryman. Thus the whole details of an account for assumed losses in timber, firewood, sugar trees, mills, etc., amounting within a trifle, to Ten thousand Pounds Sterling, were invalidated & the government released from such a heavy claim proffered against it.

I will only further state, in a brief manner, that I have ever had a great degree of confidence placed in me by my superiors in office, and that I have had the good fortune to render that satisfaction which is one of the greatest consolations to me in the fast declining stage of a career, which, through the interposition of Providential agency has already been extended to the *ninety sixth year!* The books and other official documents of the Royal Engineer Department will bear testimony, not only to the extent of the duties I have performed, but also to the protracted period to which I continued to discharge them; and if the infirmities which are peculiar to extreme-age, now constrain me to desist from my wanted exertions, I cherish a confidence that the Respective Officers will, from their knowledge of further circumstances which I have not touched upon in this place, make such a communication in my behalf to the Honourable The Master-General and Board of Ordnance, as will induce that Honourable Board to continue to me the emoluments of a situation which has received the best energies of a long life almost exclusively devoted to its interests, and the enjoyment of which emoluments, in the usual course of nature, cannot be viewed as attaching a burden upon the Public, which it might not reasonably bear for a short space of time.

    The whole respectfully submitted,
            Quebec, the 31st July, 1828.
                Ja. Thompson
                Overseer of Works

Sidenote by James Thompson Jr.:
My father's Full Pay had been 7/6 per day: In consequence of this Appeal he was allowed a Retiring Allowance of 11/4 per day. J.T.

Memorandum of services. Some years previously, James Thompson had prepared a detailed memorandum of his services, which he kept in the small, bound journal shown here. When he applied for a pension in 1828, he was asked to provide a formal document that would describe his services at Quebec. Using this small journal, and with the help of his son, Thompson put together a memorandum of his services which was then forwarded to the Board of Ordnance. It is this latter memorandum which appears in Anecdote 38. Part of the James Thompson collection acquired by BAnQ. (Photo by Earl John Chapman)

APPENDIX B

LIST OF ANECDOTES

Notes:

1. All numbered anecdotes with their original titles were taken verbatim from the original manuscript letter-books held at BAnQ and the Stewart Museum, Montreal.
2. The "Included" column indicates which anecdotes are included in this publication.
3. Unless otherwise indicated all anecdotes are oral histories of James Thompson Sr. dictated to his son, James Thompson Jr.
4. A complete verbatim transcript of the original manuscript letter-book held at BAnQ, complete with the additional anecdotes found in the original manuscript letter-book held at the Stewart Museum (and from other sources), has been deposited with BAnQ and the Stewart Museum.

No.	Title	Included
1	Anecdote of Wolfe's Army: 1758. Adventure of a Volunteer attached to the Grenadier company of Fraser's Highlanders.	Yes
2	Anecdote of Wolfe's Army. March of Fraser's Highlanders through Ireland: 1758.	Yes
3	Anecdote of Wolfe's Army. The March from Donaghadee to Cork of a Highlander, Volunteer of that Army: 1758. For Embarkation.	Yes
4	Anecdote of Wolfe's Army. Landing of Louisbourg, as related by a Volunteer attached to the Grenadier company of Fraser's Highlanders, and some previous incidents: 1758.	Yes
5	No title. [This anecdote covers a little dog which accompanied the regiment at Louisbourg.]	Yes
6	Anecdote of Wolfe's Army. Adventures of the Master-Tailor of Fraser's Highlanders: 1758.	Yes
7	General Wolfe, the Soldier's Friend: 1758.	Yes
8	Additional. [This anecdote covers Wolfe's statue which was erected at Wolfe's Corner in Quebec.]	Yes
9	Louisbourg: 1758. The great, fat, tall Savage.	Yes
10	Anecdote of Wolfe's Army: 1758 (Duncan McFee).	Yes
11	No title. [This anecdote, written by James Thompson Jr., repeats a poem on General Wolfe published in a local Quebec newspaper in 1829 – a favourite of his father.]	Yes
12	Stratford: 1758. The Dirk and the incidents to which it gave rise.	Yes
13	Anecdote of Fraser's Highlanders. Skenectady: 1758.	Yes
14	Anecdote of Wolfe's Army. Corporal McPherson, the Highland Swordsman: 1758.	Yes
15	Anecdote of Colonel Ross and the 42nd, or Old Highlanders: 1758.	Yes
16	Occurrences at Pointe Levis: 1759. As related by my Father at Quebec, in March 1828.	Yes
17	Captain Montgomerie, afterwards General in the American Service: 1759 – 1775.	Yes
18	Fraser's Highlanders in Cantonments at St. Valier: 1760.	Yes

19	No title. [This anecdote covers Thompson's stay with the Blais family in Saint-Pierre.]	Yes
20	Sergeant Ballinagagg. Fraser's Highlanders: 1760.	Yes
21	Captain McDonald: his mode of wetting both Eyes, and his cruel Death: 1760.	Yes
22	Fraser's Highlanders. St. Valier: 1760. Loss of the Grenadier's Pay in the dark, & subsequent finding.	Yes
23	Anecdote of Wolfe's Army. Quebec: 1760. (By a volunteer)	Yes
24	Anecdote of Wolfe's Army: 1760. Quebec.	Yes
25	Anecdote of Wolfe's Army: 1760. Montreal.	Yes
26	Anecdote of General Amherst, and of John Wilkie, the highland Drum-beater: 1758.	Yes
27	Anecdote of Wolfe's Army. Mons. Parant the Curé of the Parish of St. Michel: 1760.	Yes
28	Anecdote of Wolfe's Army. La mère St. Gabriel of the Hôtel-Dieu Nunnery: 1760. Quebec.	Yes
29	Quebec, 31st December 1770 – 1775. General Richard Montgomery. His Sword, &.	Yes
30	My Grand Mother's Cup.	Yes
31	His Grace the Duke of Richmond on the Esplanade at Quebec.	Yes
32	History of the Mull, Quebec: 1775-6.	Yes
33	No title. [This anecdote covers John Gawler. It also features an anecdote, written by James Thompson Jr., which discusses the close friendship which existed between his father and John Gawler.]	No
34	No title. [This anecdote, written by James Thompson Jr., discusses a silver neck stock buckle left to his father on the death of the quartermaster sergeant of the 15th Foot in 1761.]	No
35	Quebec, 8th September 1828. [This anecdote, written by James Thompson Jr., discusses the Earl of Dalhousie's departure from Canada on 8 September 1828 and the effect it had on his father.]	No
36	To the Honorable Colonel John Ramsay on board H.M.S. "the Challenger." [This anecdote, written by James Thompson Jr., discusses a package of papers (concerning his father) which were delivered to the Earl of Dalhousie on his departure from Canada.]	No
37	No title. [This anecdote, written by James Thompson Jr., discusses a visit by an American gentleman in August 1828 to pay his respects to his father.]	No
38	Memorandum of the most arduous Services performed by James Thompson, overseer of works, since his joining the Engineer Department at Quebec, in the year 1761.	Yes, see App. A
39	Copy of the Last Will and Testament of Mr. James Thompson, late overseer of Works in the Ordnance Department at Quebec: 1st June 1828. [Copied by James Thompson, Jr.]	No
40	To know how the Order of the Gâteau became first instituted.	Yes
41	No title. [This anecdote, written by James Thompson Jr., consists of his birth and baptismal entries, extracted from his father's journal.]	No
42	Propositions for a New Monument, on the Plains of Abraham, to General Wolfe. [These propositions, sent by R. Routh, D.A.C.G. in 1845 to all commissary stations in Canada, were copied by James Thompson Jr. (along with a few related letters)].	No
–	Unnumbered Anecdote. Action at Montmorency Falls, July 1759. Source: *Star and Commercial Advertiser*, 16 April 1828, under title "Miscellaneous – Anecdote of Wolfe's Army – History of Sergeant Allan Cameron."	Yes
–	Unnumbered Anecdote. Loan to General James Murray, 1760. Source: Alfred Hawkins, *Picture of Quebec: with Historical Recollections* (Quebec, 1834), 395-6.	Yes

Anecdote numbers vs page numbers

The following list enables the reader to reconstruct the anecdotes in their original sequence.

Anecdote Number	Page Numbers	Anecdote Number	Page Numbers
1	115–117, 155–160	24	185–186, 199–200, 201–203
2	117–120	25	215–218, 219–220
3	120–124	26	166–167, 218–219
4	124–125, 142–148	27	227–228
5	153	28	203–209
6	160–162, 167–169	29	231–238
7	153–155, 188–189	30	248–249
8	246–248	31	245–246
9	148–150	32	239–240
10	150–153	33	Not included
11	243–244	34	Not included
12	129–132	35	Not included
13	169–170, 128–129, 132	36	Not included
14	170–171, 214–215	37	Not included
15	162–164	38	329–335
16	176–180	39	Not included
17	184–185, 238	40	241–243
18	226–227, 229	41	Not included
19	229, 244	42	Not included
20	229–230	Unnumbered (1)	180–184
21	192–193, 197–199, 200–201	Unnumbered (2)	213–214
22	223–225		
23	191–192, 194–197, 186–188		

BIBLIOGRAPHY

Primary sources

1. Manuscripts

Archives du Séminaire de Québec.
    Recensement de la population anglais demeurant à Québec vers 1773, Polygraphie 37, no 1.

Bibliothèque et Archives nationales du Québec (BAnQ), Quebec.
    P254: James Thompson Jr. Fonds (incl. James Thompson Sr. Fonds).
    P450: Literary & Historical Society of Quebec (James Thompson Fonds).
    TL9: Register, Military Court of Quebec.
    TP5: Military Courts, 1765–1770.
    Directory, City of Quebec: 1791; 1795.
    Register Book, St. Louis Gate Cemetery.

Canadian War Museum, Ottawa.
    James T. Harrower Papers.

Centre for Kentish Studies, Maidstone.
    U1350: Amherst Family Papers.

Cumberland Papers, Windsor Castle.

Fairfield County Superior Court Files, Fairfield, Connecticut.
    RG3: George II v. Sergeant Alexander Fraser, 1757–58.

Huntington Library, San Marino, California.
    LO: Loudoun Papers.

Library and Archives Canada, Ottawa.
    MG15-T1: Treasury Records (subsistence rolls).
    MG18-D4: Arthur Dobbs fonds.
    MG18-L7: George Townshend Collection, "Military Papers."
    MG23-GIII: A Military Sketch of Colonel John Nairne.
    MG23-K2: James Thompson fonds.
    MG23-K34: Frederick Mackenzie Collection.
    MG24-A12: George Ramsay, 9th Earl of Dalhousie fonds.
    RG4-C2: Correspondence, Provincial Secretary, Lower Canada.
    RG8: "C" Series – British Military and Naval Records.
    National Map Collection.
        Mackellar, P., Plan of the Town of Quebec, the Capital of Canada in North America, with the Bason and a part of the adjacent Country, shewing the principal Encampments and Works of the British Army, commanded by

Major General Wolfe, and those of the French Army commanded by Lieut. General, the Marquis of Montcalm, during the Siege of that Place in 1759. NMC 21345.
>Sessional Papers: 16 July 1782; 31 July 1778.

Library of Congress, Washington, D.C.
>James Grant Papers.

McCord Museum, Montreal.
>P670: James Thompson Fonds.

Public Record Office of Northern Ireland.
>DOD162/77: Dobbs Collection.

Register, Église protestante de Trois-Rivières, 1767–1875.

Stewart Museum, Montreal.
>78th Fraser Highlanders Fonds.
>James Thompson letter-book.

The National Archives, Kew.
>War Office Papers.
>>4: Out-Letters, Secretary at War.
>>12: Muster Books and Pay Lists.
>>25: Succession Books.
>>34: Amherst Papers.
>>64: Manuscript Army Lists.
>>120: Out-Pension Records, Royal Hospital, Chelsea (Regimental Registers).
>
>Colonial Office Papers.
>>CO5: America and West Indies.

The National Archives of Scotland, Edinburgh.
>Gifts and Deposits
>>GD45: Papers of Maule Family, Earls of Dalhousie.
>>GD125: Rose of Kilravock Muniments.
>>GD201: Papers of the MacDonald Family of Clanranald.
>
>E769-139: Forfeited Estates: Lovat.

William L. Clements Library, Ann Arbor, Michigan.
>Murray Repetition Map No. 1, Sheet 2.
>"Croghan's Journal," Thomas Gage Papers, 1754–1783.

2. Printed original sources

"A Dialogue in Hades: A Parallel of military errors, of which the French and English armies were guilty during the Campaign of 1759 in Canada." A Narrative attributed to Chevalier James Johnstone. LHSQ, *Historical Documents*, Series 2, vol 2 (1867).

A Short Authentic Account of the Expedition against Quebec in the Year 1759 under Command of Major General James Wolfe: By a Volunteer upon That Expedition (Quebec, 1872). A narrative wrongly attributed to James Thompson. Believed to have been written by Patrick Mackellar, Wolfe's engineer-in-chief.

Armorial général de France.

British Army Lists.

Christie, R. *Memoirs of the Administration of the Colonial Government of Lower-Canada,* by Sir James Henry Craig, and Sir George Prevost; from the year 1807 until the year 1815, Comprehending the Military and Naval operations in the Canadas during the late War with the United States of America* (Quebec, 1818).

Commission Books.

Doughty, A. G., and A. Shortt, ed. *Documents Relating to the Constitutional History of Canada 1759–1791* (6-7 Edward VII, A. 1907, Sessional Paper no. 18). (Ottawa, 1907).

Doughty, A. G., ed. *An Historical Journal of the Campaigns in North America for the Years 1757, 1758, 1759, and 1760 by Captain John Knox,* 3 vols (Toronto: The Champlain Society, 1914).

Doughty, A. G., and G. W. Parmelee, eds. *The Siege of Quebec and the Battle of the Plains of Abraham,* 6 vols (Quebec, 1901).

Durnford, M., ed. *Family recollections of Lieutenant General Elias Walker Durnford, a colonel commandant of the Corps of Royal Engineers* (Montreal, 1863).

Edwards, R. F. *Roll of Officers of the Corps of Royal Engineers from 1660 to 1898* (Chatham, England, 1898).

Ferguson, James, ed. *Papers Illustrating the History of the Scots Brigade in the Service of the United Netherlands 1572-1782,* v2 (1698–1782) (Edinburgh, 1899). Extracted by permission from the Government Archives at The Hague.

Fraser, M. *Extract from a Manuscript Journal* [vol 2], *Relating to the Siege of Quebec in 1759, Kept by Colonel Malcolm Fraser, then Lieutenant of the 78th (Fraser's Highlanders) and Serving in That Campaign,* LHSQ, *Historical Documents,* Series 2, vol 1 (1867).

Hadden, Lieutenant J. M. *Hadden's Journal and Orderly Books: A Journal Kept in Canada and Upon Burgoyne's Campaign in 1776 and 1777* (Albany, 1884).

James, A. P., ed. *Writings of General John Forbes, Relating to His Service in North America* (Menasha, Wisconsin, 1938).

"Journal of the Expedition up the River St. Lawrence, republished from the New York Mercury of 31 December 1759," LHSQ, *Historical Documents,* Series 2, vol 6 (1867).

"Journal of the Principal Occurrences during the Siege of Quebec by the American Revolutionists under General Montgomery and Arnold in 1775–76," LHSQ, *Historical Documents,* Series 8 (1906).

Kane, J., and W. H. Askwith, eds. *List of Officers of the Royal Regiment of Artillery from the year 1716 to the year 1899* (London, 1900).

Kimball, G. S., ed. *The Correspondence of William Pitt, when Secretary of State, with Colonial Governors and Military and Naval Commanders in America,* 2 vols (London, 1906, reprint New York, 1969).

Livingstone, A., et al, eds. *Muster Roll of Prince Charles Edward Stuart's Army 1745–46* (Aberdeen, 1985).

Maseres, F., ed. *A Collection of Several Commissions, and Other Public Instruments, Proceeding from His Majesty's Royal Authority, and Other Papers, Relating to the State of the Province of Quebec in North America, since the Conquest of it by the British Arms in 1760* (London, 1772).

——, *Mémoire à la défence d'un plan de l'acte de parlement … contre les objections de M. François Joseph Cugnet* (London, 1773).

Murray, J. "Journal of the Siege of Quebec, 1760," LHSQ, *Historical Documents,* Series 3, vol 5 (1871).

Provost, H. *Les Premiers Anglo-Canadiens à Québec. Essai de recensement 1759–1775.* Quebec, Institut québécois de recherche sur la culture, "Documents de Recherche," no 1, 2e édition, 1984.

"The Campaign of 1760 in Canada." A Narrative attributed to Chevalier James Johnstone, LHSQ, *Historical Documents,* Second Series (1887).
Signaÿ, J. *Recensement de la ville de Québec en 1818, Cahiers d'histoire #29* (Quebec, 1976).
Webster, J. C., ed. *Journal of Jeffery Amherst: Recording the Military Career of General Amherst in America from 1758 to 1760* (Toronto, 1931).
Whitelaw, M., ed. *The Dalhousie Journals,* 3 vols (Ottawa, 1978-82).
Vialar, A., and R. Lester. "Orderly Book begun by Capt. Anthony Vialar of the British Militia in 17th September 1775, and kept by him till November 16th, when continued by Capt. Robert Lester," LHSQ, *Historical Documents,* Series 7 (1905).
Willson, B. *The Life and Letters of James Wolfe* (New York, 1909).
Wood, W., ed. *Select British Documents of the Canadian War of 1812,* 3 vols (Toronto: The Champlain Society, 1920).
———. *The Logs of the Conquest of Canada* (Toronto: The Champlain Society, 1909).

Newspapers and periodicals

Boston Newsletter, Boston: 6 July 1758.
Bytown Gazette, Ottawa: 8 August 1838.
Gazetteer & London Daily Advertiser, London: 26 December 1763.
Gentleman's Gazette, 15–17 November 1779.
La Minerve, Montreal: 30 August 1830.
Lloyd's Evening Post: 31 March 1758.
London Chronicle: 9 July 1757; 13 November 1759.
The Military Register, 23 September 1818.
Morning Chronicle, Quebec: 8 December 1869.
New York Times, New York: 6 October 1895.
Pennsylvania Gazette: 7 September 1758.
Public Advertiser: 12 July 1757; 25 September 1758.
Star and Commercial Advertiser, Quebec: 20 February 1828; 16 April 1828; 10 May 1828; 28 June 1828; 28 July 1828; 15 April 1829; 25 August 1830; 28 August 1830; 8 September 1830.
Quebec Chronicle, Quebec: 20 December 1918.
Quebec Gazette: 21 July 1768.
Quebec Mercury, Quebec: 24 August 1809; 17 May 1814; 20 June 1815; 4 July 1823.

The Gentlemen's Magazine and Historical Chronicle...
The Historical Magazine, Notes & Queries, concerning the Antiquities, History & Biography of America.
The London Gazette.
The London Magazine, or Gentleman's Monthly Intelligencer...
Manual of the Corporation of the City of New York.
New England Historical & Genealogical Register.
Notes & Queries: A Medium of Inter-Communication for Literary Men, General Readers, etc.
The Public Advertiser.
The Quebec Almanac.
The Scots Magazine.

Secondary sources

1. Books

Audet, F.-J. *Les Députés au premier Parlement de Bas-Canada* (1792–96).

The Authorship of a Journal of the Siege of Quebec in the year 1759. Prepared by an associate-member of the LHSQ (Quebec, 1872). (From a copy in the Bibliothèque, Séminaire de Québec.)

Bernier, S., et al. *Military History of Quebec City: 1608–2008* (Montreal, 2008).

Boscawen, H. G. R. *The Capture of Louisbourg, 1758* (University of Oklahoma Press, 2011).

Boswell, J. *James Boswell: The Earlier Years, 1740–1769*, F. A. Pottie, ed. (New York, 1966).

Bradley, A. G. *Sir Guy Carleton* (Toronto, 1907).

Brumwell, S. *Paths of Glory: The Life and Death of General James Wolfe* (Montreal, 2006).

——. *Redcoats: The British Soldier and the War in the Americas, 1755–1763* (Cambridge, 2002).

Burt, A. L. *The Old Province of Quebec* (Minneapolis, 1933).

Charbonneau, A., et al. *Quebec The Fortified City: From the 17th to the 19th Century* (Parks Canada, 1982).

Cockburn, J. P. *Quebec and its Environs: Being a Picturesque Guide to a Stranger* (Quebec, 1831).

Colley, L. *Britons: Forging the Nation, 1707–1837* (New Haven, 1992).

Corbett, Sir J. S. *England in the Seven Years' War: A Study in Combined Strategy*, 2 vols (London, 1907).

Currie, D., and Duncan Campbell. *The Lairds of Glenlyon: Historical Sketches Relations to the Districts of Appin, Glenlyon, and Breadalbane* (Perth, 1886).

Dalbiac, Colonel P. H. *History of the 45th: 1st Nottinghamshire Regiment (Sherwood Foresters)* (Nottingham, 1902).

Dickens, Charles. *Our Mutual Friend,* iv (New York, 1865).

Dictionary of American Biography, Williamstown, Mass.

Dictionary of Canadian Biography, Toronto.

Dictionary of National Biography, London, England.

Dionne, N.-E. *Sainte-Anne de la Pocatière, 1672–1900* (Lévis, 1900).

Doughty, A. G., and N. E. Dionne. *Quebec Under Two Flags: A Brief History of the City from its Foundation until the Present Time* (Quebec, 1903).

Everest, A. S. *Moses Hazen and the Canadian Refugees in the American Revolution* (Syracuse, 1970).

Ford, W. C., ed. *British Officers Serving in America, 1754–1774, Compiled from the Army Lists* (Boston, 1894, reprint, Oldwick, N.J., 1999).

Frégault, G. *Canada: the War of the Conquest* (Toronto, 1969).

Gibbon, J. M. *Scots in Canada* (Toronto, 1971).

Gale, G. *Historic Tales of Old Quebec* (Quebec, 1920).

——. *Quebec 'Twixt Old and New* (Quebec, 1915).

Graham, J. H. *Outlines of the History of Freemasonry in the Province of Quebec* (Montreal, 1892).

Harper, Colonel R. J. *The Fraser Highlanders* (Montreal, 1979).

——. *78th Fighting Frasers in Canada: A Short History of the Old 78th Regiment or Fraser's Highlanders, 1757–1763* (Laval, 1966).

Harris, R. C., ed. *Historical Atlas of Canada* (Toronto, 1987).
Hawkins, A. *Picture of Quebec: with Historical Recollections* (Quebec, 1834).
Heitman, F. B. *Historical Register of Officers of the Continental Army during the War of the Revolution...* (Washington, 1893).
Houlding, J. A. *Fit for Service: The Training of the British Army 1715–1795* (Oxford University Press, 1981).
Jaenen, C. J. *The Role of the Church in New France* (Toronto, 1976)
Jones, T. *A History of New York During the Revolutionary War and of Leading Events in the Other Colonies at that Period*, vol 1 (New York, 1879).
Journal of the Society for Army Historical Research (Hendon, England).
Judd, P. H., compiler/publisher. *Genealogical and Biographical Notes on the Haring-Herring, Clark, Denton, White, Griggs, Judd, and related families* (New York, 2005).
Anon. *Le Colonel Dambourgès – étude historique canadienne* (Quebec, 1866).
Lemoine, J.-M. *Histoire des fortifications et des rues de Québec* (Quebec, 1875).
——. *Maple Leaves* (Quebec, 1894).
——. *Picturesque Quebec: A Sequel to Quebec Past and Present* (Montreal, 1882).
——. *Quebec Past and Present: A History of Quebec, 1608-1876* (Quebec, 1876).
Lespérance, J. *The Bastonnais: Tale of the American Invasion of Canada in 1775–6* (Toronto, 1877).
Long, J. C. *Lord Jeffery Amherst: A Soldier of the King* (New York, 1933).
McCulloch, I. M. *Sons of the Mountains: The Highland Regiments in the French & Indian War, 1757–1767*, 2 vols (Purple Mountain Press, 2006).
McCullough, A. B. *Money and Exchange in Canada to 1900* (Dundurn Press, 1999).
McIlwraith, J. N. *Sir Frederick Haldimand* (Toronto, 1911).
Mackenzie, T. A., et al., eds. *Historical Records of the 79th Queen's Own Cameron Highlanders* (London, 1887).
McLennan, J. S. *Louisbourg: From its Foundation to its Fall, 1713–1758* (London, 1919; reprint. Halifax, 1979).
MacLeod, D. P. *Northern Armageddon: The Battle of the Plains of Abraham* (Toronto, 2008).
Macmillan, S. *Bygone Lochaber: Historial & Traditional* (Glasgow, privately printed, 1971).
MacNutt, W. S. *The Atlantic Provinces: The Emergence of Colonial Society, 1712–1857* (Toronto, 1965).
Mahon, Major General R. H. *Life of General the Honourable James Murray* (London, 1921).
Martin, A. P. *Life and Letters of the Right Honourable Robert Lowe, Viscount Sherbrooke ... with a memoir of Sir John Coape Sherbrooke...* (London, 1893).
Miller, H. *Tales and Sketches* (Edinburgh, 1872).
Mimeault, M. *Gaspésie* (Laval, 2005).
Morgan, H. J. *Sketches of Celebrated Canadians and Persons Connected with Canada...* (Quebec, 1862).
The Old Gentlemen Stood to Pray (St. Andrew's Church, Quebec, 1984).
Orcutt, Rev. S. *A History of the Old Town of Stratford and the City of Bridgeport, Connecticut* (Fairfield County Historical Society, 1886).
Pargellis, S. *Lord Loudoun in North America* (New Haven, 1933).
Parkman, F. *Montcalm and Wolfe*, 2 vols (Boston, 1884).
The Penny Cyclopaedia of the Society for the Diffusion of Useful Knowledge (London, 1837).

Porter, W., et al. *History of the Corps of Royal Engineers* (Chatham, 1889).
Quebec History Encyclopedia.
Quick, E. *James Thompson: A Highlander in Quebec* (Tain & District Museum Trust, 2009).
Reilly, R. *The Rest to Fortune: The Life of Major General James Wolfe* (London, 1960).
Reynolds, P. R. *Guy Carleton, a biography* (New York, 1980).
Roy, P.-G. *Les Cimetières de Québec* (Lévis, 1941).
Rutledge, J. L. *Century of Conflict: The Struggle Between the French and British in Colonial America* (New York, 1956).
Sadler, H. *Thomas Dunckerley: His Life, Labours and Letters* (Kessinger Publishing, 2003).
Smith, P. *Research into Early Canadian Masonry, 1759–1869* (Quality Press, 1939).
Stacey, C. P. *Quebec, 1759: The Siege and the Battle* (Toronto, 1959).
———. *Quebec, 1759: The Siege and the Battle*, revised ed., Donald E. Graves, ed. (Toronto, 2002).
Stewart, Colonel D. *Sketches of the Character, Manners and Present State of the Highlanders of Scotland, with Details of the Military Service of the Highland Regiments*, 2 vols. (Edinburgh, 1822).
Straith, Major H. *Introductory Essay to the Study of Fortification, for Young Officers of the Army*, 2nd ed. (London, 1852).
Stuart, H. C. *The Church of England in Canada, 1759–1793. From the Conquest to the Establishment of the See of Quebec* (Montreal, 1893).
Tales of Remembrances, and Historical Sketch (St. Andrew's Church, Quebec, 1828).
Todd, A. L. *Richard Montgomery: Rebel of 1775* (New York, 1966).
Townshend, Lieutenant Colonel C. V. F. *The Military Life of Field Marshal George First Marquess Townshend, 1724-1807 … From Family Documents not Hitherto Published* (London, 1902).
Trimble, W. C. *The Historical Record of the 27th Inniskilling Regiment, from the period of its Institution as a Volunteer Corps till the present time…* (London, 1876).
Vergé-Franceschi, M. *Les Officiers généraux de la marine royale: 1715–1774. Origines, conditions, services*, 7 vols (Paris, 1990).
Wright, R. *The Life of Major General James Wolfe* (London, 1864).
Würtele, F. C. *The English Cathedral of Quebec, A Monograph* (Quebec, 1891).

2. Articles

Anderson, W. J. "Canadian History: The Siege and Blockade of Quebec, by Generals Montgomery and Arnold, in 1775–76," LHSQ, *Transactions*, New Series, no. 9 (1872).
Audet, F.-J. "James Cuthbert de Berthier et sa family; notes généalogiques et biographiques," *Transactions, Royal Society of Canada*, Ser. III (1935).
Burt, A. L. "Sir Guy Carleton and his first council," *Canadian Historical Review*, IV (1923).
Casgrain, P.-B. "The Monument to Wolfe on the Plains of Abraham, and the Old Statue at 'Wolfe's Corner.'" *Transactions, Royal Society of Canada*, Ser. II (1904).
Clark, W. C. "The Early Presbyterianism of Quebec under Dr. Spark," LHSQ, *Transactions*, New Series, no. 27 (1908).
"Concerning the Journal of James Thompson: 1758–1830," *LHSQ, Transactions*, New Series, no. 22 (1898).

Elting, J. R., and F. T. Chapman. "Military Dress: The 78th (Highland) Regiment of Foot, 1757–1763 (Fraser's Highlanders)," *Military Collector and Historian*, vol 26, no. 1 (Spring 1974).

Elwood, M. "Studies in Documents: the Discovery and Repatriation of the Lord Dalhousie Collection," *Archivaria 24* (Summer, 1987).

Fraser, M. "Conquering Canada on the Plains of Germany," *Clan Fraser Society of Canada.*

Hitsman, J. M., and C. C. J. Bond. "The Assault Landing at Louisbourg, 1758," *Canadian Historical Review*, XXXV (1954).

Lemoine, J.-M. "Les sièges de 1759 et de 1775," *Bulletin des recherches historiques*, 1er vol 1, 10eme livraison (Lévis, 1895).

———. "The Scot in New France," LHSQ, *Transactions*, New Series, no. 15 (1881).

McCord, D. R. "An Historic Canadian Family, the Cuthberts of Berthier," *Dominion Illustrated* (1891).

McCulloch, I. M. "'From April Battles and Murray Generals, Good Lord Deliver Us!': The Battle of Sillery, 28 April 1760," in *More Fighting for Canada: Five Battles, 1760–1944*, Donald E. Graves, ed. (Toronto, 2004).

MacFarlane, R. "The Macdonells of Aberarder," *Clan Donald Magazine*, no. 12 (1991).

Macpherson, A. "Sketches of the Old Seats of Families and of Distinguished Soldiers, etc., connected with Badenoch," *Journal of the Clan Macpherson Association (U.S. Branch)*, no. 92 (Summer, 1999).

Milborne, A. J. B. "Miles Prentice: Soldier and Mason," *The Builder*, vol XV (1929).

———. "The Lodge in the 78th Regiment (Fraser's Highlanders), *Quatuor Coronati Lodge*, vol LXV (1952).

———. "Freemasonry at the Siege of Quebec 1759–60," *The Papers of the Canadian Masonic Research Association,* collected edition, C. E. B. LeGresley, ed., vol 1 (Toronto, 1986).

Montgomery, T. H. "Ancestry of General Richard Montgomery," *New York Genealogical and Biographical Record* (New York, 1871).

Richardson, A. J. H. "Guide to the architecturally and historically most significant buildings in the Old City of Quebec with a Biographical Dictionary of Architects and Builders and Illustrations," *Bulletin of the Association for Preservation Technology*, vol 2, nos. 3–4 (1970).

Roy, P.-G. "Les amours de Sergent James Thompson," *Bulletin des recherches historiques*, vol 42 (Lévis, 1955).

Sewell, J. "Notes upon the Dark Days of Canada," LHSQ, *Transactions,* Original Series, vol 2 (1831).

Stevenson, J. "Currency, with Reference to Card Money in Canada during the French Domination," LHSQ, *Transactions*, New Series, no. 11 (1875).

Wallace, W. S. "Some Notes on Fraser's Highlanders," *Canadian Historical Review*, vol 18 (1937).

———. "The First Scots Settlers in Canada," *Bulletin des recherches historiques*, vol 56, January-March, nos. 1–3 (Lévis, 1950).

Whitworth, R. "Field Marshal Lord Amherst, a Military Enigma," *History Today* (1959).

Würtele, F. C. "Note on Montgomery's Sword," LHSQ, *Historical Documents*, Series 7 (1905).

INDEX

Notes: 'n' following a page number denotes a footnote is referred to; page numbers in bold type indicate an illustration or map; ranks after names reflect the persons rank at the time of their first appearance in James Thompson's anecdotes; estate names after surnames, while not technically correct (e.g. Cameron of Dungallon) and usually reserved to denote the laird, have been inserted to help differentiate the many cadet branches or families that share the same surname.

abattis, 137, 145, 181
Abercrombie, Major James, 133, 162n, 256, 279
Abercromby, Major General James, 133, 141-142, 256, 298-299
Abercromby, Sir Ralph, 289
Act of Proscription, 9
Addison, Major Thomas, 210
Agnew, Major James, 210, 214n
aiguillette, 12n, 152, 154, 325
Albany, New York, 110, 126, 133, 165, 166n, 167, 256-258, 267, 275, 283, 299
Allcock, Chief Justice Henry, 309
Alexander, Gregory, 96
Allen, Ethan, 257
American Portfolio No. 1, 90n, 327
American War of Independence, *see* wars, War of American Independence
Amherst, Major General Jeffery, 23, 25, 27n, 92, 133, **134-135**, 136, 139, **140**, 141-142, 150, 162, 164-167, 171, 212, **216**, 217-218, **255**, 256, 264, 269, 273, 278-279, 281, 283, 286, 288, 296, 299-300, 304, 310, 324
Amherst, Lieutenant Colonel William, 139, **140**, 141, 157n
Anderson, Francis, 242
Angel Street (rue des Anges), Quebec, 67, **98**
Anglican Cathedral (Holy Trinity Church), Quebec, 46, 78, **98**, 291, 310, 313
Anse au Foulon, Quebec, 3, **5**, **15**, 16, 176, 186, 202, 322
Argyll, Archibald Campbell, Duke of, 112, 113, 292
Armagh, (Township), Quebec, 42, 68, 87, 244, 260, 314
"army currency," *see* currency
Arnold, Nottinghamshire, England, 310
Arnold, Brigadier General Benedict, 31-33, 97, 230, **232**, 233, 238, 256, **257**, 258, 268, 300-301, 304, 307, 331, 332
Arsenal Foundry, Quebec, 30n

Articles of War, 151, 156
artificers, 16, 32, 40, 44, 234n, 300, 331
Artillery Barracks (Nouvelles Casernes), Quebec, 18n, 30n, 202, 237
Artillery Park, Quebec, 30n, **98**
Atholl, 1st Duke of, 112
Augustinian Hospital Sisters of the Mercy of Jesus, **205**
Augustus, Brigadier General George, Lord Howe, 133
Augustus, Prince Edward, Duke of Kent and Strathearn, 30n, 68, 69, 70, 218, 220, **272**, 273
Augustus, Prince Frederick, Duke of York, 265, 290-291, 310, 321
Augustus, William, Duke of Cumberland, 255, 318-319, 323
Aylmer, Governor Lord Matthew Whitmore, 84n
Aylwin, Lieutenant Thomas, 239, 240, 258-259

Badelard, Doctor Philippe-Louis-François, 196-197, 259, 276, 277
Badge of St. Patrick, **272**
Badge of the Order of the Gâteau, *see* Order of the Gâteau
baillie (civic officer, magistrate), 8n
Baillie, Captain Charles, yr of Rosehall, xv, 6, 10-11, 16n, 113-114, 116-117, 121, 137n, 143, 155, 156, 192, 194, 249, 259-260, 275, 292
Baillie, William, of Rosehall, 10
Balan, Michel (*dit* Lacombe), 25
Ballencrieff, Lothian, Scotland, 302
Ballinagagg, Sergeant, 229-230, 290
bards, xvi, 5, **104**, 193n
Barnsfare, Captain Adam, 294, 300
Barrachois, Louisbourg, Nova Scotia, 157, 322
Barrack-Master, Quebec, 24, 59, 64, 169
Barrington, William Wildman, Lord, 111, 113, 184
battles
    Bayonne, France, 289
    Brandywine (Creek), Pennsylvania, 284
    Bunker Hill (Breed's Hill), Massachusetts, 264
    Calcavellas, Spain, 326
    Concord, Massachusetts, 31, 230
    Copenhagen, 1807 Expedition to, 73, 263
    Corunna, Spain, 326
    Culloden, Scotland, 9, 113, 116n, 153n, 277, 286, 292, 312, 318, 324-225
    Dettingen, Germany, 287, 318, 323
    Falkirk, Scotland, 324

Fontenoy, Belgium, 287
Freeman's Farm, New York, 264
Germantown, Pennsylvania, 284
Hohenfriedberg, Poland, 281
Hubbardton, New York, 264
Kesseldorf, Germany, 281
Laffeldt, Holland, 318, 324
Lake George, New York, 197n, 297
Lexington, Massachusetts, 31, 230
Louisbourg, Nova Scotia (landing and siege), xv, 11, 12, 20, 23, 87, 97, 114, 133, **138-140**, 141-150, 154, 157, 159-160, 162-164, 170, 192, 194, 200, 217-218, 220, 227, 255, 260-261, 264, 269, 273, 275-276, 278, 282-284, 287, 290, 292-293, 296, 298-299, 303-304, 306, 312, 314, 324-325, 329
Mollwitz, Poland, 281
Monmouth Court House, New Jersey, 284
Montmorency Falls, Quebec, 12, **15**, 87, 97, 174, **175**, 176, 180-181, 194, 278, 279, 298, 319
Montreal, Quebec, capture, 12, **17**, 23, 133, **135**, 163, 182, 210, **211**, 212-215, **216**, 217-218, 220, 256, 281, 283, 285, 299, 303, 312, 329
Nive, France, 326
Nivelle, France, 289, 326
Oporto, Portugal, 311
Orthez, France, 289, 326
Piacenza, Italy, 297
Plains of Abraham, Quebec, xv, 3, **15**, 16, 18, 83, 84, 86, 92, 93, **104**, 176, 185-186, 188, 203, **205**, 213, **250**, 259, **262**, 273-274, 276-277, **278**, 279, 285, 290, 292, 296, 298, 303-305, 319, 324-327
Prestonpans, Scotland, 286
Quebec, 1759 siege, 12, 97, 200-202, 218, 227, 260, 266, 269, 278, 279, 283, 286-287, 290, 303, 312, **319**, 320, 322, 329
Quebec, 1775 blockade, 31-33, 36, 76, 83, 88, **95**, 96, **104**, 132, 230, 239, 256-257, 259-260, 262, 264, 281, 286, 294, 300, 306-307, 331-333
Sackets Harbor, New York, 261, 289
Saratoga, New York, 37, 257, 321, 333
Sillery, Quebec, xv, 12, 22-23, **104**, 149, 194, **195**, 196-197, **198**, 199-201, 204, **205**, 210, 212, 223n, 269, 273-277, 279, 283, 285, 292, **303**, 304, 322
Talavera, Spain, 311
Tarbes, France, 326
Toulouse, France, 289, 326
Vellinghausen, Germany, 320
Vera, Spain, 289
Vimeira, Portugal, 326
Waterloo, Netherlands, 289, 291
bayonets, *see* weapons
Beaumont, Quebec, 172, 177n
Beauport, Quebec, **15**, 180, 227-278, **251**
Beauport Flats (heights), Quebec, 12, 174, **175**, 180, 298
Beauport House, Sussex, England, 303
Beckwith, Sir George, 80
Bell, Jane, 301
Bell, Captain Thomas, 174n
Bellamy, Mr, 43

Benet, Paul-Eugène, 322
Bernier, François, 190
Berthier, Quebec, 40, 51, 208, 267-268, 334
Berwick-upon-Tweed, England, 297
Bibliothèque et Archives nationales du Québec, xv, xvii-xviii, **xx**, **5**, 8n, 21n, 91n
Bishop's Palace, Quebec, **19**, 27, 40, 47-48, 54, 56, 64-65, **98**
Biswick, QM Sergeant, 93
"black cuffs," 53
Black, Judge Henry, 8n
Blackwood, Frederick Hamilton-Temple, Lord Dufferin, **252**
Blackwood, John, 281
Blais, Mademoiselle, 224
Blais, Captain Michel "José," 28, 42, 50, 57-58, 68, 224, 229, 244, 260
Blais, Michel (Junior), 57-58, 68, 260
Blais, Pierre, 42, 260
Bluntach, James Bruce W., 315
Board of Ordnance, 20n, 56, 58-59, 72, 89, 91, 289-290, 305, 314-315, 320, 329, 335
Bolton, Bruce, 4
Bonshaw, Dumfries, Scotland, 284
Boscawen, Vice Admiral Edward, 135-136, 141, 143n, 150n, 264, 269, 296, 322, 324
Boston, Massachusetts, 23, 133, **134**, 135-136, 142, 164, 218n, 286, 288
Boswell, James, 112
Bougainville, Colonel Louis Antoine de, 217n
Boulanger, Doctor Jacques, 95
Bouquet, Colonel Henry, 282
Boyton, Barbara, 55, 313
Brasenose College, Oxford, England, 309
Brewer, Captain John, 283
Brilliant, Monseigneur, 228
broadsword, *see* James Thompson, artefacts
broadswords, *see* weapons
Broadway, New York, 237
Brockville, Ontario, 315
Brooke, Reverend John, 37n, 301
Broun, Christian (Lady Dalhousie), 80, 84, 86, 90, 308
Bruyères, Captain Ralph Henry, 53n, 72, 74, 260-261
Bryce, Lieutenant Alexander, 67
Buade Street (rue de Buade), Quebec, 46, **98**, 307
Burford, Edward, 42-45
burgess, 6
Burgoyne, Major General John, 37, 258, 264, 296, 320-321, 333
Burton, Sir Francis, 80
Burton, Colonel Ralph, 210, 213n, 215n, 260, 319
Buttes-à-Neveu, Quebec, 22, 194, 202n, 261
Bytown Gazette, 318

Caldwell, Colonel Henry, 258, 276, 301, 304
Cambridge, Massachusetts, 309
Cambridge Military Library, Halifax, Nova Scotia, 311
Cameron, Captain Alexander, 4th of Dungallon, 133, 165, 170-171, 261-262, 276, 304

Cameron, Sergeant Allan, xvii(n), 87, 180n, 181-184
Cameron, Daniel, 42
Cameron, Lieutenant Donald, of Fassifern, 274
Campbell, Lieutenant Alexander, 138n
Campbell, Captain Archibald "Archie Roy," yr of Glenlyon, 114, 173
Campbell, Major John, 160n
Campbell, Sir John Douglas Sutherland (Marquess of Lorne, 9th Duke of Argyll), 94, **104**, 238
Campbell, Louisa, 294
Campbell, Piper Patrick, 292
Canadian War Museum, Ottawa, xvii, xxii, 55n, **103-104**, **131**, 132n, **250**
Candiac, France, 297
Caipal Mhor, *see* Reverend Robert Macpherson
canister shot, 180, 231, 298, 300
cannons, *see* weapons
cantonments, 170, 223, 227-228
Cap Rouge, Quebec, 193, 203n, 322
Cape Breton, Nova Scotia, **110**, 140, 142, 255, 269, 287, 292, 322
Cape Diamond (Cap Diamant), Quebec, 32, 41, 45, 48-49, 51-52, 56, 60, **103**, 190, 202, 231, **251**, 300, 330-331, 333
Cape Sable, Nova Scotia, 142
Cape Sambro, Nova Scotia, 125
capitaine de milice (captain of militia), 28, 42, 50, 229, 244, 260, 281
carbines, *see* weapons
Carleton, Sir Guy (later 1st Baron Dorchester), 28-29, 31, 33-35, 37, 53n, **58**, 59, 63-65, 68, **75**, **103**, 207, 234, 236-238, 257, **262**, 263, 266-267, 270, 274, 276-277, 282, 284-285, 290, 295-296, 300-302, 306, 309, 320, 330, 332
Carleton Island, New York, 304
Cartagena, Central America, 303
Castle of Saint Louis, *see* Château Saint-Louis
Cedars, (Côteau-du-Lac), Quebec, xviii, 6n, 88, 238n, 316, 321
censuses
 (1773), 30-31, 48n, 307, 312-313
 (1792), 67-68
 (1798), 67-68
 (1818), 77
Chabot, François, 300
Chaleur, Bay of, (Baie des Chaleurs) Quebec, 28, **134**, 222, 273, 277, 290, 312-313, 318, 326
Chambly, Quebec, **110**, 209, 300, 316, 318
Champlain Street (rue Champlain), Quebec, 50, 294
Chapman, Earl, 4, **5**
Charlestown, South Carolina, 114, 126
Château Frontenac Hotel, Quebec, 57, **58**, **85**
Château Haldimand, Quebec, 57, **58**, 64-65, **98**, **103**
Château de Ramezay Museum, Montreal, 275
Château Saint-Louis, Quebec, 46, 57, 63-64, 78, 84, **85**, 86, 90, **98**, **103**, 236, 248, 308, 330, 334
Chaudière River, Quebec, 32, 257, 331
Chaulette, Ives, 38, 84n, **102**, **246-247**
Chaulette, Thomas-Hyacinthe, 38, 84n, **102**, **246-247**

Cheeseman, Captain Jacob, 76, 231, 233, 238, 294, 301
Chelsea (London), England, 72
Chelsea Hospital, *see* Royal Hospital, Chelsea, London
Cheltenham, Gloucestershire, England, 327
Chien d'Or, Quebec, 33n, 234n, **235**, 307, *see also* Free Mason's Hall
Chipman, Solicitor General Ward, 309
Chisholm, John, 241
Christie, Lieutenant Colonel Gabriel, 283
Citadel, Quebec, 18n, 29n, 32n, 40, 44, 53, 57, 60, 65, 74n, **82**, **98**, **103**, 201, **251**, **271**, 296, **321**
Clephane, Major James, 160n, 165, 169n, 170n
Cockburn, Colonel James Pattison, **39**, **58**, **62**, **75**, **81**, 97, **103**, 245, 263-264
Cockpen, Scotland, 309
Coffin, Thomas Aston, **75**
cohorn mortar, *see* weapons
Collins, John, 47
Concord, Massachusetts, 230
Constitutional Act of 1791, 66, 263, 270
Continental army, 283, 286, 299
contingent men, 225
Cooper, Frances "Fanny," 36n, 45-47, 51, 52, 54-56, 60, 61n, 65-68, 87, 94, 307, 313-315, 317-318
Cork, Ireland, 11, 114-115, 124, 161, 223
Cormorant's Cove (L'Anse à la Coromandière), 137
Cornélier, Charles (*dit* Grandchamp), 66, 96
Côte de la Montagne, Quebec, *see* Mountain Street
Côté, Willy, 95
Côteau-du-Lac, Quebec, *see* Cedars
Courserac, Marie-Anne Aubert de, 152, 160, 163, 264, 269, 270
court martial, 166, 168-169, 207, 288
Craig, Sir James Henry, 71, 264, **265**, 270, 289
Craigie, Deputy Commissary General John, 199, 256-257, 315
Cramahé, Lieutenant Governor Hector, 301
Craufurd, John Walkinshaw, 21st of Craufurland, 113
Cugnet (Cuznet), François-Joseph, 203, **266**, 267-269
Cugnet, Jacques-François, 267
Culloden, battle of, *see* battles
Cushing, Lucy, 258
Cuthbert, Captain James, 51, **267**, 268, 334
Cuthbert, Lieutenant John, yr of Castlehill, 128, 137n, 143
currency
 army, 29, 30n, 69n
 "half-joe's," 223-225
 Halifax, 29n, 30n, 69, 72, 73
 Irish *vs* English, 119-120
 livre tournois, 224
 Spanish dollar, 30n

D'Auteuil Street, Quebec, **103**
D'Urban, Lieutenant General Sir Benjamin, **100**
Dalhousie Castle, Edinburgh, Scotland, 307-309
Dalhousie College, Halifax, Nova Scotia, 311
Dalhousie, Earl of, *see* George Ramsay
Dalhousie, Lady, *see* Christian Broun

Dalhousie University, Halifax, Nova Scotia, 308, 311
Dalkeith, Scotland, 326
Dambourgès, Lieutenant François, 36, **268**, 301
"Dark Day(s) of Canada," 59, 60n
Dartmouth, Nova Scotia, 142
Dauphin Gate, Louisbourg, Nova Scotia, 141, 157n
Dauphine Bastion, Quebec, 30n
David, Jacques-Louis, **34**
Davis, Lieutenant J., 42
Davis, Mr., 203
Davis, Private, 268-269
De Lanaudière, *see* Charles-François Tarieu de la Naudière
Debbig, Captain Hugh, **14**
Deblois, Joseph-François, 318
Delancey, Oliver, 126
Delezenne, Ignace François, 306
Dénéchau, Claude, 86, **102**
Des Barres, Lieutenant J.W.F., **14**
Dieppe, France, 322
Dinan, James, xxi, 4, **5**
Directory, City of Quebec (1795), 67
dirks, *see* James Thompson, artefacts; *see also* weapons
Dominica, West Indies, 295, 318
Donaghadee, Ireland, 117, 119, 121
Dorion, Isaac, 38
Dornoch, Ross-shire, Scotland, 8
Drucour (Drucourt), Augustin de Boschenry de, 137, **140**, 141, 145n, 264, 269-270, 322
Dublin, Ireland, 120-123
Duke of Athol, *see* James Murray
Duke of Clarence, *see* William Henry
Duke of Cumberland, *see* William Augustus
Duke of Kent, *see* Edward Augustus
Duke of Richmond, *see* Charles Lennox
Duke of Wellington, *see* Arthur Wellesley
Duke of York, *see* Prince Frederick Augustus
Dunbar, John Telfer, i
Dundas, General David, 289
Dunn, Henry, 234, 236-237, 242
Dunn, Judge Thomas, 234, 270, 334
Durnham, Earl of, *see* John George Lambton
Durnford, Jane, **271**
Durnford, Lieutenant Colonel Elias Walker, 72n, 74, 80, **271**
Drummondville, Quebec, 256

Easter Ross, Ross-shire, Scotland, 9
Edinburgh, Scotland, 278, 286, 288, 291, 304, 307
Emery, Christiana, 304
Epiphany, *see* Festival of Epiphany
Episcopal Palace, Quebec, *see* Bishop's Palace
Esplanade, Quebec, 18n, 20, 57, 77, **98**, **103**, 191-192, 245

Fairfield, Connecticut, 126
Farago, Pietre, 95
fascines, 20, 21, 181, 190-191, 329
Ferguson, Sergeant Alexander, 11, 116-117, 226, 229, 273, 290

Festival of Epiphany, 240-241, 243
Fisher, Captain Benjamin, 67
Fisher, Surgeon James, 259
flogging, 149, 166
Forbes, Brigadier General John, 126-127, 133
Ford, Mr, 88
fortifications (Quebec), 18, 25n, 30n, 31, 40n, 61, 61n, **98**, 190, **251-252**, 261, 330
forts
    Augustus, 114
    Beauséjour, **110**, 282, 296
    Carillon, **110**, 133, 141, 219n, 255-257, 264, 281, 298, 305, 320
    Chamby, **110**, 207, 209, 299-300
    Crown Point, 133, 162, 219, 256-257, 299
    Detroit, 256
    Duquesne (Pittsburgh), **110**, 133, 305
    Frederick, 283
    Henry, **104**
    Herkimer, 166
    Île-Ste-Hélène, **104**
    Lennox, **104**
    Lévis, 256
    Michilimackinac, 284
    Needham, 314
    Niagara, **110**, 261
    Ontario, 256
    Pitt, 256, 273
    Stanwix, **110**, 165-166, 169, 170n, 261, 304
    St. Frederic, *see* Crown Point
    Saint-Jean, 300
    Ticonderoga, *see* Carillon
    William Henry, **110**, 298
"François," (dog), 153
Franklin, Benjamin, 190
Fraser, Lieutenant Alexander, 26, 194, 221, 273-274
Fraser, Captain Alexander, 6th of Culduthel, 22, 195n, 262, 274-275
Fraser, Sergeant Alexander, **103**, 127, 129-130, **131**, 275
Fraser, Archibald Campbell, **102**
Fraser, Lieutenant Colonel Charles, yr. of Inverallochy, 278, 324
Fraser, Sergeant John, 66, 119, 196-197, 259, 276-277, 313, 315
Fraser, Lieutenant Hugh, 147-148, 242, 275
Fraser, Lieutenant John, of Culbokie, 170-171, 276-277
Fraser, Lieutenant Malcolm, 26, 35n, 172, 197n, 221, 261, 277-278, 304
Fraser, Captain Simon, 324
Fraser, Simon (11th Lord Lovat), 9, 10, **111**, 278n
Fraser, Lieutenant Colonel Simon (formerly Master of Lovat), 10, 12, 16, 21, **102**, **111**, 113-114, 125-130, 135, 138n, 148, 149n, 151, 154, 156, 160n, 161-162, 165-170, 178, 182, 192, 194, 211-212, 219, 213n, 259, 261, **278**, 279, 288, 293, 324, 329
Fraser, Lieutenant Simon, of Tenakyle, 137n
Fraser's Highlanders, *see* regiments, 78th Foot
Free Mason's Hall, Quebec, 33, 65, 76, **98**, 234, **235**, 307, 312

Freemasonry, xvii, 9, 16, 19-22, 55, 65, 86, 92, **102-104**, 197, 220-221, 240-241, 258, 259, 276-277, 279, 281, 290, 293-294, 306-307, 312-313, 327, *see also* Masonic Lodges

Gabarus Bay, Nova Scotia, 136-137, 324
Gage, Brigadier General Thomas, 256, 273, 282
Garden Street (rue des Jardins), Quebec, 196, 277
Garrison Club, Quebec, 74n, **82, 103**
Gaspé, Bay of, Quebec, 28, 222, 273, 277, 290, 312-313
Gaspé (District), Quebec, 84, **134, 317**, 318
Gâteau, Order of the, 234n, 240-241, **242**, 243
Gaubert, François, 234, 236
Gaumond, Michel, 95
Gawler, Sergeant John, 20n, 22, 36n, 48n, 279
Gawler, Felix, 22, 279
Gawler, William, 22, 279
Gazeteer & London Daily Advertiser, 96n, 221n
Gazette, Montreal, 92
General Hospital (Hôpital général), Quebec, **24**, 38, **98, 104**, 290, 298, 306, 332
gentleman volunteers, i, xv, 11n, 114, 116n
Gentlemen's Gazette, 288
George II, King, 120, 123, 329
George III, King, 65n, 68, 70-71, 96, 256, **272**, 281, 294
German mercenaries, 31, 40, 45, 49, 334
Germain, Lord George, 288
Gibraltar, Spain, 47, 74, 272-273, 308, 315, 320
Gibson, Mr., 88
Gill, James, 42
Glacière Bastion, Quebec, 23
Glasgow, Scotland, 27, 96, 114-115, 221
Glenelg, Scotland, 293
Goldsworthy, Richard, 67
Gordon Riots, 256
Gordon, William (18th Earl of Sutherland), 123, **280**, 281
Governor's Garden, Quebec, 248, 327
Grand Battery, Quebec, 48, 64
Grandchamp, *dit*, *see* Charles Cornélier
Grant, Captain Charles, 55, **103**, 239, 240, 281
Grant, William, 281
grape shot, *see* canister shot
Gravesend, Kent, England, 320
Gray, Thomas, 325
Greenbush, New York, 165, 166
Greenfield, Connecticut, 130
"Green Wood," *see* Greenbush, New York
grenadiers, function of, 10n
Grenier, Joseph, 50
Gricy, James, 66
Guernsey, Channel Islands, 285
Gugy, Conrad, 334
Guinnett, Lieutenant John Price, **102**
Gunn, "Bettee," 127
Gunn, Drum Major Daniel, 127

Haldimand, Governor Frederick, 37, 40, 50-51, 53-4, 57, **58**, 59, 63, 72, **103**, 244, 260, 267, 276, 281, **282**, 284, 296, 312, 315, 334

Haldimand Castle, *see* Château Haldimand
"half-joe's," *see* currency
Halifax, Nova Scotia, 11, 23, 32, 43, 68, **79**, 114, 124-125, **134**, 136, 142-143, 272, 284, 278, 310, 331
Halifax Citadel, Nova Scotia, 314
Halifax currency, *see* currency
Hall, William, 67
Halstead's Wharf (Champlain Street), Quebec, 50
Hamilton, Henry, 284
Hammersmith (London), England, 309
Harkness, Reverend James, 92
Harrower, Annie, 94
Harrower, James Thompson, xviii, 91n, 94, 314
Harrower, Robert, 68n, 87, 314
hatchet men (pioneers), 16, 20, 165
Haviland, Brigadier General William, 23, 217, 256, 279, 299
Havana, Cuba, 220, 256, 262, 299
Haverhill, Massachusetts, 282
Hawkins, Alfred, xvii(n), 180n, 213n
Hawley, General Henry, 278, 324
Hawley, Lieutenant Vernon, 177, 179
Hayley, Lieutenant, *see* Lieutenant Vernon Hawley
Hazen, Captain Moses, 149, 199-200, 282-283
Henry, Reverend George, 52, 56, 60, 301
Henry, Samuel, 52
Henry, Prince William (Duke of Clarence), 65
High School of Quebec, 277
Highland Battalion, 2nd, *see* regiments, 78th
Hipps, George, 38, 40, **103, 246, 247**
Historic Monuments Commission, Ministry of Cultural Affairs (Commission des Monuments Historiques, Ministère des Affaires Culturelles), 95-97
Holland, Captain Samuel, **14, 17**, 68
Holy Trinity Church, Quebec, *see* Anglican Cathedral
Hope, Captain Erskine, 313
Hope, Colonel Henry, 61, **62**, 64-65, 239n, 266, 283-284
Hope, General Sir James Archibald, 117, 313
Hope Gate (Port du Conotrie), Quebec, 61, **62**, 63, **98**, 239, **295**, 330
Hôpital général, Quebec, *see* General Hospital
Hôtel-Dieu, Quebec, **98, 100**, 196, 203-204, **205**, 206-209, 290
Hôtel-Dieu, Montreal, 306
Houlding, John, 11
Houston, Richard, 40
Howe, Colonel William, 210, 288
Hunt, Judy Barton, 94n, **104**, 238n
Hunt, Louise Livingston, **104**, 238n
Hunter, Lieutenant General Peter, 69

Île aux Coudres, Quebec, **134**, 188
Île aux Noix, Quebec, 259, 287, 304
Île d'Orléans, Quebec, **15**, 171, 176, 180, 182, 203, 211, 220, 221, 319
Île Royale (Cape Breton), Nova Scotia, 269, 287, 322
Île Saint-Ignace, Quebec, 214n
Île Saint-Jean (Prince Edward Island), Canada, 272, 287
Inglis, Bishop Charles, 302

Intendant's Palace, Quebec, 18n, 25n, 33, **98**
Inverness, Scotland, 114, 116, 163, 312-313
Irving, Major Paulus Æmilius, 174n, 178-179, 284, **285**
Ivers, Anna, 128n
Ivers, Elizabeth, 128n, 286
Ivers, Hannah, 131, 286
Ivers, Thomas, 126, 128-129, 131-132, 286

Jacobites, xv, 9, 10, 112-113, 147, 152, 163, 193, 220, 261, 277-278, 280, 286-287, 291-292, 302, 318, 323-324
Jacobs, Samuel, 281
Jacques-Cartier, Quebec, 190, 323
Jeffreys, Thomas, 83
Jenner, Doctor Edward, 63n
Jesuits' Barracks, Quebec, 20, 52n, 76, **98**, 326
Jesuits' College, Quebec, *see* Jesuits' Barracks
Jesuits' Garden, Quebec, 70
Job, Eleanor, 16
Johnson, Doctor Samuel, 112
Johnson, Sir William, 275
Johnston, James, 258
Johnstone, James (*aka* Chevalier de Johnstone), 152n, 181, 286-287, 323
Jones, Thomas, 35
Jones, Colonel Valentine, 29, 30n, 287-288, 296, 330
Judge Thompson House, Quebec, 318

Kamouraska, Quebec, 41, 277, 333
Kanavan, Corporal (Master Tailor) David, 150, 154, 160-162, 167-169, 288
Kempt, Sir James, 288, **289**
Kennington Cove, Nova Scotia, 324
Kent Gate, Quebec, **252**
King's Wharf, Quebec, 201
Kingsbridge, Westchester County, New York, 299
Kingston, Upper Canada, 91, 261, 295, 315, 318
Knox, Captain Andrew, 322
Knox, Lieutenant John, **104**, 176n, 190, 202n, 215n, 217n, 269, 287

L'Ancienne-Lorette, Quebec, 190, 259, 283
L'Ange-Gardien, Quebec, 50, 185
La Citadelle de Quebec, *see* Citadel, Quebec
La Malbaie, Quebec, 26, 41, **134**, **223**, 270, 277, 304, 333
La Pérade, Quebec, 305
"la petite guerre," 305, 325
Labrador, Newfoundland, 228
Lacey, Lieutenant Thomas, 67
Lachance, Magdelaine (Mrs Michel Balan *dit* Lacombe), 25, 28
Lachine, Quebec, 217-218
Lacombe, *dit*, *see* Michel Balan
Lacombe, Mrs, *see* Magdelaine Lachance
la grippe, 61
Lafleche, Monsieur, 331
Lajus (Lajuste), Doctor Louis-François, 65, 163, 290
Lake Killarney, County Kerry, Ireland, 45n
Lamb, Captain John, 286
Lambton, John George, 1st Earl of Durham, **103**, **251**

lanthorns (lanterns), 33, 118, 224, 231-232, 333
Laprairie, Quebec, 217
Latham, Doctor James, 63
Laval Normal School, Quebec, **58**
Lawrence, Brigadier General Charles, 136, 324
Le Chien d'Or, Quebec, 33n, 234n, **235**, 307, *see also* Free Mason's Hall
Leclerc, Captain Jacques, 226-227, 229, 273
Leguay, Monsieur, 334
Leith, Sergeant Alexander, 21, 230, 290
Leith, Mrs, 230
Lemoine, James-MacPherson, xviii, 8n, 94, 294
Lennox, Charles (Duke of Richmond and Lennox), 59, 77, **79**, 245-246, 248, 271, **291**, 311
Lévis, Quebec, *see* Pointe Lévy
Lévis, Brigadier General François-Gaston de, 22-23, 176, 180n, 190-191, 266, 269, 281, 287, 298, 303, 322
Lewis, Major General Morgan, 88-89
Lewisham (London), England, 295
Lexington, Massachusetts, 230
Library and Archives Canada, Ottawa, xvii, 94
Ligonier, General Sir John, 255, 319
Linlithgowshire, Scotland, 283
Literary & Historical Society of Quebec, xvii-xviii, xxi, 12n, 38n, **39**, 94, **247**, 310
Livingston, Janet, 237n, 299
Livingston, Lewis, 237-238
Livingston, Robert R., 299
Llanidloes, Wales, 288
London, England, 72, 86, 123, 239, 279, 301
"Long Bowles," 183
Long Island, New York, 126, 135
Lord Aylmer, *see* Matthew Whitworth-Aylmer, 5th Baron Aylmer
Lord Dorchester, *see* Guy Carleton
Lord Dufferin, *see* Frederick Hamilton-Temple-Blackwood
Lord Durham, *see* John George Lambton, 1st Earl of Durham
Lord Howe, *see* Brigadier General George Augustus
Lorette, Quebec, 283
Loudoun, John Campbell, Earl of, 114-115, 126-127, 133, 135, 279
Louis XV, 297
Louisbourg, Nova Scotia, 23, **134**, 136-137, 142, 152-153, 155, 171, 212, 264, 269, 287
Louisbourg, siege of, *see* battles
Lower Canada Rebellion (1837-38), xxi, 117n, 313, 316
Lynd, John, 46, 52, 56n, 66

Mac Shimi, *see* Lieutenant Colonel Simon Fraser
"Mack-Chesney," *see* Corporal James Macky
MacAllister, Lieutenant Archibald, of Loup (McCallister), 156
McChesney, *see* Corporal James Macky
McCord Museum, Montreal, xvii, xxi-xxii, **103**, 240n, 248n
McCurdy, Captain John, 283
Macdonald, Alexander, of Barrisdale, *see* Lieutenant

Alexander MacDonell, of Barrisdale
Macdonald, Piper Archibald, 185n
Macdonald, Lieutenant John, 138n
Macdonell, Alexander, 294
Macdonell, Captain Charles, of Glengarry, 114, 223n
MacDonell, Lieutenant Alexander, of Barrisdale, 114
Macdonell, Captain Donald "Donull Gorm," of Benbecula, 138n, 155-156, 158, 176, 190, 192-193, 195n, 199, 291-292
Macdonell, Captain John, of Lochgarry, 114, 223n
Macdonell, Captain Ranald "Raonall Oig," 18th of Keppoch, 113, 223, 225, 292-293
Macdonell, Ronald, 294
McFee, Sergeant Duncan, *see* Sergeant Duncan McPhee
McIntyre (McErtar), Alexander, 128
McKay, Hugh, 52
Mackay, Janet, 259
Mackellar, Major Patrick, xxi-xxii, **14**, **19**, 190
McKenivan, Corporal Donald, *see* Corporal David Kanavan
Mackenzie, Ensign James, 4th of Ardloch, 173
McKenzie, Janet, 208
McKenzie, Sergeant, 143
McKulloch, Jeannot (*aka* Janet McCulloch), 248, **249**
Macky, Corporal James, **103**, 127, 129-130, 192, 275
McLane, Sergeant John, 30, 241-242
Maclean, Lieutenant Colonel Allan, 36n, 300, 307, 332
MacLean, Doctor John, 196n
MacLean, Mrs, 120
Macleod, Captain John, Macleod of Macleod, 114
MacNeil, Lieutenant Roderick, of Barra, 113
McPhee (McFee), Sergeant Duncan, 84, 147-148, 151-153, 155-156, 293
McPherson, Corporal, *see* Corporal Donald Macpherson
Macpherson, Corporal Donald, 158, 170-171, 214-215, 276
Macpherson, Captain John, of Cluny, 114
Macpherson, Captain John, 231, 233, 238, 294, 301
Macpherson, Ensign Malcolm, of Phoness, **cover**
Macpherson, Reverend Robert (*Caipal Mhor*), 19, 135, 144n, 165, 220-221, 276, 293-294
Macpherson, Robert "Roby," 146n
Macpherson, William, 293
McQuarters, Sergeant Hugh, 231, 294
McRae, Aunt, 116
Maison Côté, *see* James Thompson, house
Maison historique James Thompson, *see* James Thompson, house
Maison Thompson-Côte, *see* James Thompson, house
Maltese cross, 57
Mann, Captain Gother, 53, 61, 67, 70, 261, 294, **295**
Mansback, Sergeant, 49
Market Place Street (Place Royale), Quebec, 22
marquee, 156, 161
Marquess of Lorne, *see* Sir John Douglas Sutherland Campbell
Marr, Captain John, 27, 29, 37, 295-296, **321**, 329-330
Marseille, Emile, 318

Marseille, Fanny, 318
Marseille, Mary, 318
Martello towers, 200-201, 261, 321
Martinique, Caribbean Islands, 296, 299
Maseres, F., 267
Masonic Lodges, *see also* Freemasonry
  Grand Lodge of Canada, Quebec, 86, **102**, 279, 307
  No. 1, Merchants, Quebec, 55, 307
  No. 2, St. Andrew's, Quebec, 9n, 258, 279
  No. 4, St. Peter's, Quebec, 259
  No. 6 Canada (later St. Andrew's), Quebec, 21, 192n, 220-221, 273, 277, 290, 294
  No. 11, P.G.L., Quebec, 279, 313
  No. 13, Unity, Sorel, Quebec, 259
  No. 82, St. Duthus, Ross-shire, Scotland, 9
  No. 136, Ireland, 306
  Provincial Grand, Quebec, 21n, 55, 86, 258, 313
  travelling, 19
  Quebec Select, 220, 293-294
Masonic Memorial Temple, Montreal, **102**
Massey, Colonel Eyre, 171
mastitis, infectious, 52
Mathews, Colonel Robert, 64, 72, 312, 315, 334
Maufils, Françoise, 306
Maxwell, Mary, 280
Milborne, Alfred J.B., **ii**, 91n, 96-97
miles, Irish vs. English, 122
Milford, Connecticut, 126
Mills, Catherine, 313
Minerve, La, 71n
Ministry of Cultural Affairs, Quebec, *see* Historic Monuments Commission
Minorca, Spain, 184, 303
Miré Bay, Nova Scotia, 137
Mohawk Valley, New York, 26, 221, 275
Monckton, Brigadier General Robert, 171-174, 176-180, **187**, 282-283, 296, **297**, 319
Mongan, Reverend Charles, 301-302
Monk, Attorney General James, 309
Mont Real (Mount Royal), Montreal, Quebec, **211**
Montcalm, Major General Louis-Joseph de, 22, 84, 141, 174, 176, 179-180, 196n, 287, 297, **298**, 305, 310, 325, 327
Montgomery, Captain Alexander, 184-185, 298
Montgomery, Lieutenant Colonel Archibald, 112-114, 154n
Montgomery, Brigadier General Richard, 31, 33, **34**, 35, 48n, 75-76, **82**, 88, 94, **95**, 97, **104**, 132, 185, 196n, 230-231, **232**, 233-235, **236**, 237-238, 257, 286, 294, 298, **299**, 300-301, 304, 306-307, 332
Montmollin, Reverend David-François de, 37n, 46-47, 76, 236, 301-302, 313
Montmollin, John Frederick, 302
Montmollin, John Samuel, 302
Montmorency Falls, Quebec, *see* battles
Montreal, Quebec, 23-24, 74, 183, 191, **211**, **216**, 244, 256, 260, 264, 276, 279, 283, 287, 300, 306, 315, 322
Montreal, Quebec, Capture of, *see* battles
Montreal *Gazette*, 92

Montressor, Lieutenant John, **17**
Monument, General James Wolfe (Plains of Abraham), Quebec, 40n, 84n, **100**
Monument, Wolfe–Montcalm (Government Gardens), Quebec, 84, **85**, 86, 89-91, **98**, **102**, 248, 310, 327
Morrin Centre, Quebec, *see* Literary and Historical Society of Quebec
Morrison, Doctor Donald, 196
Morrison, William, 83, 87
Moseley, QM Sergeant William, 92, **252**
Mount Murray (la Malbaie), Quebec, 277, 304
Mountain Street (côte de la Montagne), Quebec, 27n, 61n
Mukins, Captain Francis, 225
Munro, Hector, 20, 191, 194-196
Munro, Henry, **7**
Munro, Hugh, 8, 116n
Murray, Lord George, 286
Murray, James, 2nd Duke of Athol, 112
Murray, Lieutenant James, of Macgregor, 138n
Murray, Brigadier General James, **17**, 22-28, 59, 66, 183-184, 186, 190, 193-194, 197, **198**, 201, 204-206, 210-215, **216**, 217, 221, **223**, 256, 258, 262, 266-267, 270, 273, 276-277, 279, 281, 283-285, 290, 304, 306-307, 312-313, 319-320, 329
Murray Bay (la Malbaie), Quebec, 277-8, 301-302, **303-304**, 305

Nairne, Captain John, 26, 32, 36, 41, 221, **223**, 261, 277, 301, **304**, 305, 314, 331, 333
Nairnshire, Scotland, 275
Napiers, Miss, 247
National Archives of Scotland, xvii
National Battlefields Commission, Canada, 84n, 200n
National Gallery of Canada, 90n
Naudière, Charles-François Tarieu de la (*aka* de Lanaudière), 162-163, **305**, 306
neck stocks, 92
Nelson, Captain Horatio (later Admiral), xix, 312, 322
Netherlands, 260, 265, 295, 301, 321
Neuchâtel, Switzerland, 301
Neuville (Pointe-aux-Trembles), Quebec, 32n, 50
New Brunswick, 263, 283, 309, 326
New Carlisle, Quebec, 318
New France, 281, 293, 297-298
New Haven, Connecticut, 256
New Jersey, 284, 288
New Orleans, 273
New York (colony, state), 75, 94, 124, 267, 275, 278, 284-285, 288-289, 296, 298-299, 304
New York City, New York, 23, 26, 29, 54n, 75-76, 94, **110**, 124n, 125-126, 133, 141-142, 255-256, 261, 272-275, 284-286, 296, 298-299, 304-305
New York Evening Post, 286
Newfoundland, 32, 271
Niagara, New York, 261, 315
Niagara, Ontario. 315
Notre-Dame-de-l'Annonciation, Quebec, 250, 266-267, 282, 297

Norfolk, England, 318, 320
North America, xv, xxii, 256, 263, 265, 271, 274
North Carolina, 264
Northern Ireland, 284
Northwest Company, 275-276
Norwich, Connecticut, 256
Nova Scotia, 263, 265, 272, 278, 282, 284, 296, **297**, 302, 310, 314, 324, 326

Oliver, Captain, 334
Ontario (province), 264
Order of the Bath, 158n, 282, 289, 308, 311
Order of the Garter, **272**
Order of the Gâteau, Quebec, 240-241, **242**, 243
Order of Saint-Louis (Ordre Royal et Militaire de Saint-Louis), 287, 297, 305
Ordnance Department, *see* Board of Ordnance
Oswegatchie, New York, 256
Oswego, New York, 256, 281, 298
Ottawa River, 271
Oxford University, England, 309

Palace Gate, Quebec, 30-31, 61n, **98**, 313, 330-332
Palace Street (côte du Palais), Quebec, **98**, 313
palisades, 18n, 31, 300
Papineau, Louis-Joseph, 291
Parant, Monseigneur, 226-228
Paris, France, 150, 161, 259, 286-288, 306, 324
Paris, Treaty of, 26, 54n, 273
Parkman, Francis, xvii
Parks Canada, 85
Parlour Street, (place de l'Archevêché), Quebec, 25n
Pennsylvania, 256, 281
Penobscot, Maine, 265
Penobscot River, 311
Pensacola, Florida, 271, 282
Percé Rock, Quebec, 326
Perth, Scotland, 294
Petite-Rivière, Quebec, 266
Peyton, Lieutenant Henry, 176, 181-182
Philadelphia, Pennsylvania, 257-258, 296
Phillips, Major General William, 296, 320
Picard, Lieutenant Louis-Alexandre, 300, 306
Picton, General Sir Thomas, 289
pioneers, *see* hatchet men
pipers, 4, 23, 83, 119n, 121, 129, 176, 185, 186n, **195**, **198**, 200, 292
pistols, *see* weapons
Pitt, John (2nd Earl of Chatham), 72
Pitt, William, 10, 72, 114, 124, 133, 211-212, 319, 324, 326
Place d'Armes, Quebec, 57, 196n
Place Jacques-Cartier, Montreal, **322**
Plains of Abraham, Quebec, **98**, **100**
Plains of Abraham, battle of, *see* battles
Plattsburgh, New York, 257
Plymouth, England, 272, 321
Point Pleasant Park, Halifax, Nova Scotia, 314
Pointe Blanche (White Point), Louisbourg, Nova Scotia, 137

Pointe Lévy (Levi, Lévis), Quebec, **14**, 16, 60, **172**, 176, 186, **187**, 201, 284-285, 300, 324
Pointe Lévy Church (St. Joseph's), Eglise Saint-Joseph-de-la-Pointe-Lévy), Quebec, 16, 173-173, 178-179, 186, **187**
Pointe Platte (Flat Point), Louisbourg, Nova Scotia, 137
Pointe-aux-Pères, Quebec, **15**, 187n
Pointe-aux-Trembles, Quebec, 32, 45, 212, 215n, 300, 323, 332
Pointe-Pitre, Guadeloupe, 271
Pontiac Uprising, (1763-64), 256, 273-274
Portpatrick, Ireland, 115, 117n
Portsmouth, England, 53, 188n, 189n, 296-297, 310, 320-321
Portugal, 279
Prentice, Lieutenant Jonathan, 45
Prentice, Provost Marshal Miles, 33-34, 46, 51-52, 55-56, 65, 76, **102**, 234n, **235**, 306-307
Prentice, Mrs. Miles, 234
Prescott, Governor Robert, 61n, 68, 262-263
Prescott Gate, Quebec, 61n
Près-de-Ville, Quebec, **232**, 300
Prevost, General Sir George, 261
Prévost, Colonel Jacques, 281
Prince Edward Island, 272, 286
Provence, France, 298
Provincial soldiers, *see* regiments, British, other troops
Providence, Rhode Island, 135
Provost Prison (St. Roch Suburb), Quebec, 50
Pryer, Mary, 309
"punch," 118, 123, 167
Puysieux, Marquis de, 286

Quakers of England, 227
Quebec Act, 267, 270
Quebec Almanac, 259
Quebec Citadel, 271, 296, 321
Quebec City, 4-9, 11n, 12, **15**, 16n, 18, **19**, 20-37, 38n, 39-46, 48, 50, 51n, 52, 54, 56, 59-61, **62**, 63, 65-68, 70, 71-79, 82-84, 86, 88, 92-93, 95-97, **98**, **110**, 123, **134**, 135, 141, 142n, 143n, 172, 173n, 174, 176-177, 180, 181n, 184-185, 187, 188n, 190-192, 193n, 194n, 196, 197n, 198, 199n, 200n, 202, 203n, 204, 207-208, 210-212, 215, 218-228, 230-231, **232**, 233-336, 240-241, 243-247, 256, 258-260, 274, 284, 286, 295-296, 300-301, 303, 305-309, 311-312, 314-316, 325-326
Quebec (colony, province), 241, 247, 256-257, 263-265, 295
Quebec Gazette, 63n, 84n, 92, 277
Quebec Mercury, 261, 278, 313
Quebec Morning Chronicle, 317
Quebec *Star & Commercial Advertiser*, xvii, 12n, 24n, 87, 93, 96n, **101**, 142n, 145n, 180n, 243
Queen Victoria, 272-273
Quincy, Esther, 309

Racey, Mr, 238
Ramsay, George (8th Earl of Dalhousie), 307
Ramsay, George (9th Earl of Dalhousie), xvi, 6n, 65, 77-79, 80n, 94, 240n, **247**, 264, 289, 307, **308**, 310-311, **317**, 326-327
Ramsay, Colonel John, 88-89
Rangers, *see* regiments, other troops, British
rattan, 121
Raury's Brewery, 231
Raynham Hall, Norfolk, England, 320
Reay, Lord, 259
Rebellion, Lower Canada (1837-39), *see* Lower Canada Rebellion
Récollets Gate, Montreal, 23, **216**
regiments, British regular
  3rd Dragoons (Earl of Albemarle's), 307
  1st Foot Guards (later, Grenadier Guards), 255, 261-262, 319
  2nd Foot Guards, (later, Coldstream Guards), 290
  1st Royal Regiment (*aka* "The Royal" and later, "Royal Scots"), 9, 120, 123n, 142, 180n, **272**, 280, 308, 318
  3rd (Howard's, *aka* "The Buffs"), 314
  4th (Duroure's *aka* "The King's"), 310, 323-324
  5th (Bentinck's), 302
  7th (Bertie's, *aka* "The Royal Fusiliers"), 218n, 272
  8th (Wolfe's), 56, 153-154
  9th (Yorke's), 117n, 274
  10th (Pole's), 288
  12th (Napier's), 323
  15th (Amherst's), 27n, 92-93, 136, 172-174, 176-178, 180, 182, **198**, 225, 255, 260, 267, 283-284, **285**, 290, 301, 303
  16th (Robertson's), 265
  17th (Forbes), 34, 142, 185n, 234n, 298-299, 306-307
  20th (Bligh's, Cornwallis'), 153-154, 274, 318, 324
  21st (Panmure's, *aka* "Royal North British Fusiliers"), 10, 113, 259
  22nd (Whitmore's, Rollo's), 212, 285
  25th (Rothes'), 261
  26th (Anstruther's, *aka* "The Cameronians"), 117, 307-308, 313
  27th ("Inniskillens," or Blakeney's), 27n, 284
  28th (Bragg's), 181n, 210, 290
  30th (Campbell's), 264
  32nd (Leighton's), 290
  33rd (Johnson's), 287, 310
  34th (Cavendish's), 274
  35th (Otway's), 156, 210, 291
  40th (Hopson's), 212
  41st (Invalids), 120n
  42nd (Lord Murray's, The Royal Highlanders, later "The Black Watch"), 12n, 23, 133, 152, 162-164, 172, 176n, 177n, 181n, 185n, 217n, 219
  43rd (Crawford's, Sempill's, Kennedy's), 45n, 193n, 289-290, 292, 298, 306-307
  44th (Abercromby's), 283-284
  45th (Warburton's), 274
  46th (Massey's), 171
  47th (Lascelle's), 27n, 142, 165, 193n, 211, 264, 296
  48th (Webb's), 142, 193n, 210
  52nd (Sandford's), 29, 287-290

53rd (Whitmore's), 305
54th (Campbell's), 287
56th (Lord Charles Manners'), 123n, 280
58th (Anstruther's), **198**, 210, 280
60th ("Royal Americans"), 27n, 28, 147, 176, 181n, 193n, 241n, 281-**282**, 290, 302, 311
62nd (Strode's), 288
64th (Lord Loudoun's), 115n
66th (La Fausille's), 99n, 293
67th (Wolfe's), 154n, 324
68th (Lambton's), 310
71st (Fraser's), 279
72nd (Stuart's), 261
74th (Argyll Highlanders), 293
77th (Montgomery's), 12n, 23, 124n 126, 133, 159, 274, 305
78th (Fraser's), xv, xix, 10-11, 12n, 23, 26, 27n, 28, 96, 97n, **108**, 112-113, 115, 121n, 124, 125n, 126-127, 133, 135-139, 149n, 154, 159, 160n, 165, 169n, 170n, **198**, 210-211, 220-222, 241n, 255-256, 259, 261-262, 273-278, 286, 288, 290, 292-294, 299, 304-305, 312-313, 324-326
79th (Cameron Highlanders), 78, 83, 290, 326
81st (Earl of Lindsay's), 290
82nd (Prince of Wales Volunteers), 265
84th (Royal Highland Emigrants), 35n, 36n, **268**, 277, 300, 304-305
85th (Royal Volunteers), 310
91st (Campbell's), 326
95th (Burton's, later "Rifle Brigade"), 289-290
101st (Johnstone's "Highlanders"), 267, 289
103rd ("Volunteer Hunters"), 284
113th (Hamilton's), 289
other troops, British
6th Garrison Battalion, 307
British Militia, Quebec (post Conquest), 313
Corps of Engineer Invalids, 296, 309
Dutch Scots Brigade, 113, 143, 302, 304
Louisbourg Grenadiers (28th, 40th and 45th), **189**, 262
Marines, (later Royal Marines), 136, 153n, 154n, 174n, 303, 323
Massachusetts Provincials (Shirley's), 133, **257**, 282
New York Provincials (Saltonstall's), 133
Rogers' Rangers, 111, 123, 136, 146n, 172, 177n, 182, 185n, 190n, 195n, 199, 210, 256-257, 282-283
Royal Artillery, 20, 22, 30n, 53n, 72, **73**, 74n, 260, 271, 279, 294, 308, 314, 321
Royal Canadian Volunteer Regiment, 268
Royal Engineers, 18n, 20n, 32n, 37, 40n, 41, 53n, 67n, 72, **73**, 74n, 260, 271, 295, 308, 314, 321
Sedentary Militia, (post Conquest), 305
Sutherland Independent Companies, 123
Sutherland Regiment of Fencible Men, 120n, 123n, **280**, 281
regiments, French regular (*troupes de terre***)**
d'Auxerois, 297
de Berry, 259
d'Hainault, 297
de Languedoc, 197n
de la Reine, 197
other troops, French
Compagnies franches de la Marine (colonial regulars), 152n, 181n, **198**, **286**, 305
Milice canadien (Canadian Militia), 28, 42, 50, 268, 306-307
aboriginal warriors, 136, 149, 173, 185n, 190, 220
Rensselaer, Stephen van, 75
Rettleberg, Sergeant de, 49
Reynolds, Paul, 35
Rhinebeck, New York, 299
Richelieu River, 218n, 283, 287
Richmond, Ontario, 78, 291-292
Richmond, Duke of, *see* Charles Lennox
Rideau Canal, 271, 295
Rideau River, 271
Rivière-du-Loup, Quebec, 27n, 220
Robertson, Major James, 146n, 147
Robertson, John, 86
Robertson, William, 312
Robinson, Fanny, 317
Robinson, Margaret, 317
Robitaille, André, 95
Rochanplatt, Brigadier General, 334
Rochefort, France, 323-324
Rochefort, Expedition to, 303, 324
Rogers, Major Robert, 199n, 256, 282-283
Rollo, Honourable Aemilia, 284
Rollo, Andrew (3rd Lord), 284
Rollo, Lieutenant Colonel Andrew (5th Lord), 285
Romsey, England, 258
Rosehall (estate) Scotland, 259
Ross, Alexander, 315
Ross, Anne (Mrs James Thompson Jr), 315-316
Ross, Colonel, 152, 162-163, 219, 220n, 286-287
Ross, Hugh, 103, **248-249**
Ross, John, 66
Ross, Captain Thomas, of Calrossie, 133
Ross, William, Earl of, 10
Ross-shire, Scotland, 6, 9, 96, 219, 259
Royal 22nd Regiment, **251**, **271**
Royal American Regiment, *see* regiments, British regular
Royal Engineers Office, Quebec, 67, 80, **81-82**, 89, 196
Royal Engineers Yard and Complex, Quebec, 74, **98**, 196
Royal High School, Edinburgh, Scotland, 307
Royal Hospital, Chelsea, England, 185n, 293, 320
Royal Military Academy, Woolwich, England, 53n, 72, **73**, 260, 263, 271, 294, 314, **321**
Royal Navy, 33, 139, 143n, 151n, 191, 197n, 266-268, 303, 321
Rudyerd, Captain Henry, 53, 59
rum, issue of, 23, 164, 218, 220

Sacket's Harbor, New York, 261
Sackville, Lord George, 136, 324
Sainte-Anne, Quebec, 241
Saint-Eustache, France, 306

Saint-Gabriel, Sister (mère St. Gabriel), 203-204, **205**, 206-209
Saint-Jean-Port-Joli, Quebec, 68n, 87n
Salies, Bearn, France, 268
Salmon, Surgeon Edward S, 46
Sandby, Paul, 263
sangris, 239
Saratoga, campaign, *see* battles
Sault-au-Matelot, Quebec, 36, **232**, 238, 300-301
Saunders, Vice Admiral Charles, 150, 325
Saxony, Germany, 273
Schenectady, New York, 166, 169, 170n, 261, 276
Schoharie, New York, 166
"Scotch church," *see* St. Andrew's Presbyterian Church, Quebec
Scott, Major George, 261
Seminary (Séminaire), Quebec, 76, 233-234, 290
Sept-Îles, Quebec, 270
Seton, Captain Sir Henry, of Culbeg (4th Baronet Abercorn), 113, 133
Sewell, Justice Jonathan, 86, 237, **309**-310, 317
Sherbrooke, Sir John Coape, 75, 237, 310-311
Sherbrooke, Sarah, 310
Sherbrooke, William, 310
Shippen, Margaret (Peggy), 258
ships, French navy
  Appollon, 150n
  Aréthuse, 150n, 151n, 202n, 321-322
  Atalante, 203n, 266, 268, 321-323
  Biche, 150n
  Bienfaisant, 141
  Bricole, 323
  Capricieux, 150n
  Célèbre, 150n
  Chevre, 150n
  Coulisse, 323
  Echo, 150n, 151n, 160n, 264
  Entreprenant, 150n
  Fidèle, 150n
  La Marie, 323
  Lys, 197n
  Prudent, 141, 150n
  Tourterelle, 321
ships, Royal Navy
  Albemarle, 312
  Centurion, **175**
  Diana, 83, 202n, 203n, 215n, 322-323
  Dublin, 136, 143n
  Enterprise, 115
  Falkland, 115
  Hecla, 158n
  Inconstant, 38n
  Kennington, 144n
  Lawrence, 202n
  Lowestoft, 83, 188n, 201n, 202n, 203n, 322
  Namur, 136, 160n
  Norwich, 124n
  Pegasus, 65
  Penzance, 215n
  Porcupine, 215n
  Princess Amelia, 324
  Province, 136
  Racehorse, 215n
  Royal William, 16, 188
  Shannon, 141
  Southhampton, 83
  Stirling Castle, 188
  Stork, 15, 115
  Sutherland, 215n
  Terrible, 143n
  True Briton, 215n
  Vanguard, 202n, 322-323
transports, Royal Navy
  Ann, 124n
  Brotherly Love, 124n, 125n
  Duchess of Hambleton, 124n, 125n
  Kent, 124n
  Martilla (aka Martello), 124n
  Matilda, 124n, 125n
  Myrilla, 125n
  Neptune, 125n
  Russell, 175
  St. Cecilia, 124n, 125n
  Two Sisters, 175
Shirley, Governor William, 282
Short, Elizabeth, 314
Sicily, 310
Sidmouth, England, 310
Signal Hill, Newfoundland, 271
Sillery, battle of, *see* battles
Sillery, Quebec, xv, 12, 22-23, 24, 92n, 156n, 181n, 185n, 190-192, 197n, **198**, 210, 212, 223n, 241n, 269, 273-275, 278-279, 283, 285, 292, 303
Simpson, Sergeant Alexander "Sanders" (aka "Saunders"), 22, 46-47, 48n, 49, 52, 72, **102**, 178-179, 312, 321
Simpson, Mary, 50, 72, 312
Simpson, Sarah (Mrs Alexander Simpson), 22, 46-47, 49-50, 52, 65, 312
Simpson's Coffee House, Quebec, 22, 312
Sinclair, Elizabeth, 313
Sinclair, George, 313
Sinclair, Sergeant James, 117-120, 312-313
Sinclair, Brigadier General James, 117
Sise, Charles Fleetford, 38n
Skye, Scotland, 294
smallpox, 31, 63, 101n, 257
Smillie, James, 240
Smith, Caroline, 316
Smith, Eliza Julia, 316
Smith, Francis, 241
Smith, Henrietta, 309
Smith, Sergeant Lauchlan, 54, 56, 241-243, 313
Smith, William, 310
Smith, Chief Justice William, 309
Smithsonian Institution, xxii, 94, **104**, 238n, 301
Smythe, Captain Hervey, **13**, 173, 174n, **175**, 279
snuff, taking of, 239n
Sons of St. Andrew, Quebec, *see* Masonic Lodges,

No. 6, Quebec
Sorel, Quebec, 51, 208, 214, 321
"soupaun," 128, 132
South Africa, 265
Spain, 303
Spark, Reverend Alexander, 19n, 71
Spittal, Major John, 211
Springfield, Massachusetts, 165
Spry, George, 314
Spry Lieutenant General Horatio, 314
Spry, Captain William, **14**, 22, 25, 27, 59, 314, 329
Spry, Major General William, 314
St. Amable, Quebec, 276
St. Andrew's Lodge, Quebec, *see* Lodges, No. 6, Quebec
St. Andrew's Presbyterian Church, Quebec, 56n, 71, **98**, **101**, 276, 294, 317
St. Anne's (Fredericton, New Brunswick), 283
St. Anne's Church, London, England, 320
St. Anne-de-la-Pocatière (seigneury) Quebec, 313
St. Anne Street (rue Sainte-Anne), Quebec, **98**, 266, 277
St. Armand (seigneury), Quebec, 270
St. Augustin, Quebec, 323
St. Augustine, Florida, 274
St. Croix, Quebec, 212
St. Croix River, New Brunswick, 311
St. Denis and La Pocatière (seigneury), Quebec, 313
St. Duthus's Collegiate Church, Tain, Scotland, 7, 8n, 116n
St. Foy, Quebec, 190, **252**, 279
St. Francis, Quebec, 256
St. George's Chapel, Windsor, England, 273
St. Ignace, Quebec, 214n
St. James Protestant Cemetery, Trois-Rivières, Quebec, 313
St. Jean, Île de, 286
St. Johns (Saint-Jean-sur-Richelieu), Quebec, 283, 300, 316-317
St. John's College, Cambridge, England, 318
St. John Gate, Quebec, 61n, **98**, **102**, **252**, 332
St. John River, New Brunswick, 283, 305, 314
St. John Street (rue Saint-Jean), Quebec, 37-38, 65, 84n, 92n, **98**, 258, 307
St. John Street (Protestant) Cemetery, Quebec, 34n, 37n, 92, **98**, **101**, **252**
St. Joseph's Church, Point Lévy, Quebec, 76, 172, 177, 186, **187**
St. Lawrence River, Quebec, 256-257, 274, 295, 306, 319-220, 331, 324-325
St. Leger, Barrimore Matthew, 284
St. Lucia (island), 297
St. Louis Bastion, Quebec, 34-35, 37n, 74
St. Louis Gate, Quebec, 32, 61n, **75**, 76, **81**, **98**, **103**, **236**, **252**, 259, 266, 303, 312, 314, 316, 331
St. Louis Gate Cemetery, 37n, **82**, 307
St. Louis Street (rue Saint-Louis), Quebec, **98**, 259, 266, 303, 306, 312, 314
St. Margaret's Church, Westminster (London), England, 314
St. Mary's (Sault-Ste-Marie, Ontario), 295

St. Michel, Quebec, 226n, 229, 278
St. Paul's Chapel, New York City, 76, 237n
St. Peter's Street (rue Saint-Pierre), Quebec, 281
St. Pierre (Saint-Pierre-de-la-Rivière-du-Sud), Quebec, 42, 50, 260, 289
St. Roch, Quebec, 33, 61, **62**, 87, **98**, 228, 300
St. Thomas, Quebec, 40, 229-230, 268
St. Ursula Street (rue Sainte-Ursule), Quebec, 5, 66-67, 70, 75, 87, 91, 94-95, **97**, **98**, 248, 316-317
St. Vallier (St. Valier), Quebec, 221, 223, 226-227, 229, 273, 294
St. Vincent (island), 297
Stanford, Connecticut, 126
Stanwix, Brigadier General John, 296
Star & Commercial Advertiser, xvii, 12n, 24n, 87, 93, 96n, **101**, 142n, 145n, 180n, 243
Stead, Captain, 52
Stewart, James, 278
Stewart, Jessie, 292
Stewart, Colonel David, of Garth, 293
Stewart, Colonel John Roy, 287
Stewart Museum, Montreal, xv, xvii-xviii, **xx**, xxi, 4, **5**, **103-104**
Stirling, Scotland, 292
Stirling, Elizabeth "Bare Betty," 302
Stirling, Captain Thomas, 273
Stockbridge, Massachusetts, 165
Strabane, Ireland, 262
Strachronnachan, Scotland, 294
Stratford, Connecticut, **103**, 135, 275, 286
Strode, Lieutenant General William, 288
Stronach, Alexander, 7-9
Stronach, Barbara, 6, 8, 248
Stuart, Andrew, 317
Stuart, Charles Edward ("The Young Pretender"), 163, 286, 323-324
Stuart, Peter, 270
subsistence pay, 26n, 27, 222-223, 225
Sudbury, Massachusetts, 164
Sun Tavern (St. John Street), Quebec, 307
superannuation, 91
supernumeraries, 121n
Sussex, England, 291, 303, 321
Sutherland, Scotland, 267, 280
Sutherland (clan), 9-10
Sutherland, Earl of, 280
Sutherland, Sergeant, 229
"Sutherland's Rangers," *see* regiments, other troops, British
swagger stick, 121n
Swanton, Commodore Robert, 323

Tain, Ross-shire, Scotland, 6, **7**, 8-10, 93, 96-97, 116, 219, 248n, **249**, 259, 312
Tain & District Museum, Ross-shire, Scotland, xvii
Tanswell, James, 315
Tarbat, Ross-shire, Scotland, 8
Terroux, Jacques, 306
thistle cup, *see* James Thompson, artefacts

Thompson, Anne "Nancy," xviii(n), 53, 60, 63, 66n, 68n, 316, 317
Thompson, Frances "Fanny," 53, 65, 68, 317
Thompson, Lieutenant George, 53, 66n, 321
Thompson, Sergeant James
 birth in Scotland and early childhood, 6-10, 259
 volunteers for overseas service, xv, 10-11, 114, 249, 259-260, 329
 early military service, 11, 115-125, 312, 329
 adds "p" to surname, 6, 120n, 249
 winter quarters in Connecticut, 125-132
 makes his first dirk, xxii, 94, **107**, 127, 129
 dirk fight in Stratford guard house, 127, 129-132, 275
 siege and capture of Louisbourg, 11-12, 133, 138-139, 142-164, 293, 299, 329
 death of Captain Baillie, 143-144, 155
 early affection for General Wolfe, 12, 154-155, 324-326
 winter quarters in New York, 165-171, 286
 battle of Montmorency, 12, **15**, 87, 174-177, 298
 siege and battle for Quebec, 16, 173-174, 176-189, 329
 death of General Wolfe, 16, 176, 188-189
 early Freemasonry in Quebec, 9n, 19, 21, 273, 279, 290, 294
 winter garrison at Quebec and battle of Sillery, 22-23, 190-209, 274, 283
 early work with engineers, 18, 20-22, 25, 287, 314, 329
 reduction of Montreal, 23, 210, 212-220, 299, 329
 garrisoning the St. Lawrence (1760-63), 220-230, 290
 meets John Gawler, 22, 279, his grandmother's cup, xxi-xxii, **107**, 248, **249**
 offered positions in Montreal and Quebec, 24
 acquires house on St. Louis Street, 25
 discharged in Quebec, 27-28
 appointed clerk of works, 22, 27, 222, 329
 appointed overseer of works at Quebec, 29-30, 233, 296, 330
 marriage and death of first wife, 27-28, 30-31, 34, 35n, 36-37, 48n
 American Revolutionary War, 51, 75, 230-239, 300, 330-333
 salary, 30, 68-70, 72-73
 acquires Montgomery's sword, xxii, 33, 35, 76-77, 94, **95**, **107**, 233-234, 238, 301, 332
 supervises Montgomery's burial, 33-36, 48n, 234-238, 301, 332
 acquires snuff mull, xxi-xxii, 55, **107**, **239**, 240
 applies for land grant with Michel Blais, 28, 42, 50, 57-58, 68, 244, 260
 helps wood carvers execute Wolfe's statue at Wolfe's Corner, 38, **39**, 40, 84n, **106**, 246-248
 keeps work journal during construction of citadel, 41
 courtship with Fanny Cooper and marriage, 45-48
 children from union with Fanny Cooper, **vi**, xvi-xviii, 51-53, 56, 60, 65-68, 72-74, 87, **106**, 277, 313-318
 obtains Letter of Service, 69-70
 house on St. Ursula Street, 66, **70**, 94-96, **97**, 317
 meets Duke of Richmond on Esplanade (1818), 77, 245-246

 story teller to Lord Dalhousie, xvi, 6n, 77-78, **79**, 80, 83, 203n, 264, 308
 Dalhousie leaves Quebec, 90
 portrait sketched by Captain John Crawford Young, **ii**, 78, 90, 327, **back cover**
 retirement and pension, 82-83, 89, 91, 335
 Wolfe–Montcalm monument, 84, **85**, 86, 89-91, 248, 327
 last will and testament, 87
 reminiscences and anecdotes recorded by his son, xv, xvii-xix, **xx**, xxi-xxiii, 88, 94, 213n, 225n, 238n, 316
 anecdotes appear in local newspapers, xvi-xvii, 87, 142n, 145, 180n
 journals acquired by LHSQ and BAnQ, xvii-xix, **xx**, xxi, 213n
 journal acquired by Stewart Museum, xv, xvii-xviii, **xx**, xxi, **5**
 death and burial in Quebec, 5, 24n, 91-94
 death of Fanny Cooper, 94
Thompson, James, artefacts
 family broadsword, **back cover**, xxii, 94, **250**
 General Montgomery's sword, xxii, 33, 35, 76-77, 94, **95**, **104**, **107**, 232-234, 238, 301, 332
 dirks, xxii, 94, **103**, **104**, **107**, 127, 129-130, **131**, 132, 192n, 275
 snuff mull, xxii, 55, **103**, **107**, **239**
 silver (thistle) cup, xxii, **103**, **107**, 248, **249**
Thompson, James, house (Maison historique James Thompson), Quebec, xvii, xxii, 66-68, **70**, **75**, 77, 80-83, 87-88, 91, 94-96, **97**, **98**, 240-241, 248, **251**, **316-317**
Thompson, James Jr, **ii**, **vi**, xvi-xix, **xx**, xxi-xxiii, 6, 24n, 28n, 36n, 53, 56, 63, 66n, 72, 74, 77n, 88-94, **106**, 115n, 117n, 121n, 124n, **131**, 132n, 145n, 168n, 180n, 188n, 189n, 203n, 213n, 225n, 234n, 238n, 240, 249n, 313, 315-317
Thompson, John Gawler, 35, 53, 63, 65-66, 72, 84, 90n, 279, 316-318
Thompson, Rose, 53n, 67
Thompson, Samuel, 53n, 67
Thompson, William "Billy," 51-53
Thompson, William Alexander, 53, 66n, 72, 317-318
Thomson, Barbara, 6
Thomson, Christian, 6
Thomson, James, 6, **7**, 9, 248-249
Thomson, Janet, 6
Thomson, William, 6, 120n
Three Rivers, Quebec, *see* Trois-Rivières
Ticonderoga, New York, **110**, 133, 141-142, 162n, 219n, 255-257, 281, 298, 305, 320
Tisseran, Jean-François (de Montcharvaux), 25
Titchfield, Hampshire, England, 314
Tolbooth, Tain, Scotland, 7, 8n
Toronto, Ontario, 315
Tower of London, 320
Town-Major, Montreal, 24, 170n
Town-Sergeant, Quebec, 51
Townshend, Charles, (3rd Viscount), 318

Townshend, Brigadier General George (4th Viscount and 1st Marquess Townshend), 175, 186n, 318, **319**
Trahan, Joseph, 276
Travelling Masonic Lodges, *see* Masonic Lodges, travelling
Treaty of Paris, *see* Paris, Treaty of
Trinity College, Dublin, Ireland, 298
Trois-Rivières (Three Rivers), Quebec, 31, 260, 270, 282, 313, 330
Troy, New York, 283
Tullochchrom, Scotland, 294
Tunbridge Wells, Kent, England, 271
Twiss, William (father), 320
Twiss, Captain William, 27n, 37, 40, 43-44, 46-47, 51-53, 56, 59, 72, 296, 308-309, 314-315, 320, **321**, 334

United Empire Loyalists, 66, **75**, 258, 263, 309
United States, 261, 272
Unity Lodge, Quebec, *see* Masonic Lodges, Unity
Upnor Castle, Kent, England, 285
Ursuline Chapel (Chapelle des Ursulines), Quebec, 196
Ursuline Convent, Quebec, **98**, 196, 276, 298
Ursuline Lane (ruette des Ursulines), Quebec, xxii, 66n, 67, **70**, **97**
Ursuline nuns, 96

Vaillancourt, Joseph, **102**
Valcour Island, New York, 257
"Vandoos," *see* Royal 22nd Regiment
Vane, Lady Anne, 283
Vaudreuil, Pierre de Rigaud de, Marquis de, 23, 191, 281, **298**
Vauquelin, Lieutenant Jean, 150n, 202n, 203n, **322**
Vermont, 257, 274
Verrier, Louis-Guilliame, 266
Vialar, Captain Anthony, 307
Victoria, Queen, 272, 326
Victoria Cross, 158n
Virginia, 256, 274

Wade, Anne, 295
Wade, Captain John, 42-45
Walker, Alexander, 288
Walker, Rebecca, 271
Walker, Robert "Rob", 127, 130-131
Walker, Thomas, 285
warrant men, 225n
wars
    Napoleonic Wars, 263, 265, 274, 310, 321
    Seven Years' War, xv-xvii, 111, 129n, 154n, 211n, 262, **266**, 280-282, 295, 321, 324
    War of 1812, 261, 271, 281, 289, 311, 318
    War of Austrian Succession, 255, 293, 297, 319, 321-322, 324
    War of American Independence, 256, 260-268, 274-277, 283-285, 298-300, 303, 305-307, 310, 312-313, 320, 330-333
Warwick, England, 268

Washington, General George, 31, 230, 257
weapons
    bayonets, **108**, 160, 181
    cannon, 33, 60, 158, 180n, 190, 200n, 212, 294, 318, 331
    broadswords, xxii, 3, 94, 129n, 130, 143, 147, 154, 170
    carbines, 135, 136, 149n
    cohorn mortars, 141, **159**
    dirks, xxii, 94, 114, 127, 129n, 130, **131**, 132, 192n, 275
    pistols, 129n, 135, 154, **168**
Wellesley, Sir Arthur, 265, 289-291, 307-308, 310-311, 326
Wellington, Duke of, *see* Sir Arthur Wellesley
Wemyss, Lady Elizabeth, 280
Wemyss, Major James, 288
Wentworth, Sir John, 272
West Florida (colony), 271, 282
West Indies, 256, 271-272, 291, 295, 308, 316, 318
West Point, New York, 258
Westchester, New York, 299
Westerham, Kent, England, 323
Westfield, New York, 165
Wetmore, Parson Izrahiah, 128n
Wheelwright, Miss (Mother Abbess), 205-206
Whitby, England, 308
White, Abigail, 282
Whitelaw, Doctor John, 315
Whitmore, Brigadier General Edward, 141
Whitworth-Aylmer, Matthew, 5th Baron Aylmer, **100**, **103**
Wilkie, Reverend Daniel, 243, 317-318
Wilkie, Drummer John, 166-167, 218-219
Wilson, Mr (brewer), 238
Wilson, Sergeant John, 203-204, 208
Winslow, Colonel John, 282
winter quarters, 78th Regiment
    Connecticut (1757-58), 125-132, 261, 275, 278
    New York (1758-59), 164-171, 256, 276, 278, 286, 304
    Quebec (1759-60), 190-192
Wolfe, Lieutenant General Edward, 153n
Wolfe, Major General James, xx, 5, 12, **13**, 16, 34, 37-38, 40n, 77-80, 83, 86, 136, **139**, 142, 147n, 149-155, 159, 171, 174, 176, 179, 185, 187-188, **189**, 243-244, 296, 298, 302-303, 307, 319, 323-325
"Wolfe's Corner" (and statue), Quebec, 38, **39**, 40, 84n, **98**, **102**, **246-247**, 248
Wolfe's Cove, Quebec, *see* Anse au Foulon
Wolfe's Poem, 243
Wolfe–Montcalm Monument, Quebec, 84, **85**, 86, 89-91, **98**, **102**, 248, 310, 327
Woolwich Arsenal, London, England, **73**, 264
Wooster, Brigadier General David, 300
Worcester, Massachusetts, 164

York, Duke of, *see* Prince Frederick Augustus
Yorkshire, England, 321
Young, Captain John Crawford, **ii, back cover**, 78, 84, **85**, 86, 90, **102**, 326-327
Yverdon, Switzerland, 281-282

A Bard of Wolfe's Army: James Thompson, Gentleman Volunteer, 1733–1830 is published in collaboration with the Stewart Museum (The Fort, Île-Ste-Hélène, Montreal) and the 78th Fraser Highlanders.

The Stewart Museum is proud to have supported the publication of this work on James Thompson, a true Quebec Scottish pioneer. From its establishment in 1965 as the Montreal Military Museum, then the Montreal Military & Maritime Museum, the museum has highlighted the role that two of the great European cultures have had on Canadian history – France and Great Britain. David Stewart, associated with a number of businessmen, most of them Second World War veterans, saw the need for a military museum in Montreal and so began the museum's collections, with a military emphasis. To bring this military history to life, the museum undertook the recreation of the *Compagnie franche de la marine* in 1963 and, through the impetus of Colonel J. Ralph Harper, the 78th Regiment of Foot, commonly called Fraser's Highlanders, in 1965, in advance of Expo 67. These initiatives put the museum at the forefront of historical military animation, now so common at historic sites. Since then the collections have broadened to include maps, navigation instruments, scientific instruments, a large collection of kitchen and fireplace utensils and artefacts of day-to-day use, whether commonplace or for nobility. The story of James Thompson reflects this development – from the life of a common soldier in Wolfe's army to one of the most respected men in Quebec in the 18th and 19th centuries.

Readers are invited and encouraged to visit the Stewart Museum while in Montreal.

www.stewart-museum.org

The Fort, Île-Ste-Hélène, Montreal

Compagnie franche de la marine

78th Fraser Highlanders

About the Editors

Earl John Chapman of Montreal is a member of the history and heritage committee of Canada's Black Watch and has written several books on the regiment's early years. He is also historian of the 78th Fraser Highlanders, a ceremonial regiment raised in 1965 by Montreal's David M. Stewart Museum to perpetuate the history of the old 78th Regiment of Foot. He was the 2008 recipient of the prestigious Gordon Atkinson Memorial Prize in Highland Military History, awarded annually by the Quebec Thistle Council.

Ian Macpherson McCulloch, a native of Halifax, is a Canadian Forces officer who has served in a variety of regimental and staff appointments in Canada, the U.S.A. and Germany. Lieutenant Colonel McCulloch is on the directing staff of the Canadian Forces College in Toronto and is a military historian specializing in the Seven Years' War in North America. He has published numerous articles and has written or contributed to several books, the most recent being *Sons of the Mountains: A History of the Highland Regiments in North America, 1756–1767* and *Highlander in the French-Indian War, 1756–1767*. He too won the Gordon Atkinson Memorial Prize in Highland Military History, in 2009.